Brief Contents

Contents

Preface xvii

Putting It All Together   397

Preface

The gratifying response to the third edition of *Your Guide to College Success* has led to this new edition. We believe even more strongly that the college success course can be a key factor in how well students master their college experience. When adults (including your authors) reflect on their lives, they often wish they had been able to take such a course early in their college journey. We are very pleased that colleges and universities are increasingly realizing that virtually all students can significantly benefit from studying and exploring the topics in *Your Guide to College Success*—including values, goal setting, learning styles, time management, thinking and study skills, communication, diversity, relationships, physical and mental health, and careers.

What are the changes and improvements in the fourth edition of *Your Guide to College Success*? Listening carefully to feedback from instructors and students, we have had as our goal making this book even more helpful.

Text Organization

The following changes have been made to the overall organization of the text:

- The chapter "Explore Your Campus, Courses, and Computer" has been moved earlier in the text to better fit with schools' orientation programs at the beginning of the term. The content has also been revised for increased relevancy.
- We moved the chapter "Expand Your Thinking Skills" up in the text to consolidate coverage of learning and critical thinking.
- The chapter "Be A Great Money Manager" has been moved later in the text to consolidate coverage of money management and careers.
- There is expanded coverage of the important topic of memory in Chapter 7, "Enhance Your Study Skills and Memory."

Chapter Organization

The following changes have been made at the chapter-level of the text:

- The "Six Strategies for Success" model has been refined to provide more opportunities for active learning and direct application to students' lives. Each chapter begins and ends with a visual representation of these strategies, which are then integrated into each chapter's discussion. An evaluation section at the end of each chapter allows students to immediately apply what has been learned regarding important strategies.
- In addition, Chapter 1 now features a "Strategies for Success" evaluation, providing students with an opportunity to assess their strengths and weaknesses in each of the six strategy areas at the beginning of the term; they then revisit this assessment in the "Putting It All Together" section at the end of the course.
- A new feature in each chapter, "Career Connections," shows applications of chapter content to real-world job situations that students may have already experienced or could experience in the future.

- While the popular "Where Are You?" checklists at the beginning of each chapter have been retained, the follow-up "Where Are You Now?" lists have been moved to the CD-ROM where they have been consolidated into an end-of-term exercise; now students can more easily mark their progress from the beginning to the end of the course.
- We have updated the high-interest "Images of College Success" profiles at the beginning of each chapter as well as the "Take Charge," "Staying Out of the Pits," and "On Target Tips" features.
- Each chapter ends with a more extensive Chapter Summary section, and Review Questions have been revised to be more varied and interactive.
- The Learning Portfolio at the end of each chapter consists of three Self-Assessments; a variety of Journal activities organized around the principles of reflection, action, critical thinking, and creative thinking; and a new summary activity, "Applying the Six Strategies for Success," where students immediately apply what they have learned in each chapter.
- The CD-ROM that accompanies each new copy of the text has been completely revised to provide additional study opportunities for different learning styles.

Chapter-Specific Changes

The following revisions have been made within each chapter of the text:

Chapter 1   Commit to College Success

- The "Image of College Success" profile on Marian Wright Edelman has been updated.
- Figure 1.2 is revised for greater student interaction.
- A new section, "Evaluating Your Strategies" allows students to assess their strengths and weaknesses in the six key strategy areas at the beginning of the course. They will then revisit this assessment at the end of the text.

Chapter 2   Explore Your Campus, Courses, and Computer

- This was Chapter 4 in the third edition.
- A new section, "Online Education," highlights the prevalence and importance of online courses and electronic supplements which can be particularly helpful for nontraditional students.
- Coverage of health and safety as well as transfer credits has been moved within the chapter for better flow.
- A new Journal activity, "A Current Challenge in My Life," provides an opportunity for students to assess and address a stressful situation.

Chapter 3   Be a Great Time Manager

- The "Images of College Success" profile on "Flo-Jo" has been updated.
- Technological coverage has been updated with information on "smart" cell phones.
- There is expanded coverage of responsibilities of nontraditional students.
- Expanded coverage of the "ABC" method of time management is now combined with discussion of the Covey Matrix method.

- There is a new section on working backwards to meet goals.
- A new Journal activity, "The 80/20 Principle," helps students apply this concept to their own lives.

Chapter 4   Diversify Your Learning Style

- This was Chapter 2 in the third edition.
- A new table has been added that compares different learning styles and relates them to appropriate majors.
- A new section on technological facility updates technological coverage.
- Self-Assessment 2, "Sensory Preference Inventory," has been reorganized.

Chapter 5   Expand Your Thinking Skills

- This was Chapter 9 in the third edition.
- The "Food for Thought" section has been reorganized for better flow.
- A new section on critical thinking and the Internet helps students critically evaluate information they find online.
- A new Journal activity, "Your 'IDEAL'," provides students with an opportunity to practice the IDEAL method of problem solving.

Chapter 6   Take It In: Notes and Reading

- A new "Images of College Success" profile of Ann Coulter has been added.
- There is a new section on strategies for finding your place after getting lost.
- A new section on taking notes from online sources provides guidelines for using online resources.
- Coverage of active listening has been reorganized for better flow.
- Discussion of reading has been reorganized to emphasize activities that occur before, during, and after the reading process.
- A new Journal activity on notetaking allows students to practice this important skill.

Chapter 7   Enhance Your Study Skills and Memory

- The "Images of College Success" profile on Janeane Garofalo has been updated.
- Expanded coverage of memory includes new discussion of procedural versus declarative memory as well as semantic versus episodic memory, with a related figure.
- Discussion of Bloom's Taxonomy has been reorganized for greater clarity.
- There are additional suggestions for using technology while studying.

Chapter 8   Succeed on Tests

- A new Journal activity provides an opportunity for students to practice what they have learned about test preparation in a creative way.

Chapter 9   Refine Your Expression

- This was Chapter 10 in the third edition.
- Added are pointers for using notecards in preparing both written and oral presentations.

- Website addresses for APA and MLA style guidelines have been included.
- A new "On Target Tips" feature provides suggestions for delivering effective PowerPoint presentations.
- A new Journal activity, "PowerPointers," provides students with an opportunity to critique a PowerPoint lecture to improve their own skills in this area.
- A new Journal activity, "The Liberal Arts Flair," encourages students to become familiar with quotations as a way of adding flair to their writing projects.

Chapter 10 Communicate, Build Relationships, and Appreciate Diversity

- This was Chapter 11 in the third edition.
- Increased coverage of diversity is reflected in the revised chapter title, which shows the entire scope of coverage.
- Discussion of the communication loop has been included as well as increased coverage of communication skills.
- A new Journal activity helps students practice overcoming barriers to successful communication.

Chapter 11 Take Charge of Your Physical and Mental Health

- This was Chapter 12 in the third edition.
- The updated "Images of College Success" profile features Brooke Ellison.
- Table 11.1 is integrated into the main narrative.
- Coverage of obesity has been increased to reflect this growing health crisis.
- A discussion and critique of fad diets has been included, featuring the popular Atkins and South Beach diets.
- A new Journal activity, "Evaluate Your Sleep," encourages students to keep a sleep journal to better understand their sleep patterns.

Chapter 12 Be a Great Money Manager

- This was Chapter 3 in the third edition.
- A new example of a monthly budget has been added and integrated with coverage of debt-to-income ratio.
- A new Journal activity provides an opportunity for students to evaluate their values with regard to money.

Chapter 13 Explore Careers

- The "Images of College Success" profile of Giselle Fernandez has been updated.
- The section on college job experience has been moved earlier in the chapter for better flow.
- Updated references to the *Occupational Outlook Handbook* include the 2004/2005 edition.
- Figures 13.1 and 13.2 are integrated into the main narrative.
- A new Journal activity aids students in evaluating their networking potential.

Putting It All Together

- Self-Assessment 2, "What Are My Values"? has been added from Chapter 1 so that students can evaluate how their values have developed and changed throughout the course.
- Students are asked to revisit the strategies evaluation they completed in Chapter 1, repeating the exercise and comparing the visual models representing their areas of strength and weakness.

Ancillaries

For Instructors

Your Guide to College Success: Strategies for Achieving Your Goals, **Fourth Edition, Loose-leaf Advantage Edition (1-413-01365-1).** An unbound, three-hole-punched version of the text complete with front and back cover and ready to be placed into a binder. This version of the popular textbook is ideal for instructors who want to add campus-specific or other unique materials to the book.

Instructor's Manual/Test Bank for *Your Guide to College Success: Strategies for Achieving Your Goals,* **Fourth Edition (1-413-01368-6).** A comprehensive guide for teaching the Freshman Seminar course. Includes sections on using popular culture in the freshman seminar classroom, advice for first-time instructors, and hints on integrating technology resources in the classroom. Each chapter contains additional activities, collaborative learning suggestions, alternative teaching strategies, and quiz questions, including essays to be used for discussion, testing, or journal writing.

NEW: MultiMedia Manager for College Success 2.0: A Microsoft® PowerPoint® Tool (1-413-01414-3). Available upon adoption of the book, this free one-stop presentation tool contains Microsoft PowerPoint lectures, digitized CNN® Today video excerpts, color text images, and live web links.

WebTutor™ on WebCT for *Your Guide to College Success: Strategies for Achieving Your Goals,* **Fourth Edition (0-534-58425-X), or WebTutor™ on Blackboard for** *Your Guide to College Success: Strategies For Achieving Your Goals,* **Fourth Edition (0-534-58353-9).** A content-rich, Web-based teaching and learning tool. Use WebTutor to post syllabi, set up threaded discussions, track student progress on quizzes, and hold virtual office hours. WebTutor is easily customizable to specific course needs. In addition to course management capabilities, WebTutor contains an array of exercises, activities, electronic journal, and additional resources.

ExamView® for *Your Guide to College Success: Strategies for Achieving Your Goals,* **Fourth Edition (1-413-01369-4).** ExamView® enhances the range of assessment and tutorial activities by providing a way to quickly create and customize tests and quizzes. The ExamView test generator offers up to 250 questions made up of twelve different question types.

JoinIn™ on Turning Point® (1-413-01550-6). Thomson Wadsworth is now pleased to offer you book-specific JoinIn™ content for Response Systems tailored to Santrock/Halonen, allowing you to transform your classroom and assess your students' progress with instant in-class quizzes and polls. Our exclusive agreement to offer TurningPoint® software lets you pose book-specific questions and display students' answers seamlessly within the Microsoft PowerPoint slides of your own lecture, in conjunction with the "clicker" hardware of your choice. Enhance how your students interact with you, your lecture, and each other. For college and university adopters only.

Videos: See your local Wadsworth sales representative for more information.

10 Things Every Student Needs to Know to Study **(1-413-01533-6).** This 60-minute video covers such practical skills as note-taking, test-taking, and listening, among others.

CNN® Videos: 2004 Edition, 2003 Edition, and CNN® Videos: 2002 Edition. Three volumes of short, relevant clips from CNN on college success topics are available to launch lectures and stimulate discussion.

For Students

Interactive CD-ROM for *Your Guide to College Success: Strategies for Achieving Your Goals,* **Fourth edition.** A free student CD-ROM is available with the purchase of a new textbook and features a variety of interactive study aids for each chapter, including Self-Assessments, a Quiz, a Journal, exercises that allow you to Evaluate your Strategies for Success, case studies, and a Review of the concepts in the chapter.

College Success Factors Index (0-534-40457-X). Available as a special book bundle This pin-protected website is a student assessment tool that measures eight indices that can affect student adjustment to college life. An excellent pre- and posttest for incoming freshmen, this online assessment provides a way for individual instructors to tailor their course topics to the needs of the students. The data collected can also be applied to longitudinal studies of College Success and Freshman Seminars on a school-wide level. For more information about the CSFI, go to www.success.wadsworth.com.

Wadsworth Premier College Success Academic Planner (0-534-40448-0). Wadsworth is pleased to offer a spiral-bound calendar designed for first-year college students. Featuring 18-month coverage, a unique design and plenty of room for students to record their academic and personal commitments and schedule, the planner is a great way to encourage time management skills. For a minimal price, this planner can be offered as a bundle with your textbook.

Website: http://success.wadsworth.com/santrock4e/

Santrock/Halonen's YOUR GUIDE TO COLLEGE SUCCESS, Fourth Edition companion website provides access to a rich array of teaching and learning resources that you won't find anywhere else. This outstanding site features chapter-by-chapter online practice quizzes, chapter outlines, chapter review, chapter-by-chapter weblinks, flashcards, self-assessments and more!

Acknowledgments

We are fortunate to have worked with two remarkable people—Carolyn Merrill and Rebecca Pascal—whose expertise, passion, and commitment have made the fourth edition of this book far better than its predecessor.

College Success editor Carolyn Merrill provided insights and enthusiasm that helped to dramatically improve the fourth edition of this book. Rebecca Pascal, development editor, put her mind and heart into this positive revision, with the result being a much-improved book. We also appreciate the superb support of this project by Marcus Boggs, Editor-in-Chief, and Susan Badger, Thomson Higher Education CEO. We thank our spouses—Mary Jo Santrock and Brian Halonen—for their enthusiastic support of our work, patient tolerance of our work habits, and goodhumored companionship.

We also would like to extend our appreciation to the reviewers whose time, opinions, and suggestions helped to make this fourth edition a better book:

Anne Daly, *Cumberland County College*
Cynthia Desrcohers, *California State University–Northridge*
Stephen Ford, *Anne Arundel Community College*
Cheryl Fortner-Wood, *Winthrop University*
Elvira Johnson, *Central Piedmont Community College*
Laura Kauffman, *Indian River Community College*
Chris Landrum, *Mineral Area College*
Karen Siska, *Columbia State Community College*
Kathi Williams, *College of the Siskiyous*

In addition, we thank the reviewers of the previous editions:

Alicia Andrade-Owens, *California State University, Fresno*
Anne Aiken-Kush, *University of Nebraska, Omaha*
Frank Ardaiolo, *Winthrop University*
Diane D. Ashe, *Valencia Community College*
Clarence Balch, *Clemson University*
Marilyn Berrill, *Joliet Junior College*
Nate Bock, *University of Nebraska, Omaha*
Phyllis Braxton, *Pierce College, Los Angeles*
Cynthia Bryant, *Tennessee Technical University*
Tricia Bugajski, *University of Northeast Oklahoma*
Bev Cavanaugh, *Joliet Junior College*
Diana Ciesko, *Valencia Community College*
Dorothy R. Clark, *Montgomery Community College*
Carol A. Copenhefer, *Central Ohio Technical College*
Dr. Kara Craig, *University of Southern Mississippi*
Susann B. Deason, *Aiken Community College*
Cynthia Desroches, *California State University, Northridge*
Anthony R. Easley, *Valencia Community College*
Susan Epstein, *Drexel University*
Barbara Foltz, *Clemson University*
D. Allen Goedeke, *High Point University*
Lorraine Gregory, *Duquesne University*
M. Katherine Grimes, *Ferrum College*

Erica Henningsen, *Colorado School of Mines*
Hollace Hubbard, *Lander University*
Lucky Huber, *University of South Dakota*
Cynthia Jenkins, *University of Texas, Dallas*
Elvira Johnson, *Central Piedmont Community College*
Christine Landrum, *Mineral Area College*
Alice Lanning, *University of Oklahoma*
Judy Lynch, *Kansas State University*
Jeannie Manning, *University of Nebraska, Kearney*
Maritza Martinez, *State University of New York, Albany*
Kathleen McGough, *Broward Community College*
Alison Murray, *Indiana University/Purdue University Columbus*
Christina Norman, *University of Oklahoma*
Jean Oppel, *Oklahoma State University*
David M. Parry, *Pennsylvania State Altoona*
Jori Beth Psencik, *University of Texas, Dallas*
Glen Ricci, *Lake Sumter Community College*
Marti Rosen-Atherton, *University of Nebraska, Omaha*
Diane Savoca, *St. Louis Community College*
Regina C. Schmidt, *Texas Women's University*
Kathleen Speed, *Texas A&M University*
Sarah Spreda, *University of Texas, Dallas*
Nancy Taylor, *Radford University*
Karen Valencia, *South Texas Community College*
Vivian Van Donk, *Joliet Junior College*
Kimberly Vitchkoski, *University of Massachusetts, Lowell*
Mary Walz-Chojnacki, *University of Wisconsin–Milwaukee*
Vicki White, *Emmanuel College*
Donald Williams, *Grand Valley State University*
Kaye Young, *Jamestown Community College*

Your Guide to
College Success

1 Commit to College Success

Where Are You? By entering college, you've embarked on an important journey. What is life like as you make this transition? To evaluate where you stand right now, place a check next to only those items that apply to you, leaving the others blank.

- I know what I want from college and am motivated to get it.
- I have clarified my values.
- I set goals, plan how to reach them, and monitor my progress.
- I know my long-term and short-term goals.
- I take responsibility for myself and know how to be internally controlled.
- I have values that connect with college success.
- I have good thinking and learning skills as well as strong computer skills.
- I feel good about myself and have self-confidence.
- I've given some serious thought to careers I might pursue.

As you read about Marian Wright Edelman, think about what her values are and how motivated she is.

1

Images of College Success

Marian Wright Edelman

Marian Wright Edelman founded the Children's Defense Fund in 1973, an advocate group for poor, minority, and handicapped children. For more than two decades she has worked to advance the health and well-being of children in the United States. When she was 14, her father died. The last thing he told her was to let nothing get in the way of her education. Four years later she entered Spelman College in Atlanta. Challenged by college, Edelman responded by working hard. Beginning in her junior year, she won scholarships to study in Paris and Moscow. Edelman later commented that the experiences abroad showed her that she could navigate the world and do just about anything. She later graduated from Yale Law School and became the first African-American woman to pass the bar and practice law in the state of Mississippi.

In her book *The Measure of Our Success* (1992), Edelman high-lighted several lessons for life for college-aged students, including:

Create opportunities. Don't think that you are entitled to anything you don't sweat and struggle for. Take the initiative to create opportunities. Don't wait around for favors. Don't assume a door is closed. Push on it until you get it open.

Challenge yourself to do things right. Everyone makes mistakes. Don't be afraid of taking risks or being criticized. It's the way you learn to do things right. It doesn't matter how many times you fall down. What matters is how many times you get up.

Don't ever stop learning and improving your mind. College is a great investment. But you can't just park your mind there as if everything you need to know will be poured into it. Be an active learner. Be curious and ask questions. Explore every new horizon you can.

MARION WRIGHT EDELMAN (left) mastered the college experience and went on to become a powerful advocate for improving the lives of children.

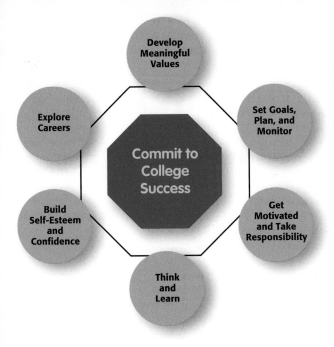

Success in college? It is not enough to just want to be successful. By taking an active role in mastering specific skills and strategies, you can actually shape your own success. The "Six Strategies for Success" listed to the left will help form the foundation of your success . . . not just in college, but in life. As you read each chapter, you will begin to see how much you can accomplish by developing meaningful values, setting and monitoring goals, getting motivated and taking responsibility, thinking and learning, building your self-esteem and confidence, and exploring careers. We will revisit these strategies at the end of each chapter.

Make the College Transition

The key to success in college is knowing what things you value and setting goals to reach them. If you know your goals, you will have no trouble deciding what you need to learn and motivating yourself to learn it. If you let your values steer you through college, you'll feel good about yourself. You'll also prepare yourself to do great things beyond college. In this and every chapter, you'll be able to assess where you are now, what you need to change, and how to change.

Life is change and college is change. Whether you have entered college right out of high school or as a returning student, you'll need to adapt to this new place. What unexpected things are going on around you? What's different? What changes are you going through as you make this transition? Consider these issues in the Journal activity "Your New Life" on page 30.

The High School–College Transition

One first-year student said that a difference between high school and college is that in high school you can't go off campus for lunch because you aren't allowed but that in college you can't do this because you can't afford it.

Another student said the difference between high school and college is that in college it's much more difficult to figure out the course schedule of the man or woman you have a crush on in order to figure out where he or she will be on campus at a certain time so you can "accidentally" say hello.

You can probably come up with many other differences between high school and college.

> Life is change.
> Growth is optional.
> Choose wisely.
> Karen Kaiser Clark
> *20th-century American author*

- *College classes are much larger, more complex, and more impersonal.* Your teachers in high school probably knew your name and maybe even your family. In college, however, your instructors may not know your name or recognize your face outside class.
- *In college, attendance may be up to you.* Although some of your instructors will require attendance, many won't. If you miss class, it's your responsibility to find out what you missed. Most instructors do not allow makeup work without a reasonable, well-documented explanation.

- *College instructors give fewer tests.* They may hold you responsible for more than what they say in class. Some won't let you make up tests.
- *In college, nobody treats you like a kid anymore.* You have more independence, choices, and responsibility. You are more on your own about how you use your time than you were in high school.
- *You have to do much more reading in college.* More of your work will need to be done outside class. You may be expected to make your own decisions about what information from your reading is most important for you to remember.
- *Good grades are harder to get in college.* In many colleges, there is more competition for grades than in high school, and instructors set the bar higher for an A or B.
- *Your college classmates may be more diverse in age and backgrounds.* Look around. You'll probably see more older individuals and more people from different cultures than you did in your high school.

Strengths of Returning Students

An increasing number of students start or finish college at an older age (Sax & others, 2004). More than one out of five full-time and two thirds of part-time students today are returning students. Some work full time, are married, have children or grandchildren, are divorced, retired, or changing careers. Some have attended college before while others have not.

If you have entered or returned to college at an older age, you may experience college differently from recent high school graduates. You may have to balance your class work with commitments to a partner, children, a job, and community responsibilities. This means you may have less flexibility about when you can attend classes. You may need child care or have special transportation needs. As an older student, you may lack confidence in your skill and abilities or undervalue your knowledge and experience.

Despite such challenges, as a returning student you bring specific strengths to campus. These include a wide range of life experiences that you can apply to issues and problems in class. Your multiple commitments may stimulate you to be more skilled than younger students in managing your time. You may have greater maturity in work habits and more experience participating in discussions. You may also face setbacks more easily. Failing a pop quiz, for instance, is not likely to feel devastating for those who have experienced greater disappointments in life. See On Target Tips, "Returning-Student Strategies" for some helpful guidelines.

ON TARGET TIPS

Returning-Student Strategies

Evaluate your support system. A strong and varied support system can help you adapt to college. If you have a partner or family, their encouragement and understanding can help a lot. Your friends also can lend support.

Make new friends. As you seek out friends of different ages, focus on meeting other older students. You'll find they also juggle responsibilities and are anxious about their classes.

Get involved in campus life. The campus is not just for younger students. Check out the organizations and groups at your college. Join one or more that interest you.

Don't be afraid to ask for help. Learn about the services your college offers. Health and counseling services can help you with the special concerns of older students. These include parenting and child care, divorce, and time management. If you have any doubts about your academic skills, get some help from the study skill professionals on your campus.

Why Are You in College?

As you make the transition to college, you need to be aware of why you're here. What are your reasons for being in college? You can complete Self-Assessment 1 "Why Am I Here?" on page 27 to evaluate your motivation. Are you here for the "right" reasons? That is, do your reasons for being in college connect with what you think is important in life? What *are* your values?

Develop Meaningful Values

What are some strengths of returning students?

Just what are "values"? Values are our beliefs and attitudes about the way we think things *should* be. They involve what is important to us. We attach values to all sorts of things: politics, religion, money, sex, education, helping others, family, friends, self-discipline, career, cheating, taking risks, self-respect, and so on. As the contemporary U.S. columnist Ellen Goodman commented, "Values are not trendy items that can be traded in."

Connect Your Values with College Success

One of the most important benefits of college is that it gives you the opportunity to explore and clarify your values. Why is this so critical? Our values represent what matters most to us, so they should guide our decisions. Without seriously reflecting on what your values are, you may spend too much time in your life on things that really aren't that important to you. Clarifying your values will help you determine which goals you really want to go after and where to direct your motivation. "Develop meaningful values" is one of the most important "Strategies for Success" listed on page 3 and explored throughout this book.

Sometimes we're not aware of our values until we find ourselves in situations that expose them. For example, you might be surprised to find yourself reacting strongly when you discuss religion or politics with other students. Spend some time thinking about and clarifying your values. This will help you determine what things in life are most important to you. Self- Assessment 2 "What Are My Values" on page 28 will help you with this process.

One of the values listed in this self-assessment is "happiness." What makes college students happy? One recent study compared very happy college students with their counterparts who were average in happiness or unhappy (Diener & Seligman, 2002). Very happy college students were more likely to be socially connected, including positive romantic and social relationships.

Many students place family relationships high on their list of values. Positive, supportive family relationships can help you through some difficult times as you go through college. One self-assessment that you can take to discover the extent of your family's involvement in your values is called the *College Success Factors Index* (Halberg & others, 2000). You can complete this self-assessment at the Wadsworth College Success website: <http://success.wadsworth.com>.

Stephen Covey, author of the highly successful book, *The 7 Habits of Highly Effective People: Powerful Lessons in Personal Change* (1989), has helped many individuals

> *Your character is what you really are.*
>
> John Wooden
> *Former UCLA basketball coach*

Clarify Your Values

Stephen Covey and his colleagues (Covey, Merrill, & Merrill, 1994) recommend the following to help you clarify your values (use your watch to go through the timed exercises):

1. Take one minute and answer this question: *If I had unlimited time and resources, what would I do?* It's okay to dream. Write down everything that comes into your mind.

2. Return to Self-Assessment 2 on page 28 and review the list of five values that are the most important to you.

3. Take several minutes to compare this list with your dreams. You may be living with unconscious dreams that don't mesh with your values. If you don't get your dreams out in the open, you may spend years living with illusions and the feeling that you somehow are settling for second best. Work on the two lists until you feel that your dreams match up with your values.

4. Take one minute to see how your values relate to four fundamental areas of human fulfillment: physical needs, social needs, mental needs, and spiritual needs. Do your values reflect these four needs? Work on your list until they do.

clarify their values. He stresses that each of us needs to identify the underlying principles that are important in our lives and then evaluate whether we are living up to those standards. Covey asks you to imagine that you are attending your own funeral and are looking down at yourself in the casket. You then take a seat, and four speakers (a family member, a friend, someone from your work, and someone from your church or community organization) are about to give their impression of you. What would you want them to say about your life? This reflective thinking exercise helps you to look into the social mirror and visualize how other people see you. See On Target Tips, "Clarify Your Values," for some other helpful tips from Covey.

Forge Academic Values

Throughout your college career, you will be making many choices that reflect your values. Although your primary goal in seeking a college education may be learning about new ideas, your journey through college can also help to build your character.

Participate Fully College involves a higher level of personal responsibility than most students experienced in high school. This freedom can be alluring, even intoxicating. Especially when instructors do not require attendance, you may be tempted to skip classes. What's wrong with skipping class?

It's expensive. See Figure 1.1 to calculate how much a skipped class will cost.
It harms your learning.
It hurts your grades.
It annoys those who end up lending you their notes to copy. (If you must miss a class, be sure to borrow notes from someone who is doing well in the course!)

You will frequently have opportunities to clarify your academic values throughout college. For example, when you make a choice to linger over a computer game rather than get to class on time, you make a statement about what really matters to you. The frivolous minutes you spend in short-term pleasures may cost you some points on the next exam. Deciding early to do your best, even if it requires sacrifice, will have the best long-term payoff.

Participate Honorably Most campuses publish their expectations about appropriate academic conduct in the college handbook. Many colleges have adopted an honor code to promote academic integrity. This represents your formal agreement to abide by rules of conduct that promote trust and high ethical standards. Typically, codes address such problems as cheating, plagiarism (submitting someone else's work for your own), or other forms of dishonest performance. When a student violates the

"*I've got the bowl, the bone, the big yard. I know I should be happy.*"

campus honor code, it dictates how severe the consequences might be. These may include something as mild as "censure," formal recognition of wrongdoing, to expulsion from school.

Why do some students make choices that put them at risk for expulsion? They engage in misdirected problem solving based on faulty conclusions:

1. *The risk of getting caught is small.* Students have witnessed lots of academic misconduct in their own careers by other students who have gotten away with it. They violate academic expectations because they assume they won't get caught either.

2. *There is no other way to be "successful."* Students may get so far behind in their work that they don't trust what they have learned to help them succeed on tests or papers. These students focus on getting an acceptable grade by any means available rather than letting the grade legitimately stand for their learning.

3. *It doesn't matter in the long run.* Some students don't see the connection between the violations of academic trust and the quality of their character development and education. Cutting corners in the classroom can eventually forge bad habits that may show up later in professional life as "cooked books," malpractice, or other violations of professional ethics.

4. *The penalty for getting caught won't be severe.* Some students take the risk because they are confident that penalties may not be imposed. They may have heard honor code procedures discourage faculty from reporting students or they simply believe that they will be able to fast-talk their professors out of taking a severe stance.

All of these examples illustrate how students can miss the point. Every academic performance you render gives you an opportunity to exercise your own values and demonstrate your character. Why should you embrace academic integrity and commit to doing your best?

1. *Practicing academic integrity builds moral character.* Doing the right thing often means doing the hard thing. It may mean sacrificing personal advantage to achieve an outcome for the benefit of others. However, doing the right things also feels good when you avoid the suspicion, guilt, and ambiguity caused by the wrong choice.

2. *Choosing moral actions builds others' trust in you.* We expect others to treat us fairly and appropriately. Violating the academic trust signals to others that the character flaw you exhibit in the classroom could carry over to other settings as well.

3. *Making fraudulent grades masks important feedback about learning.* An artificially high grade may cheat you of the opportunity to recognize your learning deficits and address them appropriately before you graduate.

4. *Improving integrity in the classroom can rebuild national character.* The recent emergence of massive corporate crimes linked to greed has prompted many social critics to suggest that the country has lost its moral compass. Embracing principles of academic integrity will be fundamental to helping us resurrect our moral foundations.

By clarifying your values, you gain a better idea of where to direct your energy and motivation. The following sections are intended to help you build a strong connection between personal values, goals, and motivation.

FIGURE 1.1 The Cost of Cutting Class

How much tuition did you pay for this term?

How many credits must you take on your campus to be considered full-time?

Divide the full-time hours into your tuition dollars (cost per credit hour):

How many credit hours does the course you're most tempted to avoid have?

Multiply the course credit hours by the cost per credit hour (cost of the course):

How many classes meet in this course over the term?

Divide the cost of the course by the number of classes:

The final calculation represents the financial loss that happens every time you cut this class.

Set Goals, Plan, and Monitor

As you have seen, college success begins with determining your personal values. The next step is to set specific goals based on these values, plan how to reach them, and monitor your progress. In the "Strategies for Success" model on page 3, setting goals is directly linked to the development of values, as they influence each other throughout life.

Set Goals and Plan How to Reach Them

> *A goal is a dream with a deadline.*
>
> Napoleon Hill
> *Contemporary American author*

How important are goals? Two sports figures expressed their thoughts about this question. Former NBA star Julius Erving, who went on to be very successful in business, summed up the importance of goals this way: "Goals determine what you are going to be." University of South Carolina football coach Lou Holtz said that if you're bored with life—you don't get up every morning with a burning desire to do things—you don't have enough goals.

Let's see how you might connect your personal values with setting goals. Suppose that one of the values you chose in Self-Assessment 2 on page 28 was being well educated. If so, then it's important for you to set educational goals and plan how to reach them. If one of the values you selected was "contributing to the welfare of others," it is then important to set goals pertaining to this, such as participating in at least one service learning activity per month like volunteering at a nursing home for the elderly.

Students vary considerably in the extent to which they set goals and plan. Those who never do these things usually don't excel in college. Those who do excel realize that the time they take to set goals will pay off in helping them get done what they need to get done on time. When students don't set goals or plan, time tends to slip away until it's too late for them to accomplish what they want or perform as well as they could.

Set Goals That Are Challenging, Reasonable, and Specific For every goal that you set, ask yourself, "Is it challenging? Is it reasonable? Is it specific?" When you set challenging goals, you commit to improving yourself. Be realistic, but stretch yourself to achieve something meaningful. Also, when you set goals, be concrete and precise. An abstract goal is, "I want to be successful," A precise, concrete goal is, "I want to achieve a 3.5 average this term." One study found that individuals who construct their goals in concrete terms were 50 percent more likely to be confident that they would attain them and 32 percent more likely to feel in control of their lives than those who created abstract goals (Howatt, 1999).

Precision is an important aspect of goal setting. If you are sloppy and haphazard in setting goals, your success will be hard to measure. Measuring the outcome of your effort will help you monitor your progress and experience the satisfaction of reaching the goal.

Set Long-Term and Short-Term Goals Have both long-term and short-term goals. Some long-term goals, such as becoming a successful teacher or getting into medical school, take years to reach. Other goals are more short-term, such as doubling study time next week or perhaps simply not drinking this weekend.

Make a Personal Plan

A goal is nothing without a means of achieving it. Good planning means getting organized mentally, which often requires writing things down. It means getting your life in order and controlling your time and your life, instead of letting your world and time control you.

Set Completion Dates for Your Goals Set completion dates for your goals and work out schedules to meet them. If you want to obtain a college degree, you might want to set a goal of four to six years from now as your completion date depending on how much time each year you can devote to college. If your goal is to make one good friend, you might want to set a time of six weeks from now for achieving it. If your goal is to become the funniest person on campus, set a date for that as well.

Create Subgoals In *Even Eagles Need a Push* (1990), David McNally suggests that as you set goals and plan, you should think in terms of intermediate steps or subgoals. McNally recommends living your life one day at a time and making your commitments in daily bite-sized chunks. Don't let long periods of time slip by when you aren't working on something that will help you reach your goals.

You don't need to do everything today, but you should do something every day. Researchers have found that people who do not feel they are taking steps toward their goals are five times more likely to give up and three times less likely to feel satisfied with their lives (Elliott, 1999). The U.S. Olympic speed-skating champion Bonnie Blair described how she thinks about and acts on goals every day: "No matter what the competition is, I try to find a goal that day and better that goal."

In many cases, reaching a goal involves several activities. Say that one of your life goals is obtaining a college degree. You can break this down into either four subgoals (if you're in a four-year degree program) or two subgoals (if you're in a community college). Each subgoal can be the successful completion of a year in your degree program. These subgoals can be broken down into exams, quizzes, term papers, amount of time you plan to study each week, and so on. Figure 1.2 illustrates this strategy.

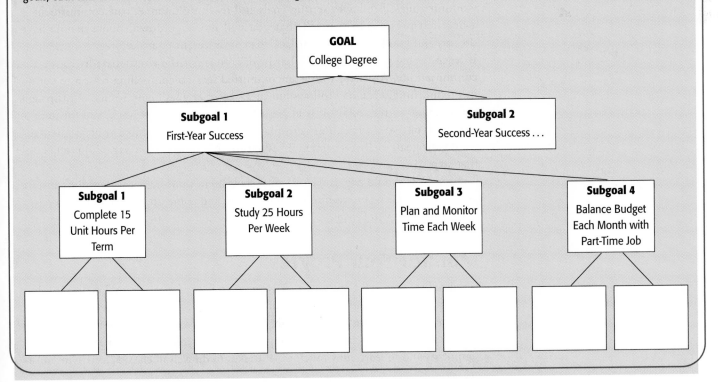

FIGURE 1.2 Creating Subgoals

You could divide your goals of college success into subgoals of success for each college year. For each year, you develop more detailed subgoals, each within its own time frame. Fill in additional subgoals in the blank spaces below.

GOAL
College Degree

Subgoal 1
First-Year Success

Subgoal 2
Second-Year Success . . .

Subgoal 1
Complete 15 Unit Hours Per Term

Subgoal 2
Study 25 Hours Per Week

Subgoal 3
Plan and Monitor Time Each Week

Subgoal 4
Balance Budget Each Month with Part-Time Job

TABLE 1.1 Steps for Completing a Term Paper

GOAL: Psychology Term Paper

Subgoals/Intermediate Steps	Deadline
1. Meet with instructor to explore topic for paper	10/1
2. Conduct library research on topic	10/15
3. Write several draft outlines of paper	10/22
4. Meet with instructor to go over topic and proposal	10/29
5. Write first draft of paper	11/15
6. Edit first draft	11/22
7. Write second draft of paper	11/29
8. Meet with instructor for further feedback on paper	12/6
9. Make final adjustments, write final draft, and proofread	12/13
10. Turn in paper	12/20

The more you can order steps or subgoals into a series, the more easily you can accomplish each. Writing a good term paper involves many tasks that you can break down into fairly orderly stages. Table 1.1 provides an example of how this might work. In your planning, work backward from the final due date, reserving enough time for each step. You can apply this same approach to many college goals.

Be sure to assign a completion date to each intermediate step. Without doing this, time often sprouts wings and flies away. Before you know it, you won't have time to do all of the tasks necessary to do well on a project. For example, in writing an important paper, you might end up doing only a crude first draft because you didn't have enough time to revise or to accept an instructor's offer to give you feedback.

Anticipate and Overcome Obstacles It not only is a good idea to develop effective strategies for overcoming obstacles when they arise, but also it is a good idea to spend time anticipating what obstacles might come up in the future. Take stock of the next week, month, and term. Think about some problems that might appear down the road, such as not having adequate math or writing skills to do well on assignments, a shortfall of money, a failed friendship, or a lost romantic relationship. Developing the skills now to deal with such problems can help you cope with such obstacles to college success if they arise in the future.

Commit and Get Started Now

Commit yourself today to setting goals and reaching them. A true commitment is a heartfelt promise to yourself that you will not back down. Some people have dreams and good intentions but lack the commitment to make dreams come true. If reaching big goals sounds like hard work, consider the alternative: living an uncommitted life. A person who is uncommitted sees no compelling reason to get up in the morning. One day follows another, the only goal being to make it through the day. Get started today on your goals for the term, for next week, and for tomorrow. Map out your plans. Put your plan into action and monitor your progress toward your goals. Self-Assessment 3 "What Are My Goals?" (on page 29) is a helpful first step.

Your goals should engage you. If your goals do not move you, if they don't inspire you to action, then you need to reevaluate them and come up with goals that do challenge and excite you (Niven, 2001).

Monitor Your Progress

It not only is critical for you to set goals and plan how to reach them, but also it is important to monitor your progress toward your goals to help you discover new courses of action for improving your academic performance. Without this monitoring, you'll likely fall behind in a class. Monitoring will improve your ability to keep up with assignments and to learn how much time it takes to do well in class. Effective monitoring lets you know whether you are spending too little time on the tasks you need to complete to accomplish your goal and involves posing questions and asking what you need to know and find out in order to draw effective conclusions about your progress toward a goal.

This even means making daily lists of things you need to do to stay on track toward your goal and monitoring whether you do these. After writing down your goals, place the list where you can easily see it, such as on a calendar or taped to the inside of your personal planner or address book. Chapter 3 discusses such strategies in more depth. If after a week or month you find that you are falling behind, evaluate what you can do to get back on track.

It is also important to look at the setbacks you experience as opportunities to learn (Niven, 2001). Not only can you learn what you might have done wrong, but also you can learn what led you to choices you have made. Are you seeking the goals you truly want? Make it a habit to gain some understanding every time things don't go your way. Many students drop out of college because they don't know how to cope with failures and learn from them. To help you anticipate obstacles to completing college successfully, complete the Journal activity "Manage Your Risk" on page 31.

Analyzing your successes and failures can help you better understand yourself and the changes you need to make in your life. One study found that a majority of students who failed in college and later returned to obtain their degree said the main difference in their second chance was better knowledge of themselves, their capabilities, and their commitments (Robeson, 1998). In sum, make it a point to learn from your losses.

Get Motivated and Take Responsibility

Consider the values and motivation that Terry Fox, a young Canadian, must have had. Fox ran 3,339 miles across Canada, averaging a marathon run each day for five months. He performed this tremendous feat as an amputee and a survivor of cancer to raise money for cancer research. Before his run, Terry had set a goal and was intensely motivated to reach it. He wanted his life to have a purpose and to make a difference in this world. He surpassed his goal.

Whether or not we can ever match Terry Fox's motivation, the lesson is clear. When we want something badly enough, we expend the energy and effort to get it. This book describes many strategies that will help you to succeed in college, but all the strategies in the world won't help you unless you become motivated to learn them and use them. In the "Six Strategies for Success" model on page 3, getting motivated and taking responsibility is directly linked with goal setting as the two go hand in hand in college and throughout life.

In national surveys, when pitted against other factors such as intelligence and ability, how motivated people are proves to be a better predictor of career success (Bradshaw & Grant, 1994). How can you become motivated to succeed?

© Bettmann/CORBIS

Terry Fox exemplifies the importance of getting motivated, planning, and setting goals in life. He spent considerable time planning his run. Although he faced some unforeseen obstacles, such as ice storms, he reached his goal.

Develop an Internal Locus of Control

If you take responsibility for your successes and failures, you would be said to have an internal locus of control. If you don't take such personal responsibility and let others, or luck, be responsible for what happens to you, you would be said to have an external locus of control. Being internally controlled means seeing yourself as responsible for your achievement, believing that your own effort is what gets you to your goals, and being self-motivated. To help determine your locus of control, complete the Self-Assessment: "Evaluating My Locus of Control" on the CD-ROM that accompanies this book.

Being internally controlled can help you succeed in college. For example, research studies have found that internally controlled students are more likely than externally controlled students to:

Have a stronger work ethic (Mendoza, 1999).
Possess high self-esteem (Stipek, 2002).
Be aware that their grades are strongly linked to how much effort they put forth (Wigfield & Eccles, 2002).
Attain a grade point average of one full letter grade higher (Niven, 2001).

Widely read author M. Scott Peck (1978, 1997) made some insightful comments in his book *The Road Less Traveled* about internal control and self-responsibility. He says that life is difficult and that each of us will experience pain and disappointment. Peck believes that we might be right that some of our problems are caused by other people, including our parents. However, you are not going to succeed in college and life thereafter by continually blaming others. Peck urges you to take responsibility for yourself. On Target Tips, "Becoming More Internally Controlled," encourages you to think critically about how to become more self-motivated.

Being internally motivated, though, does not mean doing everything in isolation. Surround yourself with other motivated people. Ask individuals who are successful how they motivate themselves. Find a mentor, such as an experienced student, an instructor, or a teaching assistant you respect, and ask his or her advice on motivation. You also can benefit from thinking about a person you would call your "hero" and "inspirational leader" by completing the Journal activity "My Hero" on page 31.

Some first-year college students lack motivation because they have not separated their parents' "shoulds" from their own, sometimes opposite, interests and motivations. Examine your motivations and interests. Are they yours, or are you currently acting as a "clone" to fulfill your parents' or someone else's motivations and interests? Your motivation will catch fire when you are doing what YOU want to do.

Because taking responsibility for yourself is such an important dimension of college success, in each chapter you will find special sections titled "Take Charge." The first one guides you through the creation of a mission statement.

Expect to Succeed and Persist until You Do

Do you expect to do poorly in college or to be highly successful? How much effort do you put into your academic work? Both expecting to succeed and persisting with a great deal of effort will positively impact how well you will do in your courses.

College students who expect to succeed are often more likely to do so than those who expect failure (Brissette, Scheier, & Carver, 2002). Consider having a long, difficult assignment due the next day. A negative expectation might be: "I'll never get this work done by tomorrow," whereas positive expectations include: "If I work really hard I think I can get this done," or "This is going to be tough but I think I'm up to the challenge." Consider also having to participate in a class discussion. A negative expectation might be: "Everyone else knows more than I do, so what's the use of saying anything" or "I'm afraid I'll say something that others will think is stupid," whereas positive expectations include: "I have as much to say as anyone in the class" and "It's okay to be nervous; I'll relax as I start talking." Complete the Journal activity "College Graduation Day" on page 31 to practice having positive expectations.

Being motivated not only involves having expectations for success, it also involves persistence. Getting through college is a marathon, not a 100-yard dash. Studying a little here and a little there won't work. To be successful you have to study often, almost every day for weeks and months at a time. You'll often need to make small sacrifices to gain long-term rewards. College is not all work and no play, but if you mainly play you will pay for it by the end of the term. Remember, from the beginning of the chapter, Marian Wright Edelman's advice not to feel entitled to anything for which you don't sweat and struggle. See "Staying Out of the Pits, Here Comes the Beer Truck" for a real-life example.

Get Involved and Tackle Boredom

Successful college students are often involved in college activities (Astin, 1993). This can be accomplished in many ways—through socializing and studying with friends, engaging in extracurricular activities, living on campus, having a part-time campus job, and interacting with faculty. Students who are not involved in college activities frequently feel socially isolated and unhappy with their college experience.

We will further examine college involvement in Chapter 2. You may be fired up about college, enjoying all your courses and socializing—you couldn't be happier. Or you may not be enjoying it at this stage. You may already feel homesick, lonely, bored, or just plain lost. If you fall into the latter camp, what can you do about it?

Explore New Avenues For starters, think more deeply about the values you listed in Self-Assessment 2 "What Are My Values?". What interests do these values suggest? To explore them, you can get to know new people, seek out new situations, ask new questions, read new books, and reexamine your school's catalog for new ideas and possibilities that turn on your mind.

Shaq Goes Back

We put in a lot of effort and believed in ourselves.

Shaquille O'Neal, *after winning the 2000 NBA Championship.*
Note: Shaq left LSU before graduating to play in the NBA but recently returned to college and obtained his undergraduate degree in 2001.

STAYING OUT OF THE PITS

It's Noon Thursday. Here Comes the Beer Truck.

One first-year student showed up at college motivated to do well. He never partied much in high school and really did not have plans to party and drink much in college. But things changed quickly. By the luck of the draw, his first roommate's father owned a major national brewery. The roommate conned one of the drivers who worked for his dad's company to deliver several kegs to him each week. Every Thursday around noon the beer truck pulled up and unloaded the kegs. And the party was on.

The student from the beer company family was a fun-loving, persuasive fellow. It didn't take long for him to convince his more naive, serious roommate that he was missing out on a lot of fun. How did it all end? Their parties went on several months before they got thrown out of the dorm. With all Fs at the end of the term, both were kicked out of school.

For several months, as they played and partied, their immediate gratification felt great. By the end of the term, they began to wonder where all the fun had gone.

Tune in to Inspiration Keep track of the moments in the day or week when you feel the most energetic and inspired because of what you are doing or what you see and hear around you. What do these moments tell you about how to become more involved and less bored or unhappy?

Think and Learn

Above all, college is a place to think and learn. More specifically, it is a place to practice thinking reflectively, critically, and productively. Keep an open mind about different ideas and decide for yourself what you believe. Evaluate, analyze, create, solve problems, and poke holes in arguments. Be prepared to show "why" and back up your assertions with solid evidence. Don't just stay on the surface of problems. Stretch your mind. Become deeply immersed in meaningful thinking. In the "Six Strategies for Success" model on page 3, thinking and learning are important strategies directly linked with motivation. Get motivated to make the most of college as an opportunity to strengthen these important skills.

You learn when you adapt and change because of experience. Make it a high priority to learn from both your successes and failures. Make a commitment not to make the same mistake twice. Identify your weaknesses and develop strategies for strengthening those weaknesses or working around them in a way that promotes your college success. For example, if you are not a good writer, take full advantage of the writing center on your campus. Begin to identify your weaknesses by completing the Journal activity "The Magic Wand" on page 31.

Focus Your Talents and Master Work Skills

Some courses may put you to sleep because they don't tie in well with your needs and current interests. Others may spark new interests and even make you passionate about a subject. Where you "catch fire" and become highly motivated to learn will point you to a successful future. Remember that not all learning takes place in the classroom. If a topic in class seems interesting to you, explore it more deeply. Scan books and journals and do online searches on the topic, picking out several articles to read more closely.

Success in college and in life requires self-discipline and good work habits. These habits will help you become not only a better student in college but also a valuable employee, a skilled professional, or a resourceful entrepreneur afterward. This book shows the best ways to stay on task, on time, and under budget. The strategies presented will give you more hours not only for study but also for play and sleep.

To succeed in college you need many work skills such as knowing how to take good notes, participate in class, collaborate with other students, and interact with instructors. You also need good study and test-taking strategies and good reading, writing, and speaking skills. The following chapters will provide you with a solid foundation and extensive strategies for improving these skills.

Explore Your Learning Styles

Some people learn mainly by doing things themselves. Others learn best by watching or listening to someone lecture. Still others learn best by reading, or doing field projects or laboratory experiments.

Your college experience will help you to sort through the ways you prefer to learn. In Chapter 4, you'll explore learning styles extensively and determine those at which you excel. You'll also learn some strategies that can improve your flexibility in using different learning styles. This exploration continues throughout the book.

Manage Your Time

Learning takes a lot of time. Your life as a college student will benefit enormously if you become a great time manager. If you waste too much time, you'll find yourself poorly prepared the night before an important exam, for instance. If you manage time well, you can relax before exams and other deadlines. Time management will help you be more productive and less stressed, with a better balance between work and play. Chapter 3 is all about managing time. Among other things, it will explain how to set priorities, eliminate procrastination, and monitor your time.

Think Critically and Creatively

There is no getting around the fact that you are going to have to spend quite a bit of time memorizing material to do well in many courses. We will discuss a number of effective memory strategies in Chapter 7. However, you will get the most out of your college experience when you go beyond just memorizing information and think critically and creatively.

"Doctor, have you any advice to offer a young man who would love to be a physician but whose crowded schedule simply doesn't permit time for medical school?"

Thinking critically involves more than learning how to make sound arguments, solve problems, and make good decisions. Thinking creatively involves coming up with unique, innovative ideas and solutions to problems. We will further explore thinking critically and thinking creatively in Chapter 5. Also, in the Learning Portfolio at the end of each chapter, you will be given opportunities to think critically and creatively.

Communicate Effectively

A very important aspect of college success and life thereafter is having effective communication skills. College will provide you with many opportunities to refine and improve your speaking, writing, and listening skills. When interviewing college graduates for prospective jobs, many employers rate communication skills as the important factor in hiring a job candidate. We will explore many aspects of speaking and writing skills in Chapter 9, and examine listening and communication skills in relationships in Chapter 10.

Use Your Resources

An important aspect of learning is figuring out what resources are available to you and the best way to use them. Family members and friends can be important resources. Your college also has many resources that can support your college success, including academic advisors, physicians, mental health counselors, and many others. Become acquainted with these resources early in your college transition and don't hesitate to use them when you think that you need help. We will extensively explore your connection to campus and ways to use college resources in the next chapter.

Join the Information Age

To get the most out of your college education, you need to be familiar with computers. We encourage you to take every opportunity to use the computer and applications such as word processing, e-mail, and the World Wide Web effectively. If you

DILBERT reprinted by permission of United Feature Syndicate, Inc.

don't already have good computer skills, developing them will make your college life much easier and improve your chances of landing a good job later. To be blunt, if you don't develop computer skills, you are likely to get left behind. Can you think of a career in which computers aren't used? From the humanities to the sciences, we now are squarely in the middle of the information age and the technological revolution.

Throughout the book, you'll find strategies using technology to your advantage in both college and your career. For example, Chapter 3 presents the benefits of electronic planners. Chapter 2 offers other strategies for using computers. On the website for this book at http://success.wadsworth.com/santrock4e/ you can connect with many other sites that have information to help you master college.

Build Self-Esteem and Confidence

Building self-esteem will improve your chances of college success. What is self-esteem? Sometimes called self-worth or self-image, it is your general evaluation of yourself—how you feel about you, the image you have of yourself. One of the important "Strategies for Success" listed on page 3, building your self-esteem and confidence will improve your performance in college and beyond, as well as make you a happier, more satisfied individual.

Evaluate Your Self-Esteem

Many things in your life contribute to your self-esteem: how much you have succeeded or failed, how much the people around you (parents, friends, peers, teachers) positively evaluate or criticize you, whether you tend to be optimistic or pessimistic, and so forth. What is your current level of self-esteem? To evaluate this, you can complete Self-Assessment "Evaluating My Self-Esteem" on your CD-ROM. You also can visit a campus counselor for a more personalized assessment.

Raising Your Self-Esteem

Building self-esteem will give you the confidence to tackle difficult tasks and create a positive vision of the future. It will help you reach your goals and give you the confidence to act on your values. If you have low self-esteem, commit to raising it. Following are some good strategies for increasing self-esteem based on a number of research studies (Bednar, Wells, & Peterson, 1995).

Have Confidence in Yourself Above all else, have confidence in yourself. Believe in your ability to succeed and do well in life. Believing that you can make changes in your life is a key aspect of improving your self-esteem. Psychologists call this ability to believe that one can make effective changes in their lives *self-efficacy* (Bandura, 2001). Individuals who don't think they can make such changes often never even take the first step to improve themselves. Researchers have found that confidence, in combination with a realistic self-appraisal, produces a 30 percent increase in college students' satisfaction with their lives (Sedlacek, 1999).

Monitor what you do and say to yourself. Putting yourself down will only lower your self-esteem. Take responsibility for yourself and believe in your abilities. Remember, though, if you have legitimate weaknesses in skill areas, such as math or English, just thinking positive thoughts won't be enough. You'll also need to work hard to improve your skills. This may involve obtaining support through tutoring, study skills workshops, and the like.

"*It took a long time before I could look myself in the mirror and say, 'I'm Frosty the Snowman, and I like me.'*"

Identify Causes of Low Self-Esteem Identifying the sources of low self-esteem is critical to increasing it. Is your low self-esteem the result of bad grades? Is it because you live with people who constantly criticize you and put you down? Explore ways to change these sources.

Define Important Areas of Competence Students have the highest self-esteem when they perform competently in the areas of their lives that matter to them. If doing well in school is important to you, then academic success will increase your self-esteem. If you value being well connected in society, having a great social life will increase your self-esteem. Consider the actor Arnold Schwarzenegger. He did not stop at his physical achievements. He also took college courses in business to give him added competence and self-esteem to launch a film career and other enterprises, and eventually he became governor of California.

> *The greatest discovery of any generation is that human beings can change their lives by changing their attitudes.*
>
> Albert Schweitzer
> *20th-century French missionary*

Get Emotional Support and Social Approval Emotional support and social approval can increase your self-esteem. When people say nice things to us, are warm and friendly, and approve of what we say and do, our self-esteem improves. Sources of emotional support and social approval include friends, family, classmates, and counselors. Seek out supportive people and find ways to give support back.

Achieve Achievement boosts self-esteem. Learning new skills can increase both achievement and self-esteem. For example, learning better study skills can improve your GPA. This, in turn, might do wonders for how you feel about yourself this term and will also pay off in the long run.

Cope Self-esteem also increases when we tackle a problem instead of fleeing. Coping makes us feel good about ourselves. When we avoid coping with problems, they mount up and lower our self-esteem. You also can evaluate your coping strategies by completing the Journal activity "Conscious Coping" on page 30.

Explore Careers

Exploring careers is a key aspect of your college experience. Take advantage of the career counseling opportunities at your college.

Exploring careers now will help you link your short-term and college goals with some of your long-term life goals and be motivated by your long-term prospects. What do you plan to make your life's work? Is there a specific career or several careers that you want to pursue? If you have a career in mind, how certain are you that it is the best one for you? Begin to explore these questions by completing the Journal activity "Toward Your Future" on page 31.

An important aspect of college is training for a career. Each of us wants to find a rewarding career and enjoy the work we do. If you're a typical first-year student, you may not have any idea yet of which particular career you would like to pursue. That's okay for right now, especially if you're currently taking a lot of general education courses. But as you move further along in college it becomes ever more important to develop such ideas about your future. The sixth and final point in the "Six Strategies for Success" model on page 3 is exploring careers. This strategy links back to the first point, developing meaningful values, demonstrating the interconnectedness of all six strategies for success.

> *As long as you keep searching, the answers will come.*
> Joan Baez
> *Contemporary American folksinger*

Connect College and Careers

Choosing a career based on a college education will likely bring you a higher income and a longer, happier life. College graduates can enter careers that will earn them considerably more money in their lifetimes than those who do not go to college (Occupational Outlook Handbook, 2004–2005). In the United States, individuals with a bachelor's degree make over $1,000 a month more on average than those with only a high school diploma. Individuals with two years of college and an associate degree make over $500 a month more than those who only graduated from high school. Over a lifetime, a college graduate will make approximately $600,000 more on average than a high school graduate will! College graduates also report being happier with their work and having more continuous work records than those who don't attend or don't finish college.

How would you like to give yourself several more years of life? One of the least-known ways to do this is to graduate from college. If you do, you will likely live longer than your less-educated counterparts. How much longer? At least one year longer. And if you go to college for five years or more, you are expected to live three years longer than you would if you had only finished high school.

Master Content and Develop Work and People Skills

A successful career often involves three things:

1. Gaining specialized knowledge of the content of a particular field (like electrical engineering or English).
2. Having good work skills, especially those involved in communication and computers.
3. Having good personal skills, including being able to get along with people, high self-esteem, and working from one's own values, motivations, and goals.

"Your son has made a career choice, Mildred. He's going to win the lottery and travel a lot."

© 2002. Reprinted courtesy of Bunny Hoest and Parade Magazine.

As a single mother of two, Simone entered Portland Community College determined to graduate in two years with the skills and background knowledge to secure a good job, something with better pay and benefits than her current position as a part-time sales clerk. She was a good salesperson, known for her up-beat personality and strong social skills. She selected the field of Alcohol and Drug Counseling because of her interest in working with people, the value she placed on helping others, and her goal of completing a career program in two years (this particular program offered lots of evening courses). Finally, the campus career counselor recommended it as a growing field with a strong demand for qualified counselors, driving her motivation to secure a good job immediately upon graduation. This type of program allowed her to gain specialized knowledge that she could immediately apply in a job setting, utilizing her strong work ethic and personal skills.

Jorge also was determined to complete a career-oriented program in two years and was interested in helping others, but he had always been interested in medicine and hoped to go to medical school some day. First, he needed to expand his experience and his savings account! The Emergency Medical Technician (EMT) program was just the ticket. It offered career training in an emergency medical setting, allowing him to expand his knowledge base and prepare for state certificate exams. Once he became a certified EMT, Jorge secured a job with a local ambulance company, providing immediate medical care and transportation and even helping with emergency childbirth on a few occasions. This foundation in emergency prehospital care was a good first step in his more long-term goal of becoming a doctor.

Your college experiences will give you plenty of opportunities to develop your talents in these three areas. Throughout this book other connections to the long-term question of careers will be made, and Chapter 13 is devoted to this topic. In addition, every chapter contains a special feature titled "Career Connections," which demonstrates how important skills and strategies are implemented in the workplace, as shown to the right.

Your Learning Portfolio

We have included a Learning Portfolio section at the end of each chapter to help you practice different types of learning and apply various strategies to help increase your chance of success in college and beyond. This section has three parts:

1. Self-Assessments
2. Your Journal
3. "Six Strategies for Success"

Self-Assessments

At the end of each chapter are three or more self-assessments related to the chapter topics that provide the opportunity to evaluate yourself in a number of areas related to your college success. At the end of each self-assessment, we give you information about how to score it or evaluate your responses. In addition, the website for this book, located at http://success.wadsworth.com/santrock4e/ contains these self-assessments in electronic format and a number of others, with customized scoring. They also are found on the CD-ROM in the front of this text. Completing these assessments will provide you with important information about your strengths and weaknesses in a variety of areas.

Your Journal

There are four types of journal exercises at the end of each chapter that will help improve your self-understanding, enhance your writing skills, and give you the other benefits of keeping a journal. For example, James Pennebaker (1990), a professor at the University of Texas at Austin, found that first-year students who write in a journal cope more effectively with stress and are healthier than those who don't. Another study revealed that individuals who regularly kept a journal that focused on their aspirations were 32 percent more likely to believe that they were making progress in their lives than those who did not (Howatt, 1999). The four types of exercises include:

Reflect These items ask you to reflect on the topics of the chapter. You will be encouraged to expand your thinking and consider issues in more depth.

Do These exercises involve action projects such as conducting interviews, participating in discussions, taking field trips, and putting together presentations. These projects help you to solve problems, practice report writing, and collaborate with others.

Think Critically These exercises help you to practice thinking more deeply, productively, and logically. In some, you will evaluate evidence. In others, you may criticize an idea. Your critical insights may be expressed in critiques, memos, reports on group discussions, and so forth.

Create These exercises will help you pursue new insights alone and with other students. You may be asked to write creatively or try your hand at drawing images, inventing quotations, or crafting posters. Some exercises will encourage you to brainstorm others.

Six Strategies for Success

"Six Strategies for Success" is the third and final part of the Learning Portfolio. It is tied to the six-point college success model that was introduced on page 3 and appears at the beginning of each chapter. In each of these exercises, you will be asked to think back on what you learned in that chapter and write down how this information relates to each of the six strategies. We hope this will help you learn to apply these strategies in your own life. For example, what did you learn in this chapter about the importance of developing meaningful values?

© 1973 News America Syndicate. Reprinted with permission of Creators Syndicate.

Evaluate Your Strategies

The "Six Strategies for Success" model visually demonstrates the interconnectedness of these important strategies that you can use to form the foundation of your success. The first step is to evaluate where you stand now with regard to implementing these strategies for success in college.

Place a checkmark next to each of the following statements that represents you and your actions now. Leave the others blank. When you are done, go back and award yourself one point for each checkmark. Then add up the points for each of the six sections. Finally, shade the "Strategies for Success" model at the end of this section with your *total* for each of the six strategies. This provides you with a visual representation of your current strengths and weaknesses in these important areas. You will be asked to repeat this after you have completed reading this text to evaluate your progress in these areas over the term.

Develop Meaningful Values

1. _____ I know what my values are.
2. _____ I feel good about my values.
3. _____ I have spent considerable time reflecting on what values I want to guide my life.
4. _____ I have discussed my values with others.
5. _____ My values are helping me succeed in college.
6. _____ My values serve as an underlying foundation for the goals I want to achieve.
7. _____ I've been in situations in which my values have been tested and I stayed with them.
8. _____ I have a clear understanding of my purpose in life.
9. _____ I am flexible and realize that as I continue through college I will likely change and grow, and my values might change.
10. _____ My values are at the core of my existence.
    _____ TOTAL

Set Goals, Plan, and Monitor

1. _____ I am good at setting goals.
2. _____ I have established some long-term goals.
3. _____ I have created subgoals to go along with my long-term goals.
4. _____ The goals I have set are challenging but reachable with considerable effort on my part.
5. _____ My goals are concrete and specific.
6. _____ I periodically monitor my progress toward reaching the goals I have set.
7. _____ I have set completion dates for these goals.
8. _____ I manage time effectively in the pursuit of my goals.
9. _____ I make lists of things I need to do to stay on track in reaching my goals.
10. _____ I anticipate and overcome obstacles on the way to reaching my goals.
    _____ TOTAL

Get Motivated and Take Responsibility

1. _____ I am internally motivated.
2. _____ I take responsibility for my actions.

3. _____ I expect to succeed.
4. _____ I am persistent at completing important tasks.
5. _____ I am passionate about succeeding in life.
6. _____ I put a lot of energy into college.
7. _____ I have a strong work ethic.
8. _____ If I get bored, it doesn't last long.
9. _____ I have a strong desire to be a competent person.
10. _____ I am good at staying on task and not being distracted from what I need to do.
_____ TOTAL

Think and Learn

1. _____ I am self-disciplined and have good work habits.
2. _____ I have good study skills.
3. _____ I know the best ways I can learn.
4. _____ I am good at managing my time.
5. _____ I think critically.
6. _____ I think creatively.
7. _____ I have good problem-solving skills.
8. _____ I communicate effectively with good speaking and listening skills.
9. _____ I know what learning resources are available to me and how to best use them.
10. _____ I have good computer skills.
_____ TOTAL

Build Self-Esteem and Confidence

1. _____ I have a lot of confidence in myself.
2. _____ I feel good about myself.
3. _____ I have a positive self-image.
4. _____ I have a lot to be proud of.
5. _____ I am a person of worth.
6. _____ When I don't feel good about myself, I can tell why and attempt to do something about it.
7. _____ If I start to feel bad about myself, it doesn't last long.
8. _____ I have a good support system and get good feedback from others.
9. _____ My achievements help me feel good about myself.
10. _____ I have good coping skills.
_____ TOTAL

Explore Careers

1. _____ I know how much more successful I am likely to be if I complete college.
2. _____ I have several careers that I would like to pursue.
3. _____ I know what my college major will be.
4. _____ My college major matches up well with the careers I am interested in.
5. _____ I have good communication skills.
6. _____ I have good personal skills, including being able to get along with others.
7. _____ I know which college experiences will help me down the road in my pursuit of a career.

8. _____ I have talked with a career counselor about careers that might interest me.
9. _____ I have set some career goals.
10. _____ I am on the right path to reaching those career goals.
_____ TOTAL

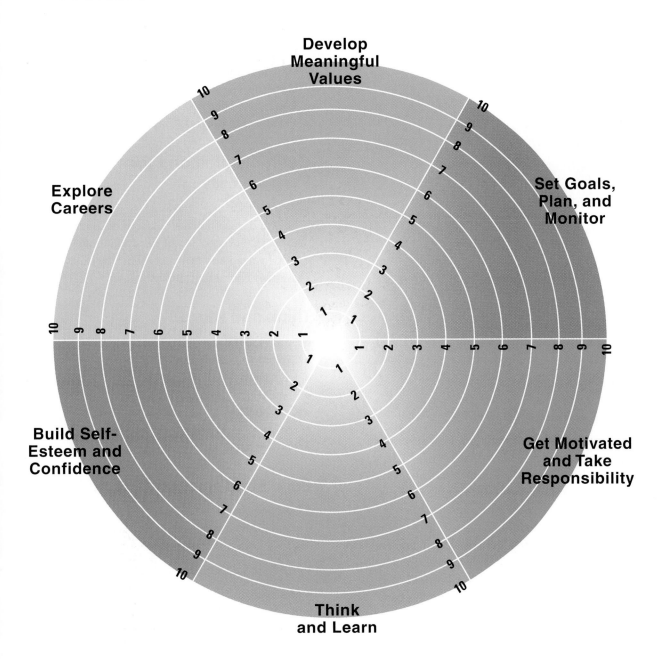

Summary Strategies for Mastering College

Know What Things You Value and Set Goals to Reach Them

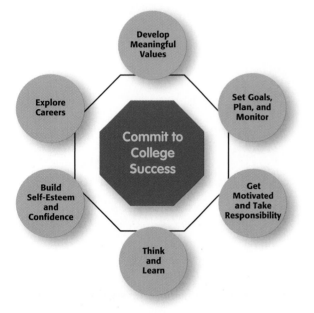

Focus on the "Six Strategies for Success" above as you read each chapter to learn how to apply these strategies to your own success.

 Make the College Transition

- If you're making the transition from high school to college, think about the ways that college differs from high school. Remind yourself that change can be challenging and requires you to adapt. Let go of some old ties and securities. Get some new friends.
- If you're a returning student, evaluate your support system, make new friends, get involved in campus life, and don't be afraid to ask for help. Evaluate how you may need to balance your class work with commitments to partners, children, jobs, and the community. Realize that you bring strengths to campus.
- Explore your motivation for being in college.

2 Develop Meaningful Values

- Examine how your values relate to college success.
- Identify the underlying principles in your life.
- Forge positive academic values.

3 Set Goals, Plan, and Monitor

- Set goals that are challenging, reasonable, and specific; plan how to reach these goals.

- Set long-term and short-term goals. Make a plan that includes completion dates and divides goals into subgoals. Know how to anticipate and overcome obstacles to reaching your goals.
- Commit and get started now.
- Monitor your progress toward your goals.

4 Get Motivated and Take Responsibility

- Be internally motivated and take responsibility. Learn how to develop an internal locus of control.
- Expect to succeed and be persistent until you do.
- Get involved and tackle boredom by exploring new avenues and tuning into inspiration.

5 Think and Learn

- Focus your talents and master work skills.
- Explore your learning styles.
- Manage your time.
- Think critically and creatively.
- Communicate effectively.
- Use your resources.
- Join the information age.

6 Build Self-Esteem and Confidence

- Evaluate your self-esteem.
- Identify how to raise your self-esteem.

7 Explore Careers

- Research, think, and talk with others about careers.
- Be aware of the advantages of a college education.
- Master content and develop work and people skills.

8 Your Learning Portfolio

- Complete self-assessments to learn about your strengths and weaknesses.
- Do the different types of Journal activities to improve self-understanding and writing skills.
- Fill out the "Six Strategies for Success" activity at the end of each chapter to learn how to apply these strategies to your own life.

Review Questions

1. Consider your roommate or another student you have met recently. How do the challenges you both face making the transition to college differ? How are they similar?

_____

_____

_____

_____

2. Imagine talking to a friend who is still in high school about the importance of setting goals, planning, and monitoring progress in college. What would you tell him or her? What would you tell an older, returning student?

_____

_____

_____

_____

3. How will your values help determine your success in college? Did you learn anything in this chapter that changed your opinion of what values are most important to you?

_____

_____

_____

_____

4. According to this chapter, can you increase your motivation to do well in college? Write down a few strategies that you can start implementing _now_.

_____

_____

_____

_____

5. Do you know anyone who suffers from low self-esteem? How would you recommend tackling this problem? Why is it important to address now?

_____

_____

_____

_____

Learning Portfolio

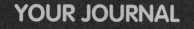
SELF-ASSESSMENTS

YOUR JOURNAL

STRATEGIES FOR SUCCESS

Develop Meaningful Values

Explore Careers

Set Goals, Plan, and Monitor

Commit to Sucess in College

Build Self-Esteem and Confidence

Get Motivated and Take Responsibility

Think and Learn

Why Am I Here?

Different individuals want different things from college. Think for a few moments about why you are here. The following items can help you to see how college might serve your needs. Place a checkmark next to any of the items that apply to you.

I'm in college because:

_____ It can help me learn and think more effectively.

_____ It can help me get a good job.

_____ It can help me make a lot of money.

_____ I'm avoiding having to find a job.

_____ It's a good place to find a mate.

_____ I want to have a good time.

_____ It's a way to prove my self-worth.

_____ It's a way to get away from home.

_____ My parents made me go.

_____ My friends are here.

_____ There are things that I can learn here better than any-where else.

_____ I want to learn more about what I can do with my life.

_____ I couldn't think of anything else to do at this point.

Reflect on which of these reasons, as well as others not listed, are motivating you to be in college. Are these the best reasons to be in college? To achieve academic success, do you need to rethink your motivation? Now group the items you selected in the categories listed below. Do you have more positive or negative reasons for attending college? What can you do to address the negatives?

Positive Motivations:

Negative Motivations:

What Are My Values?

This list presents a wide variety of values. Place a checkmark in the spaces next to the 10 values that are the most important to you. Then go back over these ten values and rank order the top five.

_____ Having good friendships and getting along well with people
_____ Having a positive relationship with a spouse or a romantic partner
_____ Self-respect
_____ Being well-off financially
_____ Having a good spiritual life
_____ Being competent at my work
_____ Having the respect of others
_____ Making an important contribution to humankind
_____ Being a moral person

_____ Feeling secure
_____ Being a great athlete
_____ Being physically attractive
_____ Being creative
_____ Having freedom and independence
_____ Being well educated
_____ Contributing to the welfare of others
_____ Having peace of mind
_____ Getting recognition or becoming famous
_____ Being happy

_____ Enjoying leisure time
_____ Being a good citizen and showing loyalty to my country
_____ Living a healthy lifestyle
_____ Being intelligent
_____ Family relationships
_____ Honesty and integrity
_____ Dedication and commitment
_____ Having personal responsibility
_____ Other values
List any values important to you
_____
_____

My five most important personal values are

1._____

2._____

3._____

4._____

5._____

As you review your selections, think about how you got these values. Did you learn them from your parents, teachers, or friends? Or did you gain them from personal experiences? How deeply have you thought about each of these values and what they mean to you? Think about whether your actions support your values. Are you truly living up to them? Do they truly reflect who you are?

What Are My Goals?

By completing the following statements, you will get a better idea of what your goals are. Earlier you examined your values. Look at your responses to Self-Assessment 2. These values should help you formulate your goals. Remember that goals can be academic (such as getting straight As this term) or personal (such as forming at least two good friendships this term). A good strategy is to set goals that are challenging but achievable. Be sure to make your goals as concrete and specific as possible.

My main goals in life are

1. _____
2. _____
3. _____
4. _____

My main goals for the term are

1. _____
2. _____
3. _____
4. _____

My main goals for tomorrow are

1. _____
2. _____
3. _____
4. _____

Return to this self-assessment tomorrow evening. How did you do in reaching your four goals for tomorrow? Are your goals for these three time frames—life, term, and tomorrow—in sync?

Your Journal

● REFLECT

1. Your New Life

Think about the changes that have taken place in your life since you started college.

- What is different?

_____

_____

- What excites you the most about your life and opportunities in college?

_____

_____

2. Conscious Coping

- Describe the most stressful experience you have had so far in college.

_____

_____

- What made it so stressful?

_____

_____

- How did you cope with it?

_____

_____

- Were you successful?

_____

_____

- If the problem still bothers you, how do you plan to cope with it in the future?

_____

_____

● DO

1. A Current Challenge in My Life

Spend a few moments and reflect on what is going on in your life right now. What is stressing you out the most? Describe that stressful, challenging circumstance:

Using the information discussed in this chapter, create at least three subgoals related to overcoming this stressful, challenging circumstance:

Subgoal 1:_____

Subgoal 2:_____

Subgoal 3:_____

Your Journal

2. Toward Your Future

Think about a career that you might want to pursue. Write it down here.

_____

_____

Search the Internet to find out as much as you can about it. Try to find out entry requirements, recommended majors, and salary ranges. Use e-mail, the phone, or personal contact to talk with someone in that field about how he or she likes it and whether it might be right for you.

● THINK CRITICALLY

1. Manage Your Risk

Many college students don't get past their first year. Think about your own risks related to dropping out of college. Make a list of the factors that could undermine your ability to succeed in college. Describe how you plan to overcome these potential obstacles.

_____

_____

2. College Graduation Day

Imagine the day you will graduate from college. Describe what you hope your family, friends, classmates, and teachers will say about you as a college student.

_____

_____

_____

● CREATE

1. The Magic Wand

Suppose your teachers granted you a magic wand to make three changes to improve your academic life. What three changes would you make and why?

_____

_____

_____

2. My Hero

As you read about the inspiring example of Terry Fox, you probably recognized how heroic his fund-raising efforts were, given his physical disability. Fox demonstrated that motivated individuals can overcome even severe limitations. Who is your hero? Who inspires you? Write about why you selected this person as your hero and inspirational model. How are you like him or her? What could you do to be more like this person? Place a photo of this individual in your journal accompanied by your answers to the questions just posed.

Applying the Six Strategies for Success

What did you learn in this chapter that you can apply to the following key strategies to help form the foundation for your success? Write down all of the major points you can remember that support the following strategies:

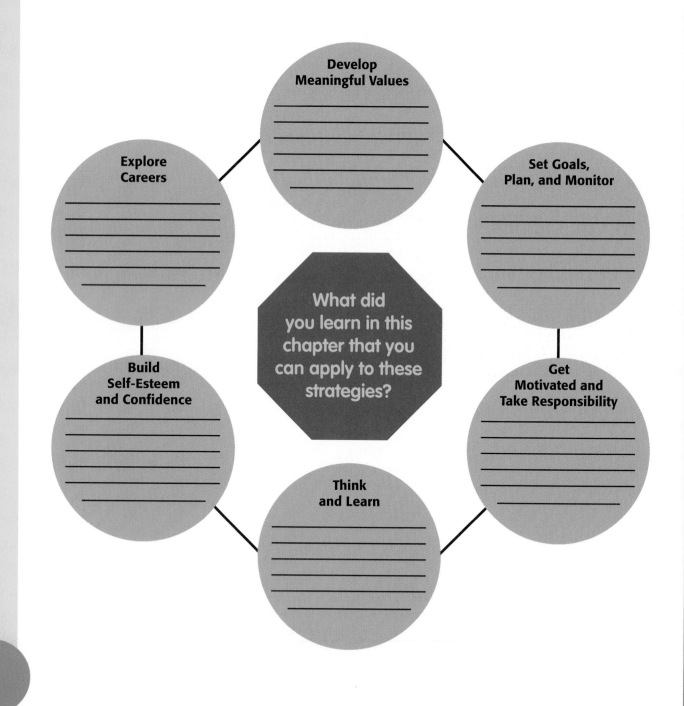

2

Explore Your Campus, Courses, and Computer

Where Are You? You want to be independent, but even the most successful college students don't do it all on their own. They get connected—find the resources that will help them master college. They know the best resources on campus for what they need.

Get to know the people on campus who can help you when you run into problems. Consult with an academic advisor, more advanced students, and others about which courses to take and how to map out an academic plan. Use computer resources to your advantage.

To evaluate your current connections place a check mark next to only those items that apply to you.

- ● I know what campus resources are available to meet my needs.
- ● I know how to use library services.
- ● I plan to participate in one or more extracurricular activities.
- ● I have spent adequate time with my academic advisor.
- ● I have studied my college catalog and use it as a resource.
- ● I know what I want my major to be.
- ● I have made a coursework plan toward a degree or certificate.
- ● I have a mentor.
- ● I use the Internet for e-mail and to search for information.
- ● I use a word-processing program for most of what I write.

As you read about David Eggers, think about how his extra-curricular activities helped him achieve success in college and a career.

33

Images of College Success

David Eggers

David Eggers, a very talented and insightful writer, is the author of *A Heartbreaking Work of Staggering Genius* (2001), which has been #1 on the *New York Times* best-seller list. Eggers began his career as cofounder of *Might* magazine, which focused on young adult issues and concerns, at the age of 24.

When *Might* folded, Eggers became editor of *McSweeney's,* a literary journal, which gives writers an opportunity to publish work that has been rejected by mainstream magazines. *McSweeney's* has published a number of intriguing books by authors who write about, among other things, a love affair with a lemon and the lives of desperate folks trapped inside a human body. Another recent Eggers project is 826 Valencia, a San Francisco location where young people can come for one-on-one guidance in their writing pursuits.

Eggers obtained his undergraduate degree in journalism from the University of Illinois. He believes that extracurricular activities helped him a great deal in college. He worked on the campus newspaper, participated in campus concert promotions, and ran the campus art gallery. In Eggers's (2000) words: "I wanted my extracurricular activities and my summer jobs to advance my career. I saw a lot of students pick interesting majors but not think at all about what they needed to do in order to make their major practical. . . . I picked up a lot of skills through my extracurricular activities in college, like computers, production, photography, and journalism" (p. 53).

Eggers's work on the student newspaper fascinated him so much that he changed his major from art to journalism. However, during his senior year of college, tragedy struck. Both his parents died of cancer, leaving Eggers, and his sister (a law student at the University of California at Berkeley), and his eight-year-old brother to watch out for each other. Eggers says that suffering through his parents' deaths motivated him to turn his dream of creating a popular magazine for young people into a reality. Eggers's creative style of writing, humor, and insights about life have become very popular with many college students.

DAVID EGGERS, author of the best-seller, *A Heartbreaking Work of Staggering Genius.* Extracurricular work on his campus newspaper helped launch his writing career.

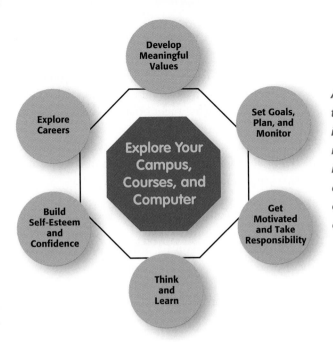

As you read, think about the "Six Strategies for Success" listed to the left and how this chapter can help you maximize success in these important areas. For example, to master college and reach your goals, you need good resources. Important resources include knowledgeable and helpful people on campus such as academic advisors, more advanced students, and mentors, and computer technology. If you connect effectively with these, your college life will be easier, less stressful, and more productive.

Connect with Your Campus

It costs you nothing to connect with your campus, yet nothing will help you more than knowing and utilizing your campus resources. You probably have visited some of them already—the book store for textbooks and study supplies, the student center or commons to check out bulletin boards or pick up a newspaper.

An important goal in college is learning how to solve your personal problems and get your needs met. Many campus resources can help you attain these goals. You can learn a great deal about the best campus resources if you make this an important goal and aren't afraid to ask questions. Complete Self-Assessment 1 "Campus Resources to Meet My Needs" on page 57 to get started. The Journal exercise "Only the Best" on page 61 will also help you locate such places as the best cheap, hot breakfast, live music, free or cheap movies, and so on. Furthermore, the Journal activity "Your Cognitive College Map" on page 61 encourages you to draw your own campus map, emphasizing the places that you need to know about the most.

Get Help from Advisors, Academic Support Services, and Counselors

Most people on campus will be eager to help you in your quest to master college. Whether you want information or training, here are some things you can do to get the help you need (Canfield & Hansen, 1995):

- *Ask as though you expect to get help.* Your tuition dollars pay for assistance in the classroom, the library, or even the cafeteria line.

© 1982 Universal Press Syndicate

Ask with authority. You may be able to enter that restricted part of the library merely by acting like you know what you're doing. High self-esteem gives you the confidence to do these kinds of things.

- *Ask someone who is in a position to help you.* You may have to do some homework to find out who can help you best. If someone you approach can't deliver, ask whether that person knows of someone else who might be able to help you. Form a network of resources.

- *Ask clear and specific questions.* Even those who enjoy helping students don't like to have their time wasted. Think ahead about what you need and what level of detail will satisfy you. Take notes so you won't have to ask twice.

- *Ask with passion, civility, humor, and creativity.* Enthusiasm goes a long way toward engaging others to want to help you. A polite request is easier to accommodate than a loud, demanding one. Sometimes problems yield more readily to a playful question. A clever request is just plain hard to turn down But size up whether your instructors will appreciate a humorous approach. If not, your good intentions and creativity may backfire. To further explore getting help with your college needs, complete the Journal activity "My Best Helpers" on page 60.

page 60.

Learn about Academic Support Services Perhaps the most important helper on campus will be your academic advisor. We will further discuss the importance of this person later in the chapter when exploring how to map out an academic plan.

Most campuses provide access to specialists who can assist you with academic problems. For example, many study skills specialists are qualified to do diagnostic testing to determine the nature of your learning difficulties, or they can refer you to specialists who provide this service. They can suggest compensating strategies for your assignments and may be able to give you some directions about taking courses with instructors who are more sympathetic with your struggle to learn. They also can set up and monitor additional study supports, including tutoring and study groups, to get you accustomed to the demands of college-level work.

Seek Counseling for Personal Concerns College life is often challenging on a personal level. Talking to a counselor or therapist may provide the relief you need. Large campuses have mental health departments or psychology clinics. They may have therapists and counselors on site who will give you the support you need on a one-to-one or a group basis. The fee for such services will be on a sliding scale (meaning that the cost is proportional to your income), covered by your health insurance policy, or covered by your tuition.

Some student services offer topic-specific support groups, such as a group for single mothers returning to college or one for students struggling with English as a second language. In support groups you can meet others who have problems similar to yours. Their advice and experience may be helpful. Ask the counseling center or dean's office about support groups on campus.

If you do not find a group that addresses your concern, consider creating one. Most support groups start from the concerns of one or two students. The student services office will usually assist you with the advertising and the room arrangements to help your group get off the ground.

Tap the Library

Libraries may not seem a likely site for adventure. But think about it. Each visit to the library can be a treasure hunt. The treasure might be a bit of information, an opportunity to go online, or a chance to check out a new book by your favorite

---

Beatles Sighting

Help!

The Beatles
20th-century British rock group

author. The sooner you get a feel for how the library works, the more useful it will be to you.

One of your classes may arrange a tour. If not, ask a librarian for help in getting oriented. Librarians can give you a schedule of library tours or provide you with maps or pamphlets to help you search independently. Although librarians may look busy when you approach them, step up and ask for help. Most of them enjoy teaching others how to use the library. If you find an especially friendly librarian, cultivate the relationship. A librarian friend can be a lifesaver.

What do you need to know in order to use the library effectively? The following questions may help you organize your first tour:

How can I check out materials?

What are the penalties for late returns?

Do instructors place materials on reserve? How does this work?

What interesting or helpful journals does the library have? Are they available online?

Is the library catalog online or on cards? What can I access electronically?

Can I arrange interlibrary loans to get materials from other libraries?

What kinds of reference materials are available? Are the abstracts of published research on microfilm or in books?

Where are "the stacks" and when can I use them?

What technological resources does the library have that will help me succeed in college?

The Journal activity "My Library Needs" on page 61 will help you to think further about library services that might benefit you.

> *Either I will find a way or I will make one.*
>
> Sir Philip Sidney
> *16th-century English poet and soldier*

Stay Healthy

Many campuses have fully equipped medical centers for students. Health care services may offer blood testing, health screenings, pregnancy tests, flu shots, and educational programs, as well as regular physicians' care. Smaller campuses may offer access to a nurse or health specialists trained in emergency care. Find out the phone numbers for these services. Carry them with you. When health emergencies arise, contact an employee of the campus or call the campus switchboard to explain the situation and request urgent help. Call 911 in the case of serious emergencies.

Keep Safe

Personal safety is an important concern on all campuses. Security personnel monitor the campus for outsiders and sometimes provide escorts after dark. If you feel unsafe or spot activities that you think may threaten the well-being or property of others, call the campus switchboard or security and report your suspicions or concerns.

Most campuses teem with activity. Unfortunately, they do attract people who find busy places ideal for stealing. No matter what the size of your campus, possessions that can be converted to cash can disappear. Keep your personal belongings locked up when you are not around. Consider insuring valuable property.

Exercise good judgment about the risks you take. You'll be meeting many people. Most of them will enrich your life, but some may try to take advantage of you. Be careful about lending money or equipment, especially to people you've just met. Exercise your street smarts on campus to avoid potential exploitation.

You may sometimes feel pressured by friends to take safety risks, such as drinking inappropriately, taking drugs, or hanging out in places that don't feel safe. Don't succumb to friendly pressures to do things that place you at risk. True friends have your best interests at heart. If you feel pressure to take risks, it's time to reevaluate your friendships.

Pursue Extracurricular Activities

Participating in extracurricular activities improves your chances of meeting people who share your interests. Activities may be listed in the campus handbook or advertised in the student newspaper. Many majors sponsor clubs that allow you to explore careers through field trips or special speakers. If you're interested in journalism, you can work on the college newspaper or yearbook. Prospective drama students can audition for plays. Students interested in business can join an entrepreneur's group to examine how business people manage their lives and work.

Intramural and campus sports also are available. Some clubs promote service to others. It may seem like your study life is too full to accommodate fun. However, leisure activities are important for balance in your life. The campus may hold dances, concerts, campuswide celebrations, or other events to help you meet people, relax, and have fun. Extracurricular activities of any kind can also help you develop leadership skills and learn to manage multiple commitments.

One decision that many first-year students face is whether to join a sorority or a fraternity, which are known as Greek organizations. They were originally established not only to enhance academic achievement but also to encourage social participation outside of the classroom. Membership in a fraternity or sorority takes place through what is known as "rush," a process of mutual selection that matches students interested in joining a Greek organization and the individual sorority or fraternity. Rush usually begins at the start of the fall or spring term.

Joining a sorority or fraternity can have advantages and disadvantages. The advantages can include becoming closely connected with a group of people who share similar interests with you. You not only are a part of a sorority or fraternity at your particular college but also a national organization with many chapters and a network of people. These contacts may be beneficial after college for social and business opportunities. Many sororities and fraternities also participate in worthwhile service activities. The disadvantages can include the extensive amount of time to pledge a sorority or fraternity, alcohol abuse and hazing that occurs in some Greek organizations, and membership expenses.

As valuable as extracurricular activities are, your involvement can also create problems. Some activities, like Greek organizations, can be expensive. If your income is limited, look for ones that don't wipe out your cash. Sometimes you also can get too involved. Before you know it, you may have more commitments than you can manage and too little time to study. Have fun, but keep your larger goals in mind.

Enrich Your Cultural Life

Your campus and community may offer unique opportunities for cultural enrichment. Because most campuses are training grounds for artists and performers, they often operate an art gallery for student work or invited artists. They also host live performances in music, dance, and theater to showcase student and faculty talent, as well as outside professional performers. In the community, museums, galleries, theaters, the symphony, and political gatherings can all enrich your learning.

Many college students also have spiritual concerns. Campus ministries usually coordinate religious activities for various denominations. These may be formal religious services or social groups where you can simply get together with others of a similar faith. You not only can practice your faith but also expand your network of friends with common values. Of course, religious services also are available off campus.

Overcome Limitations

In the last decade, the number of college students with a disability has increased dramatically. Today more than 10 percent of college students have some form of physical or mental impairment that substantially limits their major life activities. Colleges are required to make reasonable accommodations to allow students with a disability to perform up to their capacity. Accommodations can be made for motor and mobility impairments, visual and hearing deficits, physical and mental health problems, and learning disabilities.

If you have a disability, determine what support you need to succeed in college. The level of service a college provides can be classified as follows:

- *Minimal support.* Students generally adapt to the college and advocate for their own services and accommodations.
- *Moderate support.* The campus offers a service office or special staff to help students with advocacy and accommodations.
- *Intense support.* The campus provides specific programs and instructional services for students with disabilities.

Among the academic services that may be available on your campus are:

- *Referrals for testing, diagnosis, and rehabilitation.* Specialists who can help in this area may be located on or off campus.
- *Registration assistance.* This involves consideration regarding the location of classrooms, scheduling, and in some cases waivers of course requirements.
- *Accommodations for taking tests.* Instructors may allow expanded or unlimited time to complete tests and you may be able to use a word processor or other support resources during the exam.
- *Classroom assistance.* Someone may be assigned to take notes for you or translate lectures into sign language. Instructors may allow their lectures to be taped for students with impaired vision or other disabilities.
- *Special computing services and library skills.* Support services on campus are finding inventive new ways to interpret written texts to overcome reading and visual limitations.

Many individuals overcome physical disabilities and other limitations to become successful college students. What are some services that colleges provide for individuals with physical limitations?

© Jeff Greenberg/AGE Fotostock

Map Out an Academic Path

It is important for you to devote some time to designing an academic path. Your academic advisor is an important resource for helping you with this process. Contact your advisor whenever you have any questions about your academic life.

Connect with Your Academic Advisor

As discussed earlier, navigating academic life by yourself is not a good idea. Your academic advisor has important information about your course requirements that can help you realize your plans. Advisors can explain why certain courses are required and can alert you to instructors suited to your preferred learning style. Plan to confer with your advisor regularly. When it's time to register for next term's courses, schedule a meeting with your advisor early in the registration period.

A Memo to Your Advisor

When you need to contact instructors or academic staff members to help you solve a problem, notify them in advance about your needs. A standard memo format will help you set the context for the meeting. Be sure to include your telephone number, e-mail address, and good times to reach you in case a change in scheduling is necessary. For example:

Memo
To: Dr. Charles
From: Tyrell Wilkins
Re: Changing majors
Date 9/27

I would like to meet with you during your 11 A.M. office hour on Monday, 10/5. I am thinking about changing majors but I want to find out whether this could delay my graduation. Please e-mail me or call me any weekday evening after 7 P.M. if the proposed time doesn't work for you.

Thank you!
Phone: 555-3300
E-mail: tykins@omninet.edu

Find a Mentor

A *mentor* is an advisor, coach, and confidant who can help you become successful and master many of life's challenges. He or she also can advise you on career pursuits, suggest ways to cope with problem situations, and listen to what's on your mind. A mentor might be:

A student who has successfully navigated the first-year experience
A graduate student
An instructor
Someone in the community you respect and trust

If you don't have a mentor, think about the people you've met in college so far. Is there a person you admire whose advice might benefit you? If you don't have anyone in mind right now, start looking around for someone. As you talk with various people and get to know them better, one person's competence and motivation can start to rub off on you. This is the type of person who can be a good mentor.

Bring a tentative plan of the courses that you think will satisfy your requirements. Be open if the advisor offers you compelling reasons for taking other courses. For example, your advisor may suggest that by taking some harder courses than you had planned, you can prepare yourself better for the career you have chosen. Your advisor will help you reach your career objective as efficiently as possible, but not by compromising solid preparation.

Some advisors may not have regular office hours. To maximize your effectiveness and efficiency, call or e-mail your academic advisor for an appointment before dropping by. If you put your concerns in writing before the appointment, your advisor will have some time to work on your specific issues before you arrive. See On Target Tips, "A Memo to Your Advisor," to help you get started.

If the "chemistry" between you and your academic advisor isn't good, confront that problem by discussing what behaviors make you feel uncomfortable. Recognize that your own actions may have something to do with the problem. You need an advisor you can trust. If you can't work out a compromise, request a change to find an advisor who is right for you. To think further about the importance of an academic advisor, complete the Journal activity "Ask the Right Questions" on page 61.

In addition to your academic advisor, a mentor also can enhance your opportunity for college success. To think further about the person you would like to have as your mentor, read Take Charge, "Find a Mentor," and start putting together a list of individuals who might fill this role for you.

Get to Know Your College Catalog

A college catalog is a valuable resource. If you don't have one, check with your advisor or the admissions office to obtain one. An online version might also be available at the college website. College catalogs usually are published every one or two years. Be sure to save the catalog that is in effect when you enroll for the first time. Why? Because requirements for specific programs sometimes change, and you usually will be held to the degree plan that was in place when you enrolled.

Know What Is Required If you've decided on a field of study or have several in mind, turn to the part of the catalog that describes those areas and the courses required for graduation. The catalog should tell you what the core requirements are, whether there are any prerequisites for the programs, and whether there is a sequence of courses you should follow.

Prerequisites Many courses have prerequisites and other enrollment requirements, such as "consent of instructor," "enrollment limited to majors," "seniors only," "honor students," and so on. You are expected to comply with these prerequisites and enrollment requirements when you register for courses.

Core Courses *Core courses* are the central courses that must be taken by students, either for general education requirements or for a major. Especially in your first several years of college you are likely to have a number of general education core courses that you will be required to take. Also when you start taking courses in the major you have chosen, it is likely that you will have to take certain core courses before you can take more advanced courses. Become familiar with both the general education core courses and the core courses in the major in which you are interested so that you take these courses in the required sequence.

Electives In addition to core courses, you will be able to take *electives*, courses that are not required. You likely will take some of these in your major, others outside of your major. Electives provide you with an opportunity to explore your interests and expand your education. In some cases, students take an elective that interests them so much that it becomes a springboard for taking more courses in the area, establishing a major, or changing majors.

"Well, we've finally done it. We've listed two courses, each of which is a prerequisite for taking the other."

© Harald Carl Bakken.

Consider Your Major

One of the most frequent questions that you will get asked on campus is, "What is your major?" The major you select is also something that your parents or partner might show a special interest in because they want you to major in something that will link up with a successful career after college. The major or specialization that you select should match up with your career goals and values, which we discuss extensively in Chapter 13. Your academic advisor can be a good resource for finding out more about majors. Also, your college counseling or career center can help you learn more about your interests, skills, and abilities, and how these might link up with certain majors and careers. "Exploring Careers" is one of the "Six Strategies for Success" listed at the beginning of this chapter. It is never too soon to start planning ahead.

What Is a College Major? A college *major*, or field of concentration, is a series of courses that provides a foundation of learning in an academic discipline. Majors vary in the number of courses required. For example, engineering requires more major courses than does history or psychology, which allow you to choose more electives.

Some graduate programs may prefer a specific undergraduate degree, whereas others may not. For example, law schools admit students from many different undergraduate majors. In contrast, graduate schools in physics require a physics undergraduate degree or a large concentration of physics classes. If you want to be an English teacher in a public high school, you probably need to major in secondary education with a concentration in English.

Many first-year students take several general education courses such as Introductory Psychology or American History before they invest in courses in their specialty or major. This allows them to broaden their education and have more time to choose their focus. If you're not sure what you want to focus on, you're not alone. More than two thirds of first-year college students change their intended majors in the first year. Don't panic. When college administrators have you fill out forms during your first year, most let you write "undecided" or "exploring" in the column for a college major.

Some four-year institutions have a one- or two-year general curriculum you can follow before you choose a major. But if you're in a four-year program and aren't sure about a major after two years, you may end up taking extra courses that you don't need when you graduate and might have trouble fitting in all of the classes you do need to complete your major.

"Hmm, summa cum laude—very impressive. But what exactly is a Bachelor of Arts & Leisure?"

Some students don't major in a special area but instead pursue a broad range of college courses. Many four-year institutions have individualized majors that allow this. Even individualized majors, though, usually require one or two concentrations of courses to keep the coursework somewhat unified, not totally disconnected. Some students also choose a double major. If this interests you, most colleges will let you declare a single major first, then the double major when the second one is declared.

How Do You Know Whether a Major Is Right for You? Before choosing a major, make a realistic assessment of your interests, skills, and abilities. Chapter 4 allows you to explore intellectual and personality strengths and weaknesses that can influence your decision regarding your major. Are you getting Cs and Ds in biology and chemistry, although you've honestly put your full effort into those courses? Then premed or a science area may not be the best major for you. If you hate the math or computer science class you're taking, you may not be cut out for a career that requires that kind of background.

But be patient. The first year of college, especially the first term, is a time of exploration and learning how to succeed. Many first-year students who don't do well at first in courses related to a possible major adapt, meet the challenge, and go on to do extremely well in that area. A year or two into your college experience, you should have a good idea of whether the major you've chosen is a good fit. At that point, you will have had enough courses and opportunities to know whether you're in the right place.

A good strategy is to seek out students who are more advanced in the field you're considering. Ask them what it's like to specialize in that particular area, and ask them about various courses and instructors.

Unfortunately, too many students choose majors for the wrong reasons: to please their parents, follow their friends, or have a light course load. What really interests you? It's your life. You have the right to choose what you want to do with it. Reconsider your values and long-term goals listed in Chapter 1. What do you really want to major in? The courses in your major can be challenging and still be right for you, but you should have a good feeling about your match with the major program. You should be enthusiastic about it and motivated to learn more about the field. To examine some possible links between majors, skills, and careers, see Figure 2.1.

FIGURE 2.1 Choose the Best Major and Career for Your Skills

Skills	Major	Potential Occupations/Careers
Research information Analyze numerical options Perform mathematical functions and apply formulas Communicate information through written and oral presentations	Accounting	Accountant Commercial/Consumer Loan Officer Compensation & Benefits Specialist Investment Analyst
Make three-dimensional models from plans and drawings Use computer-aided design and drafting software Research codes, laws, and regulations Prepare and give presentations	Architecture	Architect Building Construction Inspector Drafter Estimator

(continued)

FIGURE 2.1 Choose the Best Major and Career for Your Skills (Continued)

Skills	Major	Potential Occupations/Careers
Use lab equipment and instruments to test materials Write articles, papers, and reports describing research Evaluate written and statistical data Develop and conduct scientific experiments	Biology	Epidemiologist Quality Control Soil Conservationist Pharmaceutical Sales
Enjoy working in team environments Focus on goals and results Analyze numerical data Lead and facilitate discussions	Business Administration	Retail Store Buyer Advertising Account Executive Production Manager Logistics Coordinator
Interpret systems analyst's program specifications Plan program logic for software applications Collaborate with team of programmers, analysts, and end users Program, test, and correct errors	Business Computer Information Systems	Programmer Systems Analyst Database Administrator Web Site Specialist
Evaluate written and statistical data Develop and conduct scientific experiments Use sensitive lab equipment to test materials Read journals and articles	Chemistry	Science Lab Scientist Chemist Toxicologist Forensic Scientist
Design integrated hardware/software system Prepare engineering specifications for performance and design Conduct research regarding various materials and components Prepare schematics of components for a computer	Computer Engineer	Computer Programmer Systems Analyst Operations Research Analyst Computer Network Analyst
Coordinate movements and choreography with others Listen to and follow director's/producer's instructions Create and develop character roles Practice complex dance patterns	Dance	Choreographer Dance Instructor Dance Therapist Arts Manager
Prepare and write reports Analyze statistical and numerical information Construct mathematical models Explain, interpret, and present information	Economics	Economist Underwriter Financial Analyst International Trade Specialist
Use computers to research databases for information Develop graphics using creative software Meet with other writers, editors, photographers, and graphic artists Pay attention to detail and style while writing	English	Continuity Writer Editor Journalist Screen Writer
Perform mathematical functions and apply formulas Analyze numerical data Use computer software to track information Present information to supervisor and committees	Finance	Treasury Management Specialist Financial Analyst Trust Officer International Trade Specialist
Use computer software to simulate three-dimensional models Analyze minerals using lab equipment Describe results in written reports and presentations Compile data from logs, articles, and research	Geology	Parks and Natural Resources Manager Hydrogeologist Park Ranger Oil Drilling Analyst

(continued)

FIGURE 2.1 **Choose the Best Major and Career for Your Skills (Continued)**

Skills	Major	Potential Occupations/Careers
Use a variety of resources and databases to research information Collaborate with various departments and people Research and prepare reports summarizing plans and projects Use computer software to develop models for projects	Government	Congressional Aide Public Administrator Urban/Regional Planner Lobbyist
Apply investigative and research skills to solving problems Synthesize data from a variety of resources Analyze and interpret data Write and present reports	History	Curator Lobbyist Paralegal Public Administrator
Coordinate with editors, graphics artists, and photographers Establish rapport with people as a part of the interview process Write and review articles Use computer databases to assist with research	Journalism	Public Relations Specialist Newspaper/Magazine Journalist Proofreader Editorial Assistant
Analyze statistical information Present information to groups of people Write papers to reinforce ideas Coordinate plans with team	Marketing	Advertising Copywriter Advertising Account Executive Distribution Manager Merchandiser
Design computer simulation models Analyze, interpret, and evaluate data Formulate and solve equations in order to explain concepts Compute and calculate applied mathematical formulas	Math	Actuary Inventory Control Specialist Investment Analyst Statistician
Make drawings using computer-aided design software Write reports outlining results of tests performed Conduct research and study effects Compare options and make recommendations to committees	Mechanical Engineering	Manufacturing Engineer Field Service Engineer Sales Engineer Industrial Designer
Follow director's instructions and composer's notations Concentrate on quality of sound during rehearsals and practices Develop new interpretation of musical compositions Collaborate with other musicians, directors, and producers	Music	Music Instructor Music Therapist Artist and Repertoire Manager Booking Manager
Observe, analyze, and interpret Resolve or mediate conflicts Listen effectively and establish rapport with people Evaluate various programs	Psychology	Human Resources Interviewer Case Worker Psychological Assistant Job Development Specialist
Interact well with diverse cultures Have insight into group dynamics Understand and improve relationships	Sociology	Demographer Market Research Analyst Nonprofit Administrator Case Worker
Establish rapport easily with people Assist people with the identification of appropriate services Consult with interdisciplinary treatment team Prepare and present reports	Social Work	Probation/Parole Officer Medical Social Worker Community Worker Training Specialist
Collaborate with directors, producers, and other actors Perform before audiences Research customs, social attitudes, and time periods Develop new ways to express character's emotions	Theatre	Set Designer Theatre Manager Television/Film Producer Stage Director

Source: © Mickey Choate, Career Specialist, University of Texas at Dallas.

Get the Right Courses

With a little effort, you can learn how to select courses that both fulfill your requirements and are enjoyable. Here are some strategies for making sound selections:

- *List your constraints.* You might have child-care responsibilities, an inflexible work schedule, or commuting issues. If so, block out the times you can't take classes.
- *Examine your interests.* Interests are activities that you like to do. In many ways, they are what you truly are passionate about (Comb, 2002). Notice how you react to different activities. When you are interested in something, you are alert, tuned in, engaged, and curious. Time often passes quickly when you are doing something you are passionate about. When you aren't interested, you become bored, your mind wanders, and you tune out. Consider Tom Hanks. He signed up for a drama class, tried out for plays, got in them, and had more fun than he ever could have imagined. Hanks turned this passion into a highly successful acting career.

In many ways, college provides an almost endless array of interests that you can explore by taking electives, participating in extracurricular activities, and signing up for internship experiences. You may find that your interests fluctuate a great deal over the course of your college experience. That's okay, but keep monitoring what interests you the most. To evaluate your interests, complete Self-Assessment 2 "What Are My Interests?" on page 58.

- *Study your options.* Colleges have lists of classes required for various specialty diplomas or majors. Examine the college catalog to determine which courses are required for both general education requirements and specific courses in the specialty or major that you want to pursue.
- *Register for a reasonable course load.* Many colleges do not charge for additional courses beyond those needed for full-time status. You might be tempted to pile on extra courses to save time and money. But think again. By taking too many courses, you may spread yourself too thin.
- *Take the right mix of courses.* Don't load up with too many really tough courses in the same term. Check into how much reading and other time is required for specific courses. If you can't find anyone else who can tell you this, make appointments with instructors. Ask them what the course requirements are, how much reading they expect, and so on.
- *Ask the pros.* The "pros" in this case are students who are already in your preferred program. Ask their advice about which courses and instructors to take. On many campuses, academic departments have undergraduate organizations that you can join. If you want to be a biology major, consider joining something like the Student Biology Association. These associations are good places to get connected with students more advanced than you are in a major. On Target Tips, "Get What You Want," provides more tips on getting the right courses.

ON TARGET TIPS

Get What You Want

1. **Register as soon as you can.** Early registration improves your chances of getting the courses you want.
2. **Use computer registration.** Many campuses encourage students to register directly by using the campus computer system. This gives you immediate feedback about your scheduling. It may even suggest alternatives if you run into closed courses.
3. **Have a backup plan.** Anticipate the courses that might close out (for example, preferred times or popular instructors). Have alternatives in mind to meet your requirements.
4. **Explore the waiting list option.** If you want to get into a closed class, find out your chances for getting into a class if you agree to be put on the waiting list. If the odds aren't good, explore other options.
5. **Plead your case.** If you get closed out of a class you really want, go directly to the instructor and ask for an exception. Base your request on your intellectual curiosity for the course content, not on scheduling convenience. Some instructors may reject your request, but others will listen and try to help you.

Explore a Certificate or AA Degree

Some students enter a community college with a clear idea of what they want to major or specialize in, but many enter with no clear idea. Some students plan to obtain an associate degree, others intend to pursue a certificate in a specialty field.

The Associate of Arts (AA) degree includes general academic courses that allow students to transfer to a four-year institution. If you plan to transfer, you'll need to select a college and study its degree requirements as soon as possible. You should consult regularly with an advisor at your community college and the four-year institution to ensure that you're enrolling in courses appropriate to your major at the new institution.

In addition to a core of general education courses, obtaining an AA degree means taking either a concentration of courses in a major (or area of emphasis) such as history, English, psychology, and so on or taking a required number of electives. In most community colleges, a minimum of 60 or more credit hours is required for an AA degree. A typical breakdown might be 45 credits in general education and 15 in your major, area of emphasis, or electives. Some community colleges also offer an Associate of Science (AS) degree that requires a heavy science concentration.

Many community colleges also offer certificate programs designed to help people reenter the job market or upgrade their skills. There are many specializations: food and hospitality, graphic communication, press operation, medical record coding, word processing, building-property management, travel management, vocational nursing, and others. The coursework in certificate programs does not include general education requirements, as Associate of Arts and Science programs do. Certificate programs focus specifically on the job skills needed in a particular occupation. The number of credits required varies but is usually fewer than the number required for an associate's degree.

If you're a community college student, whether you're enrolled in an associate's or a certificate program, it's a good idea to map out a plan that lists each of your courses until graduation. Study your college's catalog and become familiar with the requirements for your degree. With your college catalog in hand, complete the Self Assessment "Coursework for an Associate Degree or Certificate" on your CD-ROM. Use this as a starting point in discussing your plans with your academic advisor.

Create a Four- or Five-Year Plan

Even though many first-year students don't know what to major in, or find themselves changing majors in their first year, it's still a good idea to map out a four- or five-year plan for your intended major that lists each of your courses every term until graduation. Study your college's catalog and become familiar with requirements in a major that interests you. You'll need to know the general education requirements, required courses in the major, prerequisites for courses, restricted electives, free electives, and other requirements. In this way, you can take control of your academic planning and give yourself the most flexibility toward the end of your four or five years of college.

The risk in not doing so is that you'll end up in your junior or senior year with too many courses in one area and not enough in another, which will extend the time needed to get your bachelor's degree. The four- or five-year plan also lets you see which terms will be light and which will be heavy, as well as whether you'll need to take summer courses. Of course, it's unlikely that you'll carry out your plan exactly. As you make changes, the plan will allow you to see the consequences of your moves and what you have to do to stay on track to complete your degree.

The four- or five-year plan is an excellent starting point for sessions with your academic advisor. The plan can be a springboard for questions you might have about which courses to take this term, next term, and so on. If you're considering several different majors, make a four- or five-year plan for each one and use the plans to help you decide which courses to take and when. If you're in a four-year institution, begin your planning with Self-Assessment 3 "A Four- or Five-Year Academic Plan" on page 59.

Transfer Credits

If you decide to transfer to another college, you'll want to know whether the credits you've earned will transfer to the new school. How well your credits will transfer depends on the schools and on your major. Check the catalog of the new college and see how its requirements match up with those of your current college. The catalog also will describe transfer requirements. Next, be sure to talk with an advisor at the new college about which of your courses will transfer. Here are some questions you might ask the admissions advisor (Harbin, 1995):

What are the minimum admission criteria that I have to meet in order to transfer to your college?
Do I need a minimum grade point average for admission? If so, what is it?
What are the application deadlines for transfer admissions?
Where can I get a transfer application?
What else can you tell me about transferring to your college?

If you want to change colleges but aren't sure where you want to go, consult some general guides to colleges such as *Peterson's National College Data Bank* (http://www.petersons.com) or *Barron's Profiles of American Colleges* (http://www.baronseduc.com). Try to visit several campuses that might meet your needs. Talk with students there, as well as an academic advisor. Walk around and get a feel for how you like it. Be clear about what aspects of your current life are unsatisfying and why the new school will be better.

Connect with Computers

Computers can make your college life easier. They can support your efforts to think and learn, help you reach many of your college goals, and provide a foundation for building important career skills. In 2003, 85 percent of first year college students used personal computers and that number is likely to increase in the future (Sax & others, 2003).

Get Up to Speed

If you've had little chance to become familiar with computers, several strategies will help you get up to speed. You should be able to become computer literate by making good use of the free computer labs on campus. Many campus computer labs are open early and close late to promote student access. Some campuses have computer labs in the residence halls. Take a beginning computer class to start learning the skills you'll need in a computer-dependent world. Or find part-time work that involves computers so you can earn a paycheck while you learn these valuable skills. Check the computer lab for opportunities. Complete Self-Assessment "How Am I Doing with Computers?" on your CD-ROM to see where you stand regarding computer use.

Explore the Internet

The Internet is a major force in the academic world and elsewhere (Hofstetter, 2003). In 2003, 82 percent of first-year students reported that they used the Internet for research or homework and this percentage is likely to increase (Sax & others, 2003).

You've probably noticed the widespread use of World Wide Web addresses in advertising. If you are an experienced "web surfer," you know how your own work patterns have changed since you began using this tool. If you have not personally experienced the astounding capabilities of the Web, find ways to gain access and get good at using it. One way to do this is to contact the learning resources center at your college and ask about courses or tutorials on Internet use.

E-mail E-mail allows ongoing Internet conversations with people who share your interests. In 2003, 64 percent of first-year students said that they communicate via e-mail. Some of your instructors may require discussions online using a class listserve. Such discussions allow you to practice the language of the course and can improve your understanding of course concepts. Some instructors welcome questions via e-mail because it's often more convenient than office hours for both parties. Technologically oriented instructors are often remarkably open to developing online relationships with their students. Some may be even more open to online chats than face-to-face discussions.

Your campus may provide you with a free e-mail account. Most campuses that have not yet provided this service are hard at work raising funds to do so. If your campus does not offer such accounts, you can join a full-range commercial service for $20 per month or less. If you have an e-mail address, consider getting some cards printed with your name and e-mail address to facilitate building your own electronic community. Once you have your own e-mail address, it will be easy to send private e-mail to others, participate in listservs, visit websites, and download a variety of resources available on the Internet.

World Wide Web (WWW) The World Wide Web is both the most exciting and the most frustrating development on the Internet (Young, 2002). The excitement comes from the impressive variety of information presented in pictures, sounds, and dazzling graphics available to anyone with a browser. The Web lets you move easily from one piece of information to other related information by clicking "buttons" on a website. In this way you can search through a "web" of connected sites. When you find a site that you especially like and wish to revisit, you can create bookmarks that let you return there directly.

Not all computer time has to be spent in physical isolation. If you're spending too much time alone on a computer, start collaborating with others at least some of the time when using the computer.

The frustration comes from the sheer quantity of information available on the Web (Haag & Perry, 2003). Entering a key word on the search engine of a browser may result in the browser listing thousands of possible resources, or "hits." You may have no easy way to separate the valuable ones from the "junk." Visiting every site takes too long. This explains why some students report that they spent hours on the Web but still couldn't find answers to the questions that prompted their search.

Many organizations and businesses offer information on the Web that pertains to college subjects. For example, a class studying AIDS may find facts on the Web about AIDS, including current research on medication, legal concerns, and support groups. Because many web pages are updated frequently, this information may be among the most current professional research available. Unfortunately, some websites don't get updates, so their information may be out of date. The Web also contains a lot of junk. It does not currently have the same quality control procedures that you would find in the academic journals in your college library. Get in the habit of examining the information about the maintenance of the website. It will help you judge the currency and value of the information posted. On Target Tips, "Critically Evaluate Web Information," will help you judge what you read on the Web.

Surfing the Web can be a wonderful experience—sometimes too wonderful. Most users report that hours can slip away while they're online. Be prepared to invest some time if you choose to use this helpful tool.

Use a Word-Processing Program

Computer word-processing programs can make the process of writing and rewriting papers easier because you can edit without having to retype most of your work (Tiene & Ingram, 2001). You also can select different print types, called *fonts,* and use other features to highlight or underline key sections of your work. With most word-processing programs, you can incorporate headers (standard headings at the top of each page), page numbers, and footnotes easily. Many programs will also develop your reference list, placing it in the conventional format for the discipline in which you're writing. Perhaps most helpful of all are the features that allow you to check spelling, grammar, and word count when your paper is completed. Of all of the tips for success in this book, one of the most important is: *Learn to use a word processor and write all your papers on it.*

Word processing also involves some hazards. If you don't make a habit of saving your work often, you can end up with nothing to print. Spell-checkers do not substitute for good proofreading, because spell-checking will identify words that are misspelled but not words that are misused. For example, most won't catch the difference between *there* and *their* or *to, too,* and *two.* The worst problem associated with word processing is that it might encourage you to procrastinate and therefore lose revision time, because your first draft can look very professional. Better papers are better because the writer allowed some time to think again and revise.

Reprinted by permission. www.cartoonstock.com.

Online Education

Learning is less confined to the classroom now than ever before. Technology advances have spawned new online learning opportunities for students such as online courses and electronic text supplements.

Online Courses Students increasingly are taking online courses as part of their college degree plan. Benefits of taking some of your courses online include accessing learning from your home or campus living arrangement and learning on your schedule at your convenience. This flexibility gives you the opportunity to demonstrate your self-responsibility in completing assignments. In a typical online course, you will find the syllabus posted and each week's assignments and activities fully explained. However, in some cases, online courses are self-paced with all assignments due by the end of the term. You likely will be required to read a textbook and take quizzes or exams online, and in some cases participate in online discussions. An instructor will monitor your work and in most cases you will be able to contact him or her via e-mail.

Many students want and need the personal interaction that a traditional classroom provides. Good candidates for online courses are self-motivated, may travel extensively because of work, or live in remote locations. If you are interested in taking one or more courses online, ask your academic advisor about this possibility.

Electronic Text Supplements Learning materials in a course increasingly include far more than just a textbook. Increasingly, these learning materials are provided to students through an online website or a CD-ROM. For example, this book has both types of electronic text supplements. If you have not already gone to this book's website at http://success.wadsworth.com/santrock4e/ or used the CD-ROM that came packaged with the book, this is a good time to get started. Text publishers spend extensive time and effort in creating learning experiences like these to help enhance your understanding of the course material.

Electronic text supplements vary by text but most include at a minimum review sections, practice tests with various types of items (such as multiple-choice and essay questions), and opportunities to expand your learning beyond the information found in the textbook. Take advantage of these electronic supplements to make learning more effective for you.

Use Computers in Other Ways to Reach Your Goals

Using e-mail, the World Wide Web, and word-processing programs regularly will help you succeed in college and thereafter. In many careers, successful individuals rely on these computer tools on a daily basis. You may also want to consider three other tools—research databases, graphics and presentation software, and

TABLE 2.1 Helpful Library Research Databases

Research Coverage	Title
Behavioral sciences	PsychInfo/PsychLit
	Sociological Abstracts
Business	PROMT
	ABI/INFORM
Education	ERIC
Humanities	Economic Literature Index
	Historical Abstracts
	Humanities Abstracts
	Philosopher's Index
Natural science	BIOSIS
	MEDLINE
News reports	Associated Press
	NEXUS
	Reuters
Reference	Books in Print
	Dissertation Abstracts
	Academic Index
	Britannica Online

Source: "Popular Electronic Abstracts" from Mick O'Leary, *The Online100: Online Magazine's Field Guide to the 100 Most Important Online Databases.* Copyright © 1995 by Mick O'Leary. Reprinted with permission of the author and Information Today, Inc., Medford, NJ, www.infotoday.com

spreadsheet programs—that can help you enormously if the task at hand is appropriate for their use.

Research Databases Your campus library houses electronic databases that you can use for research assignments (Post, 2002). Each database uses key words, years, or authors to direct you to specific articles in the professional literature. Table 2.1 lists some of the most frequently used academic databases. You may find other uses for databases as well. For example, business classes may explore how to keep track of inventory or potential customers. If you get a part-time job at the college, you may be working with databases of alumni addresses or bookstore inventories.

Graphics and Presentation Software Graphics packages let you express yourself visually. They allow you to copy and design images, create animations, develop charts and graphs, and make impressive computer-driven presentations (Heinich & others, 2002). Some of your courses may have graphic requirements. In other classes, graphics can improve the content and aesthetic appeal of your work.

PowerPoint is an especially powerful presentation software tool. If you have to prepare a class presentation, PowerPoint can help you organize it and create a dynamic, visually attractive format for it. Many successful individuals in a wide range of careers use PowerPoint, saying that it has made the art of presenting easier and more professional, and makes presentations much more interesting for the audience. PowerPoint enables you to include a variety of visual elements that add impact to a presentation.

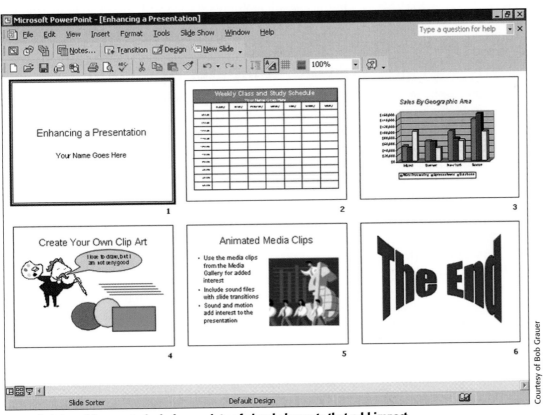

Courtesy of Bob Grauer

PowerPoint enables you to include a variety of visual elements that add impact to a presentation.

Reprinted with permission of Carole Cable.

Career Connections

When Joleen took the summer job as an office assistant, she assumed she would spend lots of time filing and answering the phones, but she thought it would still look good on her resume to have office experience. She was surprised to find herself spending most of the day on the computer. The insurance company had computerized all of its files, so the first place she looked for any information was their online database. When calls came in on the computerized switchboard, she would download the appropriate client information and later update the database with the newest developments on each case. She was expected to learn how to navigate the computer systems and have strong word-processing skills to keep up with the workload. Although it was more challenging than she expected, it certainly was more interesting than filing, and gave her real experience for an even better job after college.

Dion's job as a graphic designer also involved spending most of the day on the computer, a far cry from what he expected when deciding to major in art his first year in college. His designs were mainly computer-generated on complex systems, and then sent to clients over the Internet for their feedback. He used a spreadsheet program to track his costs versus his budget for each project and was required to produce electronic weekly reports on his progress. Occasionally he even helped produce client presentations, integrating his designs into elaborate PowerPoint presentations to demonstrate their impact and help win new business for the company. These skills made him an even more valued employee than simply someone with strong design skills. One day he hoped to manage other designers, and was well on his way.

Spreadsheet Programs Spreadsheet programs perform calculations on numerical data. For example, you can enter data from a chemistry experiment into the columns of a spreadsheet and set up the spreadsheet program to calculate and summarize the results. Students who major in business are likely to use spreadsheets in marketing analyses, business plans, and financial projections. Your instructors will probably tell you which spreadsheet programs will best suit your needs.

Avoid Computer Addiction

It's hard to pry some people away from their computers. Some computer technology fans are so dedicated to their computers that they neglect their work or studies. How can a computer be so addictive?

- *The compelling opportunity to explore the world.* Casual surfing of the Internet can take you in many directions. Anyone with a healthy curiosity can find it hard to stay away from the vast and varied sources of information that computers can reach.
- *The obsessive attraction of computer games.* The thrill of good performance is rewarding. It's easy to keep playing "just one more time" to see whether you can better your score. Hours slip by as you gradually refine your game skill and lose your real social connections.
- *The seduction of electronic relationships.* An electronic relationship between two people can feel profound, because the absence of physical cues may allow you to connect to another person in a novel way. Without the other elements of real life intruding, such exchanges can lead to deeper emotional involvement and reward than a user may currently experience in face-to-face relationships. However, this

sense of intimacy can be based on half-truths or even lies, because you have no real way of knowing who the other person is. In any case, such relationships can be compelling and time-consuming. If you find yourself favoring "e-friends" over "realfriends," think twice!

To read about one student's computer addiction, see Staying Out of the Pits, "When Computer Games Stop Being Fun." Completing the Journal activity "Dealing with Computers" on page 60 will also help you to think further about how you are doing in the computing world.

STAYING OUT OF THE PITS — When Computer Games Stop Being Fun

Dennis Bennett was failing all of his college classes, his marriage was in trouble, and he wasn't being much of a father to his one-year-old son. However, he had progressed to Level 58 as Madrid, the Great Shaman of the North, his character in the online role-playing game, *EverQuest,* and that was all that mattered at the time.

Bennett's grades and family life have improved recently, because he quit playing the game. He considers himself a recovered *EverQuest* addict, now able to control his desire to immerse himself in the game's rich fantasy world.

He says that the game almost ruined his life. "It was my life. I ceased being me; I was Madrid, the Great Shaman of the North. Thinking of it now, I almost cringe" (CNET Tech, 2002).

Summary Strategies for Mastering College

To master college and reach your goals, you need good resources.

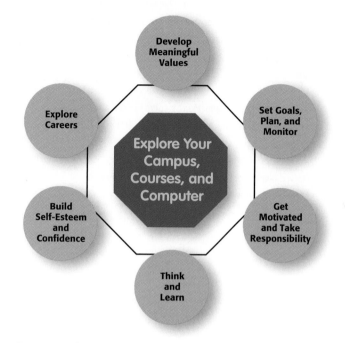

Focus on the "Six Strategies for Success" above as you read each chapter to learn how to apply these strategies to your own success.

① Connect with Your Campus

- Know which campus resources you need now or might need in the future. Find out their locations, hours, e-mail addresses, and phone numbers.
- Learn about academic support services, such as help for writing and math. Find out if tutoring and study groups are available.
- Seek counseling if you have personal concerns.
- Tap library resources and learn to use the library effectively.
- Stay healthy and use your campus health services when needed.
- Keep safe and know how to contact the campus security personnel when you need them.
- Participate in one or more extracurricular activities, but don't spend too much time on those that interfere with your academic work.
- Become culturally enriched by learning about and going to some cultural activities at your college and in the community.

- If you're a student with a physical limitation, learn about and use available campus resources.

② Map Out an Academic Plan

- Connect with your academic advisor, who can be one of your most important campus resources.
- Study the college catalog and use it as a resource. Know what is required for various aspects of your coursework, including prerequisites and core courses.
- Explore majors and plan your coursework for a degree or certificate. Create a four- or five-year plan to ensure that you take all the classes you need in a reasonable time period. Use this as a guide for regular discussions with your advisor.
- Know some good strategies for transferring to another college, if this is on your mind.
- Get the right courses by listing your constraints, studying your options, registering for a reasonable course load, taking the right mix of courses, talking with your advisor, and checking with more advanced students.

③ Connect with Computers

- Get up to speed and become computer literate. If you don't own a computer, use campus labs. Consider taking a computer class.
- Use e-mail to keep in touch with friends, classmates, and instructors.
- Learn to use the World Wide Web to support your success in college. Be sure to evaluate the accuracy and quality of information on the Web when using it for academic purposes. Explore potential online courses and utilize electronic and Web-based supplements to enhance your learning.
- Use a word-processing program for most or all of your writing. If you can't yet, learn how as soon as possible. Request help at the campus computing center. Take advantage of online education.
- Learn to use research databases, graphics spreadsheet programs, and PowerPoint.
- Avoid computer addiction by limiting your time surfing the net, playing computer games, and exploring online relationships.

Review Questions

1. What kinds of campus connections matter and why? Name at least three.

Resource: _____

Why important? _____

Resource: _____

Why important? _____

Resource: _____

Why important? _____

2. What are some key aspects of designing an academic career path? List three things you can do *now* to begin this process.

A. _____

B. _____

C. _____

3. Why is your college catalog such a valuable resource? What are some of the most important facts you can learn from this guide?

_____

_____

_____

_____

4. What are some key considerations when selecting a major? How might you know if you made an inappropriate choice?

_____

_____

_____

_____

5. List at least three important computer skills that will help you succeed in college. Which one do you think will have the greatest impact on your immediate success?

_____

_____

_____

_____

Learning Portfolio

SELF-ASSESSMENTS

YOUR JOURNAL

STRATEGIES FOR SUCCESS

Develop Meaningful Values

Explore Careers

Set Goals, Plan, and Monitor

Explore Your Campus, Courses, and Computer

Build Self-Esteem and Confidence

Get Motivated and Take Responsibility

Think and Learn

Campus Resources to Meet My Needs

First, cross off any items that you know you won't need. Add any other locations that you think you will need. Then answer yes or no after the items not crossed off. Next, write down the location of the campus resource and any notes you want to make about the resource, such as its hours, phone number, and e-mail address.

Does My Campus Have	Yes or No	Location/Notes
Career services center?		
Student testing center?		
Math laboratory?		
Performing arts center?		
Campus security?		
Financial aid office?		
ROTC service?		
TV or radio station?		
Work-study program?		
Writing lab?		
Health center?		
Travel agency?		
Mental health services?		
Language lab?		
Intramural sports office?		
Student government office?		
Post office?		
Lost and found?		
Printing service?		
Banking center?		
Computer labs?		
Multimedia and graphics lab?		
International students' center?		
College newspaper office?		
Religious services?		
Campus cinema?		
Lost and found?		
Other		
Other		
Other		

Compare your information with that of others in the class. How are you doing in discovering resources on your campus? Put the information about resources in the planner that you carry with you on campus. Note: This list is also on the website for this book, where you can easily tailor it to meet your own needs and print out a copy.

What Are My Interests?

Answering these questions can help you pinpoint your interests:

What activities do you enjoy doing the most?

_____

_____

_____

When you are doing what you want, what are you doing?

_____

_____

_____

What do you do in your leisure time?

_____

_____

_____

What are your hobbies?

_____

_____

_____

Can you relate any of the activities, hobbies, or interests to possible academic majors? If so, which ones?

_____

_____

_____

Can you link any of the activities, hobbies, or interests to possible careers? Is so, which ones?

_____

_____

_____

_____

Source: After Weston Exploration (2002). The Model for Exploration. Urbana-Champaign: Weston Exploration, University of Illinois.

A Four- or Five-Year Academic Plan

Study your college catalog to find out what courses you need to graduate in a particular major. If you have not selected a major, examine the requirements for one you're considering. Then fill in the blanks with the courses you plan to take. Use this self-assessment to discuss your decisions with your academic advisor. The plan here is for schools on a semester schedule. If your school has a quarterly system, create your own plan by listing the quarters for each of the four or five years and then filling in the courses you plan to take.

Fall	Spring	Summer
	First Year	
	Second Year	
	Third Year	
	Fourth Year	
	Fifth Year	

Your Journal

● REFLECT

1. My Best Helpers

● The names of the persons who have helped me the most on campus so far:

_____

● How they have helped me:

_____

● The aspect of college that I need the most help in right now is:

_____

● The person on campus who most likely could help me in this area is:

_____

2. Dealing with Computers

Go to the CD-ROM Learning Portfolio/Self-Assessment "How Am I Doing with Computers?"

● What computer skills do you have?

_____

_____

● Do you have any fears or problems regarding computers? What are they?

_____

_____

● How can you address them? Write down a few specific resources to help you overcome these issues:

1. _____

2. _____

3. _____

● DO

1. Explore Campus Jobs

Perhaps the fastest way to do this is to go to the financial aid office on campus. Ask for a list of available part-time jobs. Do any of these jobs appeal to you? Will any help you develop skills toward a future career? Write down at least three jobs that best link up with future careers that interest you. Include a strategy for exploring each opportunity.

1. JOB: _____

STRATEGY: _____

2. JOB: _____

STRATEGY: _____

3. JOB: _____

STRATEGY: _____

Your Journal

2. Explore Extracurricular Activities

Locate or create a list of extracurricular events or meetings on your campus. Write down a few that appeal to you most, then attend one or two. Decide whether you want to make these activities a regular part of your college life by making a list of pros and cons for such involvement.

Interesting activities:

Pros for involvement   Cons for involvement

● THINK CRITICALLY

1. My Library Needs

Libraries often provide many services that students are unaware of. What service does your library provide that you might need to use in the next year? If you can't answer this question, obtain a library brochure of services or talk with a librarian about the services. Describe them below, linked with the need they will help fulfill.

Library service: How will I use it?

2. Ask the Right Questions

Make an appointment to see your academic advisor. Create a set of questions to ask, such as:

- *What classes should I take this term and next?*
- *What sequence of classes should I take?*
- *Am I taking too many difficult classes in one term?*
- *What electives do you recommend?*
- *What career opportunities are there if I study mainly _____ or _____?*

Write about your conversation with your academic advisor below.

● CREATE

1. Only the Best

Ask students you trust and who have been on campus longer than you about where to locate at least five of the following.

- Best cheap, hot breakfast
- All-night food store
- Local businesses that give student discounts
- Best software
- Live music
- Best pizza
- Best coffee
- Free or cheap movies

- Best place for quiet conversation
- Best place to exercise
- Best bulletin board
- Best place to dance
- Discount bookstores
- Cheap photocopies
- Best place to view the stars

2. Your Cognitive College Map

You may have received a campus map as part of your orientation materials. Draw your own map as well. On it, emphasize the aspects of campus that are most important to you by drawing them larger and more stylized. You might also try constructing the map using computer graphics.

Applying the Six Strategies for Success

What did you learn in this chapter that you can apply to the following key strategies to help form the foundation for your success? Write down all of the main points you can remember that support the following strategies:

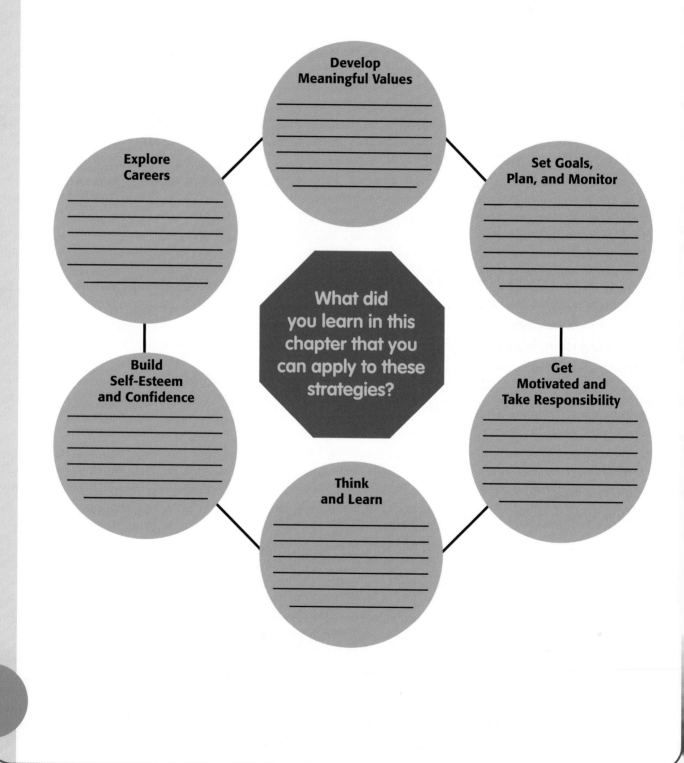

3 Be a Great Time Manager

Where Are You? What you do with your time is critical to your success in college and beyond. Highly successful scientists, business people, and other professionals say that managing their time on a daily basis is crucial to reaching their goals. How strong is your current ability to manage time effectively? Place a checkmark next to only those items that apply to you.

● I am good at spending time on activities that are related to my most important values and goals.

● I use a paper or electronic planner to manage my time effectively.

● I have created a term planner and monitor it.

● I regularly set priorities in managing my time.

● I make weekly plans, monitor how I use my time each week, and evaluate what I need to do or change in order to reach my goals.

● I complete daily to-do lists.

● I treat my academic commitment as a serious job.

● The time I spend on academics equals or exceeds the time I spend on leisure, play, recreation, sports, and watching TV.

● I don't procrastinate much.

● I'm good at balancing my academic life with other demands.

As you read about Florence Griffith-Joyner, think about what a great time manager she was and how this contributed to her success in life, competition, and career.

Images of College Success

Flo-Jo

Time is especially important in the lives of athletes who race against a clock. Florence Griffith-Joyner, or "Flo-Jo," beat the clock not only in track but also in her life.

As an Olympic athlete, Flo-Jo smashed Olympic and world records in the 100-meter and 200-meter dashes and was once considered the "fastest woman alive." In college, she had to juggle many aspects of her life to be successful. In addition to being a full-time college student and athlete, she worked and commuted to school at California State–Northridge. She managed her time well enough to run impressively in college and also to achieve high grades. Despite doing well academically as a first year student, however, Flo-Jo could not afford to return for her sophomore year, so she worked as a bank teller until the Northridge track coach helped her apply for financial aid. When her track coach took a job at UCLA, she transferred there and became the NCAA champion in the 200-meter event.

Flo-Jo's development of time-management skills in college served her well later. A typical day for her after college involved working for four hours on a public relations project for one of her sponsors, a long track workout, two hours in the weight room, a sprint home to cook dinner, a workout in the evening, and writing after dinner.

Flo-Jo grew up in poverty in the Watts area of Los Angeles as the seventh of eleven children and was intensely motivated to find a career—in sports and afterward—that would give her a more prosperous life. However, she never forgot her past and frequently gave back to the community, establishing the Florence Griffith Joyner Foundation for disadvantaged youth, among other things. She often returned to speak to children and urged them to place academics ahead of athletics in their lives. Setting priorities for her time was something that she always did well.

"WHEN YOU HAVE BEEN SECOND BEST for so long, you can either accept it or try to become the best. I made the decision to try to be the best."

—Florence Griffith-Joyner

Unfortunately, Florence Griffith-Joyner died unexpectedly of an apparent heart seizure at the age of 38. In her book, which was published after her death (Griffith-Joyner & Hanc, 1999), she talked about the importance of commitment and determining the best times of the day to do whatever is most important. "When you have been second best for so long, you can either accept it or try to become the best. I made the decision to try to be the best."

—Florence Griffith-Joyner

As you read, think about the "Six Strategies for Success" listed to the left and how this chapter can help you maximize success in these important areas. For example, to reach your goals and still be able to live a balanced life, you need to do two things:

1. Discipline yourself to plan and monitor your time with your values and goals in mind.

2. Take steps to minimize procrastination and distractions.

Take Charge of Your Life by Managing Your Time

Many college students feel overwhelmed with all they have to do. Yet some of the busiest and most successful students get good grades *and* find enough leisure time. How do they do it? They control their life by controlling their time.

How often have you said or heard people say, "I just don't have enough time"? Tough luck! Each of us has the same amount of time—24 hours, or 1,440 minutes, a day—yet individuals vary enormously in how effectively they plan and use their hours and minutes. You can't really change the nature of time or buy more of it than you're given. What you can change is how you manage *yourself* in relation to time.

You alone control how *you* use it. Once you've wasted time, it's gone and can't be replaced. Students often have ingrained habits that they practice in managing time. To evaluate your good and bad time management habits, complete the Journal activity "Change a Habit" on page 88.

Counter Time Management Misconceptions

There are a number of myths about time management. See if any of the following misconceptions ring a bell (Mackenzie, 1997):

- *Time management is nothing but common sense. I do well in school and I'm happy so I must be managing my time effectively.* Time management is simple, but it is not necessarily common sense. What is not simple is the self-discipline to use time-management strategies. Even though you might be doing well, this doesn't mean that you are managing time well. It is more likely that you are successful in spite of the way you manage time. What if you could double your productivity with more effective time-management strategies? How much more successful do you think you could be?

> *While we are postponing, life speeds by.*
> Seneca
> *1st-century Roman philosopher*

- *I work better under pressure and time management would take away that edge.* Hardly anyone works best under pressure. What really happens is that people do the best they can under stressful circumstances. Usually, this kind of thinking is nothing but a rationale for procrastinating. If you put off an important task until the last minute with the excuse that you work better under pressure, you leave yourself no time to carry out the planning that is necessary to produce outstanding results. You also leave no room for correcting mistakes or including better ideas that might come to you too late to be included. By not managing your time, you miss the opportunity to do your best.
- *People take time management too seriously and that takes all the fun out of life.* If constant stress, forgetting appointments, missing deadlines, and working feverishly through the night sound like fun, perhaps you should reconsider. Think of effective time management this way: If you had two more hours a day (good time-management strategies can do this), could you think of some enjoyable ways to spend those hours?
- *Time-management strategies take a great deal of work. I don't have time for that.* You don't have time *not* to. Once you learn how to use effective time-management techniques, like writing a daily plan and keeping a time log, they are not that time-consuming in themselves. A few minutes doing these can save you hours.

Tackle Time Wasters

There are many ways to waste time, such as surfing the Web, daydreaming, socializing, worrying, or procrastinating. Many students don't say "no" to a request for their time possibly because of their desire for approval, fear of offending, or false sense of obligation. This can lead to wasting a lot of time in low-priority rather than high-priority activities. For example, you change your plan to go to the library to study, when a friend says, "Come on with us and shoot some pool. You can afford a couple of hours with your friends."

Decide what you need to do and what you can realistically do. Say "no" to everything else. If this is difficult for you, write "NO" in large letters on a card and place it next to the phone, computer, or on your desk (Yager, 1999). You might suggest someone else who could do what is asked or offer to do it when you have more time.

Letting the telephone or e-mail interrupt you is another time waster. Instead of letting callers or instant messages control your time, try some of these strategies:

- Use an answering machine to screen incoming calls and return the calls at your convenience.
- Learn to say, "I can't talk right now. Can I call you back?" Set aside a time to return calls.
- When you leave a message, try to give a specific time for someone to return your call so that you avoid playing telephone tag.
- Set a specific time to check your e-mail every day or two rather than responding to each message as it is received.
- Consider changing your computer settings so messages don't pop up in the middle of important projects such as writing a paper or doing homework online.

Time wasters are often linked to a lack of self-discipline. To evaluate some ways and reasons that you might waste time, complete Self-Assessment 1 "Time Wasters" on page 85.

Put the 80–20 Principle into Action

You might think all of your responsibilities are so important that you can't drop any of them completely or reduce the time they take. (Davis, Eshelman, & McKay, 2000). Vilfredo Pareto, an Italian economist, conceived of the *80–20 principle.* He observed that about 80 percent of what people do yields about 20 percent of the results while about 20 percent of what people do produces about 80 percent of the results. For example, approximately 20 percent of a newspaper is worth your while to read. It is a good idea to skim the rest. At least 80 percent of people's mail (e-mail and postal mail) is junk and best not read at all.

Many people spend their time in a frenzy of activity but achieve little because they are not concentrating on the things that will produce positive results for them. Separating the important stuff from the junk will help you become a better time manager. The Journal activity "The 80/20 Principle in Your Academic Life" on page 88 will help you learn to apply this theory.

Reap the Benefits of Managing Your Time Effectively

You can reap many benefits by managing your time effectively:

- *Be more productive.* Using your time more effectively will increase your productivity in college. You'll have the hours you need to write that long term paper. Effectively managing your time will help you get better grades.
- *Reduce your stress.* Managing your time poorly will increase your stress. Imagine the day before an exam when you suddenly realize that you have a massive amount of studying to do. Panic! Tension builds and stress escalates. Effectively managing your time will help you reduce the stress in your life.
- *Improve your self-esteem.* Learning to manage time effectively will increase your self-esteem by making you feel successful and ahead of the curve. Wasting a lot of time will make you feel crummy about yourself because you are constantly playing catch up.
- *Achieve balance in your life.* Developing good time-management skills and actively using them will let you achieve a more balanced life. You'll miraculously have more time for school, work, home, family, and leisure.
- *Establish an important career skill.* College provides you with an opportunity to work on developing many skills that you can carry forward into a career. Being a great time manager is one of these. In most careers, to be successful you'll not only need to complete many different tasks, but also need to complete them quickly and by a deadline.
- *Reach your goals.* The act of setting goals and planning how to reach them will help you live the life you want to live. You need time to reach your goals, so the better you can manage time, the bigger you can dream. You

"Hey, I'll get to the meeting on time. It's those creative types you ought to be checking on."

With a Self-Contract and a Support Person

Some college students benefit from writing a contract for themselves related to their goals and time management action plan (Davis, Eschelman, & McKay, 2000). In the contract, spell out your goals, how you are going to use your time to achieve them, and how you plan to reward yourself for your self-discipline and staying on track. Sign and date your contract. To ensure that you follow through on your self-contract, choose a support person to sit down with you every other week for the next three months to evaluate your progress. following is a sample self-contract form:

I, _____ am going to do
(your name)

_____
(activity or goal)

for or by _____ .
(how long, how often, when)

I will monitor my progress by

_____
(the method that you will use)

I will evaluate my progress every

_____
(how often)

with my support person _____ .
(name)

If I stick with this plan and reach my goal, I will reward myself

with _____ .
(something that will motivate you)

don't have to reach your goals all by yourself. In many instances, it helps to have one or more support persons around you. Examine "Take Charge with a Self-Contract and a Support Person" to think further about reaching your goals.

Connect Values, Goals, and Time

In Chapter 1, we underscored the importance of knowing what your values are and creating goals that align with them. This is a good strategy to engage in before you develop plans for managing time effectively. You don't want to spend extensive time in activities that don't coincide with the values you admire the most or that don't mesh with your most important short-term and long-term goals. A key aspect of effective time management is to do so in accordance with your values and goals.

Revisit Your Values

In Self-Assessment 2 "What Are My Values?" on page 28 of Chapter 1, you were given the opportunity to determine what things in life are important to you. Recall that these things included such values as being a moral person, being competent at my work, being well educated, being well-off financially, living a healthy life-style, having a good spiritual life, and many others. This exercise was designed to help you clarify your values and you were asked to write down the five values that are most important to you. Revisit this self-assessment on page 28 and write down these five values in the space below.

The Five Values That Are Most Important to Me:

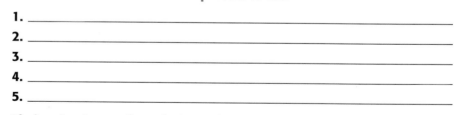

1. _____
2. _____
3. _____
4. _____
5. _____

If education is one of your highest values but you are spending the bulk of your time socializing with friends and participating in campus organizations, something is wrong. You might want to think about developing a time-management plan that involves more hours devoted to studying. Knowing what is most valuable to you gives direction to your life. Your energy should be oriented first toward your most important values with other values taking a back seat. When choosing how to spend your time, examine your values to help you make a smart decision.

Revisit Your Goals

Returning to the example of education as a high priority value, you might set a goal of attaining a 3.5 grade point average this term. It then follows that in planning to manage your time effectively, you will need to spend many more hours studying than socializing. In Chapter 1, you spent considerable time reading about the importance of setting goals to achieve college success. Let's review some important ingredients of effective goal setting:

Set goals that are challenging, reasonable, and specific.
Set long-term and short-term goals.
Set completion dates for your goals.
Create subgoals.
Anticipate and overcome obstacles.

Now complete the Journal activity "Be More Precise" on page 88 to practice making your time-management goals and plans more specific. Finally, write down one or more specific long-term (this term to more than a year) and short-term goals (from a week to a month) for each of your top five values:

	Value	Long-Term Goal	Short-Term Goal
1.	_____	_____	_____
2.	_____	_____	_____
3.	_____	_____	_____
4.	_____	_____	_____
5.	_____	_____	_____

Develop an Action Plan

Now that you have identified your most important values and related them to long- and short-term goals, the next step is to manage your time effectively so that you can reach these goals. Developing an action plan involves evaluating how you spend your time. Let's see how this could change the way you live your life this term.

> *Time moves slowly, but passes quickly.*
> Alice Walker
> Contemporary U.S. author

Plan for the Term, Week, and Day

Break down your time by term, week, and day using the following Term Planner. As you create plans for coordinating within these three time frames, always keep in mind the importance of breaking your goals down into subgoals and intermediate steps. For example, you might have a major paper in English due in three weeks that counts one third of your grade. This week you could create the following subgoals related to the paper (Winston, 1995):

First Day: go to library and survey topics.
Second Day: Narrow topics.

Third Day: Select topic.
Fourth Day: Construct outline.
Fifth Day: Write first two pages.
And so on.

Many people find it helpful to work backward to reach a goal. For example, decide on an important goal that you want to reach in one year. First, think what you need to do each month between now and then to attain that goal. Then, think about what you need to do weekly to achieve it. Finally, think what you can do in the next 24 hours to get started. In this way, you can focus on a goal and work backward to outline the steps that will enable you to reach it.

Choose the Right Planning Tools

The two basic types of planning tools you need to consider to help manage time more effectively are paper-and-pencil planners and electronic planners.

Paper-and-Pencil Planners The traditional mode of planning involves using a paper-and-pencil planner. Among the most effective and popular of these are the Franklin and Franklin Covey planners. The Franklin Covey planner especially encourages you to think about your goals and values as you set up your time-management program. For example, it asks you to set a long-range goal, write down the value of that goal or what its role is in your life, and then list the intermediate steps and their deadlines for reaching the goal. The Franklin Covey planner comes in a college version called the Franklin Covey Collegiate Planner.

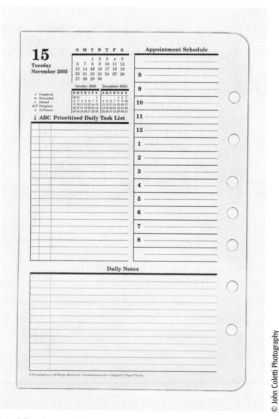

Franklin Covey Planner

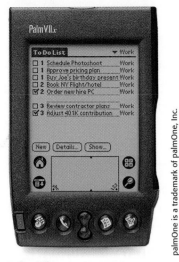

Palm Pilot

"Smart" Cell Phone

Electronic Planners Several electronic time-management systems also are available. The Franklin Covey time-management program comes in an electronic form, as do others. On the website for this book you can find links for exploring electronic planners to help determine what might work best for you. Advantages of electronic planners include:

- They are compact;
- They can sort, organize, and store information more efficiently;
- They can provide audible reminders of when to do things;
- They can easily exchange information with office and home computers.

"Smart" Cell Phones Sophisticated cell phones are increasingly being used as time-management devices. Some users say that these so-called smart cell phones more easily handle the calendar and address chores than electronic planners such as the Palm Pilot.

Which should you use—a paper-and-pencil planner, an electronic planner, or a smart cell phone? If you are gadget-oriented, learn technology easily, and can afford them, you might want to consider an electronic planner or smart cell phone. If you are not, the paper-and-pencil planner is more than sufficient.

Create a Term Planner

You'll benefit enormously by mapping out a week-by-week plan for the entire term. Some colleges provide a term calendar that identifies breaks and holidays or your college catalog may provide this information.

If you don't already have a calendar for the term, following is a grid of the days and weeks to create one. Notice that at the top of the page, it is important for you to once again list the five values that are the most important priorities of your life and then write down the five most important goals you want to attain this term.

Then, write in the weeks and number the days. Write in vacations and holidays. Next, get out your course syllabi and write down dates and deadlines for exams, major homework assignments, and papers.

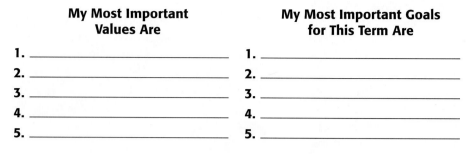

Term Planner

My Most Important Values Are	My Most Important Goals for This Term Are
1. _____	1. _____
2. _____	2. _____
3. _____	3. _____
4. _____	4. _____
5. _____	5. _____

Note: It is not necessary to have a goal for each value when listing your most important goals for the term. For example, if education is your most important value, you might have several important goals for this term related to education.

Week of	MONDAY	TUESDAY	WEDNESDAY	THURSDAY	FRIDAY	SATURDAY	SUNDAY
_____							
_____							
_____							
_____							
_____							
_____							
_____							
_____							
_____							
_____							
_____							
_____							
_____							
_____							
_____							

Consider coding different courses by color. History might be in red, English in blue, biology in green, and so on. Using colored pencils allows you to revise schedules easily. Highlight exam dates with a marker or write them in large letters.

After you've written down your exam and other task dates on the calendar, look at the dates. Think about how many days or weeks you'll need to study for major exams and write major papers. Mark the days or weeks in which these tasks will be your main priorities. Refer often to the values and goals you listed at the top of the page when allocating your time for this term. Keep in mind important nonacademic responsibilities such as employment, family commitments, commuting time, and volunteer work and make sure to mark your calendar accordingly.

Keep a spare copy of your term planner in case you lose the original. You might want to carry a copy with you when you go to classes and place one on your bulletin board or in your desk. Consider posting an electronic version on your computer where you can access and edit it easily.

Your term calendar is not etched in stone. Check it regularly and decide when it needs modification. Your circumstances may change. An instructor might add another assignment or change a test date. You might find out that you need more study time than you originally predicted for a particular course or your work schedule or family responsibilities may change during the term.

Create, Monitor, and Evaluate a Weekly Plan

In addition to creating a term plan, a weekly plan also will help you maximize your time. Former Chrysler Corporation CEO and President Lee Iacocca credited his weekly plan as the key to his success. Even if your life goal is not to run a mammoth corporation, weekly planning skills will serve you well long after college.

Following is a grid on which to map out your weekly plan. You might want to make copies or create an electronic version so that you will have one for each week of the term. You also can use the weekly planning grids in a commercial paper-and-pencil or electronic planners, as discussed earlier.

Before you start filling in the grid, again write down your five most important values at the top of the page, followed by your five most important goals (priorities) for the week.

Next, ask yourself these questions about the next week:

- What do I expect to accomplish?
- What will I have to do to reach these goals?
- What tasks are more important than others?
- How much time will each activity take?
- When will I do each activity?
- How flexible do I have to be to allow for unexpected things?

In the *Plan* column on the grid, fill in your class hours, regular work commitments, family commitments, and other routine tasks. Then fill in the remainder of the things you plan to do next week.

A good strategy is to fill in the *Plan* column at the end of the preceding week. Put it together on Friday afternoon or Sunday evening at the latest. The plan takes no more than a half hour for most students to complete, yet it can save you at least an hour a day that week!

During the week, monitor your schedule closely to see whether you carried out your plans. A good strategy is to sit down at the end of each day and write in the *Actual* column what you actually did that day compared with what you planned to do. Analyze the comparison for problems and plan some changes to solve them.

Use the weekly planner in concert with your term planner each week of the term. Every weekend, pull out your term planner and see what your most important priorities are for the following week. Make any changes that are needed and then do the same thing with your weekly planner to help stay focused.

Please. No crises next week. My schedule already is full.
Henry Kissinger
20th-century Secretary of State

		MONDAY		TUESDAY		WEDNESDAY	
		Plan	Actual	Plan	Actual	Plan	Actual
AM	6:00						
	7:00						
	8:00						
	9:00						
	10:00						
	11:00						
PM	12:00						
	1:00						
	2:00						
	3:00						
	4:00						
	5:00						
	6:00						
	7:00						
	8:00						
	9:00						
	10:00						
	11:00						
AM	12:00						
	1:00						
	2:00						
	3:00						
	4:00						
	5:00						

Weekly Plan

**My Most Important
Values Are**

1. _____
2. _____
3. _____
4. _____
5. _____

**My Most Important Goals
for This Term Are**

1. _____
2. _____
3. _____
4. _____
5. _____

Note: It is not necessary to have a goal for each value when listing your most important goals for this week. For example, if education is your most important value, you might have several important goals for this week related to education.

THURSDAY		FRIDAY		SATURDAY		SUNDAY	
Plan	Actual	Plan	Actual	Plan	Actual	Plan	Actual

Allocate Time for Studying and Other Responsibilities As you construct your weekly plan, be sure to put enough time aside for doing assignments outside of class. In a national survey, the more hours students spent studying or doing homework, the more they liked and stayed in college, improved their thinking skills, graduated with honors, and got into graduate school. Students who have higher grades and graduate with honors are less likely to watch TV or spend time partying (Astin, 1993).

To find out how much time you actually spend studying each week and whether it's enough, complete Self-Assessment: "Are You Studying Enough?" on your CD-ROM and the Journal activity "Link Goals with Time Spent in Activities" on page 89.

Swiss Cheese and Set Time Two strategies for getting the most out of your weekly plan are called *Swiss cheese* and *set time*. Time management expert Alan Lakein (1973) describes the Swiss cheese approach as poking holes in a bigger task by working on it in small bursts of time or at odd times. For example, if you have 10–15 minutes several times a day, you can work on a math problem or jot down some thoughts for an English paper. You'll be surprised at how much you can accomplish in a few minutes.

If you're not a cheese lover, the set time approach may suit you better. In this approach, you set aside a fixed amount of time to work on a task. In mapping out your weekly plans, you may decide that you need to spend six hours a week reading your biology text and doing biology homework. You could then set aside 4–6 P.M. Monday, Wednesday, and Saturday for this work. To think further about getting the most out of your weekly plan, complete the Journal activities "Put Swiss Cheese into Action" on page 88 and "A New Kind of Cheese" on page 89.

page 88 and "A New Kind of Cheese" on page 89.

ON TARGET TIPS

Setting Daily Priorities

1. **Make up your daily to-do list before you go to bed at night.** Or do the list first thing in the morning. Set priorities. Estimate how much time it will take to complete each task.

2. **Identify the top-priority tasks and try to do these first.** Do them in the morning if possible.

3. **Raise your time consciousness.** Periodically look at or think about your list. Maybe you have a few items that take only a little time. Knock them off in 10 minutes here, 15 minutes there. Keep your priorities in focus. Make sure you get your number-one priority done before it is too late in the day.

4. **Toward the end of the day, examine your to-do list.** Evaluate what you have accomplished. Challenge yourself to finish the few remaining tasks.

A Week Later: How Did You Do? After you have planned what you will do with your time for a week and monitored yourself, a very helpful exercise is to complete Self-Assessment 2 "Evaluating My Week of Time Management" on page 86 to evaluate how effectively you stayed with your plan and think about how you could better use your time.

Create a Daily Plan

Great time managers figure out what the most important things are for each day and allocate enough time to get them done. Figuring out the most important things to do involves setting priorities. An effective way to do this is to create a manageable to-do list. Your goal is to complete at least all of your priority items on the list. A no-miss day is one after which you can cross off every item. If that turns out to be impossible, make sure that you finish the most important tasks. For some good strategies, see On Target Tips, "Setting Daily Priorities."

The ABC Method A to-do list consists of listing and setting priorities for daily tasks and activities. It can help you stay focused on what is important for you to accomplish that particular day and generally does not include your classes, which should be in your weekly plan. Time management experts Stephen Covey (1989) and Alan Lakein both recommend prioritizing tasks by A, B, and C, determining whether they are:

A Vital   Extremely important tasks that affect your weekly goals and must be done today.

B Important   Tasks that need to be done soon, such as projects, class preparation, buying a birthday gift for a friend, and other time-driven activities or personal priorities.

C Optional   These also could be labeled "trivial." Examples include getting a haircut, going to a shopping mall, or rearranging your room. Do these activities when you have extra time and consider practicing the Swiss cheese method here.

Figure 3.1 shows one student's to-do list. Notice that this student has chosen one A-level *vital* task and is planning on devoting the most time to it. The student also has allotted time for two B-level *important* tasks.

You can create your own to-do list for tomorrow in Self-Assessment: "My To-Do List" on your CD-ROM. Commercial planning tools—especially electronic planners,

FIGURE 3.1 **Sample To-Do list**

To Do

A. The Most Vital:

1. Study for Biology Test

B. Next Two Most Important:

2. Go to English and History Classes

3. Make Appointment to See Advisor

C. Task	Time	Done
Study for biology test	Early morning, night	
Call home	Morning	
Buy test book	Morning	
Call Ann about test	Morning	
Make advisor appt.	Afternoon	
Do exercise workout	Afternoon	

such as the Palm Pilot—often are good for making to-do lists. Or you might just take a notepad and create a to-do list to be updated each day.

The Time Matrix Management expert Stephen Covey (1989) created a time matrix that is another way you can set and monitor priorities. This time matrix of four quadrants helps prioritize your most important and urgent activities. *Important* activities include those linked to your goals and values. *Urgent* activities require immediate attention but might not reflect those things most important to you. Following are some examples of activities that might be placed in the four quadrants.

1. IMPORTANT URGENT —Math test tomorrow —Make bank deposit today —Science project due today —Take back library book due today	**2. IMPORTANT NOT URGENT** —Date with friend —English paper due in 30 days —Call home —Visit with academic advisor today
3. NOT IMPORTANT —Ringing phone —Unnecessary work —Trivial questions —Interruptions	**4. NOT IMPORTANT NOT URGENT** —Hanging out at the student union —Watching TV —Playing computer games —Reading comic strips

Guidelines for using this matrix to manage your time include:

1. Spending time on important nonurgent things (Quadrant 2) before they become urgent (Quadrant 1).
2. Not letting yourself be ruled by urgency.
3. Never avoiding important work because of tasks that are just urgent.
4. Doing important activities early. If you wait until they are urgent, you will just increase your stress level.

5. Identifying the most important work that needs to be completed after each class.

6. Setting priorities for your tasks and completing them in order.

Source: *College Success Planner,* Wadsworth (2000), p. 6.

Get in the habit of using the Time Matrix on a regular basis. It is a great organizing tool for setting priorities.

Do successful people really use strategies like the time matrix and to-do lists in their everyday lives? For the most part, yes. These strategies help them keep track of the tasks they want to complete and monitor their progress.

Defend Your Priorities But making a list is not enough. As we mentioned earlier in this chapter, you also need to defend your priorities from unnecessary interruptions that waste time, such as telephone calls, e-mail, and drop-in visitors. To avoid such unwanted intrusions, you might:

- Unplug the phone.
- Get an answering machine.
- Ignore social e-mails and instant messages until you have a pocket of free time.
- Hang a DO NOT DISTURB sign on the door.
- Tell visitors that you're too busy to talk with them. Promise to get back to them when you've finished what you're doing.

Tune in to Your Biological Rhythms It has been said that people will accept an idea better if they're told that Benjamin Franklin said it first. Indeed, Benjamin Franklin did say, "Early to bed, early to rise, makes a man healthy, wealthy, and wise." Some of us are "morning people." However, others are "night people." That is, some students work more effectively in the morning, while others are at their best in the afternoon or evening.

Evaluate yourself. What time of day are you the most alert and focused? For example, do you have trouble getting up in the morning for early classes? Do you love getting up early but feel drowsy in the afternoon or evening?

If you're a night person, take afternoon classes. Conduct your study sessions at night. If you're a morning person, choose morning classes. Get most of your studying done by early evening.

What can you do if you hate getting up early but are stuck with early morning classes? Start your day off properly. Many students begin their day with too little sleep and a junk-food breakfast or less. Does this description fit you?

Try getting a good night's sleep and eating a good breakfast before you tackle your morning classes. You may even discover that you're not a "night person" after all. Exercise is also a great way to get some energy and be more alert when you need to be—and is often more effective than caffeine.

Never Procrastinate Again (Much)

Procrastination often hurts many students' efforts to become good time managers. Do you tend to put off until tomorrow what you need to do today?

Know What It Means to Procrastinate

Procrastination can take many forms (University of Illinois Counseling Center, 1984):

- *Ignoring the task, hoping it will go away.* A midterm test in math is not going to evaporate, no matter how much you ignore it.

- *Underestimating the work involved in the task or overestimating your abilities and resources.* Do you tell yourself that you're such a great writer that you can grind out a 20-page paper overnight?
- *Spending endless hours on computer games and surfing the Internet.* You might have fun while you're doing this, but will you have to pay a price?
- *Deceiving yourself that a mediocre or bad performance is acceptable.* You may tell yourself that a 2.8 grade point average (GPA) will get you into graduate school or a great job after graduation. This mindset may deter you from working hard enough to get the GPA you really need to succeed after college.
- *Substituting a worthy but lower-priority nonacademic activity.* You might clean your room instead of studying for a test. Some people say, "Cleanliness is next to godliness," but if it becomes important only when you need to study for a test, you are procrastinating.
- *Believing that repeated "minor" delays won't hurt you.* You might put off writing a paper so you can watch *Six Feet Under* or the World Wrestling Federation. Once the one-eyed monster has grabbed your attention, you may not be able to escape its clutches.
- *Dramatizing a commitment to a task rather than doing it.* You take your books along on a weekend trip but never open them.
- *Persevering on only one part of the task.* You write and rewrite the first paragraph of a paper, but you never get to the body of it.
- *Becoming paralyzed when having to choose between two alternatives.* You agonize over whether to do your Math or English homework first, and neither gets done.

To evaluate whether you are a procrastinator, complete Self-Assessment 3 "Are You a Procrastinator?" on page 87. Also, see the Staying Out of the Pits section for one student's best excuses for procrastinating.

Conquer Procrastination

Here are some good strategies for overcoming procrastination:

- *Put a deadline on your calendar.* This creates a sense of urgency. You might put deadline Post-its on the mirror and in other places you can see them at strategic times during the day. Think about other ways that you might create urgent reminders for yourself.
- *Get organized.* Some procrastinators don't organize things effectively. Develop an organized strategy for tackling the work you need to do. Your term planner, weekly planner, and to-do list will come in handy here.
- *Divide the task into smaller jobs.* Sometimes we procrastinate because the task seems so complex and overwhelming. Divide a larger task into smaller parts. Set subgoals of finishing one part at a time. This strategy often can make what seemed to be a completely unmanageable task an achievable one. For example, imagine that it's Thursday and you have 15 math problems due on Monday. Set subgoals of doing five by Friday evening, five more by Saturday evening, and the final five by Sunday evening. Reward yourself for completion.
- *Take a stand.* Commit yourself to doing the task. One of the best ways to do this is to write yourself a "contract" and sign it, like the self-contract we discussed earlier in the chapter. Or, tell a friend or partner about your plans.

> *Better three hours too early than a minute too late.*
>
> William Shakespeare
> *16th–17th-century English playwright and poet*

STAYING OUT OF THE PITS

Let Me Count the Ways (Instead of Working)

Here is one student's "Top 10 List" for procrastinating:

1. I work best under time pressure so I'm going to wait and study later.
2. I'm too tired.
3. It's morning and I'm a night person—my body clock is out of sync.
4. My horoscope says it's a bad day for me.
5. It's too nice outside to be in here studying.
6. Study tonight? No way, my favorite TV shows are on.
7. This is going to give me a headache. I'm going to do something else.
8. Even if I do it, it probably won't be good enough, so why do it?
9. Ten years from now, will it really matter if I don't do this right now?
10. I think I'll wait until later when I become more motivated.

- *Use positive self-statements.* Pump yourself up. Tell yourself things that will get you going, such as the following (Keller & Heyman, 1987): "There is no time like the present." "The soon I get done, the sooner I can play." "It's less painful if I do it right now. If I wait, it will get worse."
- *Build in a reward for yourself.* This gives you an incentive to complete all or part of the task. For example, if you get all of your math problems done, treat yourself tonight to a movie you've been wanting to see. What other types of rewards can you give yourself for completing an important task?

To reflect further on your procrastination tendencies, complete the Journal activity "Jump Starts" on page 89.

Balance College, Work, Family, and Commuting

Time management is particularly challenging for college students who also hold a job, have a partner or children, or commute. If you face these challenges, for the next term you can schedule your classes at the earliest possible time during registration. This will get you the classes you want at the times you want. You also can talk with other students who share similar challenges. Here are some additional time-management strategies for students with these special needs.

Career Connections

Theo never thought his part-time job as a waiter at Pizza Hut would be such a challenge to his time-management skills. In just one shift he had to take and deliver drink orders, make sure food arrived promptly from the kitchen, clear tables, and deliver dessert and the check, all while juggling similar needs for multiple tables and squeezing in some study time in the back when things were slow. He also had to make sure his shifts fit into his weekly schedule around classes and study time. Falling behind meant lost tips, something he could not afford—his long-term goal of graduating on time depended on it.

In contrast, Nancy's job as an advertising executive involved client presentations planned up to a month in advance. She had to balance all aspects of the presentation and make sure the art, slogan, and visual aids were developed simultaneously by different teams, all completed on time without procrastination. She found working backward from the due date helped her create a good time-management plan, as well as prioritizing and monitoring tasks on a daily basis. While her Business Management major helped her land the job, it was her time-management skills that helped get the job done.

Good time-management skills are essential for any job and will help make you a more valuable and successful employee now and in the future.

Balance College and Work

Managing time can be hard if you work to pay for college. Students who work full time are less likely than those working part-time or not at all to complete college, have high grade point averages, graduate with honors, or go on to graduate school (Austin, 1993). If you need to work, here are some suggestions.

Limit Work if Possible It's best not to work more than 10 to 20 hours. Full-time students who work more than 20 hours a week get lower grades than students who work fewer hours. They are also much more likely to drop out of college.

Work on Campus if Possible Whether part-time work is positive or negative for college students depends on where they work. In general, a part-time job off campus is an academic minus (Astin, 1993). However, a part-time job on campus is an academic plus. Why does it matter where you work? The answer has to do with involvement. Students who work part-time on campus will likely be connected with other students and faculty which more than compensates for the time they devote to the part-time job.

Investigate Work-Study Options Some jobs can help you develop your skills for future careers. Others are good just for the money. Some companies pay for the courses of their student employees. Look for jobs and programs that suit your needs and goals.

Evaluate Your Course Load Carefully consider how many classes you are taking and how much work each one requires. You might want to take a reduced class load to give you more time for studying and work.

Explore Financial Aid Options. You may quality for state or federal financial aid to help you afford tuition while working fewer hours. Visit your campus financial aid office or ask your advisor for more information.

Balance College and Family

Time is especially precious if you have a spouse, partner, or children. Communicating and planning are important assets in balancing your family time and academic time.

Talk with Your Partner Communicate with your partner about his or her importance in your life. Set time aside for your partner. Plan ahead for tasks that require extra study time. Inform your partner about test dates and other deadlines. After you've created your weekly and term calendars, let your partner see how you plan to use your time and consider posting a copy on the refrigerator or another prominent place. If your partner is also a student, you may be able to coordinate your schedules so you can spend free time together. If one person works and another is in school, perhaps work-related activities can be coordinated with school/study time, and vice versa.

Build in Study Time at School If you have a partner or child, try to do some studying while you're still at school. Use time between classes, for example. Possibly arrive at school 30 minutes before your first class and stay 30 minutes after your last class to squeeze in uninterrupted study time.

Be Creative in How You Manage Time with Children If your child has homework, do yours at the same time. Take a break for 10 minutes or so for each hour you study at home, and play or talk with your child. Then go back to your studying. If your children are old enough to understand, tell them what your study routine is and ask for their cooperation.

Consider having your children play with neighboring children during your study hours. If your children are young, this might be arranged under another parent's supervision. Or try to swap child care with other student parents. Also check into child care and community agencies that may provide service and activities for your children in the before-school and after-school hours.

Use Commuting Time Effectively

If you commute to class, you already know how much time disappears on the road. Commuting students also tend to have family and work commitments that cut into study time. Courses may be available only at inconvenient times. Conflicts in schedules can make it difficult for commuters to take part in study sessions and other learning opportunities. Solving such scheduling problems requires good time management. On Target Tips, "Commute Boosters," describes some good commuting strategies.

At this point, you have explored many aspects of being an effective time manager. To examine your time-management strengths and weaknesses, complete the Journal activity "Who's in Charge?" on page 88.

ON TARGET TIPS

Commute Boosters

- Save time by consistently using to-do lists and weekly plans.
- Audiotape your instructors' lectures if allowed. Play them back on the way home or on the way to school.
- Rehearse what you learned in class each day on your way to work, school, or home.
- If you carpool with classmates, use the commuting time to discuss class material with them.
- Use a backpack or briefcase to carry books and papers that you use each day. Organize these materials the night before to make sure you have everything you need.
- Exchange phone numbers and e-mail addresses with other students in your classes early in the semester. Call them if you need to discuss class issues or their notes for a class you missed.
- Create a personal commuter telephone and/or e-mail directory. Important phone numbers and addresses might include your instructors and their secretaries or teaching assistants, the library, student services, study partners, and other campus resources.

Summary Strategies for Mastering College

Managing time more effectively will help you maximize the "Six Strategies for Success."

1 Take Charge of Your Life by Managing Your Time

- Manage yourself to manage your time effectively.
- Counter time-management misconceptions.
- Tackle time wasters like unnecessary phone calls, e-mail, or social obligations.
- Put the 80–20 principle into action to concentrate on what is most important to produce results.
- Reap the benefits of managing your time effectively: Be more productive and reduce your stress; improve your self-esteem; achieve balance in your life and conquer multitasking; find career success and reach your goals.

2 Connect Values, Goals, and Time

- Revisit your values to focus on the five values that are most important. Use these values to establish your goals.
- Revisit your goals and establish five long- and short-term goals based on your most important values.
- Develop an action plan based on your values and driven by your goals.

3 Plan for the Term, Week, and Day

- Break down your time by term, week, and day, breaking goals into subgoals and intermediate steps. Consider working backward to help reach your goals.
- Choose the right planning tools including paper-and-pencil planners and electronic planners.
- Create a term calendar planner and monitor it. Make sure it is driven by your most important values and goals and includes all of your important responsibilities.
- Create, monitor, and evaluate a weekly plan. Allocate enough time for studying and other activities. Remember how many hours a week you need to study outside class to make good grades. Monitor this closely. Make sure it is driven by your most important values and goals.
- Use the Swiss cheese and set time strategies to get the most out of your weekly plan.
- Make a daily plan by setting priorities and managing to-do lists. Consider establishing a time matrix of responsibilities. Make sure you get the most vital priority done. In deciding when to carry out tasks, examine your daily biological rhythms.

4 Never Procrastinate Again (Much)

- Know what it means to procrastinate and avoid common traps.
- Conquer procrastination by engaging in such strategies as putting a deadline on your calendar, getting organized, dividing the task into smaller jobs, taking a stand, using positive self-statements, and building in rewards for accomplishments.

5 Balance College, Work, Family, and Commuting

- Balance college and work by limiting work and working on campus if possible. Evaluate your course load. Manage your time.
- Balance college and time with partners and children by practicing good communication, planning study time at school, and being creative in how you manage time with children.
- Use commuting time effectively.

Review Questions

1. How can becoming a great time manager help you control your life? What benefits does someone who effectively manages time enjoy?

_____

_____

_____

_____

2. What are some good strategies for staying on time to reach your goals?

_____

_____

_____

_____

3. What advice would you give someone who wants to create a term planner? A weekly planner? A to-do list?

_____

_____

_____

_____

4. What are some good strategies for tackling procrastination?

_____

_____

_____

_____

5. Describe ways to balance your academic responsibilities with all of the other demands in your life.

_____

_____

_____

_____

Learning Portfolio

SELF-ASSESSMENTS

YOUR JOURNAL

STRATEGIES FOR SUCCESS

Develop Meaningful Values

Explore Careers

Set Goals, Plan, and Monitor

Be a Great Time Manager

Build Self-Esteem and Confidence

Get Motivated and Take Responsibility

Think and Learn

Time Wasters

To spot some ways and reasons that you might waste time, place a check mark next to the items that apply to you.

____ Talking on the phone
____ Listening to music
____ Watching TV
____ Playing computer games
____ Surfing the Web
____ Daydreaming
____ Socializing
____ Not being able to say "no"
____ Worrying
____ Having weak reading or study skills
____ Not being able to concentrate
____ Not planning adequately
____ Not spending enough time on what's important
____ Too much time spent with friends who drop by
____ Not being organized
____ Not being able to make decisions
____ Procrastinating
____ Not being self-disciplined
____ Other

From this list select the three ways and reasons you waste the most time:

1. _____

2. _____

3. _____

What can you do to reduce the number of hours you lose in these three time wasters?

_____

_____

_____

_____

Evaluating My Week of Time Management

Earlier in this chapter you planned how to use your time for a week and then monitored what you actually did during that time period. After one week of monitoring your time, what did you learn?

I spent too much time on:

1. _____
2. _____
3. _____

I spent too little time on:

1. _____
2. _____
3. _____

Next week, I will spend more time on:

1. _____
2. _____
3. _____

Next week, I will spend less time on:

1. _____
2. _____
3. _____

After a week of managing, monitoring, and evaluating my use of time, these are the most important things I have to work on to be a great time manager:

1. _____
2. _____
3. _____

Are You a Procrastinator?

For each item, place a check mark in the column that most applies to you.

		Strongly Agree	Mildly Agree	Mildly Disagree	Strongly Disagree
1.	I usually find reasons for not acting immediately on a difficult assignment.				
2.	I know what I have to do but frequently find that I have done something else.				
3.	I carry my books/work assignments with me to various places but do not open them.				
4.	I work best at the "last minute" when the pressure is really on.				
5.	There are too many interruptions that interfere with my accomplishing my top priorities.				
6.	I avoid forthright answers when pressed for an unpleasant or difficult decision.				
7.	I take half measures which will avoid or delay unpleasant or difficult action.				
8.	I have been too tired, nervous, or upset to do the difficult task that faces me.				
9.	I like to get my room in order before starting a difficult task.				
10.	I find myself waiting for inspiration before becoming involved in important study/work tasks.				

Give yourself 4 points for each item you checked strongly agree, 3 points for each item you checked mildly agree, 2 points for each item you checked mildly disagree, and 1 point for each item you checked strongly disagree. Total your points: If you scored above 30, you likely are a severe procrastinator, 21–30 a chronic procrastinator, and 20 or below an occasional procrastinator. If your score is 21 or above, seriously consider going to the college counseling center for some guidance in conquering your procrastination.

Source: University of Texas at Austin Learning Center.

Your Journal

● REFLECT

1. Who's in Charge?

We discussed many different ideas about managing time, such as developing a term plan, creating a weekly plan, setting priorities, consistently creating to-do lists, and tackling procrastination.

- What are your current strengths and weaknesses with regard to managing time?

_____

_____

- What do you plan to do to address your weaknesses?

_____

_____

2. The 80–20 Principle in Your Academic Life

Recall our description of the 80–20 principle earlier in this chapter, which stated that approximately 80 percent of what people do produces about 20 percent of the results they achieve, and vice versa. Think about the courses you are taking this term. How might you apply the 80–20 principle to work more efficiently?

● DO

1. Change a Habit

Select a bad habit that is hurting your ability to effectively manage time. The bad habit I'm going to get rid of is:

_____

_____

Many people find that in managing time, it helps to replace a bad habit with a new, more positive habit. Instead of spending time on my old bad habit, I will commit to spending more time on this good habit:

_____

_____

2. Put Swiss Cheese into Action

The Swiss cheese approach involves poking holes in bigger tasks by working on them in small bursts or at odd times. List your biggest task for next week. You should have some set time to work on it. However, also try to work on it in small bursts when you have a little time here, a little time there. At the end of next week, come back to this activity and write down how much more time you were able to sneak in on the big task by taking the Swiss cheese approach.

● THINK CRITICALLY

1. Be More Precise

Following are some vague plans. Make them more specific.
Vague: I'm going to start getting to school on time.
Precise:

_____

_____

Your Journal

Vague: I plan to watch TV less and study more.
Precise:

_____

_____

Vague: I'm going to quit wasting my time.
Precise:

_____

_____

_____

2. Link Goals with Time Spent in Activities

- In what waking activities do you spend more than three hours a week?

_____

_____

- How does each of these activities relate to your goals?

_____

_____

- Examine your reasons for participating in activities that are unrelated to your goals.

_____

_____

_____

● CREATE

1. A New Kind of Cheese

We describe the Swiss cheese and set time approaches to using your time more productively. Come up with a catchy title for a time-management approach that works for you.
Write down its title and briefly describe it.
Title of approach:

_____

Description of approach:

_____

_____

_____

2. Jump Starts

In this chapter we described some strategies for reducing procrastination. Get together with some other students and brainstorm about strategies for reducing procrastination.
Summarize these strategies below.

_____

_____

_____

Applying the Six Strategies for Success

What did you learn in this chapter that you can apply to the following key strategies to help form the foundation for your success? Write down all of the main points you can remember that support the following strategies:

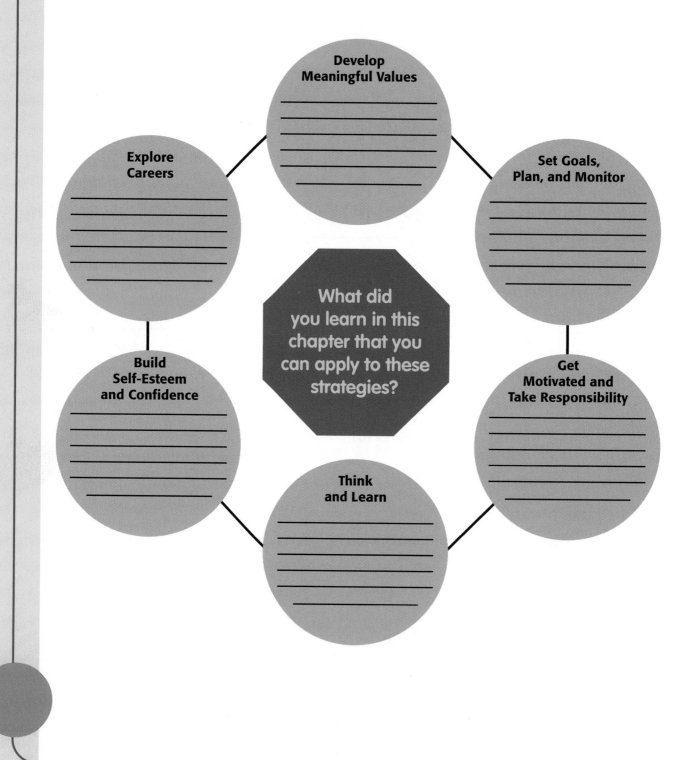

Develop Meaningful Values

Explore Careers

Set Goals, Plan, and Monitor

What did you learn in this chapter that you can apply to these strategies?

Build Self-Esteem and Confidence

Get Motivated and Take Responsibility

Think and Learn

Diversify Your Learning Style

Where Are You? Your success in the classroom will depend on several factors: how well you know your learning strengths and weaknesses, how fully you embrace personal responsibility for your actions, how effectively you relate to your instructors and classmates, and how actively you link current performance to your future plans and dreams.

To evaluate where you stand right now, place a check next to only those items that apply to you.

- I know my greatest strengths and weaknesses as a learner.
- I know whether I favor visual, auditory, or tactile sensory modes of learning.
- I can describe types of learning experiences that are easiest for me.
- I know how my personality influences my classroom success.
- I have started out my classes on the right foot.
- I deal well with different teaching styles.
- I get along well with my instructors and I know how to solve problems I may have with them.
- I can describe career options that fit with my learning style.

© Jose Luis Pelaez, Inc./CORBIS

Consider what the writer Robert Fulghum has to say about using all of your talents and preferences to get the most from college.

Images of College Success

Robert Fulghum

Robert Fulghum's amazing writing career started with a column for a newsletter at the church where he was pastor. He wrote about the lifelong value of the ideas contained in simple sayings directed toward children. "Share everything," "Play fair," and "Clean up your own mess" were lessons that Fulghum believed to be as important to helping adults get along as they were for children.

A kindergarten teacher in the congregation was so impressed by one essay that she sent it home with the children in her class. One child's parent was a literary agent who thought that Fulghum's writing would have broad appeal in such complex times. She was right. *All I Really Need to Know I Learned in Kindergarten* topped the *New York Times* bestseller lists for 209 weeks.

Is it true that Fulghum really learned everything he needed to know in kindergarten? No. But his earliest school experiences laid a foundation for the wisdom that would evolve through the rest of his education and his life. Fulghum began his college career at the University of Colorado. When his father became ill, he transferred to Baylor University to be closer to home. In these and later experiences, he developed a rare capacity to analyze his own experiences and mine them for simple truths. College also helped him learn to write and build the self-discipline to pursue a challenging career as a writer.

Fulghum observes, "The older I get, the more I realize the importance of exercising the various dimensions of my body, soul, mind, and heart. Taken together, these aspects give me a sense of wholeness. I want to be a whole human being" (Fulghum, 1997). Fulghum insists that the path to wholeness is learning to use all aspects of yourself.

ROBERT FULGHUM, author of the bestselling book *All I Really Need to Know I Learned in Kindergarten.* Did Fulghum really learn everything he needed to know in kindergarten?

All of us learn a little differently, according to individual abilities, preferences, and characteristics. To reach your goals, it's important to understand how you learn and to look for ways to become more versatile. As you read, think about the "Six Strategies for Success" listed to the left and how this chapter can help you maximize success in these important areas, particularly "Think and Learn."

Know How You Think and Learn

How you learn best is sometimes called your learning *style*. People differ in how easily they learn, but describing the differences isn't easy. Many things can simultaneously influence how well you acquire new information and skills.

This chapter will help you explore several different dimensions of your learning style to maximize your success in college and beyond. For example, your basic intellectual skill in specific areas can influence your success and even your career direction. How teachers present information also will determine how easy it is for you to learn. Your learning preferences will affect how you use that information to promote long-term learning. Your personality can also contribute to your success in the classroom. In combination, these dimensions influence how well you succeed in academic and other areas of college life. Let's start with the basic intelligence that you bring to college.

There's only one corner of the universe you can be certain of improving and that's your own self.

Aldous Huxley
20th-century British author

Your Intelligence Profile

Perhaps at some point in your past, someone measured your intelligence. On the basis of your intelligence quotient (IQ) score, you may have been able to skip a grade or qualify for special help in school. Recently, psychologists have begun to question the notion that we can capture individual intelligence with a single number.

The psychologist Howard Gardner (1989) proposed that we would be wiser to consider several types of abilities rather than a single measure of intelligence. He formulated his theory of "multiple intelligence" based on observing patterns in different sets of skills. For example, brain-damaged individuals sometimes show serious losses in certain skill sets. Child prodigies and others with exceptional talents possess or can develop superior skill sets in other specific areas.

Gardner suggested that these sorts of abilities cluster in eight different areas, or *domains:*

1. *Verbal-Linguistic Skills:* sensitivity to and appreciation of word meanings and the function of language
2. *Logical-Mathematical Skills:* orderly use of reasoning, logic, and mathematics to understand and explain abstract ideas

3. *Musical Abilities:* appreciating, performing, or creating music or the elements of music, such as rhythm or pitch

4. *Bodily-Kinesthetic Awareness:* coordinated and skilled use of objects in the environment, involving both gross and fine motor skills

5. *Spatial Skills:* accurate perception and reproduction of spatial images, including strong navigation and artistic skills

6. *Interpersonal Abilities:* meaningful discrimination and interpretation of the behavior and moods of others

7. *Interpersonal Abilities:* accurate self-perception, including a refined capacity to identify and represent complex personal emotions and motives

8. *Naturalist Abilities:* understanding, relating to, classifying, and explaining aspects of the natural world

As smart as he was, Albert Einstein could not figure out how to handle those tricky bounces at third base.

© 2003 Sidney Harris

Half of being smart is knowing what you are dumb about.
David Gerrold
Contemporary science fiction writer

Gardner argued that these domains are independent so humans can be highly developed in one area but not others. According to Gardner, most college courses tend to emphasize verbal-linguistic and logical-mathematic intelligences at the expense of other important skill areas.

You may be naturally more gifted in some areas than in others. Learning in those areas is simply easier for you. You may even resist taking required courses that don't fall within those easy areas. However, most college programs focus on developing a broad base of skills. So, for example, even if you don't have strengths in logical-mathematical skills, you'll probably have to take some basic courses that require those skills to earn your chosen degree.

Take a moment to complete Self-Assessment 1 "Your Intelligence Profile" on page 115 to help identify your intellectual strengths. It also can help you predict which courses will be relatively easy or difficult for you. For example, if your strengths lie in spatial skills, then taking an art history course may be a surprisingly happy learning experience. If the area of interpersonal abilities is your main strength, then you'll likely do well in courses that focus on group work.

By contrast, if algebra is "Greek" to you, you'll have to work much harder to grasp the concepts than will the mathematically gifted person seated next to you. You may want to get help right away before you get too far behind in a course that doesn't match your talents. Find a study partner who demonstrates the intelligence that you need to develop, or work with your study skills center on campus to help you take advantage of your learning strengths and style.

Sensory Preferences

A second dimension that contributes to your learning style is your sensory preference for receiving information. Do you prefer to get input about the world through your ears, eyes, or sense of touch? The sensory mode you prefer will influence how easily you can learn in different academic situations.

Auditory Learning The majority of your course experiences will likely be lectures. Typically, the professor talks . . . and talks . . . and talks . . . while you try to take notes on the most important ideas. This traditional approach assumes that you have skills in auditory learning.

Some lucky people are good *auditory learners.* They absorb a lecture without much effort. They may not even need to take careful notes but learn just by listening. Auditory learners may avoid making eye contact with anyone in the class so they can concentrate on catching every word and nuance.

Visual Learning Many of us have an easier time learning from lectures with visual components such as pictures, diagrams, cartoons, or demonstrations. *Visual learners* make images of words and concepts. Then they capture these images on paper for a quick review. Visual learners benefit from the use of charts, maps, notes, and flash cards when they study.

Visual learners may become distracted when professors provide no visual anchors in their lectures. They get overwhelmed when professors use slides with dense terminology and lecture at the same time. In this situation, visual learners need to tune out the auditory information and focus on what they can see for the most efficient processing.

Tactile or Kinesthetic Learning Some people are *tactile* or *kinesthetic learners*. They prefer touch as their primary mode for taking in information. Unfortunately, very few college classes provide an opportunity for tactile learners to use their preferred sensory mode. Art, recreation, and technical classes related to careers involving manual procedures are among the most prominent examples.

Tactile learners faced with auditory learning situations should write out important facts and perhaps trace the words that they have written with their fingers to give them extra sensory feedback. They can make up study sheets that connect to vivid examples. In some cases, roleplaying can help tactile learners learn and remember important ideas.

Self-Assessment 2 "Sensory Preference Inventory" on page 116 provides an opportunity to identify your preferred sensory mode for learning. Also review On Target Tips, "The Match Game," to identify strategies that can help you learn more effectively, particularly if you find yourself in situations that aren't a good fit for your learning style.

Experiential Learning Preferences

Besides differing in intelligence domains and sensory preferences, people also differ in how they like to learn and think about ideas. Here are four distinctive ways based on David Kolb's (1984) work on experiential learning. We also will explore how your experiential preferences relate to your intelligence profile and sensory preferences.

Learn by Doing Although some people can learn passively simply by listening, watching, or reading, those with active learning preferences fare better when they learn by doing through problems or games and simulations, for example. They like to apply principles through fieldwork, lab activities, projects, or discussions.

Many kinds of classes are ideal for learning by doing. These include science and math classes as well as career-oriented classes, such as business and nursing. Visual and tactile learners benefit from active learning strategies. Active learning strategies also tend to appeal to people with refined intelligence in spatial skills and bodily awareness.

Learn by Reflecting Reflecting here means having an opportunity to compare incoming information to personal experience. Reflective learners prefer classes such as the humanities that tend to be rich in emotional content. Reflective learners often show

---

ON TARGET TIPS

The Match Game

How can you adapt your skills when your instructor isn't a good match for your sensory learning style?

● If you are an **Auditory** Learner your best match will be instructors who LECTURE.

When your instructor doesn't lecture:
1. Concentrate on the spoken words.
2. Rehearse key ideas in your head.
3. Identify key concepts in your notes.
4. Summarize the key themes of the class out loud to a study partner.
5. Pay less attention to visual supports that may distract you.

● If you are a **Visual** Learner, your best match will be instructors who LECTURE WITH IMAGES.

When your instructor doesn't use visual supports:
1. Draw your own related pictures and graphs in your notes.
2. Use arrows in your notes to highlight connections.
3. Seek out related media that support or review key concepts.
4. Try to visualize imagery that will help you remember.
5. Create two or three images that capture the essence of the class.

● If you are a **Tactile** Learner, your best match will be instructors who use ACTIVE LEARNING.

When your instructor doesn't use active learning:
1. Make notes that highlight how the content is connected to you.
2. Form a study group to give you a chance to discuss key ideas.
3. Imagine how the information will have practical value for you.
4. Record class information on index cards that you can handle.
5. Select the two or three cards that represent the key ideas for each session.

"Personally I'm a doer."

preferences for learning through auditory sensory channels, because these situations provide the least interference for thoughtful, quiet reflection.

Reflective learners often demonstrate strengths in intrapersonal intelligence as well. Because they look carefully at a situation and think about its meaning, they often set reasonable goals and achieve them. Reflective students take time to respond to and reflect on the quality and accuracy of their answers (Kagan, 1965). Because they're good at problem solving and decision making, they like to set their own goals for learning (Jonassen & Grabowski, 1993). Whether or not you are primarily a reflective learner, you can probably improve your learning by noticing connections with your own experience and by staying aware of your learning goals.

Reflective students tend to enjoy journal writing, project logs, film critiques, and essay questions, and prefer intimate discussions of content to group discussions. Learners who reflect carefully about ideas may not be the quickest to answer questions in class, because a question may provoke a great deal of thinking and remembering before the learner can arrive at a conclusion.

Learn by Critical Thinking Critical thinkers like learning situations that encourage them to grapple with ideas in ways that push beyond memorizing facts. They enjoy manipulating symbols, figuring out unknowns, and making predictions. They like to analyze relationships, create and defend arguments, and make judgments. Critical thinkers often are good with abstract ideas, even in the absence of concrete examples or applications. Classes that are theoretical in nature or emphasize logical reasoning, model building, and well-organized ideas are especially appealing to critical thinkers.

Good critical thinkers perform especially well in courses that appeal to verbal-linguistic, logical-mathematical, and naturalist intelligences. They are comfortable in lecture-based classes that primarily rely on auditory sensory channels, although they also can exercise critical-thinking strategies in other learning situations to make course ideas more engaging. Debates and other opportunities to exchange ideas appeal especially to critical thinkers.

Learn by Creative Thinking In contrast, creative thinkers thrive in learning situations that offer opportunities for unique personal expression. Although humanities and arts classes particularly develop creative thinking, creative opportunities can be found in other courses, too. Creative thinkers prefer to write stories, brainstorm, solve problems in original ways, design research, and so forth. They think more holistically, meaning that they try to consider a broad range of information in their problem solving. They may even enjoy violating the rules if it helps them come up with a unique solution or viewpoint.

Creative thinking is the hallmark of artists who demonstrate musical and spatial intelligence, respectively relying on auditory and visual sensory processing. Creativity also underlies the development of new theories, research strategies, novels, and computer games. That is, creative thinking can be expressed in all domains of multiple intelligence.

What learning processes do you prefer? Complete Self-Assessment 3 "Experiential Learning Preferences" on page 117 to identify your preferences among these experiential learning processes.

Put It All Together Now that you have examined a variety of learning styles and evaluated your own preferences, you may be wondering how this all relates and what it means for *your* success in college. Table 4.1 links the intelligence profiles, sensory preferences,

TABLE 4.1 Linking Choice of Major with Learning Style Dimensions

Are there some majors that seem to be a particularly good match for specific dimensions of the various learning styles? See how the following majors might logically be linked with learning style characteristics. Do your preferences relate to the majors that you think you would find most satisfying?

Major	Intelligence Profile	Sensory Preference	Experiential Learning
Anthropology	Naturalistic	Auditory	Reflecting/Critical thinking
Archeology	Naturalistic	Tactile	Doing/Critical thinking
Art	Spatial	Visual	Doing/Creating
Biology	Naturalistic	Visual	Doing/Critical thinking
Business	Logical-math	Auditory	Doing/Creating
Chemistry	Naturalistic	Visual	Doing/Critical thinking
Criminal Justice	Interpersonal	Auditory	Critical thinking/Doing
Dance	Bodily-kinesthetic	Tactile	Doing/Creating
Education	Interpersonal	Mixed	Reflecting/Doing
Engineering	Logical-math; Spatial	Tactile	Doing/Creating
English	Verbal-linguisitic	Auditory	Reflecting/Creating
Film Studies	Verbal-linguistic; Spatial	Visual	Creating/Doing
Foreign Languages	Verbal linguistic	Auditory	Reflecting/Doing
Health Studies	Bodily-kinesthetic	Tactile	Reflecting/Doing
History	Verbal-linguistic	Auditory	Reflecting/Critical thinking
Journalism	Verbal-linguistic	Auditory	Doing/Reflecting
Mathematics	Logical-math	Visual	Critical thinking/Reflecting
Medical Technology	Logical-math	Tactile	Doing/Critical thinking
Music	Musical	Auditory	Doing/Creating
Nursing	Interpersonal	Tactile	Doing/Reflecting
Philosophy	Verbal-linguistic	Auditory	Reflecting/Critical thinking
Pharmacy	Interpersonal; Logical-math	Visual	Doing/Reflecting
Physics	Logical-math	Tactile	Doing/Critical thinking
Political Science	Verbal-linguistic	Auditory	Critical thinking/Reflecting
Pre-Law	Verbal-linguistic	Auditory	Critical thinking/Reflecting
Pre-Med/Pre-Vet	Naturalistic	Tactile	Doing/Critical thinking
Psychology	Interpersonal; Naturalistic	Mixed	Doing/Critical thinking
Religion	Intrapersonal	Auditory	Reflecting/Doing
Social Work	Interpersonal	Auditory	Reflecting/Doing
Sociology	Verbal-linguistic	Auditory	Critical thinking/Reflecting
Theatre	Bodily-kinesthetic	Tactile	Doing/Creating

and experiential learning preferences discussed above. It also lists some majors that might be appropriate for each learning style. First, go to Assessments 1, 2, and 3 to revisit your learning style preferences and circle them in the last three columns of Table 4.1. Then look in the first column to see what majors might be the best fit for you.

Personality Factors

Personality, enduring personal characteristics, also influences learning effectiveness. Your personality style can facilitate or hinder your success in the classroom. We'll examine two popular approaches to understanding how personality affects learning: the Five Factor Personality Model and the Myers-Briggs Type Inventory.

Five Factor Personality Model Many psychologists today believe that there are five basic dimensions of personality that are consistently demonstrated by people across cultures (Costa & McRae, 1995). Each dimension represents a continuum and is described below, along with an overview of how these dimensions can impact success in college. The mnemonic to remember all five dimensions is OCEAN:

O = Open to experience

High O people are adventurous, imaginative, and unconventional. They tend to enjoy classes where they can experiment with new ideas.

Low O people are conventional, conservative, and rigid in their thinking, preferring more highly structured learning situations.

C = Conscientiousness

High C people are hardworking, ambitious, and driven. They tend to have developed work habits likely to place them on the Dean's list.

Low C people are pleasure seeking, negligent, and irresponsible, making them more vulnerable to being placed on probation or being suspended.

E = Extraversion

High E individuals (extraverts) are high-spirited and energetic, thriving on the continuous opportunity that college provides to meet and work with different people.

Low E individuals (introverts) are reserved and passive, tending to seek less social stimulation to do their best work.

A = Agreeableness

High A people are good-natured, trusting, and helpful. They tend to be well liked and respected and may have an easier time negotiating positive outcomes to conflicts.

Low A people are irritable, suspicious, and vengeful. They are less likely to get any breaks when negotiating because they tend to approach conflict with a hostile attitude and low expectations of others.

N = Neuroticism

High N individuals suffer a variety of problems related to emotional instability, such as anger, depression, and impulsiveness, which can create constant chaotic conditions that can threaten academic survival.

Low N individuals adapt well, tolerate frustration, and maintain more realistic perspective. They tend to have developed personal resources that can help them garner success and rebound from failure.

> *I am an intermittent sitespecific extrovert.*
> Mike Myers
> *Contemporary actor*

Take the Self-Assessment "Your Personality Style in the Classroom" on your CD-ROM to evaluate how your personality style stacks up for classroom success. Also complete the Journal activity "Your Learning Metaphor" on page 119 to capture the essence of your personality style.

Myers-Briggs Type Inventory (MBTI) Another popular approach to understanding the role of personality in academic success is the Myers-Briggs Type Inventory (MBTI) (Myers, 1962). The MBTI measures four dimensions of personality functioning by measuring responses to a series of questions that ask for a preference between two alternatives:

1. *Extraversion/Introversion (E/I)* measures students' social orientation. Extraverts (E) like talking with others and taking action. Introverts (I) prefer to have others do the talking. (This is similar to the "open to experience" dimension addressed in the Five Factor Model.)
2. *Sensing/Intuiting (S/N)* explores how students process information. Sensers (S) are most at home with facts and examples; they are drawn to realistic, practical applications. Intuiters (N) prefer concepts and theories, which can give greater play to imagination and inspiration.

3. *Thinking/Feeling (T/F)* emphasizes how students make decisions. Thinkers (T) like to take an objective approach and emphasize logic and analysis in their decisions. Feelers (F) prefer emotion to logic; they give greater weight to the impact of relationships in their decisions.

4. *Judging/Perceiving (J/P)* taps how students achieve their goals. Judgers (J) prefer clearly defined strategies to achieve their goals and may jump to closure too quickly. Perceivers (P) like to consider all sides to a problem and may be at some risk for not completing their work. (This also taps similar characteristics to the "openness to experience" dimension in the Five Factor Model.)

Your personality profile can be configured from your preferences on the four dimensions of the MBTI. The test captures your style using a four-letter code that communicates your preferences on each dimension. For example, the "ENTJ" code reveals an extravert with a preference for an orderly pursuit of concrete details but a reliance on intuitive decision making. In contrast, the "ISFP" represents the style of someone who is drawn to solitary activities, relying on facts and emotions.

As you can imagine, students with these contrasting styles are unlikely to be equally happy in any class. For example, consider how students with different personality styles might relate to a highly structured classroom. Structure would be much more appealing to the introvert who relies more on orderly process than the extravert who prefers spontaneity; the extravert would have to do much more work to adapt to the highly structured classroom. See Figure 4.1, "MBTI Styles in the Classroom," for more examples.

Find out about your MBTI profile from the campus counseling or career center. The inventory should be administered and interpreted by trained MBTI examiners, although an online version of this inventory, the Keirsey Temperament scale, can be found on the Internet at <http://Keirsey.com/frame.html>. However, beware of relying on the results of personality tests in a way that restricts your options or limits your horizons. Instead, use personality test results to help you avoid blind spots in your thinking and increase your adaptability. To pull together insights from all of the self-assessments in this chapter, complete the Journal activity "A Matter of Style" on page 118.

FIGURE 4.1 MBTI Styles in the Classroom

This Style . . .	Prefers classes that emphasize . . .	But can adapt best to unfavorable conditions by . . .
Extraverts	active learning, group projects	forming a study group to meet their social needs
Introverts	lectures, structured tasks	setting manageable social goals (for example, contribute to discussions once every two weeks)
Sensers	memorizable facts, concrete questions	identifying key abstract ideas and theories along with their practical implications
Intuiters	interpretation, imagination	identifying the most important facts and figures
Thinkers	objective feedback, pressure to succeed	seeking extra feedback from instructor to create feeling of external pressure
Feelers	positive feedback, individual recognition	seeking extra time from instructor to create personal connection
Judgers	orderliness, structure, and deadlines	setting own deadlines and structure
Perceivers	spontaneity, flexibility	assuming a temporary role of a student who must be rigidly organized to be successful

Technological Facility

One final difference in learning style is becoming increasingly important for success in college: the relative comfort you have with the variety of technological challenges that you will face. You have probably always experienced computers as a meaningful part of your life. However, not everyone is completely comfortable with the widespread involvement all of us face with computers. If you enjoy the challenge of learning new technology, you will have a definite advantage in enhancing your learning. For example, skilled use of technology can save time, expand your access to ideas, and open whole new worlds for you to explore from your keyboard. If you are not enamored with technology, you may end up doing many things in college the hard way. You will learn more about the role that technology plays in college and why it is so important to develop a technological comfort zone throughout this book.

Think Strategically about Your Learning

As you meet each challenge that college classes offer, your learning resources will expand and so will your self-confidence. You may discover abilities you never thought you had. Working harder on skills that don't come easily can improve your academic success.

Understand How Effort Relates to Learning Style

Success in college depends on more than your natural talents and preferences. You must take responsibility for your learning and that requires making some important decisions and choices about how and when to apply yourself. Depending on your learning style, some of the questions below might be on your mind.

How hard do I want to work?

Some college courses will be so intriguing that you'll naturally be drawn in deeply. It will be easy to learn because the content and instructor's approach match your interests, learning style, and abilities, making the material a breeze to learn. It's easy to be conscientious when your interests are such a good match to the class. However, you may find yourself wanting to devote just enough time and energy to get by. This choice will be tempting in courses that have little bearing on your ultimate career goals or when you're short on time.

Surface Learning

This strategy involves studying the minimum amount you need to learn. Surface learners rely primarily on rote memory, often exercised at the last minute. They tend to be motivated by grades or feedback from the teacher rather than intrinsic interest in the course.

Surface learning can be risky. Surface learners are much less likely than deep learners to do well in college. Ultimately, surface learners may have serious problems in their chosen major if they need to remember what they learned at a shallow level in prior courses. Still, you may choose to be a surface learner in some courses so that you can devote more time to *deep learning* in other courses.

Deep Learning

Deep learners accept personal responsibility for truly understanding the course ideas. They construct their learning experiences actively. They enjoy the process of learning for its own sake and use a lot of thinking skills. Deep learners remember what they learn longer. If your interests parallel those of the course, deep learning may not be much effort. It might even be fun. The Journal activity "The Deep End of the Pool" on page 118 asks you to think about the courses you are taking, and the type of learning you are doing in each.

Every time you're confronted with a learning opportunity, you must decide how deeply you wish to learn in order to succeed in college overall. Do you need to work hard in this particular course, or do you need merely to break the surface? Keep your level of effort and motivation in line with your broader goals and values.

I can already tell I won't have enough time to do well in my classes. How should I choose where to work hardest?

It's a bad idea to do poorly in many classes when you can improve your standing by dropping a class or two. If you find that you're giving short shrift to several classes, consult with your advisor about dropping the course that will have the least negative impact on your schedule. To build your confidence, stay in courses that overlap your natural talents.

I have trouble jumping into class discussions, because they seem to take off before I'm ready! Is there such a thing as being too reflective?

Students process information at various speeds. This style can create some interesting class conditions. Some people respond quickly and are accurate and insightful in their contributions. Sometimes rapid responding is impulsive, producing ill-formed, off-target ideas.

In general, impulsive students tend to make more mistakes than students who carefully reflect on their experience (Jonassen & Grabowski, 1993). However, some reflective individuals, especially those with more introverted social styles, may think forever about a problem and not ever speak.

If the course rewards contributions other than class discussion, participating in class may not be required for success. However, if you don't routinely participate in class, here is an area where you can expand your skills. Make a note of the kinds of questions the instructor presents for discussion. Prepare answers based on what you think your instructor will ask. By carefully reflecting ahead of time, you should be able to cut your processing time in class and give voice to your good ideas. Success in the classroom can make it easier to join in the conversation in other settings, giving you more social options as well.

I am often annoyed by my classmates because they refuse to get involved in class. It seems like I'm the only one who ever volunteers to answer any questions. What's wrong with them?

Probably nothing, but they may have learned already that your willingness to carry the burden relieves them of sharing the load. If you are a fast-responding extrovert, your pursuit of the spotlight may seem like "sucking up" to your less involved classmates.

Rethink your role. You may want to sit on your hands and practice a longer reaction time. That will give your classmates a chance to get involved and also may help your own ideas to be more fully developed and useful when you do volunteer.

Group work makes me crazy. How will I survive classes that require group projects?

In almost every career domain, working with people is a requirement. This is a skill that is worth developing but a challenge for students who are introverted or who tend to have difficulties getting along with others. Think of your peers as additional resource people who can help you learn. In groups, volunteer to do tasks that allow you to contribute from your areas of strength.

Amateurs hope.
Professionals work.
Garson Kanin
20th-century playwright

For example, you may show great attention to detail so you can volunteer to summarize the action of the group. Monitor each group situation for what doesn't work and engage the members to address the quality of the process.

I feel stifled by detailed assignments. Can I get away with being creative?

Intuitive thinkers crave creative experience, but that can create problems for you in some classes. If you stray in a way that enhances the point of the assignment, the instructor may be pleased with your initiative.

If you exceed the minimum criteria, most instructors will think of you as hardworking and creative. However, if you drift from the intended purpose, the instructor will see your work as deficient and possibly defiant. Check with your instructor ahead of time to make sure that your creative approach gets the right reception.

How do I decide when to stay safe and when to take a risk?
What will happen if I fail?

Many students just starting out in college feel like imposters. They worry that giving the wrong answer in class will forever brand them as stupid and alienate them from the other students. It's normal to feel a little anxiety about your performance, but you can't let neurotic behavior keep you from doing your best.

Going to college isn't just about acquiring knowledge; it's about personal change. The impact of a single failure can be a more powerful lesson than a string of successes. College should be a safe place in which to take thoughtful risks as you learn and change from both success and failure.

There may be other questions that have occurred to you as you strategize how to get the most out of your college classes. See the Journal activity "Everything I Need to Know I Plan to Learn in College" on page 119 to help you latch on to some simple but enduring strategies to help you succeed.

Use the Features of This Book

This text and its accompanying supplements offer many features to help students of all learning styles succeed now and in the future.

Chapter Features. Each chapter starts with a mini-assessment to help you anticipate areas of strength and weakness before you read, particularly good in promoting reflective learning. The "Images of Success" profile tells a story relating to the main topic of the chapter to help you view the material more creatively and visualize success. The "On-Target Tips" sections provide hands-on practice in experimenting with new strategies.

Visual learners will benefit from a variety of features in the book, including figures, tables, photos and cartoons. The use of quotations through history and across cultures will be especially helpful to those with strong verbal learning skills. "Career Connections" encourages your creativity by helping you imagine how the principles in the chapter can help you secure the kind of future you want. Finally, the "Six Strategies for Success" model visually links the six most important strategies for success, good for visual and tactile learners.

The Learning Portfolio. As discussed in Chapter 1, the Learning Portfolio sections at the end of each chapter build on the processes of learning that you just read about. The Self-Assessments provide an opportunity to learn by doing as you apply chapter content to your own experiences. The Journal activities are built around Kolb's work in experiential learning, described earlier in the chapter. As you may have noticed, these exercises ask you to "Reflect," "Do," "Think Critically," and "Create."

> *The reward of a thing well done is to have done it.*
> Ralph Waldo Emerson
> *American philosopher*

Finally, the "Applying the Six Strategies for Success" section encourages you to think critically about what you have read and creatively apply topics to each of the strategies. Choose Learning Portfolio activities that will help you stretch and grow in new ways. Don't choose only activities or assignments that let you stay in your comfort zone. Your investment will make you more versatile as you face new learning challenges in the future.

This text adapts to different learning style preferences in one other important way. You can complete many of the assessments and exercises in the text in the traditional manner with "low tech," using a pencil or pen. Or you can use the CD-ROM or website for a high tech opportunity to improve your learning.

Build Positive Relationships with Instructors

Much of college is about interactions with your professors, and the success of these interactions will have a major impact on your overall success in college.

Now that you know more about how to assess your personality and learning preferences, you will be much better equipped to deal with your instructors. Also, this knowledge should provide you with a bit more feeling of control. If you know what your strengths and weaknesses are, you are better able to improve on the weaknesses and build on the strengths.

Don't let your learning style or personality preferences control your behavior. Your natural inclinations might not always lead to success in school or work settings. Take responsibility for relating to your instructors in a way that will be most beneficial to you. They will be more responsive to you if you appear to be confident and in control.

Reconcile Your Learning Style with Your Instructor's Teaching Style

The next time you register for class, invest your time in identifying which instructors have a teaching style that suits your learning style. Interview seasoned students. Go beyond questions about whether the instructor is "good." You can guess by now that "good instructor" means different things to people with different learning styles. Ask *how* they teach. For example, does the instructor

- Lecture the entire period?
- Involve the class in discussion?
- Use active learning strategies?
- Offer any note-taking supports such as outlines?
- Show enthusiasm for students?

Teaching styles are every bit as diverse as learning styles. Teachers will vary not only in their disciplines but also in their enthusiasm, competence, warmth, eccentricities, and humor. Although you probably won't have access to your instructors' MBTI profiles, invest some time to maximize the match between their teaching style and your learning needs. What about your teachers will matter the most to you? How do these variations among your instructors relate to your learning style?

The Student-Centered Teacher Some instructors focus more on developing students' intellectual growth. They run their classes with a variety of activities chosen to motivate student interest and heighten learning. They might use small group discussions, film clips, technology, and student performance as part of their teaching. Finally, such instructors often depart from their original plans because they believe that a new direction serves the students' learning better; in these cases, class can be spontaneous. The student-centered teacher tends to appeal to individuals who are open to experience, like hands-on activities, and have energetic, extraverted approaches to learning.

If you learn best when you have the opportunity to apply course concepts to practical examples, then student-centered approaches probably will appeal to you. Your obligation to learn in such classes is simple: Work at as deep a level as you can manage. Because the instructor will include activities that appeal to your learning preferences, chances are good that you will succeed in the course.

However, you might prefer the structure and efficiency of a well-designed lecture, particularly if you're a good auditory learner, you like to memorize "the facts," or you tend to be introverted. If so, what can you do to survive the student-centered class?

- Outline your reading.
- Try to anticipate what the course will cover.
- Talk with the instructor about the course and how it's working for you.
- Form a study group to work more systematically on the key ideas.

The Content-Centered Teacher Content-centered teachers typically use lectures as their primary teaching method. The learning climate in lecture-based courses is highly structured, paced by the lecturer's strategy for covering material in a meaningful way. Instructors expect students to take careful notes to prepare for tests. Most college classes are lectures. Thankfully, there are good lecturers who tell stories and use humor to get their information across in an interesting way.

Some learning preferences fit well with lecturing. The content-centered approach tends to appeal to auditory learners who prefer classes that minimize involvement with peers. In fact, students who thrive in these environments might well consider college teaching as a potential career.

Visual and tactile learners or learners who prefer active or more social learning experiences simply have to work harder to adapt their learning style to the demands of content-centered courses. If you face this challenge, what can you do to succeed in a content-centered class?

- Learn to make systematic, creative notes or at least work with the notes creatively when you study.
- Generate practical examples that help you form concrete connections with the course material.
- Form a study group that can help you talk about and play with course concepts.

Create a Good First Impression

College instructors expect you to have academic common sense. Knowing how to develop relationships with your instructors is an important part of that common sense. Here are some Fulghum-like guidelines that can help you get off on the right foot.

- *Buy the right stuff.* You won't look like a serious student if you don't have the required books.
- *Be prepared.* If you read assignments *before* class, you'll ask better questions and impress your instructors with your motivation to learn. You'll also get more out of the lecture or discussion.
- *Make contact.* Is it possible to get acquainted with your instructors in large classes? The answer is yes, although it may be challenging. By asking intelligent questions during class or visiting during office hours, you can stand out even in

very large classes. Interviewing an instructor for this course can help you practice getting to know your instructors on an informal basis.

Complete the Journal activity "Connect with a Special Teacher" on page 118 to get some guidance on how to get acquainted with an instructor. Seeking contact with faculty outside the classroom is associated with staying in college and graduating with honors (Astin, 1993). How can you get your instructors to take a special interest in you? On Target Tips, "Become a Distinctive Student," gives some sound advice.

Maintain the Connection

Instructors respond most positively to students who show interest and enthusiasm for their course. Later in the term, instructors have an easier time cutting some slack for students who have been responsive and responsible in the earlier weeks. When test scores fall between two grades, those students who seem to care about their work are often the ones who get bumped up instead of down.

What are some other strategies that will help you develop a stronger connection to your instructors?

- *Stay on task.* It is easy to get distracted and disengage, but it is just as easy for the instructor to notice and take offense. Concentrate on keeping the connection between you and the instructor personal and lively.

- *Do the work on time.* Coping with deadlines is serious business in college. Many students are surprised when they learn that college deadlines are not as flexible as they were in high school. If you miss a deadline, you may not be able to negotiate an extension. Most instructors do not extend deadlines to individuals without justification. Many believe that doing so isn't fair to students who do their work on time.

- *Use the syllabus.* A course syllabus comprehensively describes how the instructor expects the course to proceed. The syllabus can include the course objectives, reading list, grading policies, and other information that applies throughout the term.

  The syllabus also can give hints about the instructor's teaching style. It may contain helpful hints on how to study for tests. Some instructors hold students responsible for reading all materials listed in the syllabus. This can be a surprise at test time if you thought that your class notes would be enough. The Journal activity "Review a Syllabus" on page 118 will help you reflect carefully on how to use a syllabus profitably even in your most challenging courses.

- *Ask it this way.* When you can't attend a class, don't ask your instructor, *"Did I miss anything important?"* Although it may be innocent, your question implies that your instructor regularly spends time on unimportant information. Instead, ask, *"Can I make up any of the work I missed?"* Or you can talk with a classmate or borrow notes to help you get caught up.

ON TARGET TIPS

Become a Distinctive Student

- **Sit in the front.** The most motivated and interested students often sit close to the instructor to minimize distractions and create the opportunity for informal discussion before or after class.

- **Bring articles or clippings to class related to the course.** Instructors like to see you make independent connections between what you're learning and your life outside the classroom. They may incorporate your ideas into the class and remember you for making the contribution.

- **Take advantage of existing opportunities to get to know your instructors informally.** On some campuses, faculty sponsor informal gatherings to help you network with others. You also can join student clubs with faculty sponsors. These are great opportunities to get to know the faculty as people.

- **Visit during your instructor's office hours.** Most instructors identify their office hours when the course begins. Check in with your instructor about something you found interesting or were confused about from class discussion. Ask the instructor to review your notes to see whether your note-taking skills are on target.

- **Use e-mail to connect, if that is an option.** Many instructors like to communicate with their students via email. This is a great option if you're shy or the instructor seems hard to approach.

- **Actively seek a mentor.** After you engage an instructor's interest in you, find out about the instructor's availability to serve as your mentor, someone who can give you guidance beyond the classroom and help you find other opportunities to develop. This can be the most meaningful connection you make in college in person.

© Spencer Grant/Photo Edit

Just when you think you can speak in a private conversation in the middle of class, you are likely to be wrong. This photograph illustrates why. Off-task students tend to stand out against the sea of faces paying attention.

TAKE CHARGE

Develop Your Academic Integrity Pledge

Track down the rules that govern academic integrity on your campus. Read the rules carefully. Do you agree with the position taken by your campus regarding the consequences for academic dishonesty? In what ways do you think the rules could be improved? If possible, arrange to talk with a student who serves in the capacity of hearing complaints regarding integrity violations. Compare that student's experience to your own speculations about the effectiveness of the rules. Then formulate your own personal pledge based on your study. You may want to print the pledge and hang it near your primary study area to help keep you on course.

- *Stay straight.* Even when instructors don't explicitly mention their expectations about your ethical performance, they will assume that you have read, understood, and will abide by the campus academic integrity code.

  Nothing ruins relationships with both your current and future professors than the cloud of suspicion that develops around questionable integrity. Plan your work so that you aren't tempted to take short cuts that could cut short your reputation. To help you resist such temptations, refer to Take Charge, "Develop Your Academic Integrity Pledge," which will help you clarify your personal commitment to staying straight.

- *Stay cool.* The best classes run on respectful and civil behavior. Respect does *not* mean that you can't challenge or ask questions. In fact, many instructors (but not all) regard student questions as an essential part of classroom learning. However, all instructors expect participation to be civil (calm, polite, and efficient rather than prolonged, pointless, or profane). Figure 4.2, "How to Get on the Wrong Side of an Instructor," describes other behaviors that can get in the way.

Solve Problems with Instructors

If you're lucky, you may not have to solve relationship problems with your instructors. However, four problems may prompt you to take action:

1. Your abilities are mismatched to the course.
2. You feel challenged by the instructor's professional boundary—or lack of it.

FIGURE 4.2 How to Get on the Wrong Side of an Instructor

Behaviors That Show Questionable Maturity

Talking during lectures
Chewing gum, eating, or drinking noisily
Being late and leaving early
Creating disturbances
Wearing hats
Putting feet on desks or tables
Being insincere or "brownnosing"
Complaining about work load
Acting like a know-it-all
Wearing headphones

Behaviors That Show Inattention

Sleeping during class
Cutting class
Acting bored or apathetic
Not paying attention
Being unprepared

Packing up books and materials before class is over
Asking already answered questions
Sitting in the back rows when there are empty seats in front
Yawning obviously
Slouching in seat
Asking "Did we do anything important?" after missing class
Not asking questions
Doing work for other classes in class
Reading the newspaper in class

Miscellaneous Irritating Behaviors

Cheating
Asking "Will this be on the test?"
Being more interested in grades than in learning
Pretending to understand
Blaming teachers for poor grades
Giving unbelievable excuses
Wearing tasteless T-shirts

From "Faculty and staff perceptions of irritating behaviors in the college classroom," from *Journal of Staff, Program, and Organizational Development*, 8, pp. 41–46. Copyright © 1990. Reprinted with permission of New Forum Press.

---

3. You and your instructor disagree about the completion status of your work.
4. You need to make a complaint about an instructor's actions.

Resolve a Mismatch Courses are unsatisfying when the instructor does not teach at a level the students can handle. In some of these courses students feel overwhelmed by an instructor who talks over their heads. In other cases, instructors offer too little challenge and students feel cheated.

To resolve either problem, first talk with your classmates to verify that others are struggling too. Then, preferably with one or two other concerned students, request an appointment with the instructor and present your concerns directly. Many instructors will be pleased with your initiative and grateful for the feedback. Others will be less enthusiastic but can give you suggestions about how to cope with their demands. If you can't resolve the mismatch through talking with the instructor, consider withdrawing from the course. If necessary, you can take it again later with a different instructor.

"Is the homework fresh?"

Manage Boundaries Most instructors give clear signals about how and when they can be contacted. Instructors usually have office hours. They can and should respond to student questions or concerns during those periods as part of their professional responsibilities.

Instructors differ in their enthusiasm about being contacted outside class or office hours. Some provide home phone numbers and encourage you to call whenever you have questions. Others request not to be disturbed at home, because they want to separate their professional and personal lives. It is easy to see how students get confused about how and when to contact their instructors. If your instructors have not specified that they can be reached at home, use memos, voice mail, office-hour visits, or the time just after class to ask questions or maintain contact.

Friendship between instructors and students pose an especially complex boundary problem. Many instructors believe that friendships with students is a bad idea. They do not want to do anything that could compromise their objectivity. Other instructors believe that they can be objective in grading the work of a student-friend so they aren't as rigorous about observing that boundary.

Keep Copies of Your Work When an instructor and student dispute whether work has been completed, the burden of proof falls on the student. Get in the habit of making copies of your papers. Then, if a paper gets lost or misplaced, you can easily replace it. Keep returned projects in a safe place so you can retrieve them if the instructor has failed to record and grade them.

If you have a complaint about a class, start by talking directly with your instructor. By describing the problem and offering your interpretation, you may be able to solve the problem quickly and fairly.

When the term is over and your instructor has filed your grades, retain your best work for your academic portfolio. This habit will help you track your progress over time and will give you samples that may help in future job applications.

Know Your Rights As a student, you are guaranteed certain rights. For example, you have the right to privacy. How you perform in class should remain a private matter. Most campuses foster an atmosphere of respect for and equitable treatment of students to promote their taking responsibility. However, you may experience circumstances in which you believe your rights have been violated.

You have several options when an instructor's conduct upsets you. First, recognize that the instructor is the authority in the class. Weigh carefully how upset you are against the possible consequences of confronting an instructor who holds greater power and probably more credibility than you do.

If you decide to complain, explain your concerns directly to the instructor. Ask for an appointment. Present your concerns and offer evidence to support it. If unsuccessful, appeal in writing to the instructor's immediate supervisor. In most cases, this supervisor is the department head or coordinator, who will hear you out and determine what steps to take. If the supervisor fails to take action and you still need further resolution, ask for an appointment with that person's supervisor, most likely the academic dean. At each stage of the chain of command, the person will review what attempts you have made already to resolve the problem before he or she does anything about it.

As one cautionary note, you're unlikely to have much luck appealing a final grade unless you can identify discriminatory treatment or a specific error in the instructor's judgment. Most college officials regard instructors as the final authority in grading and rarely overturn their grades. See Staying out of the Pits, "0.25 Away from Glory," for an example of an unsuccessful grade appeal.

STAYING OUT OF THE PITS

0.25 Away from Glory

Blaine was a little nervous about doing it, but he thought it would be the best way to rectify a serious problem. He had worked hard in his calculus class. When all his points were totaled, he missed an A by one quarter of a point. Unfortunately, his straight-laced professor made a point of offering no extra credit and didn't seem open to negotiation. Blaine decided to go see the head of the department and plead his case.

The department head listened to his story carefully. "Did you talk with the professor?" the department head asked. "No," Blaine said. "The prof made a big deal about not offering extra credit. But I thought there was something you could do. All I need is a quarter of a point. . . ." "Two important questions!" the department head exclaimed. "Were the grading standards clear in the syllabus? Were you treated like everyone else in the class?" Blaine reluctantly said "Yes" to both questions. "Nothing I can do then," said the department head. She explained that all grade negotiations must start with a conversation with the instructor, but added that it was unlikely that personal appeal would work in this case. "If the instructor gives you the opportunity to enhance your grade, then technically that chance must be extended to everyone in the class or the instructor is unfairly discriminating. So I wouldn't encourage you to get your hopes up." Then she added, "Good *try*, though!"

Choose a Major That Fits Your Learning Style

A college degree can be a passport to a professional career, but a well-chosen major can also produce a great number of opportunities that are linked to your interests and skills. Your learning style should influence which career you pursue and the major you choose to help you get there.

Target an Intelligent Career

One way to start planning your future is to link your natural intellectual talents to possible career options. Gardner's theory of multiple intelligences has been used to explore the relationship between intellectual ability and career choice. See Figure 4.3, "Intelligent Career Choices," for some typical and creative career choices based on the multiple intelligence model. Revisit your intelligence profile in Assessment 1 on page 115 and think about how well your profile matches up with these choices.

FIGURE 4.3 Intelligent Career Choices

The theory of multiple intelligences suggests that intellectual strengths predict career choices. Review some traditional and less-conventional careers linked to different domains of intelligence.

Intelligence Domain	Traditional Careers	Less-Conventional Careers	Intelligence Domain	Traditional Careers	Less-Conventional Careers
Verbal-Linguistic	author reporter teacher librarian attorney advertising specialist politician	talk-show host poet children's book writer crossword puzzle maker campaign manager	Musical	performer singer music teacher	composer conductor sound effects specialist
Logical-Mathematical	engineer scientist mathematician statistician insurance specialist computer expert claims adjuster	physicist astronomer astronaut	Spatial	engineer architect surgeon painter sailor Web designer fashion designer	mapmaker sculptor billboard designer
Intrapersonal	novelist psychologist philosopher	advice columnist feature writer	Bodily-Kinesthetic	artisan actor athlete dancer coach	professional juggler professional skater health writer
Interpersonal	politician social worker sales manager psychologist public relations specialist nurse, doctor, or other health care giver	religious leader	Naturalist	conservationist agricultural specialist floral designer museum curator librarian botanist	safari director antique specialist baseball card expert game-show winner

Find the Right Mix

Every college major tends to emphasize certain intellectual strengths, learning preferences, and personality styles more than others. Consider these examples:

- Marcia has a particular talent for music. She prefers the kind of hands-on learning in her music classes over courses where she passively takes notes on concepts. Her auditory skills are especially well developed. Because she is also effective at working with others, her major of music education represents a natural outgrowth of her skills *(musical and interpersonal intelligences + auditory sensory preferences + active-learning preferences + extroversion/agreeableness personality style).*

- Darnell enjoys classes where he can sit, listen, and think carefully about the issues. He especially enjoys writing assignments that allow him to reflect on the significance of ideas, particularly if he has to take apart an issue and form some judgments. He enjoys learning new and complex words. He is thinking about opting for a journalism major *(verbal-linguistic and intrapersonal skills + auditory sensory preference + reflecting and critical-thinking preferences + thinking/perceptive personality style).*

- Carra enjoys taking risks. She likes to combine her strengths in mathematics and her growing ability to deal effectively with others in action-oriented projects. She learns best when she can apply principles in hands-on situations. Carra believes a business major will complement her entrepreneurial style *(logical-mathematical and interpersonal intelligences + tactile sensory preference + active-learning preference + open to experience personality style).*

- Bruce has never been a big fan of reading or writing, but he keenly appreciates courses that allow him to be physically active. He likes the hands-on activities that his kinesiology classes offer and is considering a career in recreation management *(bodily awareness intelligence + tactile sensory preference + active-learning preference + extroversion/sensing personality style).*

- Portia has a vivid visual imagination. She prefers classes where she can express her creative impulses. She is thinking about a career in graphic design but knows she has some work to do to develop her interaction skills for business success *(spatial intelligence + visual sensory preference + creative-thinking preference + intuitive/disagreeable personality style).*

Earlier in the chapter, you learned about the Myers-Briggs Type Indicator. Career counselors have used the MBTI to provide some direction to career selection. See Figure 4.4, "The Myers-Briggs Type Indicator and Potential Career Links," to learn how MBTI codes and personality factors predict professional styles that seem to be well suited to different occupational profiles.

Review the results of your self-assessments in this chapter one final time. What career directions and majors does your learning style suggest? If no obvious directions appear, consider consulting with a career-counseling specialist on campus who can help you make more concrete links between your learning style and possible majors and careers. Now complete the Journal activity "The Stylish Major" on page 119 to further assess your best potential major.

Keep a Flexible Outlook

You may be fortunate to have natural talents in many areas. You may discover many new abilities through your college experiences. Don't close off your options by locking yourself into a career path too soon. After you commit to a specific major, stay flexible about what the future may bring. The career you ultimately pursue may not even have emerged yet as a viable option. Versatility as a learner will give you more choices about where you want to go in your major and your career. Consider the Journal activity "Career Cruising on the Web" on page 119 to assist you in thinking through some new options based on your learning profile.

Career Connections

Sandra's story offers a good example about why it is so important to stay flexible about your options. Both of her parents and her older brothers were lawyers. Like them, she was especially skilled in verbal-linguistic intelligence and enjoyed a good debate. But she was surprised to discover how much she enjoyed the community service work that she was required to do in her sociology class. By her junior year, she abandoned her prelaw major in favor of social work. Eventually she found great career satisfaction in managing a residential home for delinquent teenagers.

Seth wasn't too sure he would like college. He had always nurtured fantasies of being a cartoonist, but drawing was not something for which Seth ever earned positive feedback. After a few frustrating semesters in art classes, he sought some career counseling to figure out other alternatives. Career testing demonstrated that Seth had a knack for business and solid social skills. He recognized that these abilities, honed by a major in business, would help him develop into being an entrepreneur. In college, he started putting together a business plan that would help him establish a string of successful hobby shops where he would have the opportunity to work in cartoons in a dramatically different but highly profitable manner.

Myers-Briggs Code	Description	Possible Career Matches
ISTJ	Quiet, serious, responsible, sensible, patient, conservative, and loyal	police and protective services, administrators and managers, engineers, military personnel, scientists, physicians
ISTP	Factual, sensible, logical, and reflective	farming, mechanics, military personnel, engineering and science technicians, optometrists
ISFP	Quiet, practical, sensitive, and spontaneous	Nursing, secretarial, health service workers, clerical, technicians, forestry
ISFJ	Private, faithful, sensible, and sensitive	Nursing, clerical, teachers, librarians, physicians, health service workers
INFJ	Intuitive, caring, quiet, and peace-loving	Consultants, clergy, teachers, media specialists, physicians, social workers, marketing personnel, psychologists
INFP	Quiet, creative, sensitive, and perceptive	Physicians, editors and reporters, writers, journalists, psychologists
INTJ	Independent, innovative, logical, and driven by the inner world of ideas	Lawyers, scientists, research workers, engineers, computer systems analysts
INTP	Private, intellectual, impersonal, analytical, and reflective	Lawyers, scientists, research workers, engineers, computer programmers and analysts
ESTP	Outgoing, practical thinkers who are masters of experience and observation. They don't rely on their emotions to make decisions.	Marketing personnel, sales, police and detectives, public service and community workers, computer specialists and programmers
ESTJ	Assertive, practical, rational, loyal, opinionated, and decisive	Teachers, managerial and administration, sales, insurance and banking, military personnel, computer analyst, public relations
ESFP	Warm, outgoing, optimistic, and caring	Receptionist, hospitality and catering, designers, teachers, sales, artists and entertainers
ESFJ	Outgoing, sociable, practical, and organized	Receptionists, restaurant workers, sales, teachers, health service workers
ENFJ	Sociable, intuitive, sensitive, and organized	Teachers, actors, musicians, artists, counselors, writers, nurses, marketing personnel
ENTP	Enthusiastic, outgoing, analytical, multi-talented, independent	Marketing personnel, sales, journalists, actors, computer systems analysts, public relations
ENTJ	Outgoing, logical, decisive	Managerial and administrative, marketing personnel, sales
ENFP	Open-minded, imaginative, caring, and outgoing	Journalists, counselors, teachers, writers, social scientists

Note: The characteristics described and the occupations listed are provided to stimulate your thinking about your personality and possible links with careers. They are not intended as a formal testing of your personality and career interests.

Source: www.personalitypathways.com.

Summary Strategies for Mastering College

Diversify your learning style to get the most from college

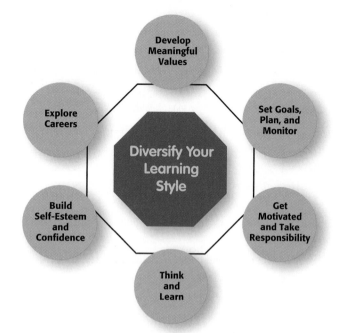

Focus on the "Six Strategies for Success" above as you read each chapter to learn how to apply these strategies to your own success.

1 Know How You Think and Learn

- Identify your intellectual strengths and weaknesses.
- Understand how your sensory preferences shape your learning.
- Recognize what learning processes help you learn best.
- Understand what courses and majors are the best fit based on your intellectual profile, sensory preferences, and learning processes.
- Link your personality style to your classroom success.

2 Think Strategically about Your Learning

- Understand how effort relates to learning style.
- Recognize the difference between surface and deep learning.
- Commit to deep learning when time and resources permit.
- Develop adaptive strategies based on your learning style.
- Learn how the features of this book can impact your success in the course.

3 Build Positive Relationships with Instructors

- Select teachers whose style works well with your own.
- Understand the difference between a student-centered teacher and one who is content-centered.
- Make a good first impression to establish yourself with your instructors.
- Maintain strong connections through conscientious and ethical behavior.
- Solve problems through effective interpersonal skills.

4 Choose a Major That Fits Your Learning Style

- Consider majors with courses that match your learning style.
- Stretch your ability to use different learning styles to have more career options later.

Review Questions

1. List the eight types of intelligence that Gardner identified and circle the one that best represents you. How can you use this information to enhance your success in college?

   1. _____
   2. _____
   3. _____
   4. _____
   5. _____
   6. _____
   7. _____
   8. _____

2. List the three types of sensory preferences for learning below and circle the one that best represents you. How can you also use this to enhance your college success?

   1. _____
   2. _____
   3. _____

3. List the four types of experiential learning preferences below and circle the one that best represents you. Now consider the preferences you circled above. What does this imply about the types of courses in which you might be most successful?

   1. _____
   2. _____
   3. _____
   4. _____

4. In what ways can personality factors contribute positively and negatively to success in the classroom?

   _____

   _____

5. What are some important things to do to get off on the right foot in class? List at least three strategies you can do now to make the best possible impression on your teachers.

   1. _____
   2. _____
   3. _____

Learning Portfolio

SELF-ASSESSMENTS

YOUR JOURNAL

STRATEGIES FOR SUCCESS

Develop
Meaningful
Values

Explore
Careers

Set Goals
Plan, and
Monitor

Diversify Your
Learning
Style

Build
Self-Esteem
and
Confidence

Get
Motivated
and Take
Responsibility

Think
and
Learn

Your Intelligence Profile

Beginning courses in college will give you an opportunity to experiment with and improve different kinds of intelligence. See how different college courses promote specific kinds of intelligence. Then indicate your strengths by identifying all the characteristics that apply to you.

Mark the space using the following codes: 2 _ very much like me 1 _ somewhat like me 0 _ not like me.

Verbal-Linguistic (Great Books, Composition, History)
6
- _1_ I like to read.
- _1_ I enjoy finding out the meanings of new words.
- _2_ I appreciate humor involving wordplay.
- _1_ I enjoy telling or writing poems or stories.
- _1_ I recall written or verbal material well.

Logical-Mathematical (Algebra, Philosophy, Chemistry)
3
- _0_ I like working with symbols.
- _1_ Math comes fairly easy to me.
- _0_ I like to analyze and solve problems.
- _1_ I like to discover logical weaknesses in an argument.
- _1_ I enjoy listening to a good debate.

Musical (Music Appreciation, Orchestra)
10
- _2_ I enjoy singing or making rhythmic sounds.
- _2_ I like to listen to favorite tapes and records.
- _2_ I sometimes make up my own tunes.
- _2_ I would enjoy learning to play a new musical instrument.
- _2_ I enjoy music deeply even when it has no lyrics.

Bodily-Kinesthetic (Recreation Studies, Engineering)
7
- _2_ I enjoy working with my hands.
- _2_ It's hard for me to sit still for long periods of time.
- _2_ I am good in at least one sport.
- _1_ I enjoy a well-executed physical movement.
- _0_ I'm physically comfortable with my body.

Spatial (Geometry, Art, Computer Science)
6
- _1_ I can easily visualize objects.
- _2_ I tend to find beauty in things that others don't.
- _1_ I can usually get around without going the wrong way.
- _1_ I enjoy working on arts, crafts, or drawing.
- _1_ People often comment on my "good taste."

Interpersonal (Psychology, Sociology, Nursing)
9
- _2_ I like to be around people, and I make friends easily.
- _1_ I have a knack for remembering names and faces.
- _2_ I have demonstrated natural leadership tendencies.
- _2_ I notice subtle differences among people.
- _2_ I understand people better than many other people do.

Intrapersonal (Religious Studies, Film Studies)
6
- _0_ I prefer solitary activities to group work.
- _1_ I enjoy quiet time.
- _2_ I am very sensitive to emotional experiences.
- _2_ I know myself very well.
- _1_ I prefer to have a few deep friendships rather than lots of friends.

Naturalist (Biology, Evolution, Forensic Science)
0
- _0_ I have a strong curiosity about how nature works.
- _0_ I enjoy looking for patterns in things.
- _0_ I can learn more easily outdoors than indoors.
- _0_ Science classes tend to be easy for me.
- _0_ I have at least one collection that I keep in careful order.

Add up your scores in each category. This inventory can reveal which multiple intelligence area is a relative strength and which is a relative weakness. In which dimensions did you score the highest? In which did you score the lowest?

Sensory Preference Inventory

Using the scale below enter the appropriate rating to each self-description in the open box.

Often = 5 points
Sometimes = 3 points
Seldom = 1 point

Then add up the numbers in each column to find out your dominant sensory preference.

		VISUAL	AUDITORY	TACTILE
1.	I can remember best about a subject by listening to a lecture that includes information, explanations, and discussion.		1	
2.	I prefer to see information written on a chalkboard and supplemented by visual aids and assigned readings.	5		
3.	I like to write things down or take notes for visual review.	5		
4.	I prefer to use posters, models, or actual practice and do other activities in class.			5
5.	I require explanations of diagrams, graphs, or visual directions.		5	
6.	I enjoy working with my hands or making things.			3
7.	I am skillful with and enjoy developing and making graphs and charts.	3		
8.	I can tell if sounds match when presented with pairs of sounds.		1	
9.	I remember best by writing things down several times.			3
10.	I can easily understand and follow directions on maps.	3		
11.	I do best in academic subjects by listening to lectures and tapes.		1	
12.	I play with coins or keys in my pockets.			5
13.	I learn to spell better by repeating words out loud than by writing the words on paper.		5	
14.	I can understand a news article better by reading about it in the newspaper than by listening to a report about it on the radio.	1		
15.	I chew gum, smoke, or snack while studying.			5
16.	I think the best way to remember something is to picture it in your head.	1		
17.	I learn the spelling of words by "finger spelling" them.			1
18.	I would rather listen to a good lecture or speech than read about the same material in a textbook.		3	
19.	I am good at working and solving jigsaw puzzles and mazes.	3		
20.	I grip objects in my hands during learning periods.			1
21.	I prefer listening to the news on the radio rather than reading about it in the newspaper.		5	
22.	I prefer obtaining information about an interesting subject by reading about it.	1		
23.	I feel very comfortable touching others, hugging, handshaking, etc.			3
24.	I follow oral directions better than written ones.		3	
Total each column of numbers to find your stronger sensory preference.		Visual Total 22	Auditory Total 24	Tactile Total 26

Experiential Learning Preferences

Each choice here captures an aspect of how people prefer to learn. Think about each choice in relation to yourself and circle the number in front of all of those items that apply to you.

When I have to learn how to operate a new piece of equipment, I
1. watch someone who knows how to operate the equipment.
2. carefully study the owner's manual.
3. fiddle with the dials until I produce a desired effect.
4. ignore the instructions and make the equipment suit my purposes.

What I like best about lectures is (are)
1. the chance to record the ideas of an expert.
2. a well-constructed argument about a controversial issue.
3. illustrations using real-life examples.
4. inspiration to come up with my own vision.

My class notes usually look like
1. faithful recordings of what the instructor said.
2. notes embellished with my own questions and evaluations.
3. outlines that capture key ideas.
4. notes with drawings, doodles, and other loosely related ideas or images.

I prefer assignments that involve
1. emotional expression.
2. analysis and evaluation.
3. solving practical problems.
4. creative expression.

In class discussion
1. I'm a watcher rather than a direct participant.
2. I'm an active, sometimes argumentative participant.
3. I get involved especially when we discuss real-life issues.
4. I like to contribute ideas that no one else thinks about.

I would rather work with
1. stories about individual lives.
2. abstract ideas.
3. practical problems.
4. creative ideas.

My learning motto is
1. "Tell me."
2. "Let me think this out for myself."
3. "Let me experiment."
4. "How can I do this uniquely?"

Interpretation: Look over your responses and add up the number of times you circled each number:

1 ____ *(learn by reflecting)*
2 ____ *(learn by critical thinking)*
3 ____ *(learn by doing)*
4 ____ *(learn by creative thinking)*

The alternative you circled the most is your preferred learning process. You may discover that you strongly favor a particular approach. Or you may find that your preferences are spread across several categories. Your experiences in college will help you develop your skills in all areas so you will become more flexible and more resourceful.

Your Journal

● REFLECT

1. A Matter of Style

You have had the opportunity to complete self-assessments designed to capture your strengths and style.

- List your strengths and weaknesses across the inventories.

_____

- What new insights do you have about your learning potential?

_____

- Did you learn anything that was distressing to you?

_____

- Considering your whole profile, what is one positive change you might make based on your knowledge that will enhance your success?

_____

2. The Deep End of the Pool

You probably recognized when you read about deep and surface learning that how comfortable you are as a learner may depend on the context. For example, you may easily comprehend complex ideas in a subject that you find intrinsically interesting. When subjects don't intrigue you, your efforts may feel shallow.

Think about the courses you are registered for this semester.

- Rank order the courses in terms of how deeply you plan to learn in the courses.
- See if you can identify the factors that will influence your decision in each course. For example,
  - Is the course intrinsically interesting?
  - Are you drawn to the teaching style of the instructor?
  - Is a good performance in the course essential for making progress in your major?
- If you get into a bind this term, can you withdraw from the course in which your learning is the most shallow?

● DO

1. Connect with a Special Teacher

Make an appointment with the instructor who seems most approachable to you. Interview that instructor and see if you can find out the following information:

- How did your instructor's interest in the discipline begin?

_____

- What does your instructor remember about being a first-year college student from personal experience?

_____

- What advice would the instructor offer on how to get the most from college and how to avoid pitfalls?

_____

- How would your instructor describe his or her own learning style and how does that influence course planning?

_____

- How good is the match between the instructor's intention and your learning style?

_____

Your Journal

2. Review a Syllabus

Consult the syllabus from the course you expect to be the most difficult for you. Examine it carefully, then try to predict how the class will proceed. What clues does the syllabus offer about how well the class demands will fit with your learning style? Ask yourself questions like these:

- How labor intensive will the course be?
- Where will the peak periods of effort occur?
- How should I pace my reading?
- Will there be an opportunity to develop my group work skills?
- How can I connect with the instructor if I run into a problem?

● THINK CRITICALLY

1. The Stylish Major

You have probably given some thought to the kind of major for which you would be best suited. Think about whether the major you've declared or to which you're most inclined is best suited to your learning style.

- What major are you considering?
- What intelligences fit best with this major?
- What sensory preferences might work best in this major?
- What learning process might be most emphasized in this major: reflection, active learning, critical thinking, or creative thinking?
- Does your personality style lend itself to the demands of the career?
- What is your conclusion about how well you might be suited to this major based on your learning style?

_____

_____

2. Career Cruising on the Web

Instead of starting with the careers that you have been considering, go at it from another direction. Conduct a Web search to identify five career options that would fit well with your learning style. Be sure to include some unconventional career choices. Explain what you think the connection is between the career choice and your learning style.

● CREATE

1. Everything I Need to Know I Plan to Learn in College

Look through Robert Fulghum's book, *Everything I Need to Know I Learned in Kindergarten.* Write down 10 simple truths that might serve as the draft for a college-level version of his book. Especially if your personality style leans toward greater structure, your ten simple truths may be useful to post somewhere near your preferred study area.

2. Your Learning Metaphor

Think about what it feels like for you to learn in the college classroom. Do you feel like a sponge, soaking up every detail you can? Do you feel like a juggler? A prisoner? A butterfly?
Are there other metaphors that describe your student experience? Describe or draw your metaphor and explain its significance. Go one step further and think about what your metaphor communicates regarding your personality style.

Applying the Six Strategies for Success

What did you learn in this chapter that you can apply to the following key strategies to help form the foundation for your success? Write down all of the main points you can remember that support the following strategies:

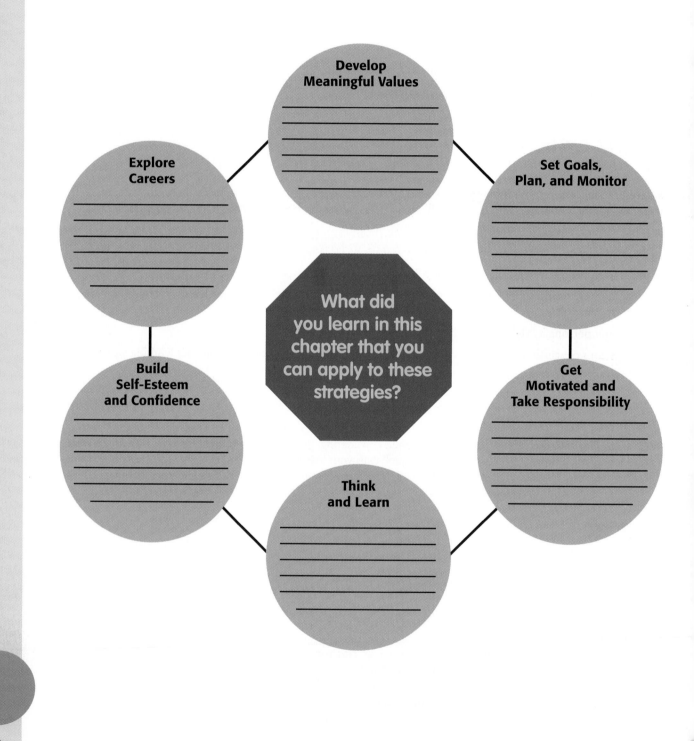

Develop Meaningful Values

Explore Careers

Set Goals, Plan, and Monitor

What did you learn in this chapter that you can apply to these strategies?

Build Self-Esteem and Confidence

Get Motivated and Take Responsibility

Think and Learn

5

Expand Your Thinking Skills

Where Are You? One of your primary purposes in college is to become a better thinker. In this chapter, you'll explore ways to move beyond memorization to refine your thinking skills, including improving critical thinking, developing strong arguments, solving problems, making sound decisions, and becoming more creative.

To get a current picture of your thinking skills, place a check mark next to only those items that apply to you.

- I can tell the difference between critical and uncritical thinking.
- I know how to ask good questions.
- I argue well.
- I use systematic strategies to solve problems.
- I practice mindful thinking to improve my quality of life.
- I regularly make sound decisions.
- I can avoid routine thinking problems that prevent good decisions.
- I strive to be creative.

Consider how cartoonist Gary Larson combines disciplinary expertise with an unusual degree of creativity that has captured the imagination of millions of people.

121

Images of College Success

Gary Larson

People Magazine described Gary Larson, one of the most distinctive cartoonists of our time, as having an "eerily unconventional mind." When he retired from cartooning in 1994 after 14 years, *The Far Side* had been featured in more than 1,900 daily and Sunday newspapers worldwide, including translation into 17 languages. His cartoon collections, 22 in all, have each become *New York Times* "bestsellers," selling more than 31 million books.

As a child, Larson was an avid comics reader, but his real love was biology. He became an enthusiast about natural selection, and his early observations would leave an indelible mark on his evolving cartoon style. Although he took every biology course he could, his college experiences took him in another direction. He majored in communications at Washington State University with hopes of a future career in advertising. However, on graduation, he played guitar in a jazz duo for three years until he went to work in a music store.

Larson reminisced about a special day at the store: "I had a sudden revelation. As I stood next to the cash register, the sky seemed to suddenly open up over my head, and a throng of beautiful angels came flying down and swirled around me. In glorious, lilting tones, their voices rang out, 'You haaaaaate your job, you haaaaaate your job'." Convinced that "angels don't lie," he quit his job. Larson took a sample of his cartoons to an editor of a Seattle nature magazine and sold six for $90. He subsequently got a job with the *Seattle Times*, but that lasted just one year because of complaints about his subject matter.

Then he became an animal-rights investigator for the Humane Society, but eventually signed with the *San Francisco Chronicle* to produce *The Far Side*. His primitive cartooning style has both devout fans and ardent critics, the latter group including pet owners, animal-rights activists, educators, clergy, lawyers, biologists, and even Amnesty International. He routinely depicts animals as smarter than their human counterparts. Cows and "weiner dogs" seem to be his favorite targets for humor. His innovative work has been recognized with a variety of awards. The scientific community honored him by naming two species—a butterfly and a biting louse—after Gary Larson.

Although **GARY LARSON** was a communications major in college, his expanded interest in biology is apparent in his cartoons.

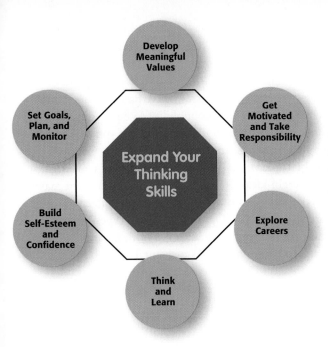

Develop
Meaningful
Values

Set Goals,
Plan, and
Monitor

Get
Motivated
and Take
Responsibility

Expand Your
Thinking
Skills

Build
Self-Esteem
and
Confidence

Explore
Careers

Think
and
Learn

Learning to think well provides a solid foundation for succeeding in college assignments and in any current or future career. As you read, think about the "Six Strategies for Success" listed to the left and how this chapter can help you maximize success in these important areas, particularly "Think and Learn."

Think Critically

College may not prepare you for a specific career but it will teach you how to think more effectively to prepare you for a broad range of career choices. Consider Gary Larson's career pursuit. He could not really major in cartooning, but his coursework in communications and biology provided exposure to content that gave him a foundation for his career. More important, his college courses gave him the opportunity to develop the thinking skills that would serve him well as a cartoonist.

During college you will learn innumerable facts and concepts that you may never use in your career, but the powerful by-product of that process should be refinement of your thinking skills. The array of courses that you take will provide much practice in developing critical thinking, reasoning, and problem solving. Along the way you also will make significant decisions and experience your creative potential. Let's explore the ways that college will help you become a more effective and powerful thinker.

You've probably heard the term *critical thinking*. It refers to the use of purposeful, reasoned thinking to reach your goals (Halpern, 1997). Among other benefits, when you think critically you improve your ability to learn and retain new information. Clearly, this will benefit you in college and beyond.

The complexities of life in the 21st century underscore the need for critical thinking skills. Conserving the environment, managing nuclear energy, and staying a competitive economic force are just a few of the tasks that require our best collective thinking. Such concerns have prompted national discussions about the role of colleges in helping citizens develop better thinking skills. One aim of a liberal arts education is to help you develop broad critical-thinking skills by sampling the various ways of thinking required in different disciplines (Beyer, 1998). Different disciplines tend to approach critical thinking in distinctive ways.

For example, the natural sciences often emphasize critical thinking skills as they relate to problem solving. The humanities focus on the critical analysis of expressive works.

To achieve, you need thought. You have to know what you are doing and that's real power.
Ayn Rand
20th-century philosopher

© Carol Cable. Used with permission of the cartoonist.

Exposure to various disciplines should help you develop a broad base of perspectives that will serve as the basis for expert critical thinking.

Your own knack for critical thinking will depend on your learning style and the successes you've had in various thinking challenges. For example, your ability to be effective as a critical thinker will vary with the commitment you make to study a discipline in depth. In some situations, your intrinsic interest in the topic matter will make it easy for you to grapple with the main ideas. In other situations, the content may feel hard to penetrate so it may be more manageable to engage at a more shallow level. Figure 5.1, "Two Types of Thinkers," summarizes the general qualities of both passive and critical thinkers. In addition, Self-Assessment 1 "The Critical Difference" on page 145 gives you an opportunity to evaluate how well your characteristics match those of good critical thinkers.

Ask Questions

One sign of a good critical thinker is the ability to ask on-target questions. When you were little, you were probably constantly asking questions. But as you got older, you

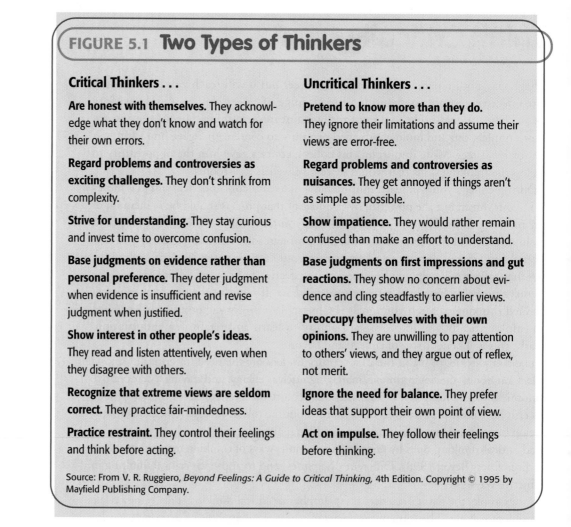

FIGURE 5.1 Two Types of Thinkers

Critical Thinkers . . .

Are honest with themselves. They acknowledge what they don't know and watch for their own errors.

Regard problems and controversies as exciting challenges. They don't shrink from complexity.

Strive for understanding. They stay curious and invest time to overcome confusion.

Base judgments on evidence rather than personal preference. They deter judgment when evidence is insufficient and revise judgment when justified.

Show interest in other people's ideas. They read and listen attentively, even when they disagree with others.

Recognize that extreme views are seldom correct. They practice fair-mindedness.

Practice restraint. They control their feelings and think before acting.

Uncritical Thinkers . . .

Pretend to know more than they do. They ignore their limitations and assume their views are error-free.

Regard problems and controversies as nuisances. They get annoyed if things aren't as simple as possible.

Show impatience. They would rather remain confused than make an effort to understand.

Base judgments on first impressions and gut reactions. They show no concern about evidence and cling steadfastly to earlier views.

Preoccupy themselves with their own opinions. They are unwilling to pay attention to others' views, and they argue out of reflex, not merit.

Ignore the need for balance. They prefer ideas that support their own point of view.

Act on impulse. They follow their feelings before thinking.

Source: From V. R. Ruggiero, *Beyond Feelings: A Guide to Critical Thinking,* 4th Edition. Copyright © 1995 by Mayfield Publishing Company.

may have acquired more passive learning habits. Unfortunately, if you haven't been asking questions often, these skills may be dormant.

The problem may be fear of embarrassment. You may think of good questions to ask but worry about what others will think of you. Perhaps the instructor will think your question comes from left field. Or maybe other students will think you are showing off what you know. The problem with worrying so much about what others think is that you sacrifice chances to improve your own thinking and speaking skills. It's *your* education. If you don't take risks, you won't get to develop your mind as much as you deserve. The Journal activity "A Question a Day" on page 148 provides the opportunity to brush up on your question-asking skills.

Another problem students have is not being sure what kind of questions to ask. Your question type will depend on what kind of information you are trying to learn. Your question can:

- *Read the lines.* These questions concentrate on identifying critical features or concepts. *What are the most important ideas being presented?*
- *React to the lines.* These questions facilitate an emotional response to the content. *How does the issue or concept make you feel?*
- *Read between the lines.* These questions emphasize your ability to analyze the content into component parts. *What factors explain how the key ideas developed?*
- *Read beyond the lines.* These questions prompt you to think about alternatives or future possibilities. *What difference will the ideas make in the long run* (Strong, Silver, Perini, & Tuculescu, 2002)?

Suppose you are studying the history of cartooning in an arts appreciation course. What kinds of questions illustrate these distinctions?

- *Read the lines.* What role does cartooning play in modern culture?
- *React to the lines.* What range of emotions do cartoons stir?
- *Read between the lines.* What political agenda might be expressed by a particular editorial cartoon regarding conflict in the Middle East?
- *Read beyond the lines.* Would you anticipate that cartoons will become more or less powerful as social change agents over the next decade?

Get your curiosity out in the open. If you recapture your enthusiasm for asking questions, your college years will be more interesting and fun. A special kind of thrill occurs when your thinking generates good questions. Have you ever gotten chills when your question elicits a "Good question!" response from your instructor? On Target Tips, "I Have a Question," gives some more tips on how to ask good questions.

Although instructors may reassure you that "there's no such thing as a stupid question," there are *unwelcome* questions. These include questions that detract from the momentum of the class, focus more on self-concerns than on the needs of the class, or demonstrate that the questioner has failed to pay attention. See Staying out of the Pits, "It's Not Therapy," for some strategies to help you discern if your questions stray off course.

> Too often we . . . enjoy the comfort of opinion without the discomfort of thought.
>
> John F. Kennedy
> 20th-century U.S. president

ON TARGET TIPS

I Have a Question

You can improve your analytic skills by learning to ask questions that will help you break open the ideas you're studying (Browne & Keeley, 1990). Here are some questions that can help you strengthen these important skills.

- What are the issues and the conclusion?
- What are the reasons?
- What words or phrases are ambiguous?
- Are there value conflicts?
- What assumptions are being made?
- What is the evidence?
- Are there other ways to explain the results?
- Are there flaws in the reasoning?
- Is any information missing?
- Do the conclusions fit the reasons?
- How do the results fit with my own values?

Source: From M. N. Browne & S. M. Keeley, *Asking the Right Questions: A Guide to Critical Thinking*, 3rd Edition. Copyright © 1990 by Prentice-Hall, Inc.

Offer Criticism

Dr. Gray shuts off the videotape of the president's State of the Union address, then turns to the class and says, "What do you think?" Jeff dreads moments like this, because the question feels so open-ended. He's never sure what instructors want.

When a teacher offers you a chance to practice the higher-order skill of thinking critically and evaluating, it's easy to feel intimidated. However, some strategies can help you handle it.

1. *Decide whether you like what you're being asked to judge.* Your general reaction can set the stage for detailed analysis later on. For example, were you smiling or frowning during the State of the Union address?

2. *Look for both positive and negative attributes.* Some people unnecessarily limit their thinking by focusing only on the attributes that support their emotional response. If you were thrilled by what the president said, try to find some weaknesses in the address. If you were dissatisfied, look also for positive features in what you heard.

3. *Use criteria to stimulate your thinking.* To what degree is the work you are evaluating

effective?	*sufficient?*
efficient?	*adequate?*
reasonable?	*logical?*
beautiful?	*sensitive?*
practical?	*accurate?*
thought-provoking?	*stimulating?*
justifiable?	*comprehensive?*
understandable?	*relevant?*

Which of the criteria would apply to a presidential address? A work of art? A symphony? A public policy?

4. *Use examples to support your judgment.* Expect to explain your judgment. Which phrases or examples in the State of the Union stayed with you? What made the examples compelling? The Journal activity "The Great Debate" on page 149 gives you an opportunity to hone your critical thinking skills.

Critical Thinking and the Internet

The Internet has transformed nearly every aspect of our lives. Although it has dramatically expanded our access to information, surfing the net can produce a quagmire of data. An uncritical user can end up with too much, too little, or invalid information. This problem poses a special threat for students who like the convenience of doing research on the Internet but may not have developed the critical thinking skills necessary to track down the valid and valuable from the massive material than can show up on the computer screen. Thinking critically about your search strategy will make your surfing profitable.

Locating What You Need Allow yourself a reasonable amount of time to play with different strategies to produce the best results. Identify and enter key concepts in a search engine. If you are operating in a particular discipline-based database, you may have the best luck by entering the basic concepts of the discipline to begin tracking down information. If you get an excess number of hits, refine your search by adding more parameters.

For example, you might limit your search to articles printed only in the last five years. Or you might conduct a Boolean search by combining two key terms. A Boolean search that specifies "OR" as an operator will hit any article in which either term is present. "First Ladies"—or—"foreign policy" will produce a broad search, identifying any net resource that addresses either term. By contrast, using "AND" as the operator will narrow your hits to any resources that deal both with first ladies AND foreign policy. You should be able to narrow down efficiently which first ladies had an influence on foreign policy.

What happens if you come up with too few hits to be helpful? Go back to the conceptual drawing board and expand your search. Think about an overarching term in which the key concept you have already tried could be embedded. Suppose you need to find information about an obscure tree disease for a botany class. If you come up empty-handed by entering the name of the disease, enlarge your search to "tree disease." Usually, however, the problem is too much rather than too little information.

Finding the Best Data Determining what is sufficiently high quality is another challenge. What are some pointers to ensure your resources will be credible?

- *Avoid opinion pieces that can't be substantiated.* The Internet does not police itself. It is the perfect vehicle for anyone with a point of view and a computer to try to capture and persuade an audience. Be vigilant about entries that appear to offer facts that can't be corroborated.
- *Identify the author and verify the author's expertise.* The most valuable websites will be those that present information by experts in the specific discipline in which you are conducting your search. Individuals with scholarly degrees, affiliations with well-known institutions, or well-established reputations will be easier for you to claim as credible sources. If the author's name is present, you can do an additional search to identify the author's credentials if those were not available on the website. web pages that do not credit an author are suspect.
- *Check the date.* Information on older websites may be sufficiently outdated that your including them will demonstrate that your search wasn't thorough.
- *Trace information to its original source to strengthen your confidence.* One of the best features of the Internet is that it can direct you toward original citations in published journals. Many of those may be online.
- *Don't be taken in by aesthetically pleasing websites.* Websites can be highly attractive but seductive if the information isn't sound. Look for indicators that the scholarship is solid, such as well-defined concepts, charts and tables, sponsorship by reputable organizations, and so forth.

Reason

Sometimes you may find that you don't have all the information you need to understand a phenomenon, make a prediction, or solve a problem. Through reasoning, you can derive the missing elements. Reasoning represents a special kind of critical thinking that you will often have to use as your course demands get more sophisticated. Good reasoners effectively make inferences, use logic, and create and defend arguments (Beyer, 1998). Good reasoning isn't always easy, but it can be learned.

Change your thoughts and you change your whole world.
Norman Vincent Peale
20th-century American philosopher

Make the Right Inferences

As you head for class early in the morning during finals week, suppose you come across a student whom you don't know, who is out cold, sprawled across the sidewalk,

What happened here? Your conclusions come from inferences you make from the clues in the scene.

his books scattered on the ground (Halonen & Gray, 2001). What do you think? There are many inferences you might draw based on what you observed. *Inferences* are interpretations that you derive from processing cues in a situation.

For example, you could infer that your fallen campus colleague might be:

1. exhausted from studying for finals.
2. suffering from a serious health problem.
3. passed out from drinking until the wee hours.
4. a psychology major doing an experiment.

All of the inferences are plausible, meaning that they are logical, potentially accurate ways to explain what you saw. However, it's likely that one explanation is better than the others. You constantly make inferences.

- Your roommate is scowling so you infer she failed a test.
- You find the dishes piled up so you infer that you'll have to do them.
- You get an unsigned note asking you to go out for coffee and you infer who was the most likely to have invited you.

Your interpretations of the events around you are based on your collected experiences. Therefore, your inferences will reflect that experience and sometimes produce biases in interpretation. Go back to the example of the fallen colleague. If you inferred that the individual might be recovering from a hangover, your past experiences may have created a predisposition or bias in how you make sense of what you see in this situation. You may have heard about a huge frat party the night before, where everyone got totally wasted. But aren't you forgetting the books on the ground? Why would someone who is passed out from drinking too much be carrying books? To test this proposition further, imagine that the fallen colleague is female, not male. How does simply changing the sex of the person change your interpretive bias? Would a woman be as likely to pass out from drinking too much? You can see how bias and previous knowledge can shape and possibly distort the reality that you experience.

Your ability to make accurate inferences is probably very good in most situations. However, inferences can be tricky. Notice in the examples given how easy it is to be wrong. In fact, think about a recent situation in which you jumped to the wrong conclusion. A faulty inference was probably to blame. Sometimes inferences become *assumptions*, an inference that we accept as the truth. This assumption is not based on fact or reason and may be false. Yet, you may not recognize that you're operating from a faulty assumption until you learn otherwise.

Learn How to Handle Claims

Instructors may challenge you to sort fact from fiction. They may ask you to judge the *validity* (truthfulness) of a *claim* (a statement that can be either true or false but not both) (Epstein, 2000). Claims are different from *facts*, which are truths that can't be disputed.

> *Fact:* The moon is full at least once a month.
> *Claim:* The full moon makes people a little crazy.

Notice how the claim is debatable and requires evidence before we can determine its validity; the fact cannot be challenged. When you evaluate a claim, you have three choices:

1. Accept the claim.
2. Reject the claim.
3. Suspend judgment until you have more information.

How will you rise to this challenge?

When to Accept a Claim There are three circumstances in which it's reasonable to accept a claim:

1. *Personal experience.* Trust your personal experience when your confidence level is high and there isn't a good contradictory explanation. For example, you may have been warned about the "freshmen 15," the tendency for students to put on weight during the first year of college. Despite the warning, you notice the scale is starting to creep upward, which you attribute to increased snacking during study sessions. Although there may be some exceptions, in general, you may notice many of your peers are struggling with extra weight gain as well. Your personal experience suggests the claim that the first year can layer on pounds seems true.

2. *Trustworthy expert.* If a claim is made by someone with a trustworthy track record or other similar credentials such as expertise, it's reasonable to accept the claim as true. This includes claims made in reputable journals and references. For example, claims about damage from smoking that are reported in the *New England Journal of Medicine* are usually trustworthy. Claims by your next-door neighbor about the value of vitamin B may not be as valid.

3. *Reliable media sources.* Unless the media source is going to profit from the claim presented, it's reasonable to accept the claim. For example, local weather forecasters regularly make claims about future weather patterns that generally are accurate. Some newscasters demonstrate their reliability with the accuracy of their predictions. However, just because someone is on the news doesn't make that person a reliable source.

When to Question a Claim Question claims that:

- *Come from "unnamed sources."* If you can't verify the source, you shouldn't readily accept the claim.
- *Confer an advantage.* Experts sometimes make large profits by supporting certain claims. Be suspicious of claims that can be linked to payoff. Jennifer Love Hewitt may be a beauty, but her endorsement of a beauty product is likely to be more of an advantage to her than to you.
- *Are used to sell a product.* Advertisements and commercials are always making claims, which are often reputed to be based on solid research. However, the research may be biased, or there may be contradictory findings that are not reported. For example, influenced by claims in advertising, millions of Americans take herbal supplements to enhance their memory. Only recently has conflicting evidence suggested that the supplements are a waste of time and money.
- *Offer personal experience as "proof."* Human memory can sometimes introduce distortions that can lead you to endorse a claim that simply isn't true. For example, the psychologist Elizabeth Loftus (1993) demonstrated that people can be tricked into recalling events in their childhood that never happened. The people in her study confidently recalled getting lost in a mall based on hearing others report the experience. Loftus suggested that we "reconstruct" memories that represent a blend of the truth, perceptual distortions, and wishes.
- *Appeal to common beliefs and practice.* Just because "everybody does it" doesn't make it right or truthful.
- *Use language in misleading ways.* Politicians are often accused of putting a "spin" on their claims. For example, they might report that the "vast majority" of Americans believe in vouchers for private school, when the actual statistic in favor might be 51 percent at the time. Beware of overblown language that can disguise the truth. Self-Assessment "Claim Check" on your CD-ROM provides additional examples.

> *To swallow and follow, whether old doctrine or new propaganda, is a weakness still dominating the human mind.*
>
> Charlotte Gilman Perkins
> *20th-century American social critic*

Form Strong Arguments In formal reasoning, an *argument* is a set of claims. The argument begins with *premises*, initial claims that lead to a final claim called the *conclusion* of the argument (Epstein, 2000). A good argument is one in which the premises (1) are true and (2) lead logically to the truth of the conclusion. Good arguments are also called *strong* or *valid* arguments.

Here's an example of a good argument:

> *Premise:* All healthy dogs have fur.
> *Premise:* Spot is a healthy dog.
> *Conclusion:* Therefore, Spot has fur.

Some good arguments are reasonable because the premises and conclusion are sound, even though the conclusion may not be as absolute as the one in the example. In most cases, these plausible arguments deal with probable outcomes instead of definitive ones.

> *Premise:* Most dogs who live outside have fleas.
> *Premise:* Spot lives outside in a doghouse.
> *Conclusion:* Therefore, Spot probably has fleas.

Spot could be the rare exception, but the conclusion is logical if the first two premises are true. Here are some simple suggestions that will help you develop the most persuasive arguments.

1. Be sure that the conclusion follows logically from the premises.
2. Leave out faulty or dubious premises.
3. Use precise language to pinpoint your claim. (Vague or ambiguous language makes your position easier to challenge.)
4. Avoid making claims you can't prove.

The Journal Activity "Claims Detector" on page 148 allows you to practice evaluating claims made by commercials and developing convincing premises and conclusions.

Form Counterarguments In many classes you may be asked to find flaws in an argument. A counterargument challenges an argument by showing:

1. a premise is false
2. the conclusion is false
3. the reasoning is weak or faulty.

In Figure 5.2, "Arguments: The Good, the Bad, and the Goofy," see if you can determine exactly what weakens each argument.

Some counterargument strategies are ineffective. For example, ridicule is not a good way to counterargue. Ridicule or criticism of the person making the argument disrupts communication without improving anyone's understanding. Refer to Staying Out of the Pits, "Offensive Defense" for an illustration.

Another ineffective strategy is restating the original argument in a distorted way and then disproving the distortion. Suppose you are debating with a classmate the need for welfare reform to improve employment opportunities. Your classmate introduces a recent study that suggests children on welfare perform poorly in school. He concludes that past welfare reform has been harmful to academic achievement and concludes that there is no basis to believe additional reform will enhance children's achievement. Note the drift and distortion in the argument. To be effective, your

STAYING OUT OF THE PITS **Offensive Defense**

What began as a simple exchange about an application of supply-and-demand principles in their marketing class had suddenly escalated. Tony was feeling pretty frustrated that Taneesha not only didn't understand what he was saying, but kept asking for examples that would provide convincing evidence for his point of view. No matter what example he generated, Taneesha rejected the example, shaking her head. In the heat of the moment, Tony lost his cool. "Well, who is doing better in this course then? I got an A on the last exam. What did you get?" When he calmed down, he recognized that he had violated a fundamental principle of making good arguments.

You attack the argument, not the arguer.

FIGURE 5.2 Arguments: The Good, the Bad, and the Goofy

See if you can spot ways to challenge the following arguments.

© 2003 Sidney Harris.

Example 1

Premise: All cats have four legs.
Premise: I have four legs.
Conclusion: Therefore, I am a cat.
Both premises are true, but together they do not produce a logical conclusion, because the first premise does not state that *only* cats have four legs. The conclusion must follow logically from the premises.

Example 2

Premise: All birds have fur.
Premise: Tweetie is a bird.
Conclusion: Tweetie has fur.
The first premise is false, so the conclusion is implausible.

Example 3

Premise: Good dogs sit on command.
Premise: Spot sits on command.
Conclusion: Spot is a good dog.
Although the premises may both be true, the conclusion isn't supported. Spot may engage in other behavior that makes him a bad dog.

Example 4

Premise: The dog show winner is the best dog in the country.
Premise: Spot won first place in the dog show.
Conclusion: Spot is the best dog in the country.
The conclusion follows logically, but what exactly is meant by "best"? And is the first claim likely to be true? There are many dog shows every year. Was the show that Spot won really the Super Bowl of dog shows? In other words, the first premise is suspect, so the conclusion is as well.

counterargument must accurately represent the original argument and defend against only that argument.

Refine Your Reasoning

You can improve your reasoning skills in the following ways.

Be Willing to Argue You may have to present a position in a term paper, in a speech, or in answer to a complex question in class. Students study reasoning as a formal science in logic classes, but you'll certainly have opportunities to create and defend arguments in many other formal and informal situations. Don't shrink from those opportunities, even if you have negative feelings about the word *argument* based on the tension that you've felt when in conflict with a friend or loved one. Intellectual arguments can generate passion, too, but they need not have the same emotional intensity or feelings of personal risk as differences you have with loved ones.

Use Inductive and Deductive Reasoning There are two types of argument: induction and deduction. *Induction* involves generalizing from specific instances to broad principles. For example, perhaps you really enjoyed your first college foreign language class. Based on that experience, you might reason inductively that *all* language classes in college are great. Notice that your conclusion or rule—your *induction*—might be incorrect, because your next course may turn out to be disappointing. Inductive arguments are never 100 percent certain. They can be weak or strong.

In contrast, *deduction* moves from general situations or rules to specific predictions or applications. Deductive reasoning parallels the hypothesis testing procedures used in the sciences. For example, your chemistry professor may ask you to identify an unknown substance. By applying specific strategies of analysis, you narrow the possibilities until you know what the substance is. A deductive argument is 100 percent true if the premises are true and the reasoning is sound. When the premises are untrue or the logical connection between the premises and the conclusion is shaky, a deductive argument may be false. Look at the deductive examples in Figure 5.3, "Using Induction and Deduction." Is any one of these arguments completely convincing? Why or why not?

Check Your Assumptions It's easy to reach wrong conclusions from wrong assumptions. For example, the satirist Jonathan Swift caused a stir in the 18th century when he proposed one solution for two serious problems facing British society: too many orphaned children and not enough food. Swift proposed that both problems could be solved if the orphans were eaten! Those who *assumed* Swift was putting forward a serious position were outraged. Those who carefully examined Swift's real purpose, and discovered that he meant to bring serious attention to these social problems, were amused by his wit and sensitized to the problem. Identify your assumptions and then do your best to verify them.

FIGURE 5.3 Using Induction and Deduction

From specific observations	→	to general principles	=	INDUCTIVE REASONING
1. Maria has red hair and a bad temper.	----→	Most redheads probably have bad tempers.		
2. Waking up on the past three Mondays was a hard thing to do.	---→	Waking up on Mondays will probably always be a hard thing to do.		
3. T. S. Eliot's *The Wasteland* is a masterpiece.	---→	The rest of Eliot's poetry should be impressive.		

From broad generalizations, observations	→	to specific conclusions	=	DEDUCTIVE REASONING
1. Butlers tend to have evil minds.	----→	The butler may have been the murderer!		
2. All cats have scratchy tongues.	----→	This is a cat. It must have a scratchy tongue.		
3. My roommate Ted seems really cranky after math class.	---→	He may have flunked his math test.		

Know Your Own Bias We all have strong preferences and prejudices that may prevent us from evaluating an argument fairly. By acknowledging your own preferences and prejudices, you can increase the likelihood of coming up with more effective arguments. For example, if you know that you feel strong sympathies for single parents, you can take this bias into account when you evaluate government policies that affect their lives. Good reasoners guard against their own "soft spots" to increase their objectivity. For example, if you know your political leanings are conservative, you may be less likely to scrutinize arguments and claims that come from well-known conservatives. You can guard against your political soft spot by paying even closer attention to the claims made by those with whom you fundamentally agree.

Take Time before Concluding Sometimes we short-circuit our reasoning. It's easy to get excited about a bright idea and stop the hard analytic work involved in thinking the problem through to the end. A premature judgment may work out, but it tends to make us even less exacting the next time we analyze a problem. Careful reasoners resist impulsive judgments. They thoroughly review an argument to make sure they have addressed all questions.

Solve Problems

The humorist Russell Baker once quipped, "I've had an unhappy life, thank God." His observation underscores the importance that problems play in building our character and resilience. You might think that living a problem-free existence would feel terrific. Maybe it would . . . briefly. Problems add vigor and vibrance to our lives; solid solutions bring a sense of accomplishment that makes the ordeal worthwhile. Wobbly or ineffective solutions provide an opportunity to learn new and better ways for the future.

Being in college will offer an array of problem-solving circumstances. Where do I get the cheapest textbooks? What field should be my major? How will I make friends who will support my academic goals and future dreams? How will I ever complete three term papers at the same time? Where can I park without getting a ticket? And the "Grand Problem" you will eventually have to solve: What will I do *after* college? One of the life lessons from Gary Larson's opening story is that you may solve this problem many times before finding the best solution. Your experience in solving problems in college will be critical to your future success in professional life.

Find the IDEAL Solution

Once a problem gets on your radar screen, it's tempting to hope that you can solve it without much thought. The fact is that good problem solving requires a great deal of thought, and a step-by-step approach often facilitates that thought process. Many people find it helpful to use a specific problem-solving system, such as the five-step IDEAL method (Bransford & Stein, 1984): Let's see how that might apply to Gary Larson's career problems:

1. *Identify the problem (Identification).* Something wasn't right about Larson's job in the music store.
2. *Define the problem (Definition).* Larson recognized that his current occupation, working in a music store, was not

Solving problems efficiently and effectively takes thoughtful consideration and a systematic approach.

sufficiently satisfying. (His version included a chorus of angels.) He decided a new direction was in order.

3. *Explore alternative approaches (Evaluation).* He considered many options about how to make a more satisfying living.

4. *Act on the best strategy (Action).* While Larson was still a clerk in the music store, he ventured forth to show his work to a publisher and felt some optimism about his work when the editor purchased his cartoons. Then he quit his job.

5. *Look back to evaluate the effects (Looking Back).* He realized the solution to become a cartoonist might have been premature since he was struggling to make a living. Taking a different job until success struck seemed to be an even better solution.

How might this approach work to solve a common problem in a college setting? Let's look at a typical case. Then go to Journal activity "Your IDEAL" on page 149 for more practice applying this strategy to an issue in your life.

1. *Identify the problem.* Bernita discovered when she arrived at her first art appreciation class that her instructor had already started. The instructor looked distinctively displeased as Bernita took a seat in the back of the class. When she looked at her watch, Bernita discovered that she was two minutes late. Obviously, she didn't want to annoy her instructor by arriving late to class each day. How could she avoid being late?

2. *Define the problem.* Be as specific and comprehensive as you can in defining a problem. Outline the contributing factors. There are two parts to this problem. First is the fact that the professor is clearly a stickler about being on time to his class. The second is Bernita's lateness. Why does the professor start right on time? Does he always? What made Bernita late to class? Was her watch broken? Was she carrying 60 pounds of books? Did she walk too slowly? Probably the main factor was the distance between the art class and the English class that Bernita had on the other side of the campus in the previous period. Even if she walked at top speed, she couldn't get to the art class on time.

3. *Explore alternative approaches.* Systematically gather and explore alternative solutions to isolate the best approach. Assuming that arriving late to class makes her uncomfortable enough to take action, what are some reasonable alternatives that Bernita could pursue? She can drop either class, or transfer into another section that prevents the conflict. She can talk to the instructor in her art class. Maybe there was something unusual about this day and he is usually more relaxed. He may be understanding about her arriving a couple of minutes late if he sees that there is a legitimate reason. Or she can ask the instructor to wait until she gets there (maybe not). Or perhaps she can talk to the English professor about leaving a couple of minutes early. On Target Tips, "Coming up with Alternatives," suggests ways to generate solutions.

4. *Act on the best strategy.* Take specific action to resolve the problem. Include more than one strategy. Bernita decided to explain to her art instructor why she would be a few minutes late to class, added that she would do her best to get there on time, and asked for her instructor's support. The instructor verified that Bernita would be late only by two minutes and asked that she sit near the door to minimize disruptions. He also thanked Bernita for her courtesy.

5. *Look back to evaluate the effects.* The final step is to evaluate whether or not your solution works. You might be thrilled

ON TARGET TIPS

Coming up with Alternatives

These approaches may help you generate new ideas for resolving problems:

- Examine how you feel about the situation.
- Collect opinions about possible approaches.
- Research what the experts would do.
- Break the problem up into smaller pieces.
- Think through the consequences of leaving the problem alone.
- Work backward from the preferred outcome.

with how well it works and feel free to move on to your next challenge. Or you might discover that the solution didn't work. In this instance, Bernita's problem solving was successful. Her solution not only saved her from the trouble and expense of dropping the class but also gave her a better personal connection with her instructor. Complete Self-Assessment 2 "How Systematically Do I Solve Problems?" on page 146 to assess your own problem solving strengths and weaknesses.

Problem-Solver Characteristics

What are some other ways you can maximize your problem-solving skills (Whimbey & Lochhead, 1991)?

- *Observe carefully.* Try to identify all the relevant factors in a problem from the outset. Superficial observation misses factors that hold keys to ultimate solutions. Careful observation involves analysis—identifying the relationships among the elements of the problem.
- *Stay positive and persistent.* Don't be beaten by frustration. Search for ways to make the struggle invigorating rather than frustrating.
- *Show concern for accuracy.* Pay attention to detail. It's easy to let small errors occur in moments of inattention. Take care not to leave out crucial information. Proofread statements and recheck calculations before submitting your work for review.

> *You see, but you do not observe.*
>
> Sherlock Holmes
> *19th-century fictional detective*

Practice Mindfulness

Developing the right frame of mind about possibilities is an essential ingredient in improving your ability to solve problems. There are many ways to practice mindfulness to improve your problem-solving skills (Langer, 1997). Here are several that are particularly helpful in a college setting.

- *Create new categories.* We often dismiss things by categorizing them in a global way. For example, you might dismiss a "bad" instructor as not worthy of attention. However, if you look more closely at the various aspects of teaching, your perceptions will be richer. For example, perhaps the instructor's delivery is plodding but his choice of words is rich. Or his ideas are delivered without enthusiasm but his precise examples always make things easier to understand. A closer look can make us less judgmental and more tolerant.
- *Take control over context.* The Bird Man of Alcatraz overcame a narrowed context. When an injured bird found its way into his prison cell, the Bird Man nursed it to health. This act began a love of learning about birds that helped him to transcend confinement. When you feel like your own options have been constrained, reexamine your circumstances to see whether you have overlooked some aspect of the situation that could make it more palatable or more rewarding.
- *Welcome new information.* We tend to disregard information that does not fit with what we already know. This is an especially important tendency to overcome when you conduct research. Staying open to new information maximizes your pool of ideas. You may begin with one idea of what you want to prove, but find that another possibility is actually more exciting.
- *Use technology.* The world is at your mouse's command through the Internet. The World Wide Web offers unlimited examples of good and bad problem solving. The Journal activity "Creative Surfing" on page 149 explores what the Internet can tell you about human problem solving.

- *Enjoy the process.* It's easy to become so single-minded about solving a problem that you forget to pay attention to the process of achieving it. Remember that the process is just as important as the outcome. At times the task before you may seem too large to finish. By taking a large project and breaking it into smaller, achievable deadlines and goals, you'll also stay mindful of the learning that occurs along the way. The Journal activity "Minding the Store" on page 148 will help you evaluate your mindfulness.

Make Good Decisions

> *All things are possible until they are proved impossible— even the impossible may only be so, for now.*
>
> Pearl S. Buck
> *American writer and missionary*

Solving problems often requires making good decisions. Some decisions have far-reaching consequences. For example, you decided where to go to college. To make that decision, you may have used some systematic criteria. Perhaps you wanted a college close to home with low tuition costs and specific majors. Or you may have decided to go to the campus you liked best when you visited or the one that was just the right distance from home. How satisfied you are now with your college experience may reflect how carefully you made that decision.

Four common problems interfere with good decision making (Swartz, 2001). The following explores how these approaches might influence your own future career decisions.

Avoid Snap Decisions

We are inclined to make decisions too quickly, before we have had time to consider all of the options. Hasty decisions are much more likely when we are trying to solve short-term problems, leaving us vulnerable for long-term problems. You might take the first job offer you get. Although the offer might be a good match for your skills, such a quick decision precludes another alternative that might be even better.

Expand Narrow Thinking

We may simplify choices in a way that overlooks a broader array of options. Our rush to choose from column A or B may keep us from turning the page to see many other options in columns C–F. Many students feel pressured to establish their careers. You might decide advertising is the way to proceed and not consider any other options that might be more satisfying.

Contain Sprawling Thinking

We may entertain too many options. By attending to too many possibilities, we may neglect the in-depth consideration that might make the best option stand out. If you find yourself making job interview appointments with more recruiters than you reasonably can prepare for, you may be suffering from thinking sprawl.

"You take all the time you need, Larry—this certainly is a big decision."

Clarify Fuzzy Thinking

We may not think through a problem carefully to isolate the key factors that will lead to a solution. Sadly, many students complete their majors using fuzzy thinking. They may graduate without any distinct ideas about what they can legitimately pursue as employment options.

But let's look at an example that might feel closer to home. If you find yourself struggling at midterm with diffuse feelings of failure, fuzzy thinking can be a problem. You can wallow in the mire or you can systematically think through what factors might be contributing to your problem. Perhaps you are taking too many credits to be successful? Maybe there is an instructor whose methods set your teeth on edge? You might be struggling from sleep deprivation linked to your roommates' snoring. Perhaps a broken heart might be distracting your concentration. The more specifically you can differentiate relevant factors, the more easily you can come up with a game plan that might address the issue.

Factors in Good Decision Making

In contrast, good decision makers know why they need to make a decision and examine as many options as appropriate. They consider both short- and long-term consequences of their decisions. Good decision makers articulate the pros and cons of each option and weigh the advantages and disadvantages according to their values. They choose an option that makes the most sense given the significance of the decision.

Making decisions involves not only using higher-order thinking skills but also integrating those skills with your own values and knowledge about yourself. Good decisions solve problems and make your life better. Bad ones often make a mess. See Staying out of the Pits, "We're Only Human," for some additional tips on avoiding bad decisions Then complete the Journal activity "No Regrets" on page 148 to explore how those principles apply to your own life.

Career Connections

As soon as she was old enough to work, Rachel pursued a string of jobs to give her some spending money. Whether she was a receptionist in a hair salon, a shoe clerk, or a waitress, she seemed to take special joy in identifying, figuring out, and solving problems. Her employers commented on her initiative and regularly benefited from the creative suggestions she came up with to improve customer service. It was no surprise to those who knew her that computer studies would be a perfect match for her talents in problem solving. Her employment history and her liberal arts training gave her just the right background to thrive in her major and set her sights appropriately on a career in software engineering. That job provided an endless string of fascinating problems for her to solve.

Andy was just like most students who cringed in horror when they learned they had to give their first speech in college. Much to his surprise, he actually enjoyed making his first class presentation. He liked the challenge of coming up with an original idea, building an argument, and defending his position when challenged by classmates. He recognized that his careful research made him a real expert for the first time and he liked the feeling. By the time his college career came to an end, he decided the career that was best suited for his needs was becoming a college professor, a career that would allow him to recapture regularly the great feeling of expertise that he was introduced to in that first college assignment.

Think Creatively

College abounds with opportunities for you to build self-esteem by expanding your creative abilities. Start to become more creative by motivating yourself to exercise your creativity whenever you can. Figure 5.4, "Young Inventors," (page 139) spotlights past winners of the Collegiate Inventors Competition sponsored by the National Inventors Hall of Fame. Although you might not have the scientific creativity of an accomplished Young Inventor or the visual creativity of someone like Gary Larson, seizing opportunities to develop your creative flair will go a long way toward building your self-confidence and self-esteem.

Creative people tend to have some common characteristics (Perkins, 1984):

- They actively pursue experiences that are aesthetically pleasing. For example, they enjoy experiencing beauty in art or elegance in a scientific theory.
- They enjoy taking a unique approach to research, choosing new and exciting topics rather than going over more familiar territory that other students might address.

Creativity is allowing yourself to make mistakes. Art is knowing which ones to keep.

Scott Adams
Contemporary American cartoonist

We're Only Human

All of us make bad decisions from time to time. How can you avoid everyday errors that produce bad decisions? See the following for some helpful answers (Halpern, 1997).

- **Avoid overconfidence.** We tend to be overconfident about the correctness of our past decisions. Usually we neglect to notice that a path not taken might have been better than the one we chose. For example, you may be convinced that you chose exactly the right place to start your college education. However, you can't be completely positive, because you won't have any way to compare how you might have felt starting on other campuses. Be a little skeptical when you evaluate how wise your past decisions have been.

- **Look for evidence to disconfirm.** We tend to look for evidence to support the outcome that we prefer. We also tend to ignore information that might change our minds. For example, you may be eager to take a particular course because you have heard great things about the instructor. You pay close attention to every glowing tribute, making you feel even more motivated to get in the course. However, you may not have thought to ask questions that might weaken the case: Just how long *is* the required term paper? When buying a new car, we may pay close attention to consumer reports on what a great buy the car is but still ignore the reports that discuss the car's safety problems.

  Good decision makers actively look for evidence that could prove them wrong so that their final decisions cover all the bases.

- **Distinguish wishes from reality.** If you believe that things are always going to turn out positively, you're in for some surprises! People who expect only positive outcomes are sometimes referred to as "Pollyannas." Pollyanna is a fictional character who always finds something to be chipper about no matter how ugly her circumstances. In the throes of optimism, we can mistakenly assume that we can will what we want to happen. For example, you may think that

because you worked so hard your instructor couldn't possibly hand out the grade that your test scores predict. Think again. Good decision makers recognize that merely wishing for positive outcomes won't make it so.

- **Abandon sunken costs.** Once you've embarked on a course of action, especially if you've had to invest time or money, it may be hard to recognize a bad decision and choose a different course. For example, if you've worked your hardest and just can't seem to do well in a particular class, don't stay there just because of the time you have already invested unless you have a good strategy that could make things change positively.

  Forget the time and energy you've already sunk—they're gone!

- **Don't overreact to forceful positions.** Most Americans hate to be told what to do. Even if we might actually like a course of action, our preferences get squashed when someone tells us we *must* take that course of action. Suppose your older brother forcefully tells you to major in political science. You might think, "Not on your life!" and begin to look for other majors just to show him your independence. Despite the way he told you, your brother might be right. Good decision makers don't choose a lesser-quality alternative just to demonstrate their freedom of choice. They evaluate the quality of the suggestion apart from the manner of the person making the suggestion.

- **Overcome hindsight bias.** Suppose you're in a class where the instructor seems a bit erratic. Toward the end of the term, he fails to show up for class and another instructor reports that he quit for mental health reasons. You might think, "I knew it all along." This pattern is referred to as *hindsight bias*. One anonymous observer reported, "Hindsight bias is 20/20." It's easy to claim that we could have predicted something *after* it has already happened. Good decision makers don't waste time claiming they predicted what has become obvious.

Source: Diane Halpern, *Critical Thinking across the Curriculum.* Copyright © 1997 by Lawrence Erlbaum Associates, Inc. Reprinted by permission of the publisher.

- They love the process of creating. For example, creative students may feel as good when they turn their work in as when they get back a successful grade.
- They are flexible and like to play with problems. Although creativity is hard work, the work goes more smoothly when taken lightly; humor greases the wheels (Goleman, Kaufmann, & Ray, 1992). Playing helps them stay open to more possibilities and disarms the inner censor that often condemns ideas as off-base.

> *Don't be afraid to go on a wild goose chase. That's what wild geese are for.*
> Anonymous

Despite the stereotype that creative people are eccentric, most strive to evaluate their work fairly. Whether they use an established set of criteria or generate their own, they themselves ultimately judge the value of what they have created. Creative students thrive when they think of guidelines for assignments as a launching point for their imagination. To evaluate your own creative style, complete Self-Assessment 3 "My Creative Profile" on page 147.

FIGURE 5.4 **Winners of the 1999 Collegiate Inventors Competition**

Amy B. Smith developed an incubator that can run without electricity, which will be helpful in remote areas or developing countries in medical work and water-quality testing.

Courtesy of National Inventors Hall of Fame

William C. W. Chan developed an ultrasensitive dye that will help in the detection of a variety of diseases, including cancer, AIDS, or Down's syndrome.

Courtesy of National Inventors Hall of Fame

Tobin J. Fisher designed a new hull shape that can increase the mid- to high-wind speed performance of catamarans because it incorporates some of the design features of windsurfing.

Courtesy of National Inventors Hall of Fame

Jennifer E. Davis produces the "Twistmaster," a device that can help people with limited dexterity or arthritis open any kind of twist-off cap, including prescription containers.

Courtesy of National Inventors Hall of Fame

Source: *http://www.invent.org/induction99/collegiate.html*.

Break the Locks

Many people believe that they can't lead creative lives. You may be one of them. Despite childhoods filled with imaginative play, many of us surrender our sense of curiosity over time, harming our capacity for creativity. A variety of "mental locks" can prevent us from pursuing creative responses. Some of these locks and the "keys" for opening your mind include:

- I have to have the right answer.

  Sometimes the "right" answer isn't as much fun or as satisfying as an alternative.

- I must be logical.

  But I need to get in touch with my emotional side.

● I must follow the rules.	But breaking the rules can be really liberating!
● I have to be practical.	But not in every situation.
● Play is frivolous and wastes time.	And I miss it! I want those feelings back!
● That's not my area.	But it could be!
● I must avoid ambiguity.	But ambiguity can open new doors.
● I can't appear to be foolish.	But foolishness can be fun.
● To err is wrong.	I'm designed to derail from time to time.
● I'm not creative.	But I could be!

(Source: Derived from Roger Van Oech, *A Whack on the Side of the Head: How You Can Be More Creative*, Copyright © 1998 by Roger Van Oech. Reprinted with permission of Warner Books, Inc.)

A flexible attitude sets the stage for creativity in school and throughout your life.

Foster Creativity

Psychologists affirm that anyone can be creative if they adopt the right attitudes and behaviors (Sternberg & Lubart, 1995). The following basic steps can contribute to more creative and fulfilling lives:

1. *Don't accept other peoples' blueprints.* Question assumptions. Constantly look through and around problems to find a new approach. By moving away from how most people approach things, you may find yourself in the lead. For example, if everyone executes a PowerPoint presentation for a speaking assignment in a class, you will stand out by using the blackboard or newsprint to support your key ideas. Think about how others will execute an assignment and, within reason, choose a course that makes your work stand out positively.

2. *Be vigilant about what others can't see.* Look for new and intriguing ways to redefine the environment. Use your unique past experiences to help you pick up on things that other people will miss.

3. *Differentiate the good from the bad.* Creative people will generate many possibilities but not all of them will be appropriate. Don't linger on the ideas that don't have strong potential.

4. *Take the plunge* before *you are expert.* You don't really need to know absolutely everything about something before coming up with some new connections. In fact, sometimes too much knowledge can produce stereotyped ways of looking at the relevant facts and lead to more mundane solutions.

5. *Concentrate on the big picture.* Attending to details will help you get your creative idea across the finish line, but adopting a more holistic, global approach will help you pursue a creative lifestyle.

6. *Take sensible risks.* All creative people will face obstacles. Successful creative people will overcome them. Having courage and staying open to new experiences will contribute to selecting reasonable risks. Creative people take risks and learn from their mistakes. Picasso created more than 20,000 paintings; not all of them are masterpieces. Your learning will be limited if you don't stick out your neck once in a while. If you're considering a particularly creative approach to an assignment, however, share your plan ahead of time.

7. *Motivate yourself intrinsically.* If you concentrate on the joy of the process rather than the prospect of rewards, your creative approaches are likely to feel much more rewarding and easier to sustain over time.

8. *Shape environments that will support your creativity.* Find friends who will recognize your distinctiveness. Choose a major in which your individuality can shine. Avoid work environments that feel oppressive, mechanical, or uninspired.

Adventure is worthwhile in itself.

Amelia Earhart
American aviator

9. *Actively pursue the creative life.* If you accept the proposition that you are not creative, then you won't be. If you open yourself to maximizing your creative potential, you begin the journey. See Take Charge Of Your Imagination to help you make the commitment.

Discover "Flow"

Creative people regularly experience a heightened state of pleasure from being completely absorbed in mental and physical challenges. Mihaly Csikszentmihalyi (pronounced ME-high CHICK-sent-me-high-ee) (1995/1997) interviewed 90 prominent people in art, business, government, education, and science in a study on this subject and coined the term *flow* to describe this special state. He believes that everyone is capable of achieving flow. Some practices that can facilitate this state include:

- *Seek a surprise every day.* Maybe the surprise will be something you see, hear, or read about. Become absorbed in a lecture or a book. Be open to what the world is telling you. Life is a stream of experiences. If you swim widely and deeply, your life will be enriched.
- *Surprise at least one person every day.* In many tasks and roles you have to be predictable and patterned. Do something different for a change. Ask a question you normally would not ask. Invite someone to go to a show or a museum you've never visited. Buy a bagel for someone who shares your commute.
- *Write down each day what surprised you and how you surprised others.* Most creative people keep a diary, notes, or lab records to ensure that their experiences are not fleeting or forgotten. Start with a specific task. Each evening record the most surprising event that occurred that day and your most surprising action. After a few days, reread your notes and reflect on the past experiences. After a few weeks, you might see a pattern of interest emerging in your notes, one that may suggest an area to explore in greater depth.
- *When something sparks your interest, follow it.* Usually when something captures our attention, it's short-lived—an idea, a song, a flower. Often we're too busy to explore it further or we think we can't because we're not experts. It's none of our business. But the world *is* our business. We can't know which part of it is best suited to our interests until we make a serious effort to learn as much about as many aspects of it as possible.
- *Wake up in the morning with a specific goal.* Creative people wake up eager to start the day. Why? It's not necessarily that they are cheerful, enthusiastic types but because they know that there is something meaningful to accomplish each day and can't wait to get started.
- *Take charge of your schedule.* Figure out which time of the day is your most creative time. Some of us are most creative late at night, others early in the morning. Carve out some time for yourself when your creative energy is greatest.

Try it out. Explore the Journal activity "I Wonder . . . " on page 149 to enhance your flow.

TAKE CHARGE Of Your Imagination

If you accept the proposition that everyone has the potential to be creative, this means you, too! But you may need to rethink your environment to promote a more creative style. Here are some simple ideas to experience greater creativity on a day-to-day basis.

- *Decorate your door or bathroom mirror.* Find images, cartoons, headlines, and pictures that express who you are and put them up. The images will express to others your personality and values. You may generate some conversation with new acquaintances based on what images you post. The images can also remind you of your commitment to live a more creative life.
- *Use a thesaurus.* In writing projects, come up with new words that may have a stronger impact on your readers.
- *Use titles with pizzazz.* Don't settle for a mundane introduction to work that you have written. Imagine what ideas might be most captivating. Devote some time to helping your work stand out.
- *Sit in a different place.* Unless you are restricted by a seating chart, move around in classes or in the lunch room. Humans are creatures of habit. Break your habit. It may produce new perspective and new friends.
- *Think "connections."* Explore how what you are learning in one class might inform what you are learning in another. These connections may provide you with some novel insights that you can share during class discussion.
- *Go with your second impulse.* Your first impulse is likely to represent an easier path, perhaps arising from routine ways that you approach problems. Go with an approach that is less characteristic of your style.

Summary Strategies for Mastering College

Motivate yourself to expand and deepen your thinking skills by taking advantage of all the opportunities you'll have in and out of the classroom.

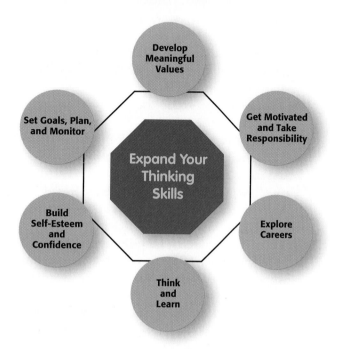

Focus on the "Six Strategies for Success" above as you read each chapter to learn how to apply these strategies to your own success.

1 Think Critically

- Recognize the role that college plays in promoting better thinking.
- Understand what critical thinking is and how it can benefit you now and in the future.
- Recognize the common features of good critical thinkers.
- Understand the different kinds of effective questions you can ask.
- Know how offering criticism can enhance critical thinking.

2 Reason

- Make accurate inferences by attending to the proper cues.
- Reject claims that mislead, give an advantage, or have no valid source.
- Accept claims based on personal experience, expert opinion, or reliable media sources.
- Evaluate arguments by looking at the logic of the premises and conclusion.
- Refine your reasoning by being open to argument, using inductive and deductive thinking, checking your assumptions, understanding your biases, and taking time before reaching conclusions.

3 Solve Problems

- Use a systematic approach to problem solving, including evaluating the consequences.
- Demonstrate good observational skills, strategic approaches, persistence, and attention to detail.
- Practice mindfulness to improve your problem-solving skills.

4 Make Good Decisions

- Practice decision-making skills that integrate your knowledge, values, and thinking skills.
- Work systematically to create the most effective decisions.
- Avoid making snap decisions or applying narrow, sprawling, or fuzzy thinking.
- Overcome personal biases.

5 Think Creatively

- Understand and imitate people with creative characteristics.
- Adopt the attitude that creativity is possible.
- Live creatively to produce a state of "flow."

Review Questions

1. List three things that distinguish good critical thinkers from bad ones. Do these characteristics apply to you? If not, how can you improve your critical thinking skills?

   1. _____
   2. _____
   3. _____

2. Write down a question you have about something you are currently studying. Is it a "good" question based on what you have read in this chapter? Analyze why or why not.

Your question: _____

Your analysis: _____

3. What steps can you take to construct a good argument?

_____

_____

_____

4. Describe the IDEAL problem-solving strategy below.
   What are some other strategies for successful problem solving?

I: _____

D: _____

E: _____

A: _____

L: _____

Additional Strategies: _____

_____

_____

_____

5. List some steps you can take now to improve your creativity.
   How can this help you achieve "flow"?

_____

_____

_____

Learning Portfolio

SELF-ASSESSMENTS

YOUR JOURNAL

STRATEGIES FOR SUCCESS

Develop Meaningful Values

Get Motivated and Take Responsibility

Set Goals, Plan, and Monitor

Expand Your Thinking Skills

Build Self-Esteem and Confidence

Explore Careers

Think and Learn

The Critical Difference

Review your general approach to intellectual challenges. Check the category that most closely corresponds with your usual pattern of critical thinking.

	Always	Usually	Sometimes	Rarely
I like to talk about topics that I know a great deal about.				
I don't pretend to know more than I really do.				
I feel energized by differences in opinion.				
I become more enthusiastic as ideas get more complicated.				
I regularly go over my thinking to spot errors.				
I like to look more deeply into things to obtain greater insight.				
I'm not afraid to change my mind.				
I prefer evidence over intuition as a way to persuade others.				
I can spot flaws in arguments.				

If you marked most of the columns "always" or "usually," you demonstrate the characteristics of a good critical thinker. Those marked "sometimes" show some room for improvement. Work on items marked "rarely" to maximize your ability to think critically.

How Systematically Do I Solve Problems?

Think about the problems you've faced in your academic and personal life in the last month. Review how regularly you went through each of the stages of the IDEAL model.

	Usually	Not Usually	Explain
Identification: I accurately identify when something needs attention.			
Definition: I describe problems comprehensively, including all factors that might influence the problem.			
Evaluation: I figure out different approaches to take and decide on the best alternative.			
Action: I put my plans into action.			
Looking back: I purposefully examine how effective my chosen solutions are.			

As you examine the results of your review, which aspects of problem solving are your strengths? What elements do you need to practice to become more systematic in your problem solving? What ideas do you have for incorporating these skills into your problem-solving style?

My Creative Profile

To get some measure of your creative potential, answer the following:

1. If you were managing a rock group, what original name would you give them?

2. You've been asked to plan a birthday party for your five-year-old nephew. How would you make it different from other parties his friends have attended?

3. How many uses can you think of for a pencil?

4. What kind of musical instrument could you make out of the contents of the junk drawer in your family's kitchen?

5. You've just been invited to a costume party. What will you wear?

6. What theme would you propose for a sales campaign for your favorite shoe?

7. What business could you establish that would make the lives of your classmates easier? What would you call the business? How would you promote and develop it?

8. What is one strategy you could develop that would make people less afraid of failure?

9. You have to negotiate a late deadline for a paper with your professor. How might you do that creatively?

10. How many creative uses can you think of for a remote control unit?

This assessment highlights flexible thinking. If you found yourself stumped by most of the items, then you may not have developed the flexible mindset that helps creative people. If you answered a few of the questions, then you can probably point to a few creative areas in your life. If you felt exhilarated by the questions, chances are good that you're often creative.

Your Journal

● REFLECT

1. No Regrets

Do a postmortem about an important decision you made that was very satisfying to you. For example, did you select the right college to begin your academic career? What about the process helped to ensure that your decision would be right? What aspects of this process can you practice regularly in making sound decisions in the future?

_____

_____

2. Minding the Store

How often do you find yourself slipping up by not paying full attention to what you are doing? On a scale of 1 to 10, rate how "mindful" you are on a day-to-day basis. Next, think about the circumstances that tend to trigger greater mindfulness. When are you in top form functioning in a mindful manner? What situations encourage you to be mindless? Speculate about some of the losses you may have incurred from mindless behavior. What would you have to do to make mindfulness your standard way of operating?

_____

_____

● DO

1. A Question a Day

Sometimes it's hard to overcome the impression that if you ask questions, other people will think you don't know what's going on. Good questions show just the opposite—that you're alert, thoughtful, and invested. For at least one week, make a point to ask a good question in each of your classes. Bring it up in class, ask your instructor after class, or e-mail your question. How did this improve your ability to ask questions? How did you feel about becoming more actively involved in your learning?

_____

_____

2. Claims Detector

Record the claims you hear in the media for one day. Commercials are especially good targets for this activity. Pick the claim that is most interesting to you and see if you can convert the commercial claims into premises and conclusions. Should you accept the claim, reject the claim, or suspend judgment based on the evidence offered?

CLAIM:_____

PREMISES:_____

_____

_____

CONCLUSION:_____

ACCEPT, REJECT, OR SUSPEND JUDGMENT:_____

Your Journal

● THINK CRITICALLY

1. The Great Debate

Think about an issue or controversy that stirred your feelings in one of your classes and record it below. Perhaps it was a political concern or a strong reaction you had to a poem or painting. Briefly map your position on this issue by providing the key ideas that support it. Now assume you've been assigned to argue the opposite side in a debate. Map this position as well. Did careful mapping of the opposing side do anything to weaken your commitment to the original position?

Your Issue:_____

Your Position:_____

Key Ideas:_____

_____

_____

Opposing Position:_____

Key Ideas:_____

_____

_____

2. Your "IDEAL"

Consider an important issue in your life right now and apply the "IDEAL" problem-solving strategy listed below. Did this help you come up with some ideas for resolving this issue? Why or why not?

Identify the Problem: _____

Define the Problem: _____

Explore Alternative Approaches: _____

Act on the Best Strategy:_____

Look Back to Evaluate the Effects:_____

● CREATE

1. "I Wonder . . ."

Here is a simple exercise to increase your creative thinking. Each day for a week, take a few minutes to ask yourself a question that begins with "I wonder . . ." Ask this question about a particular aspect of your life. It's important not to censor yourself, no matter how impractical or outlandish the question sounds. After you practice doing this, pose your questions to your friends. Focus on something that you're sincerely curious about and that matters to others. Listen carefully to your friends' responses. You'll probably discover that your questions have some assumptions that deserve to be challenged or fine-tuned (Goleman, Kaufman, & Ray, 1993).

2. Creative Surfing

Find out what the Internet has to offer concerning problem solving. Enter "problem solving" into a search engine and visit at least three sites that address the issue. List the sites and their main premises below. What did you learn about problem solving? Why has the Internet become such a boon to problem solving?

Site #1:_____

Site#2:_____

Site #3:_____

Applying the Six Strategies for Success

What did you learn in this chapter that you can apply to the following key strategies to help form the foundation for your success? Write down all of the main points you can remember that support the following strategies:

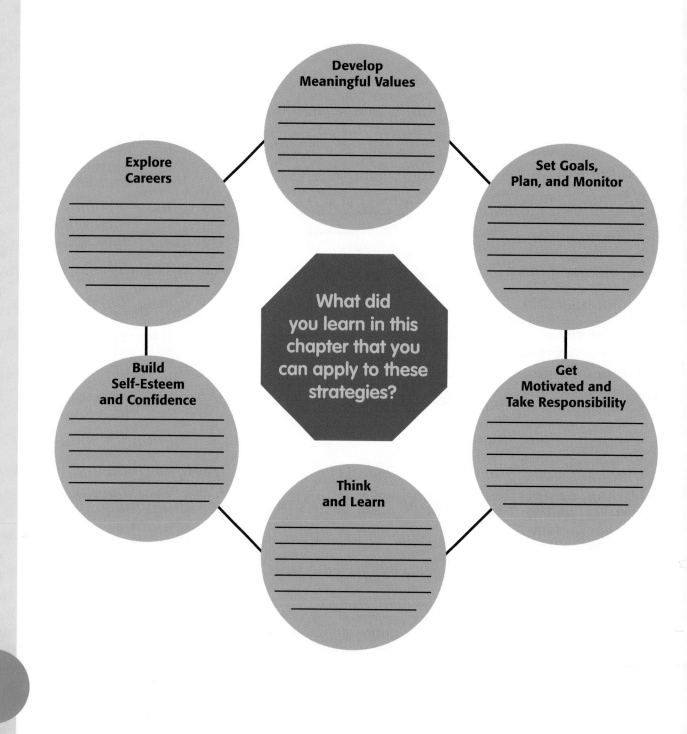

6

Take It In: Notes and Reading

Where Are You? To succeed in college, you need to take charge of new ideas and make good judgments about their importance to your learning. In other words, learn strategies for being *selective* about the information you take in.

To see where you are right now, place a check mark next to only those items that apply to you.

- I'm very organized about the way I absorb information from lectures, group work, and textbooks.

- I use many different strategies to figure out what's most important to learn.

- I know how to keep myself focused during difficult lectures.

- I'm familiar with different note-taking methods.

- I know the difference between primary and secondary research sources and the value of each.

- I use various strategies to read more effectively and efficiently.

- I use my notes to improve my learning as well as my test performance.

As you read the following profile of Ann Coulter, consider how you could benefit from the successful strategies she used to gather information and use it in original ways.

Images of College Success

Ann Coulter

If you are a fan of *West Wing* reruns, no doubt you have been impressed by the quick-witted, acid tongued Ainsley Hayes, a staunch conservative coping with the stresses of working in a liberal White House. Many social critics have speculated that attorney Ann Coulter is the model for the *West Wing* character. An author and frequent guest on news talk shows, Coulter's facile mind and confident expression comes from having done her homework.

Ann grew up in Connecticut and attended Cornell University. Following graduation, she enrolled in the University of Michigan Law School where she served as editor of the law review. Her earliest legal assignments for the Department of Justice Honors program involved child pornography.

She first captured public attention when she came to the defense of Paula Jones, a young woman who charged President Clinton with sexual harassment. Her "take-no-prisoners" approach to political rhetoric caused an uproar when she suggested the British handled impeachment most wisely by treating it as a hanging offense (Friedland, 2003).

Coulter's ability to speak in unvarnished ways have won her many friends and a host of enemies. Some see her as the female counterpart to Rush Limbaugh. Her column is carried by conservative news magazines. Her book, *Treason: Liberal Treachery From The Cold War To The War On Terrorism,* made it to the top of the *New York Times* bestselling nonfiction list.

Being able to champion a distinctive viewpoint comes from her ability to identify critical pieces of research, track down sometimes obscure documents, sift through the information carefully, and interpret these findings.

Revered by conservatives and reviled by liberals, **ANN COULTER** built an impressive career in the media based on her ability to capture ideas.

Identify Meaningful Values

Explore Careers

Set Goals, Plan, and Monitor

Take It In

Build Self-Esteem and Confidence

Get Motivated and Take Responsibility

Think and Learn

Motivate yourself by adopting helpful strategies to select, think about, and learn new ideas that college has to offer. As you read, think about the "Six Strategies for Success" listed to the left and how this chapter can help you maximize success in these important areas, particularly "Think and Learn."

Commit, Concentrate, Capture, Connect

College requires you to sift through and master an extraordinary amount of information. Extracting what you need from lectures and textbooks is no small feat, especially given differences in learning styles that make some tasks more challenging for you than others.

This chapter describes a simple, easy-to-remember approach for sorting through information and making good decisions about what you need to learn and how to best learn it—the "four C's":

- *Commit* yourself to do your best work.
- *Concentrate* to eliminate distractions and focus on the material.
- *Capture* critical information.
- *Connect* new ideas to what you already know.

This approach can be applied to your classes and reading assignments to help you learn more effectively.

Take Charge of Lectures

First let's apply the four C's to getting the most from classes.

Commit to Class

Some classes will be exciting from start to finish. You'll look forward to these lectures and linger after each. It's easy to follow through on your commitment to learning when courses match your learning style or personal interest. When the content of the class or the style of the lecturer is not a good match, making a strong commitment to attend class is even more important. This commitment involves more than just showing up, however. You commit to the work involved as well. Before each class, get ready to learn.

> *The only place you find success before work is in the dictionary.*
> May V. Smith
> *American government specialist*

Anticipate Review your notes from the last class as well as your reading assignment. Identify any areas that are difficult to understand and think about questions that could clarify them. Or search the Web to find other sources that might clarify these areas. Read your syllabus to determine the topics for discussion in class, and make sure you have done any reading associated with these lecture topics.

Think about the format for the class, and prepare appropriately. Will it be a lecture, lab, or seminar? A seminar requires a different type of attention than a lecture. These strategies will help you anticipate how the class will flow and what ideas will be most important.

Be on Time Even better, arrive a few minutes early. This gives you a chance to review your notes before class, and be ready to go as soon as the instructor begins. Well-organized instructors often use the first few minutes of class to review the previous class. This allows you to rehearse what you've been learning. Like reviewing your notes, it also sets the stage for how the upcoming class will unfold, which will help you get organized and figure out what's most important.

Don't Miss Classes The best way to be prepared is to attend all your classes. Even if you haven't done the assigned reading, the class will still be worthwhile. The lecture may be so fascinating that it makes it easier to sit down and do a double dose of reading in preparation for the next class. If you can't attend class, use good judgment about how to compensate. See Staying out of the Pits, "Any Old Notes Won't Do," for some good advice.

Do the Assignments Assignments aren't usually optional. Instructors design assignments to help students develop expertise in the content and skills that the course has to offer. If you decide not to submit an assignment, you don't just lose points. You lose ground. From the outset of the class, plan how to complete all of your assignments to get the most from your courses.

Some students assume that reading assignments aren't all that important because the instructor will cover the material in class. This is not a wise assumption. Many instructors assign reading as a related but independent resource; they do not review them. Successful students complete assigned readings, *before* class to better understand the lecture. Connections and overlaps between the lecture and reading reinforce their learning. Another reason to complete reading assignments is that you may be called on to report your impressions. It's embarrassing when you haven't got a clue what to say.

Concentrate

Many things influence concentration. For example, if you're an auditory learner or have a natural interest in the topic, extracting what you need from a lecture may not be hard. Other circumstances, though, will require you to take a more strategic approach to concentration.

Minimize Distractions You can do many things to minimize distractions:

1. *Sit near the front.* If you can't see or hear clearly, find a spot where you can.
2. *Reduce noise.* The instructor may not realize how noisy the room is for you, so do what you need to ensure your best hearing.

Close doors and windows to reduce unwanted noise. Move away from chatty neighbors.

3. *Reduce off-task pressures.* Get the sleep you need, and eat before class to quiet a growling stomach. If a specific worry keeps bothering you, write it down separately from your notes. Promise yourself that you'll worry about it later, so you can let it go for now.

4. *Stay tuned in.* If something in the lecture distresses you—either content or delivery style—concentrate on identifying more precisely what bothers you and how you can best resolve the problem. Focus on hearing what you most likely will be tested on. Breathe deeply and use other stress management techniques to stay in tune. If you tend to get off track from too much daydreaming, see the Journal activity "Daydream Believer" on page 184 to help you conquer your drift.

5. *Track your progress.* Keep records of how much time you spend paying attention. At the end of each class, estimate what percentage of time you were on track and write it in the upper right-hand corner of your notes. Try to make regular improvements in your rate.

Instructors differ in their ability to lecture. Some make learning easy; others make it tough. Sometimes students react differently to the same lecturer. For example, some lecturers enchant students by sharing personal anecdotes, but some students find these examples annoying and time wasting. Develop your skills at listening so that you can compensate for any skills in speaking that the instructor may lack. See On Target Tips, "Tame That Tough Lecture," for some pointers.

Listen Actively To succeed you need to concentrate. One way to do this is to listen actively. On average, speakers talk using about 150 words per minute, and listeners can process about 500 words per minute, more than three times the speed of speech (Nichols, 1961). This means that even when instructors talk very fast, you should have plenty of time to understand them. Put that extra time to best use through *active listening.*

Active listeners sort through the information they hear and figure out what's most important. They connect what they hear with things they already know. Although it's hard work, active listening is an efficient way to get the most from a lecture. The next sections provide some specific strategies to build your active learning skills.

In contrast, passive listeners merely write down the instructor's words without necessarily understanding the ideas or making judgments about their importance. This approach shifts actual learning to a later time, when the ideas have already faded. Don't delay the job of understanding. Putting it off not only makes ideas harder to learn, it also takes time from preparations for the next assignment.

Capture Key Ideas

Some instructors will help you spot their main ideas by starting with a preview, outline, or map of the material that a lecture will cover. Others won't, but they will still expect you to grasp their organization (even when it's obscure) and recognize key ideas. Successful note taking involves your flexible use of structures

> *The first duty of a lecturer—to hand you after an hour's discourse a nugget of pure truth to wrap up between the pages of your notebooks and keep on your mantelpiece forever.*
>
> Virginia Woolf
> *20th-century British novelist and literary critic*

ON TARGET TIPS

Tame That Tough Lecture

THE FAST-TALKING LECTURER

Enthusiastic instructors may talk too fast for you to catch what they're saying. When you're confronted with a fast talker:

- **Say "Slow down."** Most fast-talking instructors know that they talk too fast. Many appreciate getting feedback so they can adjust their pace.
- **Encourage the instructor to write down the key terms.** Seeing them written down will help you understand them. Also, when the instructor writes on the board, you may be able to catch up.
- **Focus on the major thrust, not the detail.** Fast talkers are hardest for students who attempt to take notes word for word. Concentrate on the major ideas instead.

THE BEWILDERING LECTURER

Some instructors simply use more sophisticated language than you may be used to hearing. When your instructor is hard to understand,

- **Prepare for class carefully.** If you do the assigned readings before class, you'll already be familiar with many key terms.
- **Ask for restatements.** If you persist in asking for interpretations when instructors' language is too complex, many will simplify it to avoid losing the time it takes to reexplain.
- **Change your attitude.** Think about this kind of instructor as eloquent rather than obtuse. He or she gives you extra education for your tuition dollar. You may emerge from the class with an enriched vocabulary.

(Continued)

ON TARGET TIPS

Tame That Tough Lecture (Continued)

THE DISORGANIZED LECTURER

Some lecturers organize poorly. They go off on tangents or don't teach from an organized plan. If you have a chaotic instructor:

- **Look at the big picture.** Concentrate on the larger themes so that you won't feel overwhelmed by disconnected details.
- **Form a study group.** Pool your resources to make sense of the teaching.
- **Impose organization.** Use note-taking strategies that will help you see the connections between the ideas. Try to organize the lecture materials to give them some structure, such as creating an outline.

THE TEDIOUS LECTURER

Instructors give boring lectures because they have lost interest in their work or don't understand classroom dynamics well. Some instructors even suffer from stage fright. If you have a boring instructor,

- **Make connections.** Breathe more life into the lecture by applying what you hear to what you already know.
- **Ask questions that encourage examples.** Stories have a natural appeal. They can arouse and sustain attention. By requesting an illustration of a key point, you may help the instructor add life to the lecture. Although this may be easiest to accomplish in small classes, you can also ask for examples in visits during office hours.
- **Show active interest in the lecture.** Sit in the front row, maintain good eye contact, nod your head, and smile occasionally to motivate teachers to give you their best work.

and format that will best serve your learning. You may need to experiment in each class until you find just the right notetaking groove. What are some strategies you can use to recognize key points?

Identify Key Words, Themes, and Main Points Often these are ideas that the instructor repeats, highlights, illustrates with examples, supports with related facts, or displays on a blackboard or screen.

Most instructors organize courses around a central set of terms. Any unfamiliar term or phrase is a new idea you need to learn. Such terms often represent the specialized language of the discipline you're studying. Recognizing broader themes may be more challenging. Sometimes your instructor will give you an overarching theme to help you organize what you're about to hear. If the instructor does not, make a point to think about what theme the details of the lecture suggest and how they relate to themes from previous lectures. Try to keep the big picture in mind so you don't feel overwhelmed by the details.

How can you tell the difference between a central idea and the details used to support the idea? Facts, stories, predictions, analogies, statistics, opinions, comparisons, and explanations provide the details to drive the main point home.

Recognize Organization Patterns in the Lecture Academic information comes in predictable patterns (Strong, Silver, Perini, & Tuculescu, 2002). Listen for some key words that will signal these patterns of how main points and supporting details relate. This anticipation will help you to grasp the logic and flow of the lecture and minimize the tendency to get lost in details and digressions. Some examples of such patterns include:

- *Listing Patterns:* All of the relevant facts, concepts, and events are presented in simple lists that reflect order of importance. Signal words include *first, second, also, in addition, another, moreover, next, furthermore.*
- *Comparison Patterns:* This pattern focuses on similarities and differences. Signal words include *on one hand, similarly, in contrast, but, then, either, or, compared to, opposite of, like.*
- *Sequence Patterns:* Many times instructors will incorporate timelines, chronologies, or procedural steps or stages to show how things are fixed in a certain order. Signal words include *first, second, finally, while, now, then, next.*
- *Cycle Patterns:* Cycle patterns of organization show how trends end up where they started. Signal words include *first, second, finally, while, now, then, same, circular.*
- *Problem-Solving Patterns:* In this type of organization, the instructor identifies a problem, establishes conditions for solving the problem, explains the solution, and predicts the aftereffects. Signal words include *since, resulting, hypothesis, leading to, because, so, if . . . then, solution.*
- *Cause-Effect Patterns:* This pattern involves showing causal connections between two events. Signal words include *prediction, effect, causation, control.*
- *Example Patterns:* This pattern involves defining a concept and then offering examples or illustrations to clarify or explain the term. Signal words include *for example, for instance, other examples include, such as.*

Reprinted by permission of Vivian Scott Hixon.

Relate Details to the Main Point Instructors use stories, examples, or analogies to reinforce your learning of main points. They usually intend their stories to do more than entertain. Check to make sure you understand why the instructor chose a particular story or example. Pay attention to how much the instructor relies on important details at test time. Some instructors may expect you to be accountable for all of the details. Others will pay less attention to your rote recall of minutiae, but will instead emphasize your ability to communicate your understanding of the main ideas with the most important details.

Listen for Clues Pay special attention to words that signal a change of direction or special emphasis. For example, note when a concept or topic comes up more than once. Such a topic is likely to show up on an exam. Transition speech, such as "in contrast to" or "let's move on to" or even "this will be on the next exam," signals the change of topics or emergence of new key points. Lists usually signify important material that is also easy to test. Instructors are most likely to test for ideas that they consider exciting, so listen for any special enthusiasm.

Work on Your "Sixth Sense" Some students just know when an instructor is covering key ideas, especially material that's likely to be on the test. They sit, pencils poised, and wait for the instructor to get to the good stuff. Actively categorize what your instructor is saying by asking questions such as

- Is this statement central to my understanding of today's topic?
- Does this example help clarify the main ideas?
- Is this a tangent (an aside) that may not help me learn the central ideas?

To get some practice refining your ability to predict test questions, see the Journal activity "Analyze the Sixth Sense" on page 185.

Save Your Energy Don't write down what you already know. Besides covering new material, lectures usually overlap some with material in required textbooks. If you have read your assignment, you should be able to recognize when the lecture overlaps the text. Open your text and follow along, making notes in the margins where the instructor stays close to the text. Pay closer attention when what you hear sounds unfamiliar.

Connect Ideas

The best listeners don't just check in with the speaker from time to time. They work at listening by using strategies to create more enduring impressions of the lecture and to escape daydreaming.

Paraphrase What You Hear If you can't translate the ideas from a lecture into your own words, you may need to do more reading or ask more questions until you are able to do so.

Relate Key Ideas to What You Already Know When you can see how the course ideas connect to other aspects of your life, including your experiences in other courses or contemporary events, the ideas will be easier to remember. For example, if you're studying in sociology how societies organize into different economic classes, think about how those ideas apply to the neighborhood where you grew up.

Make a Note of Unknown Words Sometimes unknown words are a signal that you've missed something in a previous lecture. If you take notes on a laptop, you may be able to look up meanings in an electronic dictionary as you go. Consider making a file in your word processing program to store these terms for easy review. If not, write the word at the top of your notes and look it up right after class. Keep a running list of the words that gave you trouble. Your list becomes a natural tool for review before exams.

Own Your Confusion It's inevitable. Sometimes you will be confused. The instructor may use terms you don't understand or present relationships that may be too subtle to grasp the first time you hear them. If English is your second language, there may be other reasons why you lose your way. The instructor may speak too fast for you to process the information. Clearly mark your notes with a question mark or other code that identifies this is an area you need to revisit. Make a point to confer with classmates, check on the internet, explore your text for backup support, or even talk with instructor after class until you get back on the right path.

Get Involved When you determine the direction that the class will take, you can come up with examples that make ideas more compelling. Suggest those examples to the instructor. Say, "Would this be an example of what you are talking about?" Ask questions. Answer questions when the instructor asks them. Participate in discussions that are prompted by the lecture. No matter what form your involvement takes, it will help you stay engaged with the ideas in the lecture.

Take Great Lecture Notes

Taking great notes is your opportunity to think and learn actively during your time in class. With proper planning and monitoring, great notes will cut your review time and help consolidate your learning.

Develop Your Style

Successful students take good notes. The quality of their work is based on the quality of their drive. By connecting your work during lectures with your future prospects, you can find the energy to excel.

A successful note-taking style reflects not just the complexity of the course content and lecturer's style but your own learning preferences as well. If you're a visual learner, use images, arrows, or other graphic organizers to help you remember the important material more easily. Color-code parts of your notes or draw sketches. Use any strategy that will help the key ideas stand out. If you're an auditory learner, you may thrive in lectures; however, you may be tempted to take down every word. See Staying out of the Pits, "It's Not Dictation," for some good advice.

Sometimes students use note taking to dodge the hard work of paying careful attention in class. Writing notes occupies their attention when their learning might be better served by devoting 100 percent attention to the lecture. Experiment with your ability to concentrate in class. Make a prior arrangement with a classmate who takes notes successfully to show you what has been recorded. Rather than taking notes yourself, attend completely to the lecture. Then examine the notes afterward to see how effectively you have learned. Taking responsibility to learn—rather than record—may make some permanent changes in how you approach note taking.

Choose the Best Method

Once you get beyond the idea of taking notes verbatim, you have numerous good options. Choose one that suits your learning needs and preferences. Here are several popular note-taking methods.

Summary Method In this approach, monitor the lecture for critical ideas and pause at intervals to summarize what you think is most important. Summarizing appeals most to students with auditory learning preferences. They are comfortable in the world of words and have learned to trust that they can extract the key ideas after the fact. Translating the material into their own words provides great writing practice.

Writing summaries may be somewhat time-consuming, but it helps you take responsibility for judging what is crucial and relating that to other aspects of the course. It's also an effective way to handle a disorganized lecturer. However, with the summary method you run the risk that some key ideas might be overlooked.

Outlining An outline summarizes key points and sub-points as demonstrated in Figure 6.1. The summary of headings at the beginning of each chapter of this book is another example of an outline. When you use an outline form, the results are neat and well organized. Naturally, outlines are easiest to create when the lecture itself is well organized. Some outliners don't use numbers and letters because the task is too distracting. They simply use indentations to signify sub-points. What kind of learner likes to outline? The distinctiveness of an outline appeals to students who are especially good at analysis and critical thinking.

Students who like to analyze tend to enjoy constructing a representation of the lecture that clearly highlights the main points with supportive details tucked neatly under subheadings. The outline shows the relationship among ideas and reduces distracting verbiage to its key points, showcased by a systematic visual display that can be easier for visual than auditory learners.

However, it may not always be easy to impose a crisp outline on a messy presentation. That challenge can sometimes divert the outliner's attention from listening to the

FIGURE 6.1 Take It In

This format organizes lecture coverage by main headings and subheadings.

Chapter 6

Target Information

I. Commit, Concentrate, Capture, Connect
   A. Identifying what you need is hard work
      1. From lecture
      2. From text
   B. 4-part approach can help make good decisions

II. Take Charge of Lectures
   A. Commit to the course
      1. Not hard to commit when interest is high
      2. When not a good match . . .
         a. Be present
         b. Be ready
         c. Be punctual

   B. Concentrate
      1. Overcome distractions
         a. Sit near front
         b. Reduce noise
         c. Reduce off-task pressures
         d. Stay tuned in
         e. Track your progress
      2. Adapt to Teaching Styles
         a. To cope with fast talkers
            (1) Tell them "Slow down"
            (2) Ask them to write down key words
            (3) Focus on key ideas
         b. To cope with bewildering lecturers . . .

content of the lecture to the process of creating an acceptable outline. However, outlining will sharpen critical thinking skills because it provides practice in analyzing the course content when done properly.

The Cornell System Draw a vertical line down your looseleaf or notebook page about 2½ inches from the left edge of the page as shown in Figure 6.2. Draw a horizontal line across the page about two inches from the bottom. Use the largest area on the right side of the page to take your notes during class. After class is over, use the blank left side of the page to write short headings or questions for each part of your notes. Use the bottom of the page for a summary or other comments and questions.

The Cornell system creates a great tool for reviewing. Cover up the right-hand portion of the page and use the phrases or questions on the left side as prompts. As you read each prompt, practice recalling the details on the right. Choose the Cornell Method if you demonstrate a preference for auditory learning and show conscientiousness about review. The format commits you to working actively with verbal representation of the notes, capturing themes, analyzing trends, and generating questions. The Cornell Method can also be combined with summarizing or outlining to take advantage of the strengths of those approaches.

Concept Maps A concept map provides visual cues about how ideas are related, as shown in Figure 6.3. Some students construct concept maps during class from lecture notes. Others may draw concept maps after class as a way to review the material.

Concept maps appeal to visual learners with a creative flair. They are more engaging to create and facilitate recall better than other formats for visual learners. A risk with this method, however, is that the concept mapper can be more drawn to the creative process and committed to making an aesthetically pleasing map than in listening to the content of the lecture and correctly identifying the relationships being represented.

FIGURE 6.2 The Cornell Method

The Cornell method separates running notes taken during class from summary phrases and an overall summary or comments added after class. To review, cover the material on the right and practice recalling it from the cues on the left.

Cues	Notes
	Dr. King -- Psychology 21 Tues. 9-14-02
	Topic: Optimism & Pessimism -- Seligman's theory
Success: 2 keys or 3?	Talent and desire, 2 keys to success. Is there a 3rd key-- "optimism"? (=expecting to succeed)? The real test=how you react when something bad happens. Give up or fight on?
Lab studies on learning/unlearning helplessness	Psych lab experiments can teach dogs to be helpless. If dog is trained to think it has no control over when it will get shocked, it starts acting helpless even when it could jump away & not get shocked. Same type thing happens to people in childhood. If they don't think they can change things, they act helpless: pessimistic. But you can also train a dog out of being helpless. All depends on expecting to be or not be in control.
	How optimists vs. pessimists explain bad events.
	Pessimist:
"P P P"	1. Personal-- "Bad things are my fault."
	2. Permanent-- "Can't get better."
	3. Pervasive-- "Affects everything I do."
	Optimist:
	1. Impersonal-- "Bad things not my fault."
	2. Momentary-- "Can change tomorrow."
	3. Particular-- "Doesn't affect the rest of me."
Pessimism → depression	Everyone can get depressed, but pessimists stay depressed longer. Why? Because of how they explain things.
Therapy = Change explanations	Cognitive therapy: Change the way pessimist explains things to cure their depression. How? First get them to hear what they tell themselves when things go bad. Then get them to change what they say.

Seligman found that desire and talent don't always win. Optimism also important. Pessimists can become "helpless" in hard times. Optimists recover faster. Training pessimists to think more optimistically might reduce depression. Q: But how does it work? Find out Thursday!

FIGURE 6.3 The Concept Map

A concept map is a helpful tool for visual learners. It displays the key ideas in a lecture or resource and shows how the ideas relate to each other.

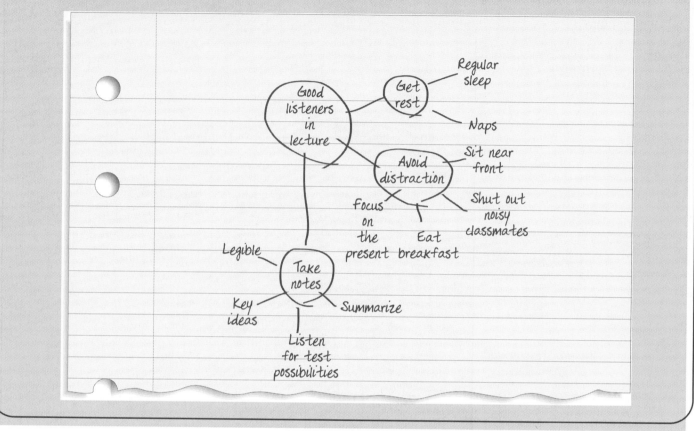

Master Note-Taking Strategies

You'll learn a great deal by taking careful notes. Whichever format you choose, combine it with the following strategies:

Clearly Identify the Class Be sure to include the topic or title of the lecture, if any, along with its date. This notation will make it easier to track down specific information in sequential order when it's time to review. Include your name and e-mail address or phone number in case you lend your notes to a classmate or they become lost.

Reduce to Key Ideas Simplify what you record from lectures to the fewest words possible in order to capture the key ideas. Shorter notes will facilitate easier review and allow you to concentrate on the most critical details.

Take Notes from All Relevant Input Some students believe that only the instructor's input is worth recording. However, the instructor may treat any class material as fair game for testing, even when other students introduce the ideas. Also remember to summarize the relevant details from videos or films that are shown in class.

Don't Erase Mistakes Erasing takes more time than crossing out an error. Drawing a line also lets you restore the information later if you need it.

FIGURE 6.4 Common Abbreviations for Notes

Using your own abbreviations or the standard abbreviations in this list will save you time when you take notes.

i.e.	= that is (to clarify by restating a point)	<	= less than
e.g.	= for example (to clarify by adding a typical case)	>	= more than
vs.	= versus (to identify a contrasting point)	k	= $1,000 (as in 10 k for 10 thousand; k = kilo)
∴	= therefore (to come to a conclusion)	~	= approximately
∵	= because	??	= I'm confused
w/	= with	*	= important, testable
w/o	= without	@	= at
→	= leads to		

Use Abbreviations Use standard abbreviations to record information quickly. Figure 6.4, "Common Abbreviations for Notes" suggests some simple substitutions. Develop your own abbreviations for words that you need to write often. For example, you can abbreviate academic disciplines, such as *PSY, BIO, EN,* and *LIT.* When instructors use terms regularly throughout the course, develop abbreviations for them as well. For example, *EV* might stand for *evolution* or *A/R* for *accounts receivable.* When you use personalized abbreviations, write their meanings inside the cover of your notebook as a handy reference.

Review Your Notes Often Review your notes right after class whenever possible. Some students like to rewrite or type up their notes after class as a way of consolidating information. If you don't rewrite, at least reread your notes to add whatever might be missing. Highlight certain phrases, identify the key points, or revise notes that are unclear. Review your notes between classes to consolidate your learning. Some students review notes from the previous class just before the next meeting as a way to get back into the subject.

Tape Lectures Selectively Some students like to tape lectures as a backup for the notes, but it isn't always a good idea. Tape the lecture only if you

- Need the complete text of a lecture, as when the content is extremely difficult or tricky
- Have a learning disability that hinders listening carefully or accurately
- Have a plan for how to listen regularly to the tapes
- Take advantage of commuting time to listen
- Must be absent but can get a classmate to tape for you

Without a plan or special need to justify taping, you will end up with a pile of cassettes that you never listen to. You also may not listen as carefully as you might the first time but still not use the tape.

Organize Your Materials for Easy Retrieval A separate notebook or compartment in a binder for each subject can improve your efficiency. Three-ring binders allow you to rearrange and add pages. Write on only one side of the page to make your notes easy to arrange and review later. Some students, especially tactile learners, use index cards because they're easy to carry, organize, and review.

Request Feedback about Your Notes Especially in classes where you struggle with note taking, see your instructor during office hours and ask for help. Ask whether you are capturing the main ideas in your notes; if not, discuss ways to improve your note taking. Complete the Journal activity "Show and Tell" on page 184 to prepare you to get that extra support.

Evaluate Your Note-Taking Strategy When you get a test back, examine the structure of your notes to see what accounted for your success. Continue to practice the strategies that served you well. Modify practices that may have made it hard for you to learn or test well. Evaluate your own style of listening by completing Self-Assessment 1 "Auditing Your Note-Taking Style for Lectures" on page 181. The results will show where you can improve.

Take Charge of Your Reading

The four C's—Commit, Concentrate, Capture, and Connect—work as well for reading as for note taking. A systematic approach to reading will allow you to achieve your reading goals and make your learning more efficient.

Commit to Reading Goals

Use Self-Assessment 2 "What's Your Reader Profile?" on page 182 to see how your reading skills stack up. Then consider these additional strategies for improving your these skills.

- *Stay positive.* Keep a positive attitude. Others have succeeded before you. If they could manage, so can you. If you approach your reading with a feeling of defeat, you may give up instead of pulling through.
- *Make the author your companion.* Most authors envision themselves talking to their readers as they write. As you read, imagine talking to the author as a way of making your reading more lively. When you approach reading as one end of a conversation, it may be easier to make comments, to see relationships, and to be critical.
- *Pace yourself according to the difficulty level.* When you're naturally drawn to a reading or it fits in well with your abilities or interests, you may not have to struggle to get the key ideas. However, you may need to read some difficult writing three or four times before it begins to make sense. When you have two or more kinds of reading to complete, read the harder or duller one first, while your concentration is strongest. We all struggle with hard material—that's normal.
- *Take breaks.* Plan to take breaks at regular intervals throughout a reading session. How long you can read between breaks depends on how hard you have to work to grasp the ideas. Examine the material to see whether there are natural breaks, such as the ends of sections, that correspond to your attention span. Reward yourself when you've completed each reading goal. Go for a walk, visit briefly with someone, or do some pleasure reading.
- *Shift gears when you do not make progress.* A fresh start may be required if you find yourself reading and rereading the same passage. Try writing a note on the reading. Take a break. Get something to drink. Call a classmate to confer about your struggle. Return to the passage with an intention to read more slowly until the clouds part.
- *Find other sources if the reading is confusing.* Sometimes an author's style is hard to comprehend. For nonfiction, find a clearer book on the same topic at the library

or bookstore. Make sure that it covers things similar to your assigned test. Browsing the Internet may be helpful as well. Some bookstores sell guides to certain disciplines that may help to clarify basic ideas. Keep your introductory textbooks as references for when you are challenged in later, tougher courses. Get help from an instructor or tutor in finding other sources.

- *Build your vocabulary.* College is a great place to expand your vocabulary. In the process of learning the specialized languages in a discipline, you'll also expand your general vocabulary. Get a dictionary or use the electronic version on your computer to look up words you don't know. Once you look up a word, practice using the word to help you remember it. Visualize some situation related to the word. Keep a list of new words and their meanings on an index card to use as a bookmark or in an electronic file on your computer.

If you don't have a dictionary nearby when you need it, you may be able to use "word attack" skills to understand a word. That is, you can often divide a word into parts that give you hints about the meaning. Knowing common prefixes and suffixes (word beginnings and endings) can help. See Figure 6.5, "Word Attack Skills," for some common examples. Sometimes you can also determine the meaning of a word from the context of the sentence.

- *Work on reading faster.* Fast readers tend to be more effective learners than slow readers, not only because they remember more of what they read but also because they save valuable time (Armstrong & Lampe, 1990). Evaluate your reading speed by completing Self-Assessment 3 "How Fast Do You Read?" on page 183.

  Improve your reading speed by concentrating on processing more words with each sweep of your eye across a line of text. For example, if you normally scan three words at a time, practice taking in four words with each scan or scan to read whole phrases instead of individual words. You can also ask to have your reading abilities tested formally by reading specialists at the college. They can help you identify specific problems and solutions. See Staying out of the Pits, "Watch What You Say," for some other pointers about reading speed.

- *Set goals.* Make commitments that will help you feel more responsible for what you've read. Join a study group or promise to tutor another student who needs to help. Some students negotiate with their instructors about how they can contribute to class on a given day. This strategy is especially helpful for shy students.

Plan Time and Space to Concentrate

College reading takes concentration. Schedule blocks of time for reading in a place where you won't be interrupted. On your main schedule, set aside times for study. Clear other concerns from your mind so you can concentrate.

Students differ about where they prefer to read. Many like the library. Others find it *too* quiet or too full of distracting people. Try out a few settings to find out which ones work best for you.

STAYING OUT OF THE PITS
Watch What You Say

One bad habit that many students fall into is *subvocalizing,* or concentrating on sounding out words as they read. Some students actually mouth words as they read, which is quite inefficient. However, others subvocalize with their mouths closed. Subvocalizing dramatically slows down your reading because it limits your reading speed to how fast you talk. Concentrating on reading phrases or passages is much more efficient. Your reward for "keeping your mouth closed" is faster reading with more time to spare.

© Francis Hogan/Electronic Publishing Services

If you have to read in distracting environments, minimize the distraction. For example, on a crowded bus you might want to read while listening to music played at a low level on headphones.

FIGURE 6.5 Word Attack Skills

Prefixes (word beginnings) and suffixes (word endings) provide clues about word meanings. Here are some common examples from Latin and Greek.

Prefixes	Meaning	Example
a, ab	without or not	*a*theist: nonbeliever in God
ad	to	*ad*vocate: to speak for
ambi	both	*ambi*valent: uncommitted
can	together	*con*vention: formal gathering
de	from or down	*de*spicable: abhorrent
dis	not	*dis*interest: boredom
ex	over	*ex*aggerate: to magnify
hyper	above	*hyper*active: overactive
hypo	under	*hypo*dermic: under skin
mono	single	*mono*lingual: speaking one language
non	not	*non*responsive: not reacting
pro	forward	*pro*duction: process of making
re	back, again	*re*vert: return to former state
sub, sup	under	*sub*ordinate: in a lower position
trans	across	*trans*pose: to change places

Suffixes	Meaning	Example
-able, -ible (adjective)	capable of	respon*sible*: in charge
-ac, -al, -il (adjective)	pertaining to	natur*al*: related to nature
-ance, -ence (noun)	state or status	dalli*ance*: playful activity
-ant, -ent (noun)	one who does	serv*ant*: person who waits on others
-er, -or (noun)	one who does	contract*or*: one who builds
-ive (adjective)	state or status	fest*ive*: partylike
-ish (adjective)	quality of	fool*ish*: like a fool
-less (adjective)	without	heart*less*: harsh, unfeeling
-ly (adjective/adverb)	like	miser*ly*: like a miser
-ness (noun)	state of	peaceful*ness*: state of peace

If you can spend only a little time on campus, you may face particular challenges in securing quiet space and uninterrupted time. Some commuters on public transportation can read and review while they travel. If you're stuck with reading an assignment in a noisy environment, you may want to wear headphones with familiar instrumental music just loud enough to block distractions. If you have a long drive to school, you can listen to taped classes.

If you have to combine reading with child care,

- Plan to read during nap times, after the children have gone to bed, or before they get up.
- Set a timer for 15 minutes and provide activities that your children can do at the table with you. Let them know that at the end of 15 minutes—when the timer goes off—everyone will take a play break.

- Find other students with similar child-care needs. Pool your resources to hire a regular baby-sitter or trade baby-sitting services to free up more time for reading.

Capture and Connect

How well you read will depend on your interest level, the complexity of the material, the time you have to do the reading, and your reading skill. If you're very interested in a topic and already know something about it, you may not need specific strategies to comprehend the reading. Just dive in and take appropriate notes. But what if the reading is unfamiliar and difficult? Read both selectively and systematically. Your system will probably include some of the following types of reading: preview, skimming, active reading, analytic reading, and reviewing. Figure 6.6 demonstrates how these different strategies are related.

Before You Read It is always a good idea to preview the material before you sit down to read. This helps you estimate how intense your reading effort will need to be and how much time it will take to complete the assignment. It also gives you a broad overview of the material that can make it easier to understand and remember the details.

Preview Dave, an education major, always previews his reading assignment no matter what the subject. During the preview, Dave looks at:

- *The context for the assignment.* To see how the assignment fits into the course, Dave thinks about the class activities that have led up to the assignment.

FIGURE 6.6 Elements of Your Reading Plan

Approaching your reading assignments strategically means adopting different reading strategies. The type of reading you choose depends on your available time, the complexity of the material, and your motivation to master the ideas. As you go from the top to the bottom of the pyramid, the intensity of your effort increases: You become more involved with the material, and the reading task becomes more demanding. The consequences of your review may return you to the reading to skim, read actively, or read analytically.

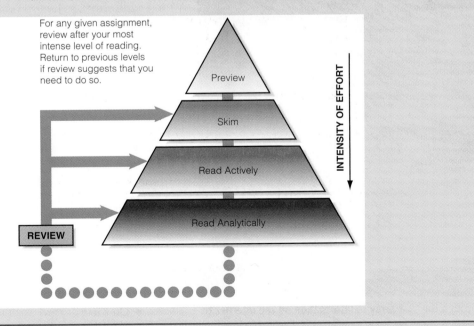

- *The length of the reading.* By applying his reading speed to the number of pages in the assignment, Dave can estimate how long he will need to devote to the job.
- *The structure and features of the reading.* A good time to take a reading break is at the end of a section. Knowing a text's structure can help Dave plan ahead. Textbook features such as summaries can help him rehearse his learning.
- *The difficulty of the reading.* Higher-level material may require more than one reading.

While You Read There are several different levels at which you can read, depending on the difficulty and importance of the material and the time you have to devote to the task.

Skimming Whereas previewing helps you size up the reading, skimming covers the content at a general level. When you skim, you read at about twice your average rate. Focus on introductory statements, topic sentences (usually the first sentence in the paragraph), and boldface terms. Slow down to examine summaries carefully. Make sure you understand the points that the author intends.

Karen, a management major, likes to skim a text before she settles down to read more intensely. Skimming gives her a sense of the kind of information her assignment contains. She recognizes that the concepts in many of her courses overlap. By skimming the material, she can see where the assignment contains new ideas that she'll have to read more carefully.

Markie, a full-time communications major with a half-time job, doesn't always have the time to read her assignments as thoroughly as she should. Rather than abandoning her reading, she skims some assignments. She usually reserves the strategy for easier courses so she can concentrate more intensely on her tougher ones.

You don't always need to read every word of every assignment (Frank, 1996). Your ability to read selectively improves as you grow accustomed to how readings relate to a course and how your instructor chooses test material. Skimming provides you with the surface structure of the ideas in the text when that is all you have time for. Successful skimmers can usually participate in class discussions with some confidence if they rehearse the main ideas and have read some key passages.

Active Reading Takima, a music major, was distressed to reach the bottom of a page of her science book only to discover that she had absorbed no information from her reading. You've probably experienced something similar. It's easy to engage in empty reading. Your eyes track across the lines of text but your brain fails to register anything meaningful.

Read texts *actively* to prevent the wasted time of empty reading or to avoid having to read the same material again. Immerse yourself in what the author is trying to say. Identify the main ideas and understand how the supporting points reinforce those ideas. Also construct the meaning in what you read by linking the information to your own personal knowledge or experience. Use these questions as guidelines for active reading:

- Have I ever experienced anything similar to what is described in the reading?
- How does this relate to things I already know?
- How might this be useful for me to know?
- Do I like or agree with these ideas?
- How does the reading relate to current events?

Sifting through the vast array of information on the Internet to get what you need takes time, energy, and careful attention.

Active readers form as many links as possible between their personal experience and knowledge and what they're reading.

Analytic Reading Joshua, majoring in pre-med, likes to read his assignments intensely. Like other analytic readers, he likes to break ideas open or dig underneath their surface. He tries to spot flaws in the writer's logic and identifies which elements are clear and which are confusing. He compares the quality of the work to that of other works he has read. He examines whether the materials are persuasive enough to change his own viewpoint. Good analytic readers question both the author and themselves as they dig their way through a reading. The following questions may help you become an analytic reader:

- What are the author's values and background? Do these influence the writing? How?
- Does the author's bias taint the truthfulness of what I'm reading?
- What implicit (unstated) assumptions does the author make?
- Do I believe the evidence?
- Is the author's position valid?
- Are the arguments logically developed?
- What predictions follow from the argument?
- What are the strengths and weaknesses of the argument?
- Is anything missing from the position?
- What questions would I want to ask the author?
- Is there a different way to look at the facts or ideas?
- Would these ideas apply to all people in all cultures or in all situations?

> *Reading a book is like re-writing it for yourself. You bring to a novel, anything you read, all your experience of the world. You bring your history and you read it in your own terms.*
>
> Angela Carter
> *20th-century British writer and educator*

After You Read The final step in a successful reading plan is to review the material after it has been read. There are several different strategies for reviewing.

Review An anthropology major, Sanjay likes to review his reading assignments to help consolidate his learning. He reviews his notes immediately after class and before he begins his next reading assignment. Reviewing the assignment makes the main points stand out and makes them easier to remember.

Think of reviewing as an opportunity to test yourself on your own comprehension. Question yourself on details or write out summaries of what you've read. The quality of your notes can make all the difference when it's time to study for a test. With well-constructed notes that you have reviewed systematically after your classes, your final review should be a breeze. On Target Tips, "Reading Strategies for Different Situations," recommends some combinations for different reading tasks. To understand your own reading patterns, complete the Journal activity "How Do You Read?" on page 184.

Know How to Read Primary and Secondary Sources

There are two general types of readings for courses: primary sources and secondary sources. A *primary source* is material written in some original form such as autobiographies, speeches, research reports, scholarly articles, government documents, and historical journal articles. For example, you may read the U.S. Constitution as a primary source in your political science class.

ON TARGET TIPS

Reading Strategies for Different Situations

- When you want to develop understanding of the ideas:
  Preview → Active reading → Review
- When you want to practice critical thinking about your reading:
  Preview → Analytic reading → Review
- When you have trouble retaining what you read:
  Preview → Skim → Active reading → Review → Review
- When you don't have time to read for mastery:
  Skim → Review
  (pay close attention to summaries and boldface terms)

Secondary sources summarize or interpret these primary sources. A magazine article that discussed politicians' interpretations of the Constitution generally would be considered a secondary source. Textbooks are secondary sources that try to give a comprehensive view of information from numerous primary works.

You have many more opportunities to read primary sources in college than you did in high school. Most people find reading original works exhilarating. For example, reading a speech by Frederick Douglass about the abolition of slavery will likely stimulate you more than reading interpretations of his speeches. However, primary sources may be more difficult to read than secondary sources because a secondary source often summarizes and interprets the meaning of the primary source. If original works must be chewed and digested; the secondary source does some of the chewing and digesting for you.

Interpreting original ideas is also more challenging than accepting others' interpretations. When reading primary sources, learn as much as you can about the intentions of the authors and the historical context in which they were writing. Understanding a historical period will help you interpret texts written at that time. Check out the Journal activity "Primary versus Secondary Accounts" on page 184 to clarify how these differ.

Master Reading in Different Disciplines

As you've already discovered, some readings are harder than others for you. Obviously, you'll learn material more easily if it matches an area in which you have special interests and intellectual strengths. However, liberal arts programs almost always require reading about topics that don't come naturally. In some readings, technical terms may slow you down. Other readings may require more imagination. Let's explore some tips that will help you read more efficiently in a variety of disciplines, some of which will be more challenging for you than others.

Literature In literature courses, you study poetry, novels, plays, and short stories. Appreciation of these forms comes most easily to people who enjoy reflective learning and who like to think critically. For them, many great works provide delight. But what strategies can help you when reading literature is challenging?

- *Use your imagination.* Visualize the action. Participate at the level the author intended: Use as many senses as the author used—taste, smell, sound—as you recreate the author's world in your imagination.
- *Look for connections.* Are any of the experiences like your own? Do the characters remind you of anyone you know?
- *Make the author real.* Search the Internet for a good biography or personal details about the author that might help you understand the author's motivation to create the work.
- *Make a chart.* If the reading is complex, make a list of key figures as they are introduced so you can easily review as the story progresses.
- *Predict what will happen.* Once you understand the direction the work is taking, see if you can anticipate what happens next.
- *Read aloud.* Some great works are savored best when read aloud. Find a study partner and share the task.

History Some students love history because they believe that we are all the walking expression of history. History texts provide a great opportunity to use your imagination and it will come alive if you let it. Good readers in history put conscientious effort into seeing how events, places, and people interconnect.

- *Put yourself in the picture.* As you read about events, think about how you might have reacted to them at the time.
- *Change history.* Predict an alternative course of history by changing a critical event or two. How might the ripple effect have changed some element of your life?
- *Imagine or draw the timeline.* Articulate a causal link from one event to the next over time.
- *Make it into a movie.* Imagine a cast of film stars in the roles of the historical figures you're reading about. It may help you visualize the action better.
- *Don't forget the big picture.* Keep in mind how each new event or person you encounter in your learning adds to your understanding of the grander historic scale.

Natural and Social Science The sciences can be especially challenging because of the level of abstraction in some scientific writing. The terminology presented in the sciences represents a kind of shorthand that allows scientists to communicate with each other. Learning these terms can be a challenge without some helpful strategies.

- *Keep a running glossary of terms.* Treat the sciences like a foreign language. Each new term stands for a concept. Study the meaning of each.
- *Accept the role of numbers.* If you aren't comfortable with numbers, you may be turned off by the practice of measurement and statistics that pervades most sciences. When numbers accompany text, spend extra time understanding their significance.
- *Think practically.* See if you can come up with a practical application of the scientific relationships you're reading about.
- *Look for links in the news.* The sciences regularly issue progress reports that may enhance your understanding or clarify concepts.
- *Cruise the Internet.* Chances are good that the Internet will provide ideas that will help you with the terms. Find information about the scientists themselves that will help make the enterprise feel more real to you.
- *Look for overlaps.* Where does your life intersect with the scientific ideas you're trying to learn?

Take Great Reading Notes

The expertise you develop in taking good notes during lectures can also help you take effective notes from reading assignments. The principles are the same:

- Capture the main ideas.
- Show how secondary information connects and supports main ideas.
- Choose a note-taking format that maximizes your retention and learning.

If you don't have the time to read, you don't have the time or the tools to write.
Stephen King
Contemporary American novelist

Choose the Best Method

There are three general strategies for taking reading notes: highlighting the text, personalizing it, and making external notes as you read.

Highlight Text Using a highlighter helps many students concentrate as they read and makes it easier for them to review for tests. Ideally, highlight topic sentences, key words, and conclusions, which usually make up much less than one quarter of a text.

"All very well and good—but now we come to chart B."

© Gahan Wilson.

Although this strategy may keep you engaged with the reading, it presents several hazards. You may highlight too much material so that you are faced with rereading nearly the entire text when you review. It's easy to find yourself mindlessly highlighting text, giving you the illusion of reading when you haven't really absorbed the key ideas. Also, simply highlighting does not show why you thought that passage was important. And when it's time to review, you still need to carry the complete text with you. Finally, if you sell your text after the course is over, the highlighting may reduce its value. Other strategies that promote greater involvement are likely to be more helpful in the long run. See Figure 6.7, "Highlighted Notes," for a model of effective highlights.

Personalize the Text Some students find that they can absorb a text more easily by using the margins to simulate an interaction with the author. Think of the margin notes as your opportunity to engage in an imaginary conversation with the text's author. Contemplate what questions you would like to ask. Identify areas that might not make sense to you. Jot down a personal example that illustrates a key point. Fill the margins with your good connections. To make your learning more vivid, you can draw arrows or thumbs-down signs when you disagree, and circle key terms. Draw symbols. Write summary notes. Although this practice may reduce the book's resale value, your gain in knowledge should compensate for lost profits.

Take Notes as You Read Earlier in the chapter, you learned about four techniques for taking notes from lecture: summarizing, outlining, the Cornell Method, and concept-mapping. These techniques also work for notes that you take from reading. What are some advantages of applying these methods to taking notes from texts?

Summarizing This technique helps you extract the key ideas from passages and put them in your own words. Plan to summarize after each major subdivision in your reading. If the text has no headings, try to summarize after you have read a small or sufficient number of pages. Summaries will highlight the important key ideas, but may glance over details that could be critical to your success at exam time.

Outlining This strategy imposes a systematic organization with predictable headings (I, A, 1, a . . .) to represent faithfully the complexity of the materials you read. Outlines distinguish main points (headings I and A) from support points (1 and a) and facilitate quick review for exams. Outlining tends to be a preferred note-taking mode for people who enjoy making explicit the nature of the relationship among concepts in the reading. Outlining from texts works best when the assigned reading materials are logically organized. If they are not, less rigid strategies will work better.

I had the worst study habits and the lowest grades. Then I found out what I was doing wrong. I had been highlighting with a black magic marker.

Jeff Altman
Contemporary U.S. comedian

FIGURE 6.7 Highlighted Notes

Minorities and Stardom

Stark, R. (1994). *Sociology.* 5th Edition.

NBA = African-American?

The majority of players on every team in the National Basketball Association are African American. White boxing champions are rare. A far greater proportion of professional football players are African American than would be expected based on the size of the African-American population. Furthermore, African Americans began to excel in sports long before the Civil Rights Movement broke down barriers excluding them from many other occupations. This has led many people, both African American and white, to conclude that African Americans are born with a natural talent for athletics. How else could they have come to dominate the ranks of superstars?

main question

The trouble with this biological explanation of African Americans in sports is that it ignores an obvious historical fact: It is typical for minorities in North America to make their first substantial progress in sports (and, for similar reasons, in entertainment). Who today would suggest that Jews have a biological advantage in athletics? Yet at the turn of the century, the number of Jews who excelled in sports far exceeded their proportion in the population. And late in the 19th century, the Irish dominated sports to almost the same extent as African Americans have done in recent decades.

example: Jews showed same pattern 19th cent.

By examining an encyclopedia of boxing, for example, we can draw accurate conclusions about patterns of immigration and periods at which ethnic groups were on the bottom of the stratification system. The Irish domination of boxing in the latter half of the 19th century is obvious from the names of heavyweight champions, beginning with bareknuckle champ Ned O'Baldwin in 1867 and including Mike McCoole in 1869, Paddy Ryan in 1880, John L. Sullivan in 1889, and Jim Corbett in 1892. The list of champions in lower-weight divisions during the same era is dominated by fighters named Ryan, Murphy, Delaney, Lynch, O'Brien, and McCoy.

Early in the 20th century, Irish names became much less common among boxing champions, even though many fighters who were not Irish took Irish ring names. Suddenly, champions had names like Battling Levinsky, Maxie Rosenbloom, Benny Leonard, Abe Goldstein, Kid Kaplan, and Izzy Schwartz. This was the Jewish era in boxing. Then Jewish names dropped out of the lists, and Italian and eastern European names came to the fore: Canzoneri, Battalino, LaMotta, Graziano, and Basilio; Yarosz, Lesnevich, Zale, Risko, Hostak, and Servo. By the 1940s, fighters were disproportionately African American. Today, African-American domination of boxing has already peaked, and Hispanic names have begun to prevail.

history of boxing:
Irish
Jews
Italians
Af. Am.

The current overrepresentation of African Americans in sports reflects two things: first, a *lack of other avenues to wealth and fame,* and, second, the fact that minority groups can overcome discrimination most easily in occupations in which *the quality of individual performance is most easily and accurately assessed* (Blalock, 1967). These same factors led to the overrepresentation of other ethnic groups in sports earlier in history.

1.
2.
key ideas

It often is difficult to know which applicants to a law school or a pilot training school are the most capable. But we can see who can box or hit a baseball. The demonstration of talent, especially in sports and entertainment, tends to break down barriers of discrimination. As these fall, opportunities in these areas for wealth and fame open up, while other opportunities remain closed. Thus, minority groups will aspire to those areas in which the opportunities are open and will tend to overachieve in these areas.

this is why

The Cornell Method When applied to notes from texts, this combines the best features of creating external notes with the personalization of making notes in the margin of your book. When you use this method, you subdivide the note page into a main portion summarizing what you read and a smaller sections for your responses, answers, questions, and connections, as discussed earlier.

By making freestanding notes that are systematic and personalized, you can maximize the resale value of your texts and maintain a record of your impressions after the course is over. Figure 6.8, "Cornell Notes on Reading," provides good examples of note taking.

Concept-mapping This strategy turns the content from the reading into a visual representation. Developing maps strongly appeals to visual learners. Concept maps can get messy if the text contains dense, interrelated content, but they also provide a great tool for review. Consider the Journal activity "Note-taking Now" on page 185 to practice some of these methods.

Other Note-Taking Tips

Regardless of the method you choose, there are some general strategies that will maximize your effectiveness.

- *Write your notes in your own words.* Translating an author's words into your own increases the personal connections you make to the material and makes it easier to remember. It also helps you avoid plagiarism when you use the notes to write a paper. When you literally lift the words of an author from a text and later present these words as your own, you are stealing the thoughts and expressions of another. Instructors may view this as laziness or deceit and may penalize you.
- *Avoid writing things down that you don't understand.* You simply won't understand some ideas on a first reading. You may feel tempted to write down unclear ideas with the intention of returning to them later. Don't. Instead, mark the passage with a question mark and do what you can to clarify it before you record it and move on.
- *Think and record in pictures.* Try to turn information from the text into some other form, such as a list, table, graph, or picture, to make it easier for you to recall. Diagrams and tables also can be tools for summarizing.
- *Explain yourself.* College reading is often complex and abstract. It's easy to read a mass of material and think you understand what you've read when in fact you missed a key idea. Imagine that you have a study companion who doesn't read as well as you do and struggles to understand the central ideas in assignments. Regularly explain the key ideas in the reading to your "friend," particularly when the material is harder or less interesting for you than usual. When you can't explain the passage easily, you need to review it. Of course, if you use this strategy, please tell your roommates about it so they won't think you're cracking up!
- *Periodically evaluate the quality of your notes.* Especially after an exam, review your notes to see how well they worked. To make some comparisons of note-taking strategies across different course contexts, complete the Journal activity "A Shared Path to Success" on page 185.

Take What You Need from the Internet

The Internet is one of your best learning resources, but you have to use it properly at the college level to maximize your benefits.

> *Laziness may appear attractive, but work gives satisfaction.*
> Anne Frank
> *German diarist killed in the Holocaust*

FIGURE 6.8 **Cornell Notes on Reading**

Stark, R. (1994), _Sociology._ Belmont, CA: Wadsworth. p.333

Minorities and sports

"Natural talent" of A-A's in sports? | Popular biological view: African-Americans born with natural athletic talent because so many pro athletes are A-A, compared with their percentage in U.S. pop.

But similar pattern for other minorities | But other minorities also made their first big progress in sports (& entertainment). See lists of boxing champions:
* Irish dominate last half 19th century
* Jews around 1900
* Italians dominate after Jews
* A-A dominate after Italians
* Hispanic champions now (& future)?

Proposed sociological reason for numbers of A-A in pro sports?

Real reasons for current number of A-A's in sports? |
1. "Lack of other avenues to wealth and fame"
2. "Quality of individual performance easily and accurately assessed" in sports.

Importance of talent in sports & entertainment tends to break down discrimination barriers in these areas before other areas of life.

People say A-A's excel in pro sports now due just to "biology." But other minorities have gone though the same pattern of excellence in sports until they were accepted in other fields. In sports individual talents can be seen, so discrimination barriers not as bad as in other fields.

Q: What about other sports beside boxing? What about music? Same pattern? How much are opportunities changing for A-A's outside sports?

Check before you search. You may plan to conduct your research process completely online for your convenience. Although there is a lot of valuable information on the internet, many instructors have strict requirements about what may or may not be used in their assignments. Many exclude internet sources because of uncertainty about quality.

Navigate to the right spot. If you are starting a cold search on the Internet, you may have to spend some time playing with the key terms to help you find the most valuable resources. An ambiguous or poorly defined search can produce too many hits for you to review, especially if you are in a time crunch. Cut back on your harvest of information by adding some terms to the search or more sharply define the key terms you are using.

Monitor quality of the resource. Not everything on the internet is credible. Some sites are simply not appropriate for work you need to submit at the college level. Your best bet will be using information developed by recognized experts in the field. If you have questions about the suitability of a resource, ask your instructor.

Beware of "cut and paste" strategies. The information on the Internet is so easy transport from one context to another that it may be tempting just to capture the information by executing a "cut and paste" command from the Internet to your computer. Although you will be in possession of the data you need, this approach can promote plagiarism. When you intend to use the information in your own paper, be careful to paraphrase what you have captured. Many instructors use special programs to detect materials that have been downloaded from the Internet into student papers, and the penalty for evidence of plagiarism can be severe.

Cite your sources. Not matter how you capture information, write down the "URL" carefully so that you can cite your source. If your thinking has benefited from what you captured, you will need to give the author of the website proper credit.

"Bookmark" important resources. Sometimes you get lucky. You may find a superb website that will continue to provide helpful information to you for the duration of a course. Enter the site into your list of favorite websites so you don't have to reproduce the search or even retype the website address when you return to the site.

Process Information Professionally

When you think about how much time you will spend over the course of your college career learning from text and lectures, you may feel a bit resentful. Sometimes such systematic study can feel like busy work, especially if the process you go through doesn't quite translate into the grades that you want. However, think again.

Any profession that you pursue will test you regularly on how well you can read and listen. The good habits that you develop in college should carry over into successful work contexts. Remember

Career Connections

Marty loved to read. He saw research assignments as a great opportunity to test his detective skills and especially enjoyed projects that allowed him to find obscure information. He honed his research skills so well that he embarked on an unusual career path that regularly gave him the opportunity to read and conduct research as a lifestyle. He became a fact-checker for novelists. One of his clients liked to write complex techno-thrillers that required a lot of technological background. Marty routinely might figure out how to incorporate the latest developments in bioterrorism or nuclear weaponry to help his clients produce bestselling, but factually accurate works.

Kirsten liked the intellectual challenge of taking good lecture notes. Early in her college career she prided herself on her ability to deal with the most complex lectures. She worked out an extensive personal coding system to maximize her efficiency in recording key ideas and distinguishing her interpretations from the facts of the matter. Because she was so curious about human nature, she pursued a job in journalism, where her exceptional ability to identify and report key themes were essential to her success.

that "exploring careers" is one of your six key strategies for success—it is never too soon to start preparing for the future. Among other responsibilities, you may need to:

- record and implement a medical program for a client
- absorb the key points from a proposal to increase sales, based on what you hear at a marketing meeting
- extract principles from a legal precedent to prepare a legal brief
- identify, communicate accurately, and take action on the primary complaints of a dissatisfied customer
- cruise the Internet to find news relevant to a current dilemma that influences social policy

Note how each of these situations will benefit from conscientious practice at being a good listener, note-taker, and reader. See the Journal activity "Taking Advantage" on page 185 to size up how your future plans might benefit from refining your skills in information processing.

> *Do what you can, with what you have, where you are.*
> Theodore Roosevelt
> *U.S. President*

Summary Strategies for Mastering College

Recognizing and capturing key information from your courses will help you reach your academic goals.

Focus on the "Six Strategies for Success" above as you read each chapter to learn how to apply these strategies to your own success.

Commit, Concentrate, Capture, Connect

- Summarize information in ways that fit your learning style.
- To make your strategies successful, you need to make a commitment, concentrate, capture key ideas, and make connections.

Take Charge of Lectures

- Commit to attending class to get the most out of lectures.
- Overcome distractions to improve your concentration.
- Adapt your listening skills to the demands of the course and the style of the teacher.

3 Take Great Lecture Notes

- Find a note-taking format that works well with your learning style.
- Use your notes strategically to improve your ability to recall information.

4 Take Charge of Your Reading

- Find the right time and space to make your reading effective and efficient.
- Tailor your reading intensity and speed to the course requirements.

5 Mark or Take Notes from Readings

- Experiment with note-taking strategies that will help you identify and retain the most important ideas.
- Use your own words to record ideas from texts in order to learn the material well and avoid plagiarism.

6 Process Information Professionally

- Show patience with how much effort will be required in information processing in your classes.
- Imagine how refined note-taking and reading skills will benefit you in the future.

Review Questions

1. Write down the four Cs of learning new information. Also include a few ways each can be applied to learning from lectures and reading assignments.

   1. C:＿＿＿＿＿＿＿＿＿＿＿＿＿＿＿＿＿＿＿＿＿＿＿＿＿＿＿＿
   2. C:＿＿＿＿＿＿＿＿＿＿＿＿＿＿＿＿＿＿＿＿＿＿＿＿＿＿＿＿
   3. C:＿＿＿＿＿＿＿＿＿＿＿＿＿＿＿＿＿＿＿＿＿＿＿＿＿＿＿＿
   4. C:＿＿＿＿＿＿＿＿＿＿＿＿＿＿＿＿＿＿＿＿＿＿＿＿＿＿＿＿

2. What are three tips for listening most effectively to challenging lectures? How can these tips also be applied to absorbing information for difficult readings?

   1. ＿＿＿＿＿＿＿＿＿＿＿＿＿＿＿＿＿＿＿＿＿＿＿＿＿＿＿＿＿＿
   2. ＿＿＿＿＿＿＿＿＿＿＿＿＿＿＿＿＿＿＿＿＿＿＿＿＿＿＿＿＿＿
   3. ＿＿＿＿＿＿＿＿＿＿＿＿＿＿＿＿＿＿＿＿＿＿＿＿＿＿＿＿＿＿

3. What style of note-taking makes the most sense for each of the classes you're currently taking? List your classes below, followed by the best method.

   1. ＿＿＿＿＿＿＿＿＿＿＿＿＿＿＿＿＿＿＿＿＿＿＿＿＿＿＿＿＿＿
   2. ＿＿＿＿＿＿＿＿＿＿＿＿＿＿＿＿＿＿＿＿＿＿＿＿＿＿＿＿＿＿
   3. ＿＿＿＿＿＿＿＿＿＿＿＿＿＿＿＿＿＿＿＿＿＿＿＿＿＿＿＿＿＿
   4. ＿＿＿＿＿＿＿＿＿＿＿＿＿＿＿＿＿＿＿＿＿＿＿＿＿＿＿＿＿＿
   5. ＿＿＿＿＿＿＿＿＿＿＿＿＿＿＿＿＿＿＿＿＿＿＿＿＿＿＿＿＿＿
   ＿＿＿＿＿＿＿＿＿＿＿＿＿＿＿＿＿＿＿＿＿＿＿＿＿＿＿＿＿＿＿＿
   ＿＿＿＿＿＿＿＿＿＿＿＿＿＿＿＿＿＿＿＿＿＿＿＿＿＿＿＿＿＿＿＿

4. List the three different ways to process information as you read. How can each style help you succeed in your various college courses? What type do you currently use most often and why?

   1. ＿＿＿＿＿＿＿＿＿＿＿＿＿＿＿＿＿＿＿＿＿＿＿＿＿＿＿＿＿＿
   2. ＿＿＿＿＿＿＿＿＿＿＿＿＿＿＿＿＿＿＿＿＿＿＿＿＿＿＿＿＿＿
   3. ＿＿＿＿＿＿＿＿＿＿＿＿＿＿＿＿＿＿＿＿＿＿＿＿＿＿＿＿＿＿
   ＿＿＿＿＿＿＿＿＿＿＿＿＿＿＿＿＿＿＿＿＿＿＿＿＿＿＿＿＿＿＿＿
   ＿＿＿＿＿＿＿＿＿＿＿＿＿＿＿＿＿＿＿＿＿＿＿＿＿＿＿＿＿＿＿＿

5. What are some good strategies for taking notes on your readings? List a few pros and cons of each.

＿＿＿＿＿＿＿＿＿＿＿＿＿＿＿＿＿＿＿＿＿＿＿＿＿＿＿＿＿＿＿＿＿＿
＿＿＿＿＿＿＿＿＿＿＿＿＿＿＿＿＿＿＿＿＿＿＿＿＿＿＿＿＿＿＿＿＿＿
＿＿＿＿＿＿＿＿＿＿＿＿＿＿＿＿＿＿＿＿＿＿＿＿＿＿＿＿＿＿＿＿＿＿
＿＿＿＿＿＿＿＿＿＿＿＿＿＿＿＿＿＿＿＿＿＿＿＿＿＿＿＿＿＿＿＿＿＿
＿＿＿＿＿＿＿＿＿＿＿＿＿＿＿＿＿＿＿＿＿＿＿＿＿＿＿＿＿＿＿＿＿＿
＿＿＿＿＿＿＿＿＿＿＿＿＿＿＿＿＿＿＿＿＿＿＿＿＿＿＿＿＿＿＿＿＿＿

Learning Portfolio

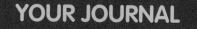
SELF-ASSESSMENTS

YOUR JOURNAL

STRATEGIES FOR SUCCESS

Develop Meaningful Values

Set Goals, Plan, and Monitor

Explore Careers

Take It In

Get Motivated and Take Responsibility

Build Self-Esteem and Confidence

Think and Learn

Auditing Your Note-Taking Style for Lectures

	Always	Sometimes	Never
I approach listening actively.			
I select note-taking formats to suit the various courses I take.			
I organize my notes in one place.			
I label the lecture with title and date.			
I take notes from all participants in class.			
I concentrate during class.			
I work to build my vocabulary.			
I cross out errors instead of erasing them.			
I try not to write dense notes. I leave space for adding more later.			
I listen for directional cues or emphasis.			
I avoid shutting down when I have a negative reaction to what I hear.			
I highlight key ideas or themes.			
I use abbreviations to save time.			
I personalize my notes.			
I review my notes after class.			
I pay attention to the quality of my note-taking process as I go.			
I would consider asking the instructor for help in constructing better notes.			

Results: Look at the pattern of the responses that you made on this assessment. Your best note-taking strategies are reflected in checks in the Always column on the left. If the majority of your checks fall in the Always column, you are establishing a good foundation for study with your note-taking practices. Now look at the items marked Never. What would it take for you to add each of these items to your note-taking toolbox?

What's Your Reader Profile?

Circle the alternative that best describes you as a reader.

1. When I have an assignment to read,

    a. I'm usually enthusiastic about what I'll learn.

    b. I like to wait to see whether what I have read will be valuable.

    c. I'm generally apprehensive about reading assignments because I'm afraid I won't understand them.

2. What is my attitude toward the authors of my college books?

    a. I think of them as human beings with an interesting story to tell.

    b. I haven't really given the writers much thought.

    c. I think of them as people who will probably talk over my head.

3. When I plan my reading,

    a. I think about how the assignment fits in with the objectives of the course.

    b. I review the prior assignment to set the stage for current work.

    c. I plunge in so I can get it done.

4. I take breaks

    a. To consolidate the information I read.

    b. To help me study longer and more productively.

    c. Whenever I lose interest in my reading.

5. When I don't know a word,

    a. I look it up, write it down, and practice it.

    b. I try to figure it out from the context of the sentence.

    c. I usually skip over it and hope it won't make too much difference in the meaning.

6. When I can't understand a sentence,

    a. I reread the sentence more carefully.

    b. I try to figure out the sentence from the context of the paragraph.

    c. I skip the sentence, hoping it will make sense later.

7. When the whole assignment confuses me,

    a. I try to find more materials that will shed some light on my confusion.

    b. I ask the instructor or someone else for ideas about how to cope with the assignment.

    c. I tend to give up on it.

8. When I read,

    a. I try to read as fast as I can while still understanding the meaning.

    b. I try to sweep as many words as I can at a glance.

    c. I take it one word at a time—speed doesn't matter to me.

Results: Alternatives "a" and "b" of each question indicate successful reading habits. Revisit any "c" alternatives that you marked. Think about possible causes of these less successful patterns. You may benefit from a visit with a reading specialist on campus who can help you figure out how to make As and Bs by practicing more "a"s and "b"s.

How Fast Do You Read?

Select a text from one of your courses. Set a timer for five minutes and start reading. When the timer goes off, stop reading. Count the number of lines you read in the five-minute period. Pick several lines at random in the text and count the number of words in the lines. Multiply the number of lines you read by the average number of words per line. This will give you an approximation of the total of words you read in the five-minute period. Finally, divide by five to produce your reading speed in words per minute.

Content area: _____

Date of assessment: _____

Number of lines read: _____

× Number of words per line: _____

= Approximate total words _____

Divided by 5 (minutes) _____

Approximate words per minute _____

How does your reading speed compare with these average speeds for different kinds of reading (Skinner, 1997)?

Skimming	800 words per minute
Active reading	100–200 words per minute
Analytic reading	under 100 words per minute

Results: Use this estimate as a baseline for your reading speed. If the material was well suited to your interest areas, you were probably able to read within the range for effective active reading. If the material was very familiar, your rate was probably higher, approaching the rates found in skimming. If your reading rate was below 100 words per minute, this may be a cause for concern. Although that reading rate is acceptable for complex materials, a slower reading rate on routine materials predicts that you may have difficulty keeping up with your reading assignments. Consider going for a more thorough evaluation of your reading strengths and weaknesses at the campus study skill center. Professional assistance can pinpoint the problem and make your future reading strategies much more successful.

Your Journal

● REFLECT

1. Show and Tell

Carefully look over the notes that you have taken in a course where your learning isn't coming easily. Think about what clues to your struggle may be present in how you take notes. For example,

- Are you staying tuned in throughout the class?

_____

- Are you writing down words that you don't understand?

_____

- Do the lecture notes fit with the big picture?

_____

Then follow up on your reflection by visiting your instructor during posted office hours. Take your notes and your observations with you. Ask the instructor to review your approach to see if other suggestions might improve your gains from note-taking.

2. Daydream Believer

One of the biggest obstacles to successful listening in class is the tendency to daydream. Monitor your listening in your current courses for one week. In which class did you daydream the most? Why do you think this is happening? Perhaps the room is too hot or the lecture falls right after lunch. List some possible reasons below. Now list some strategies for conquering your daydreams and implement these strategies next week.

Daydreaming in class:

Possible reasons: _____

Strategies: _____

● DO

1. Primary versus Secondary Accounts

Read a newspaper account (a secondary source) of a recent scientific achievement or issue and list it below. Then ask a librarian to help you track down the original work (the primary source) in a scientific journal at the library or on-line. Compare the length of the reports, the language level difficulty, the order of importance of ideas, and any other contrasting features. Based on your observations, how would you say that primary and secondary sources differ?

Scientific achievement or issue: _____

Focus of secondary source: _____

Focus of primary source: _____

How do they differ? _____

2. How Do You Read?

Monitor how you read your assignments for one week. Then rate how regularly you engage in different kinds of reading:

	Regularly	Sometimes	Rarely
Previewing:	_____	_____	_____
Skimming:	_____	_____	_____
Active reading:	_____	_____	_____
Analytical reading:	_____	_____	_____
Reviewing:	_____	_____	_____

Your Journal

In what area are you the strongest and how might this impact your academic performance? In what area do you need the most practice?

_____

_____

● THINK CRITICALLY

1. A Shared Path to Success

Form a small group in your College Success class to compare your strategies for taking notes in this course. If you have another course in common, compare your approaches to that content area as well. See whether as a group you can determine which approaches are most effective in capturing the critical ideas in these contexts. How does the type of course influence note-taking strategies?

_____

_____

2. Analyze the Sixth Sense

Some students seem to have an uncanny ability to figure out what information given in class will show up on the tests. Think about what kinds of cues they're picking up on in class and apply them to one of your courses.

● How do the instructor's vocal cues tell you what's important?

_____

● What kinds of words show an instructor's intent?

_____

● What behaviors show an instructor's excitement about concepts?

_____

● How does your instructor tend to stress important concepts?

_____

● CREATE

1. Taking Advantage

Effective organizational strategies will serve you well not only in college but also throughout life. Think about your future. How will the ability to process information effectively and efficiently influence the quality of your work? Think about the advantages you can gain by developing good information-processing skills now.

_____

_____

2. Note-taking Now

Spend the next ten minutes skimming the next chapter in this text and creating an outline of its content. After you are done, compare your outline with the one the authors' provide on the first page of the chapter. How was your outline similar or different? Did you miss any main ideas or capture any additional points? Think about how your presentation of content might differ if you had made a concept map or summary. What strategy do you think works best for you?

_____

_____

Applying the Six Strategies for Success

What did you learn in this chapter that you can apply to the following key strategies to help form the foundation for your success? Write down all of the main points you can remember that support the following strategies:

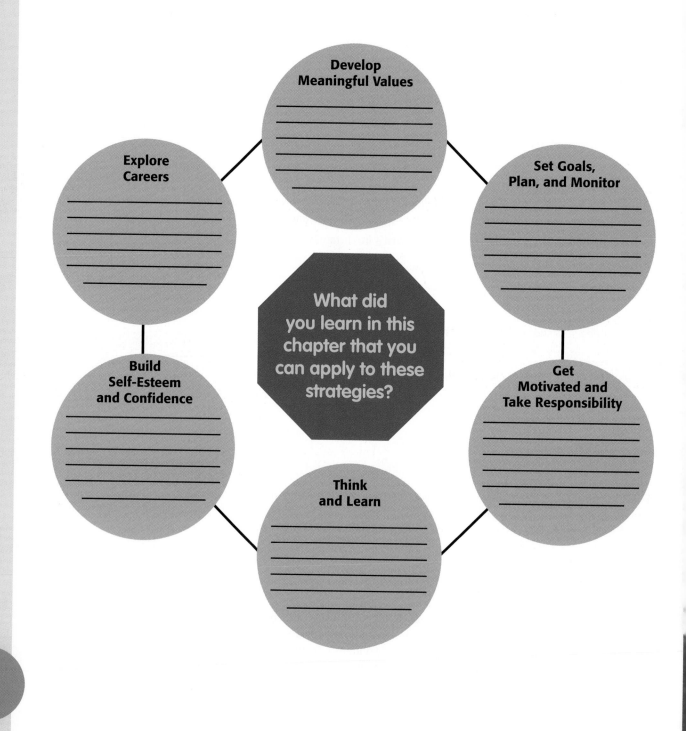

Develop
Meaningful Values
_____
_____
_____
_____
_____
_____

Explore
Careers
_____
_____
_____
_____
_____
_____

Set Goals,
Plan, and Monitor
_____
_____
_____
_____
_____
_____

What did
you learn in this
chapter that you
can apply to these
strategies?

Build
Self-Esteem
and Confidence
_____
_____
_____
_____
_____

Get
Motivated and
Take Responsibility
_____
_____
_____
_____
_____
_____

Think
and Learn
_____
_____
_____
_____
_____
_____

7

Enhance Your Study Skills and Memory

Where Are You? Studying works best when you know how to make good use of your study time. This chapter explores ways to bring your study habits under your control, improve your memory, and get the most from your study of various disciplines.

To evaluate where you stand right now, place a check next to only those items that apply to you.

- I choose appropriate places and times to study.

- I set reasonable goals for study sessions.

- I review regularly to learn course information better.

- I organize materials and use strategies to make ideas easier to learn and remember.

- I pursue deeper learning strategies when I can.

- I adapt my study strategies to suit different disciplines.

- I take my learning style into account when I study.

- I form study groups to expand my learning resources.

Think about how Janeane Garofalo's life illustrates some important features of effective learning.

187

Images of College Success

Janeane Garofalo

At 5'1", Janeane Garofalo is a surprising comedy giant (Kappes, 2001). Her alternative stand-up, a refreshing mix of jokes and self-deprecation that Janeane describes as "hit-and-run confession," has won fans across generations. Janeane's most popular film, *The Truth about Cats and Dogs*, cast her as a veterinarian who hosts a successful talk show about managing pet problems but has dubious success managing her own love life. This breakout role established her on- and offscreen persona as hip, sarcastic, and smart. She went on to win several Emmy nominations for her work as a wise-cracking assistant in *The Larry Sanders Show*.

More recently, Janeane has emerged as a political force due to her outspoken opposition to America's military activities in Iraq. Shortly after the tragedy of 9-11, she began making the rounds of talk shows to advocate for peaceful resolution to the conflict. Her latest gig is co-hosting a radio show, *The Majority Report*, on the new Air America network. She has described this opportunity of being able to share her "jaundiced" view of the world as fulfilling a lifelong dream.

Although she originally aspired to be a secretary, like her mother, her family's move from New Jersey to Houston disrupted Janeane's career plans during her senior year in high school. She began to study popular comedy styles and memorized the routines she liked best. During her senior year at Providence College, she participated in an open-mike night at a comedy club. Eventually she was voted "the Funniest Person in Rhode Island," which she describes as "a testament to the lack of talent among the other participants."

Janeane works hard to keep her stand-up fresh. She carries a notebook to record elements that will become the heart of her future monologues. To make sure that the delivery of her carefully memorized observations will appeal to the audience, she continuously reorganizes the materials, changing the order of what she has stored in memory, making new connections among the ideas and creating the impression that the connections are new. She also reads extensively. She claims that waiting around for filming to start is a great way to stay on top of the stack of books she wants to read. Her favorite book, Viktor Frankl's *Man's Search for Meaning*, is a classic that is often assigned during first-year humanities courses. She reportedly sports a tattoo that says "Think!"

Janeane Garofalo's successful stand-up routine is based on a disciplined approach to memorizing skills.

Identify
Meaningful
Values

Set Goals,
Plan, and
Monitor

Get
Motivated
and Take
Responsibility

Enhance Your
Study Skills
and Memory

Build
Self-Esteem
and
Confidence

Explore
Careers

Think
and
Learn

As you read, think about the "Six Strategies for Success" listed to the left and how this chapter can help you maximize success in these important areas. For example, effective study flows from solid planning based on your goals. Use these goals to motivate yourself to maximize your study skills and resources.

Plan Your Attack

To do well in college, most of us need concentrated study time with notes we've made from readings and classes. A systematic study strategy will make your investment of time and effort pay off. Studying accomplishes many objectives. It makes recalling the core material of the course easier. It helps you develop richer insights. It also promotes good work habits that will carry over into your career.

The amount of time students report doing assignments or studying is related to many aspects of college success (Astin, 1993). Students who study more hours say they are more satisfied with college than do students who study less. Also, those who invest more time studying report that college improves their cognitive skills and emotional life. But studying *more* is only one way to improve. Studying *more effectively* also can help. Among other benefits, sensible study methods save you time so you have more of it for social life and other interests.

Motivation also is a key to effective studying and an important part of one of the six strategies for success listed above. Imagine the motivation that it took for Janeane Garofalo to learn the comedy routines she memorized. Garofalo was motivated because she loved performing the routines and imagined that it would make her feel good to get up in front of an audience and make people laugh. Visualizing success made the process easier to accomplish.

Now imagine yourself, after a good study session, coming to class and participating actively in a discussion. Imagine raising your hand to answer one question after another and contributing to the class discussion so effectively that the entire class is responding to your comments. Would that make you feel good? How about getting back a test with a big fat "A—Good Job" on the top? If you can't get motivated to study, just imagine the positive outcomes that can make you feel at the top of your game to help you manage the hard work in between.

Action is eloquence.
William Shakespeare
British playwright

Where to Study

The phone rings. Your downstairs neighbor is throwing a noisy party. The television in the living room is blaring a *Friends* rerun. And your relentless appetite demands a hot fudge sundae. At times the world is so full of distractions that it seems impossible to find the right time and place to study. But your success as a student depends on conquering these distractions and sticking to a good study routine.

The Best Available Space Find the best place you can to work, and study there consistently. The best place is usually private, quiet, well lit, and provides a comfortable temperature. For many students, the best place will also involve access to a computer, including an online connection. That way you can have Internet resources available to support your work and still maintain a quick fix for the social deprivation that can happen during long periods of study.

Narrow your study sites to one of a few places that provide you with the working space, storage space, and electronic access that will make your work efficient. Finding a study space at home is easiest, but you have other options as well. Colleges usually try to maintain other quiet spaces on campus, including access to general use computer labs, wireless hubs, or laptop hookups to facilitate your study and maintaining your personal network. You may find just the setup you need in the library, a dedicated purpose lab, or even quiet but wired hallways of some campuses. Residence halls often set aside study spaces away from noisy roommates. Ask other seasoned students about good study places on campus to find the most promising and productive sites.

Commuters can use driving time to review audiotapes of complicated lectures or carpool with someone in class to provide review time. Commuters often find that they can use laptop computers effectively as long as they take precautions regarding computer safety and power needs. Riding on a bus or train, especially if the commute is long, also provides blocks of study time, if you can study well in this type of environment.

The Right Conditions Although some students can concentrate in strange places and odd postures, most find that sitting at a desk improves concentration. Desks provide storage for study materials and help you stay organized. If you don't have a desk, use boxes or crates to contain and organize your supplies and books. Set up a simple filing system if you can. See Staying Out of the Pits, "Home Schooling," to see how to adapt to challenging conditions at home.

Wherever you study, minimize noise. Many people study best when the CD player, radio, and television are off. Some people like music in the background to mask other sounds and give a sense of control over the environment. If you can't control the noise around you, use headphones and soft instrumental music to minimize distraction. How can you pull together these ideas to develop the most supportive study environment? See the Journal activity "Creative Space Management" on page 215 for help.

© Barbara Stitzer/PhotoEdit

Some students can study effectively in uncomfortable postures and distracting environments, but many students prefer to study at a desk or a table. Have you figured out where you study best?

When to Study

Allocate several hours outside class for every hour you spend in class. Outstanding students often put in even more time. Although some study strategies can make you a better learner, there is no denying the need to study long hours for academic success. How can you best use those hours wisely?

When to Review Review your notes immediately after class. This practice allows you to rehearse new ideas and identify unclear ones while they are fresh, so you can then clarify them with your instructor or in your reading. See On Target Tips, "After Class Is Over," for tips on how to review. Reviewing your class notes and notes on reading assignments before the class meets again adds another rehearsal session that prepares you to participate in the next class more effectively. It also reinforces your memory on those concepts. Successful students often get to class about 10 minutes early to review their notes. Taking this preparation time to anticipate class events can save you time in the long run.

Schedule regular cumulative review sessions. Devote some time to seeing the big picture in each of your courses. Look at how each lecture fits the broader course objective. If you regularly review your notes during the term, you'll need less review time right before exams.

Listen to Your Body Pay attention to your natural rhythms. Research suggests that many young adults undergo developmental changes that predispose them to being night people (Carskadon, 1990). They require more rest to cope with those changes and may not get in sync until later in the day. Sometimes that preference lingers so that even older students may feel more functional later in the day than early in the morning.

If you're a night person, review sessions may be most effective after supper and late into the evening. If you're a morning person, you need to study earlier in the day to maximize your attention and concentration. Complete Self-Assessment 1 "Early Bird or Night Owl?" on page 211 to evaluate your high- and low-energy periods.

If you aren't getting the proper amount of rest, studying will be very difficult. You should be able to stay awake and alert if you have had sufficient sleep (Maas, 1988). But what if the demands of your schedule prevent you from getting all the sleep that you want or need? Avoid getting too comfortable; it is just an invitation to doze. See On Target Tips, "Stave off the Sleep Invasion," for other ways to beat the urge to sleep while studying.

What to Study

Use the daily and weekly calendar you established in Chapter 2 to decide when your activities must intensify or when you can take a much needed recreation break. Keep your long-term goals posted in your study area or use them as your computer screen saver so you can have easy access to reminders about what your commitments will require.

STAYING OUT OF THE PITS

Home Schooling

What if you have to share study space at home with others, even children? Family squabbles over space can subtract dramatically from your study time. Together, figure out how best to share the space.

- Assign desk drawers to everyone who will be sharing the space.
- Hang a bulletin board near the workspace to display everyone's best work to promote good motivation.
- Tidy up after each study session, especially if you are using the kitchen table, unless you make other arrangements with your family.
- Develop a schedule for access to the family computer. Practice saving your work and respect the privacy of others who share your equipment.

ON TARGET TIPS

After Class Is Over

1. **Rewrite and reorganize your notes.** This not only allows you to create a neater, clearer set of ideas for study but also provides an immediate review to help you take in and organize information.
2. **Highlight the most important ideas.** Underline or color-code the ideas you think may appear on a test. Write notes in the margins that will make the material more meaningful to you.
3. **Write a summary paragraph of the main ideas.** What were the main points covered in class? How did this class fit into the overall course?
4. **Identify any ideas that are still confusing.** Make notes about what remains unclear so you can look up the answer in your reading. You also can ask other students or the instructor.

Stave off the Sleep Invasion

ON TARGET TIPS

1. **Use your desk *only* for studying.** When you drift asleep at your desk, you learn to associate your desk with napping, a cue you may not be able to afford.

2. **Set an alarm.** Buy a wristwatch that can signal you at reasonable intervals to keep you focused.

3. **Make a commitment to others.** Study with others and use the social contact to keep you from dozing off.

4. **Take a five-minute fresh-air break.** A brisk walk can clear your mind so you can focus better when you return to your studies.

5. **Stay involved in your reading.** The more invested you are, the less tempting it is to give in to sleepy feelings.

6. **Get enough sleep to begin with.** You can manage a late night every once in a while, but a steady diet of all-nighters guarantees that you'll be fighting off the sandman.

Set subgoals for each study session. Plan how long your study session will be as well as what specific tasks you want to accomplish and in what order. Build in some break time to help your concentration stay fresh. Monitor how well you're achieving these subgoals and adapt your planning and resources accordingly.

Original Bloom's Taxonomy College instructors sometimes rely on a framework, Bloom's Taxonomy, which clarifies different kinds of learning and organizes them according to complexity.

Benjamin Bloom and his colleagues (1956) developed their hierarchy of cognitive skills to describe the kind of work that college courses require. Bloom and his colleagues originally distinguished *lower-order thinking skills*, such as knowledge and comprehension, from *higher-order thinking skills*, such as application, analysis, synthesis, and evaluation. Some instructors introduce Bloom's Taxonomy as a framework to help you understand how to delve more deeply into your studies.

Beginning courses tend to emphasize the *lower-order* cognitive skill of remembering, which is usually assessed using multiple-choice tests. To study for tests that involve lower-order learning, rely on effective memory strategies discussed later in this chapter.

Advanced courses tend to emphasize *higher-order* cognitive skills include applying, analyzing, evaluating, and creating. Application skills help you transfer your knowledge to novel examples. Practice in analysis contributes to your effectiveness in reasoning and asking questions. Evaluating requires making decisions or judgments. Creating involves the integration of ideas into a new creation or perspective. Higher-order tasks require you to show greater independence and creativity in your thinking.

The New Bloom's Taxonomy Recently, Bloom's colleagues (Anderson & Krathwohl, 2001) modernized the original taxonomy with the following, arranged from lower-order to higher-order cognitive skills.

- **Remember** Retrieve pertinent acts from long-term memory *(recognize, recall)*
- **Understand** Construct new meaning by mixing new material with existing ideas *(interpret, exemplify, classify, summarize, infer, compare, explain)*
- **Apply**   Use procedures to solve problems or complete tasks *(execute, implement)*
- **Analyze** Subdivide content into meaningful parts and relate the parts *(differentiating, organizing, attributing)*
- **Evaluate** Come to a conclusion about something based on standards/criteria *(checking, critiquing, judging)*
- **Create** Reorganize elements into a new pattern, structure, or purpose *(generate, plan, produce)*

Source: Wilbert J. McKeachie, *Teaching Tips* Eleventh Edition. Copyright © 2002 by Houghton Mifflin Company. Reprinted with permission.

You can follow the spirit of Bloom's Taxonomy in your own approach to studying. Challenge yourself to go one level above what the course requires. For example, if your instructor emphasizes the learning of facts and figures in assignments, practice applying course materials to new situations. This emphasis will promote learning that endures. Try the Journal activity "Deep Study" on page 214 to see how Bloom's Taxonomy can help you study more effectively for exams.

Master the Disciplines

If you're majoring in an area that will train you for a specific profession such as business or medicine, you may wonder why you also need to take liberal arts courses. Each discipline represents a specialized way of thinking about human experience that should help you develop a richer perspective on life and more ways to view and handle problems. According to Gardner (1999), students must get beyond memorizing facts and concepts to understand how disciplines uniquely flavor the interpretation of fact. Gardner suggested that proper education provides a "shopping mall of the disciplines," which ultimately can help students choose which ones they will master.

Courses differ in how much they make you think. You may have already noticed that you have to adjust your study strategies to different disciplines, especially when it isn't a great match for your learning style. Here is a four-part framework that we will apply to the major disciplines to help you adjust to these differences and maximize your results:

- *The Rules*. Although each discipline requires memorizing new content, each also has sophisticated frameworks and theories that require deeper levels of thinking and understanding.
- *The Risks*. Each discipline tends to have special challenges associated with developing mastery.
- *The Resources*. Your learning style will make some disciplines more successful than others for you. Which elements of your learning style facilitate that success?
- *The Remedy*. If you're studying a discipline that doesn't match your learning style, there are things you can do to improve your efficiency and effectiveness.

The Humanities

Humanities courses develop your understanding of human experience. Most emphasize exploring your subjective experience as you read literature, examine specific periods in history, or evaluate the ideas of philosophers.

The Rules Typically each humanities course is built around a particular *framework*, or set of concepts or theories, that will help you develop a new perspective or richer appreciation for the human condition. For example, learning about literature will expose you to various frameworks of literary criticism, such as psychoanalytic or feminist criticism. Each framework in turn is built on a distinct set of values and assumptions.

Applying the frameworks to literature will probably lead you to different kinds of conclusions. A psychoanalytic framework prompts you to look at unconscious motivations; a feminist framework sensitizes you to social forces that create different options for women and men. You can apply these frameworks to expand your personal insight. Humanities instructors look to your insights as evidence that you understand the frameworks.

The Risks You may fear that your personal interpretations will get you in trouble in humanities courses. You may assume that there is only one right answer and may be afraid that you'll look

ON TARGET TIPS

Deep Study Strategies for the Humanities

Suppose you've enrolled in a film appreciation class. You've just read a chapter about the works of Steven Spielberg. Asking the following (or similar) questions during your review session will help you probe the material most deeply (questions based on Bloom and others, 1956):

Remember	What are the names of Spielberg's past films? When did his first film debut?
Understand	Name the ways his films could be regarded as successful. What themes does he regularly present in his films?
Apply	What other filmmakers tend to borrow from Spielberg's methods? Think about how a different director might have directed the film *E.T.*
Analyze	Why are his films so financially successful? What role has technology played in his productions?
Evaluate	In what ways do you think his work is unique? Rank order Spielberg's films from best to worst.
Create	Propose a story line that would be intriguing to Spielberg. How might his films be different if he'd been born 20 years earlier?

Source: From B. S. Bloom, et al, *Taxonomy of Educational Objectives: Cognitive Domain.* © 1956, renewed 1984 by Benjamin S. Bloom and David R. Krathwohl. Reprinted with permission of Longman Publishing Group.

foolish if what you say is "wrong." However, the objective of most humanities courses is to encourage breadth of thinking. Take the risk of sharing your insights. You may end up offering ideas that your class members have never heard. On Target Tips, "Deep Study Strategies for the Humanities," illustrates one helpful approach based on Bloom's Taxonomy.

Notice that by using your imagination to think about your assignments, you also make new connections to the assigned material. The more connections you make, the easier it will be for you to recall information. This strategy also helps you anticipate and practice for essay tests.

The Resources Because of their learning styles, some students have a natural advantage in humanities courses. For example, Janeane Garofalo declared history as her major in college. During one of her first humanities assignments she wrote an essay about Bill Murray, filling an entire blue book about his comedic gifts.

Not only was she able to star in a movie with her comedic idol later in life, she's proud that she gets to "hang" with him, but she reports that it feels "surreal." She also claims that she's glad that the essay has gotten lost, as "he'd probably think I was the biggest loser in the world." Not many of us will realize such an ironic outcome connected to a first-year assignment. However, like Janeane, those who will be drawn to humanities as a major tend to have the following characteristics:

- If you have verbal-linguistic intelligence, you bring a love of words and their meanings to complex humanities assignments.
- If you're skilled in auditory processing, you can track difficult lectures with ease.
- If you enjoy assignments that emphasize reflection and creative learning styles as well, humanities assignments offer you wide latitude for personal interpretation.
- If you like to think critically and creatively, you'll have many opportunities to create and defend your perspective.

The Remedy Not everyone has a learning style that makes learning in the humanities easy. What are some strategies you can use to enhance your success in humanities classes?

- *Keep a dictionary close.* You're bound to run into new terms that will slow down your reading.
- *Compare ideas.* Exploit any opportunity to discuss central ideas or identify challenging concepts.
- *Practice making conclusions.* Rehearse aloud or on paper the key ideas and principles you draw from the assignment.
- *Read to make connections.* The more you read about a topic, the more you'll have to reflect on.

> *The answers you get from literature depend on the questions you pose.*
> Margaret Atwood
> *Contemporary Canadian novelist*

Natural Science and Math

Natural science courses such as chemistry or physics explain the natural phenomena of the world, including everything from how fast an apple falls from a tree to the mysteries of the cell. Mathematics provides the tools to measure observations and assess change.

The Rules Natural science and math are loaded with theorems, laws, and formulas that you'll probably need to memorize, but comprehension should be your primary objective. Most of the activities that you undertake in science and math provide practice in application; you apply the rules to produce a specific outcome or solution.

Obviously, the more you practice applying the principles or formulas, the more enduring your learning will be.

The Risks Natural science and math often have an unappealing reputation. The stereotype is that only science and math "geeks" do well in these courses. It will help if you deflate your images about science slightly. For example, you regularly act like a scientist does when you figure out how things work, although you may not be as systematic or careful in your observations as scientists are. With some practice, you too, can do real science.

The Resources The natural sciences and mathematics attract students who have particular strengths in the logical-mathematical and naturalist dimensions of intelligence. Although the stereotype suggests that scientists do their work alone, progress in science depends on collaboration. Therefore, interpersonal intelligence also facilitates discovering and sharing new scientific knowledge.

Visual learners manage the challenges of mathematical formulas and also bring strong observational skills to science problems. Kinesthetic learners function well in laboratory exercises or field applications. Solving problems in natural science and mathematics also offers opportunities to exercise critical and creative thinking, thoughtful reflection, and active learning.

The Remedy If you don't have natural abilities to support your learning in the natural sciences and mathematics, see On Target Tips, "Improve in Science and Math," for some ideas that can help.

ON TARGET TIPS

Improve in Science and Math

- **Talk about what you already believe.** Sometimes pre-existing notions can interfere with learning new ideas in science (Treagust, Duit, & Fraser, 1996). If you state what you really know or think about a scientific event, it may be easier for you to see where your explanation may not be adequate. Scientific explanations may then offer a clear improvement.
- **Collaborate with others.** Most scientists do not work in isolation. Collaboration is a good model for beginners as well. By talking through problems with other students, you can improve your scientific problem solving.
- **Change representational strategies.** Some students find science and math too abstract. By changing the format of the problem, you may discover a clue about how to work with the ideas involved. For example, if a problem is presented in pictures or symbols, translate those to words. If you have a difficult word problem, try using pictures or symbols.
- **Know why you're studying.** Keep the big picture in mind. What will you accomplish by learning the skills involved in any given assignment?
- **If you get confused, find another class section and sit in.** Sometimes it helps to sit through a class twice, which may be possible if your instructor teaches multiple sections.
- **Be persistent and check your work.** Some problems don't yield a fast answer. Keep working, seeking, and persisting until you gain the insight you need to crack the problem. Be sure to check your answers so you don't lose credit because of carelessness.
- **Don't let anxiety overwhelm you.** Practice the skills and try to relax. If that doesn't work, seek counseling or tutoring.

Social Science

Because the social sciences use scientific methods to understand human experience, they often draw on both the sciences and the humanities.

The Rules The social sciences produce laws and theories to explain the behavior of individuals and groups. Concepts in the social sciences often serve as shorthand for complex patterns of behavior. For example, *social stratification*, a sociological concept, refers to how people in a society can be classified into groups according to how much money they make, what types of jobs they have, how much power they wield, and so forth. Much of what students need to memorize in social science courses has to do with learning new terms such as stratification that explain human behavior.

The Risks Learning in the social sciences can be challenging because what you are expected to learn may conflict with what you previously believed. Say, for example, that you heard on television and from your Uncle Ernie that it's dangerous to wake up a sleepwalker. It made sense to you, so you believe it. In your psychology class, however, you discover that this knowledge is inaccurate, and that it is more dangerous

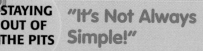
"It's Not Always Simple!"

Trudy's really frustrated. "I don't get it," she says. "I asked my psychology teacher why I can't get along with my sister and she says, 'It depends on lots of things.' It can be frustrating to look for a simple answer and end up with five explanations, but Trudy's frustration was prompting her to reconsider her major. Frustration in learning to cope with complexity is normal. For most social science majors, learning to expect and eventually enjoy complexity is part of the process for developing disciplinary expertise. Trudy probably just needs to hang in there.

to allow a sleepwalker freedom to walk into trouble. You have to reject some things you thought were true—such as opinions from Uncle Ernie—to make room for new ideas derived from social science research. See Staying Out of the Pits, "It's Not Always Simple!," for an illustration.

Social scientists draw on multiple theories to explain the same thing. Social science is considered to be a "soft" science, because it has to explain many deeply complex problems that depend on numerous circumstances.

The Resources Both interpersonal and intrapersonal intelligence can help you understand the social part of social science. Logical-mathematical and naturalist intelligence support the science part of social science. Auditory and visual sensory styles help social scientists do what they do. The strong analytic requirements of social science tend to reward critical thinking, although other kinds of processing can also help.

The Remedy

- *Expect complexity.* You're less likely to be disappointed by the limits of social science if you understand that not all your questions will have clean answers. The most interesting topics are complex and do not present simple answers.
- *Use your own experience.* Most of the topics you'll study correspond to things you've already experienced. When you connect concepts to your experiences, you can bring additional associations that will make them easier to learn. However, don't restrict yourself to understanding only what you've personally experienced.
- *Stay open to alternative explanations.* Recognize that your experience may not be typical of the systematic observations in science. You'll need to practice staying objective as you evaluate evidence, which may include reevaluating the firm conclusions you have drawn from your personal experience.

"I'm a social scientist, Michael. That means I can't explain electricity or anything like that, but if you ever want to know about people, I'm your man."

Foreign Languages

Many colleges require students to study a foreign language to help them step outside their own culture and develop a broader perspective.

The Rules The study of a foreign language is loaded with rules. Proper grammar, verb tenses, and noun forms such as "feminine" and "masculine" all represent rules that you must learn to acquire a new language. This may also include the norms and practices of the culture in which the language is practiced.

The Risks Many foreign languages have new sounds that may not be natural to you. You may fear revealing any shortcomings in your "ear" for language. The amount of time you have to spend drilling can also be daunting. Overcoming the risks and succeeding in foreign language classes involve understanding and memorizing as much as you can.

The Resources If you're blessed with a good ear for language, chances are good that you have a strong auditory sensory preference. Your fascination with words and meanings in another language point to verbal-linguistic intelligence. Because learning a new language requires a lot of memorization, the learning process of reflection may be the best tool available to help you learn a new language.

The Remedy

- *Use color-coded materials.* Color-coded flash cards may give you additional cues about the kinds of words you're trying to learn. For example, use blue cards for verbs, yellow for nouns, and so on.
- *Construct outrageous images.* Construct an image from the sounds of the language that will help you recall the vocabulary. For example, if you want to learn the word for "dinner" in Portuguese (*jantar*), picture John eating a plate full of tar at the dinner table.
- *Talk out loud.* Label objects that you know. Rehearse routine conversations and stage practices with classmates when you can. Read your assignments aloud to improve your ear for the language.
- *Don't get behind.* Keep up, because this type of classwork will pile up fast.
- *Distribute your practice sessions.* Although using shorter but frequent study sessions to memorize college material is good in general, it's *essential* when you're learning a foreign language. Regular practice sessions make your learning last longer.
- *Immerse yourself.* Try to find some natural exposure to the language you're studying. Find a pen pal. Watch movies or television programs that feature the language you're studying.

Now that you have had the opportunity to explore how to develop effective study strategies across the different disciplines, complete the Journal activity "Reduce Your Disciplinary Risks" on page 214 to facilitate your best study habits in disciplines that you find challenging.

Join a Study Group

Working in a study group adds a vital element to your education and expands your resources. Besides learning the course content better, study groups can improve your ability to communicate, develop your project skills, and help you deal with conflict. How can you make group work most efficient and effective?

Don't wait for an instructor to convene a study group. Find interested and competent classmates to meet regularly and talk about a challenging course. Once you have made the commitment, stay the course. Some additional strategies include:

- Identify the hardest concepts or ideas you've encountered.
- Talk about the problems or ideas you especially like or dislike.
- Discuss which parts of the readings interest you the most.
- Help one another share and clarify everyone's understanding of the material.
- Discuss strategies for remembering course material.

> *A special kind of beauty exists which is born in language, of language, and for language.*
> Gaston Bachelard
> 20th-century French scientist

- Generate questions to prepare for tests.
- Keep your commitments.

Read Staying Out of the Pits, "Voted Off the Island," for a description of some of the hazards of disappointing your study group members

Voted Off the Island

Molly decided to take a course in small group behavior to improve her ability to relate to others. She knew that people sometimes found her challenging and a bit disagreeable. The instructor of the course required participation in a study group to give students an opportunity to practice what he was preaching. Although Molly liked her group mates well enough, she often found that she had conflicts that prevented her from making the meetings.

When it came time to calculate grades for the course, Molly's study group members went en masse to the instructor and provided evidence that she had not carried her weight in the group. She got a big fat zero for the applied portion of the course. Not only did her final grade suffer, but so did the learning that she set out to achieve by registering for the course.

Making Study Groups Work

Whether the group is working on a 10-minute discussion project in class or a challenge that spans several weeks, effective groups usually work in stages such as the following:

1. *Plan the task.* As the group convenes, lay the groundwork for working together efficiently by doing four things:
   - Introduce group members ("Who are we?")
   - Identify the purpose of meeting by agreeing on goals and objectives ("What tasks do we need to do?")
   - Create a plan for working together ("How can we work together efficiently?")
   - Set criteria for success ("How will we know we've succeeded in our task?")

2. *Come to a consensus.* Once the ground rules have been established, your group can address the specific task at hand. You don't have to choose a formal leader, although that might be helpful. Group members who ask questions and move the group along help through informal guidance.

3. *Evaluate the results.* In the final stage of the discussion, summarize what has been accomplished and evaluate how well the group has performed so you can improve its efficiency. Then, plan your next meeting. To determine how useful study group strategies might be for you personally, complete the Journal activity "Study-Group Savvy" on page 214.

Overcoming Group Work Obstacles

Group work can provide some of your most exciting—and most frustrating—learning. When you join others to solve a problem or explore the meaning of a work of art, your pooled brainpower can result in insights you might never have had on your own. Effective groups tend to bring out the best in their members.

However, people regularly have problems working in groups. Figure 7.1, "Common Problems and Sensible Solutions for Study Groups," describes some common group work problems and what to do about them. In addition, the Journal activity "Call Waiting" on page 215 provides a common example of problems that arise in study groups to help you polish your social problem-solving skills and build your self-confidence.

> *Muddle is the extra unknown personality in any committee.*
>
> Anthony Sampson
> *Contemporary British social historian*

Overcome Learning Disabilities

Nearly 1 in 10 people in the United States experience complications in learning caused by a learning disability. Learning disabilities can interfere with incoming information

FIGURE 7.1 Common Problems and Sensible Solutions for Study Groups

PROBLEM ⟶ **SOLUTION**

Failure to do groundwork
Group members may be so eager to get on with the task that they jump into a chaotic and unsatisfying discussion.

Establish goals
Your group will collaborate more efficiently if you have a clear picture of what the group wants to achieve and how you hope to achieve it.

Conflict avoidance
Some groups become disorganized as disagreements emerge. Conflict is valuable because differences of opinion can lead to a better discussion or well-considered solution.

Legitimize difference of opinion
When conflict emerges, ask group members to support their opinions with evidence. Let the quality of evidence persuade the group.

Unequal participation
When groups are large and some members take charge, shy or unprepared members may be less likely to participate.

Specify useful roles
Ask quiet members to serve the group by taking notes or summarizing the key ideas. Ask them directly about their opinions.

Domination by one member
Sometimes leaders push too hard and end up alienating other group members. They may not recognize the value of involving all members to improve the quality of the group's conclusion.

Ask for space and cooperation
When leaders get too pushy, suggest that other members need more time and space to express their ideas. If this gentle confrontation does not work, be more forceful. Point out what the group may lose when some don't participate.

Off-task behavior
Less committed members may engage in behaviors (such as popping gum) that distract the group.

Ask for concentrated effort
Suggest that the offending person change the behavior to help promote a more favorable, quiet working environment.

Members who coast
Some group members may not contribute once they sense that the group will succeed by the work of the more energetic or motivated members.

Clarify expectations
Express your disappointment and anger about the unfair distribution of work. Propose some consequences for those who aren't doing their fair share.

---

by scrambling printed words, garbling spoken words, or causing confusion regarding numbers. As a result of confused input, people show problems in expression, including impaired short-term memory, problematic spelling, confusion about terminology, substandard grammar, and poor math skills.

Clearly, students with learning disabilities face daunting problems, including some unfounded prejudices from professors and students who equate learning disability with low intelligence. However, many find great success in school and afterward in their careers.

One of the most common learning disabilities, dyslexia, interferes with a person's ability to read. People with dyslexia report that words and sentences are hard to decode. Because they worry about performance and their slower rate of reading, students with dyslexia often feel singled out in classes for "not trying" or "failing to live up to their potential" despite the fact that they try hard to keep up.

Evaluate Your Issues

Many students think they might have learning disabilities when they really don't. Sometimes they simply don't put in enough study time or their anxiety sabotages them on tests. When you confer with your advisor about your academic struggles, prepare an honest evaluation of how much work you're putting in on your studies. Your problems may lie in ineffective study strategies rather than a learning disability.

If you've experienced criticisms about your performance even though you're trying hard, you may find it helpful to complete Self-Assessment 3 "Could I Have a Learning Disability?" on page 213, which identifies many characteristics of learning disabilities. This inventory will not tell you if you have a learning disability; it merely provides a rough outline of concerns that you can raise with your academic advisor to sort out whether more diagnostic testing is in order.

Know Your Rights

If you have a learning disability, your academic outlook can still be good. Students whose learning difference can be verified by a qualified examiner may apply for special

Learning disabilities do not prevent professional success. Businessman Charles Schwab and actors Tom Cruise, Jay Leno, and Whoopi Goldberg have all revealed their struggles with learning disabilities

education support through the Education for All Handi-capped Children Act of 1975. In addition, the Americans with Disability Act encourages campuses to support the special needs of students with disabilities. Many instructors have developed their own strategies to assist students. For example, they may offer longer test periods for students with language processing problems. Take Charge of Learning Disability Accommodation Requests offers some questions you might pursue with your instructor to help you stay competitive. Then complete the Journal activity "Thrive Even with Disability" on page 214 to round out your strategy.

Compensate

If you do have a learning disability, you'll need to develop a set of strategies to compensate for the challenges your learning style presents. Among other things, you can:

- Set up a study group to discuss course material with others.
- Compare your notes with a friend's after each class to see if you've missed any important details.
- Use audio versions of textbooks when available.
- Use a spell-checker.
- Get support from the campus study skills center.
- Ask friends to proofread your written work.
- Alert your instructors to your special needs.

The compensating strategies that you develop in college will continue to serve you throughout life.

TAKE CHARGE Of Learning Disability Accommodation Requests

If you do have a learning disability, exercise your right to level the playing field by asking for appropriate accommodations from your instructors. Here are some questions you can ask your instructor to help you stay competitive and show your intention to do your best in spite of your limitations.

- Do you mind if I audiotape your lecture?
- Have you worked with learning disabled students before?
- Do you have any special advice to help me stay current in the course?
- May I use a spelling device to help me during testing?
- May I arrange for extended time to finish exams? Can we arrange for someone to monitor me?
- Can you recommend a tutor in case I run into difficulties in your course?
- When would be a good time for me to talk with you to clarify concepts I've learned in class?
- Would you like to have more information about my learning disability?

Improve Your Memory

No matter what your learning profile, you will spend a substantial amount of time in college committing important facts, idea, and theories to memory. Memorizing is a fundamental skill that expands your knowledge base and lays a foundation for more sophisticated thinking skills as you learn about different disciplines. Especially in your early courses, your tests may depend entirely on memorization; for example, naming the levels of the phylogenetic scale in zoology or recognizing the musical instruments in a symphony requires memorization. Let's explore how memory works before we look at methods for improving your memory.

How Memory Works

Two important memory systems are involved in academic learning: *short-term memory* and *long-term memory*.

Short-Term Memory Short-term memory ("working memory") enables us to get some work done without cluttering up our minds. For example, when you look up a new phone number, it doesn't automatically go into your long-term memory for important numbers. Short-term memory lets you retain it briefly, for 30 seconds or so, just long enough to get the number dialed. Then it vanishes. Besides being brief, short-term memory has other features:

- *It's fragile.* Unless you rehearse the information in short-term memory, it will disappear. If you're interrupted while rehearsing the information—suppose someone asks you a question after you have looked up a phone number—your short-term memory will be disrupted and you'll probably lose the information.
- *It has limited capacity.* Short-term memory can hold approximately seven "chunks" of information before the system becomes overtaxed and information is dumped out of awareness (Miller, 1956). Have you ever wondered why telephone numbers have seven digits?
- *It can be tricked.* You may be able to trick short-term memory into holding more detail through a process called "chunking": making each memory "chunk" represent more than one piece of information. This is the basis for the *mnemonics*, or memory aids, discussed later.

Long-Term Memory You've already stored a mountain of facts and impressions in your long-term memory from your education and life experience. Cognitive scientists describe long-term memory as partitioned into two special functions:

- *Procedural memory:* consists of the "how" of memory, the repository of directions for various activities that you have internalized. When you enact a protocol for finding something on the Internet, climb onto a bicycle seat and begin pedaling, or put in a contact lens, you are exercising procedural memory.
- *Declarative memory:* consists of the "what" of memory, the great store of facts and ideas that constitute your personal encyclopedia. Declarative memory is further subdivided into two more functions (Tulving, 1972):

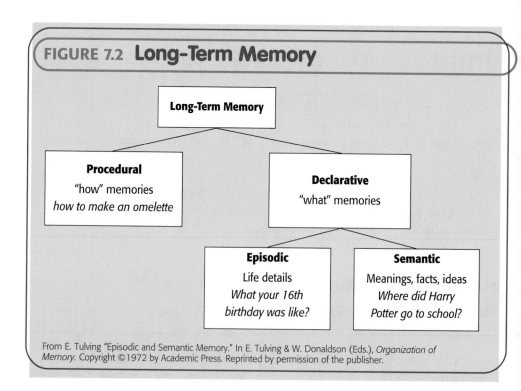

FIGURE 7.2 **Long-Term Memory**

Long-Term Memory

Procedural
"how" memories
how to make an omelette

Declarative
"what" memories

Episodic
Life details
What your 16th birthday was like?

Semantic
Meanings, facts, ideas
Where did Harry Potter go to school?

From E. Tulving "Episodic and Semantic Memory." In E. Tulving & W. Donaldson (Eds.), *Organization of Memory.* Copyright ©1972 by Academic Press. Reprinted by permission of the publisher.

- *Semantic memory:* represents your recall of basic facts and ideas. What is the meaning of *prerequisite*? When did the Great Depression begin? What was Edgar Allen Poe's most famous poem? The content of semantic memory is routinely the target of game shows such as *Jeopardy* and *Who Wants to Be a Millionaire?*
- *Episodic memory:* consists of your recall of personal details in your life What was the best movie you ever saw? Where did you go on your last group date? When did you last see your car keys?

Each memory exists in your long-term memory. Ideally, you can *retrieve* it as needed. What are some other features of long-term memory?

How we remember, what we remember, and why we remember form the most personal map of our individuality.

Christina Baldwin
20th-century American author

- *It appears to have no limits.* Many long-term memories endure. For example, you may be able to recall the name of your first-grade teacher even though you haven't thought of him or her in a long time. We can also remember vivid information without much practice.
- *It's built through association.* The more you know about a topic, the easier it is to learn more, because you have more ways to make associations between new ideas and what you already know. For example, if you're a fan of old movies, you may devote a great deal of memory storage to retaining odd facts about directors, movie locations, and favorite actors. If you're *not* a sports fan, then you'll feel bewildered when your sports-focused friends discuss obscure statistics related to the Super Bowl. People easily store vast quantities of information in long-term memory on the topics that interest them most.

  If you don't know much about a subject, then your task is harder. You'll be building your concept base from the ground up. This is why some course materials are harder to learn than others. You have to work harder to make associations.
- *It can be tricked.* Memory research suggests that long-term memory can be remarkably creative . . . and deceptive. In a series of clever experiments, Elizabeth Loftus (1980) demonstrated that people could report vividly recalling events that had never really happened to them. Once we are convinced that we know something, we may fill in the gaps without realizing how much we've invented.
- *It can fail.* Unfortunately, no matter how hard you study, you're bound to forget some things you learn. There are two main reasons why we forget: *interference* and *decay*.

Interference can crowd out memories, making them difficult to retrieve. For example, when you take a full academic load, the sheer volume of the material may cause interference among the subjects, especially when courses use similar terms for different purposes.

Memory decay is the disintegration of memory that occurs when the ideas are not kept active through use. If you fail to review regularly or do not practice retrieving information, you may find it impossible to recall it when you want it, such as during a test. This is why it is important to regularly review what you have learned.

Ideally, learning strategies should be geared toward building your long-term memory with important and meaningful information. Learn course information so you can recall it not just for tests but well beyond the end of the course.

How to Memorize

There are two general ways to add information to long-term memory (Minninger, 1984): *rote rehearsal* or *comprehensive understanding*. For example, if you're trying to learn a new procedure on your computer, you can either memorize the sequence of things you have to do to accomplish the job or strive to learn what each step accomplishes in relation to your goal. As you can imagine, the first approach leads to superficial learning. Rote learning tends not to last. The next time you have to repeat the procedure on the computer, you'll probably have to relearn it. Learning through understanding initially may require more work, but the learning sticks. What strategies can help?

Adopt the Right Attitude Memorizing new material is a challenge, but a positive attitude helps. Make a serious effort to develop interest in the subject you must study. Study to meet specific learning objectives. Think about the potential professional value the course may provide, even if you have to use your imagination a bit.

Pay Close Attention Don't allow yourself to be distracted when you're processing information about things you must do or remember. Some absentmindedness is caused by failing to absorb the information in the first place.

Concentrate on one thing at a time. You may have to study multiple subjects in one session. If so, try to focus your attention on the subject at hand. Study the most difficult subjects first because you need more energy for harder material. Reward yourself at the end by saving the subject you enjoy most for last.

If you're taking two similar subjects, they may offer overlapping or conflicting ideas. To keep the ideas separate in your mind and reduce the amount of interference between them, space these subjects apart when you study. If you must study for multiple tests in a short time frame, schedule your final study session in a particular subject as the last thing you do before the test.

Involve Yourself in Your Studies Look for personal connections. This will make learning and recalling unfamiliar or abstract ideas easier (Matlin, 1998), especially if you're a visual learner. For example, in history you may have to learn about periods that seem quite remote to you. Think about how these periods might have involved your own ancestors. For example, would your great-grandmother have been a flapper during the Roaring '20s, or would she have led a different life? Make her the focal point of your learning about this era. If you don't know anything about her, imagine her.

Ask yourself questions about what you've read or what you've recorded about class activities. Expand the number of associations you make with the information. This makes the ideas easier to recall. Add this activity to your rehearsal time. The following questions, and others like it, can help you create additional links to course concepts:

- Have I ever seen this concept before?
  - Do I like or dislike the ideas?
  - What are some practical examples of the concept?
  - Are there other ways to explain the concept?

This practice will improve not only your memory for course concepts but also your ability to think critically about them.

Create Memory Prompts Organize concepts in a tree diagram or concept map, as shown in Figure 7.3, to provide additional cues for remembering ideas. For example, suppose you're studying important events in U.S. history in the 1950s. Construct a map that captures the important, related details of the period to make them easier to remember.

Use Mnemonics *Mnemonics* (ne-mon-ix) are strategies that expand visual or auditory associations and help you learn. They involve linking something you want to remember to images, letters, or words that you already know or that are easy to recall because of how you've constructed the mnemonic. They can be visual or text based, logical or goofy, complex or simple. See Figure 7.4 for some examples of mnemonics from a variety of disciplines.

©2003 by Sidney Harris.

FIGURE 7.3 Tree Diagrams

Tree diagrams or concept maps branch out to organize important information.

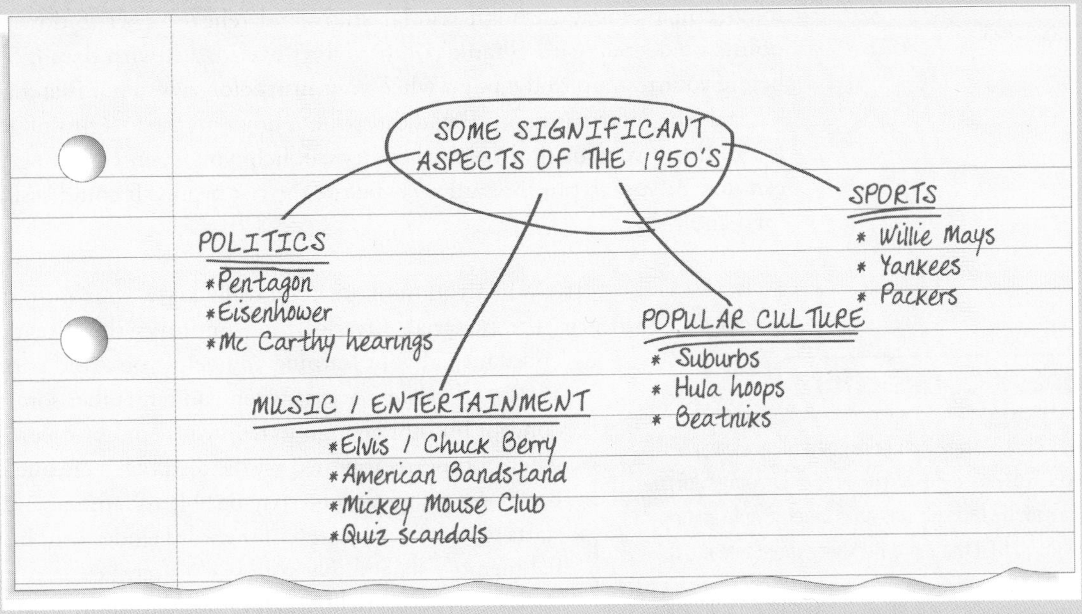

```
        SOME SIGNIFICANT
        ASPECTS OF THE 1950'S

                                              SPORTS
   POLITICS                                    * Willie Mays
    *Pentagon                                  * Yankees
    *Eisenhower                                * Packers
    *Mc Carthy hearings      POPULAR CULTURE
                              * Suburbs
         MUSIC / ENTERTAINMENT    * Hula hoops
                              * Beatniks
             *Elvis / Chuck Berry
             *American Bandstand
             *Mickey Mouse Club
             *Quiz scandals
```

FIGURE 7.4 Examples of Mnemonics from Various Disciplines

Discipline	Mnemonic	Meaning
Business	SWOT	Strengths, weaknesses, opportunities, threats (a technique for analyzing problems)
Physics	ROY G. BIV	Red, orange, yellow, green, blue, violet (visible colors in the light spectrum)
Geography	HOMES	Huron, Ontario, Michigan, Erie, Superior (the Great Lakes)
Music	Every	E
	good	G
	boy	B
	does	D
	fine	F (the lines of the treble clef)
Astronomy	My	Mercury
	very	Venus
	elegant	Earth
	mother	Mars
	just	Jupiter
	served	Saturn
	us	Uranus
	nine	Neptune
	pickles	Pluto (nine planets in order from the sun)

Use Props Create a set of flash cards and carry them with you. Rehearse while you wait in grocery store lines, at the laudromat, and at doctors' offices. Consider creating audio-tapes of the ideas you want to memorize, and review those while driving or doing chores.

Construct a "Cram Card" Whenever you can't commit important information to long-term memory through regular study and rehearsal, write down the essential points on a small card (Frank, 1996). Don't overload it with detail. Study the card before your test, up to the point when your instructor says to put materials away. Then rehearse the information until you can write it down in the margins of your test book-let. In this way, your short-term memory can help you when your long-term memory can not. Be sure to put the card away before the test begins. It could easily be mistaken for a cheat sheet.

Strive to Overlearn When you think that you really know your stuff, study just a bit longer to "overlearn" the material. Overlearning improves the integration and the endurance of your learning and helps you avoid partial memories.

Partial memory occurs when you remember something about a concept but not enough to help you. For example, you may recall where a concept appeared on the textbook page but fail to remember its meaning. Or you may be able to remember that a concept starts with "p" but the rest of the word eludes you. Instances of par-tial memory suggest that your study strategies need more work.

When you partially recall important information, you may be able to retrieve the whole of what you stored in memory if you temporarily change the direction of your thinking. Focusing away from the problem gives your mental circuits more time to "warm up," sometimes causing a term or name to surface.

Exploit Situational Cues If you can, when you take an exam, sit in the seat you normally sit in for class. Being in the same place may help you dredge up memories that might be hard to remember without context cues. The Journal activity "What's in a Name?" on page 215 also will give you an advantage in dealing with the enormous amount of memorizing that lies ahead.

Additional Memory Strategies

The following strategies provide additional help for memoriz-ing different types of information.

Rhymes. If you were raised in the United States, you most likely learned when Columbus came to America through rhyme: "Columbus sailed the ocean blue/In fourteen hundred ninety-two." The rhyme leaves an indelible impression. Eventually you do not have to repeat the rhyme to remember the date. Here's another example from first aid: "When the face is red, raise the head. When the face is pale, raise the tail." Remembering the rhyme allows you to make a swift decision about appropriate treatment.

Songs. Melodies also can produce enduring memories. A genera-tion of U.S. children learned how to spell *encyclopedia* by singing its spelling along with Jiminy Cricket on *The Mickey Mouse Club* in the early days of television. Many children learn their phone

Career Connections

Alan was almost supernaturally good in recalling obscure sports facts. Early on in his life he amazed people with the quantity and quality of the facts he was able to retrieve from his memory. He recognized that the more he knew about a team, the easier it was to attach additional interesting, related details to his fact warehouse. He was happiest when he could engage in discus-sion with other sports enthusiasts, comparing the details of what they could recall. Alan was surprised and disappointed to discover that memorizing facts in his college courses was not as easy. How-ever, he recognized that he could pursue a career in sports broad-casting that would make the most of his skills and interests.

He opted for a major in Communication Arts with an emphasis in broadcasting. His senior internship allowed him to live the life of a broadcaster for 10 hours a week. His knowledge and enthusiasm were so impressive that Alan received a job offer shortly after grad-uation. Within a few years, he was a sports reporter in a small mar-ket station, living the life about which he had dreamed.

Julia had always wanted to be a teacher. She thought it would be very gratifying to teach children about music and watch the impact of their new appreciation of cultural activities on their lives. She was profoundly disappointed when she took her Music Appreciation course in college because the professor required that her students memorize long passages of music so they could recognize them at test time in as few bars as possible. Although she understood recog-nizing music from memory could enhance musical appreciation, she doubted that it would produce the kind of transforming effect on children that she wanted to produce.

In her field placement, she began experimenting with ways to allow children to create music and to criticize what they heard. She began to see the kinds of excitement that she thought could sustain her in her teaching career. To no one's surprise, Julia easily captured her dream job after graduation and also went on to earn teaching awards that recognized her creativity.

numbers or addresses when parents sing the information to them using a familiar melody.

Acronyms. Acronyms are special words (or sentences) that you construct using the first letter from each word in the list you wish to memorize. (See Figure 7.4 for some examples.) The acronym cues you not only to the items on the list but also to their proper order.

Method of loci. In another mnemonic, you associate the parts of a list with a physical sequence of activities or a specific location that you know well. For example, you can remember a long and difficult speech by thinking about walking through your home and associating a piece of the speech with each of the rooms. Another example of the method of loci can be found in a creative pharmacy major's attempt to remember the path of a red blood cell by imagining an oversized body on a familiar floor and walking her or his way through the heart, arteries, and veins.

Visualization. Using your imagination to come up with provocative images can provide memory cues. Making visualizations ridiculous is the best way to make them memorable (Lorayne & Lucas, 1996). Substitute or combine objects, exaggerate their features, make them disproportionate, or involve action in an image to make it distinctive. For example, you could remember elected representatives by combining symbols that represent them in some outrageous way. The Wisconsin senators Feingold and Kohl become easy to remember if you picture the Senate filled with coal dipped in 14K (fine) gold.

Drawings or diagrams. You don't have to be artistic to draw pictures, make arrows, or create stars in the margins of books or notes. Adding images can make recalling details easier. Draw pictures of the comparisons that your instructor uses to clarify concepts. For example, if your psychology instructor describes Freud's view of the unconscious as similar to an iceberg, draw a large iceberg in the background of your notes. Drawings are especially helpful for visual learners.

Evaluate Your Progress

How skilled are you in using memory-enhancing strategies to achieve your goals? Complete Self-Assessment 2 "Am I Ready to Learn and Remember?" on page 212 to identify strategies that you use now and ones that show promise for helping you study more effectively in the future. Another way to evaluate your progress involves examining your test results to determine whether your strategies worked. You may need to study for longer periods or seek new, more efficient methods for learning new ideas.

If you prefer memorizing information to other kinds of academic work, you're in good company. Most beginning students prefer well-structured, simple learning tasks (Baxter Magolda, 1992). Memorizing basic facts feels like a manageable challenge in most courses. However, college courses will routinely challenge you to go beyond rote memory and learn more deeply. One reason to accept these challenges now is that they can build your confidence for upper-level courses that you'll take later on. Overall, you'll emerge from college with greater pride in what you've accomplished. Now complete the Journal activity "How to Remember" on page 215 to further practice some strategies for improving your memory.

Summary Strategies for Mastering College

Enhance your study skills by using strategies that match your resources to the demands of the work.

Focus on the "Six Strategies for Success" above as you read each chapter to learn how to apply these strategies to your own success.

1 Plan Your Attack

- Recognize that study has more positive effects than good grades.
- Find a quiet place and use it consistently.
- Schedule study times that work with your energy level and course demands.
- Set goals for what you want to accomplish in a study session.
- Recognize how surface and deep learning differ.
- Push yourself to work at deeper levels to help learning endure.
- Consider Bloom's Taxonomy to maximize study gains.

2 Master the Disciplines

- Prepare to think more abstractly as coursework deepens.

- Understand the rules, risks, resources, and remedy for each discipline.
- Know how your learning style fits with a given discipline.
- Share your personal insights in humanities courses.
- Strengthen your logic and math skills to succeed in science and math.
- Expect complexity and a blend of science and the humanities in social science.
- Memorize rules and terminology to optimize language learning.

3 Join a Study Group

- Form study groups to learn course concepts.
- Assign roles, plan tasks, set criteria for success, and evaluate your progress to ensure an effective study group.
- Solve routine problems that compromise group progress.

4 Overcome Learning Disabilities

- Recognize how confused input affects student performance.
- Undergo special testing if your results don't match your effort.
- Rely on the Disabilities Act to secure the help you need.
- Develop compensating strategies to minimize the effects of a learning difference.

5 Improve Your Memory

- Know the differences between short- and long-term memory.
- Approach memorizing with the right attitude.
- Attend, concentrate, and minimize interference among subjects.
- Use mnemonics to build personal connections to your coursework.

Review Questions

1. List a few important issues to consider when deciding where to study, when to study, and what to study.

_____

_____

_____

2. What is the difference between lower-order and higher-order cognitive skills? Provide a few examples of each.

_____

_____

_____

3. How do the different disciplines encourage different kinds of study? List some specific strategies for success in the discipline area you are considering for your major.

_____

_____

_____

4. List three pros and three cons of working in study groups. Now write down a strategy for addressing each con.

Pro: _____

Pro: _____

Pro: _____

Con:_____   Strategy: _____

Con:_____   Strategy: _____

Con:_____   Strategy: _____

5. How can learning disabilities influence study success? What can be done to address such disabilities?

_____

_____

_____

6. Describe the difference between short-term memory and long-term memory. How can you use this information to improve your study strategies in the future?

_____

_____

_____

_____

Learning Portfolio

SELF-ASSESSMENTS

YOUR JOURNAL

STRATEGIES FOR SUCCESS

Identify Meaningful Values

Set Goals, Plan, and Monitor

Get Motivated and Take Responsibility

Build Self-Esteem and Confidence

Enhance Your Study Skills and Memory

Explore Careers

Think and Learn

Early Bird or Night Owl?

To determine your typical energy level, check all the characteristics that apply to you. Then consider the strategies listed below for each type.

How's Your Energy?	Respect Your Natural Energy
____ I roll out of bed eager to face the day.	• Schedule classes as early as you can.
____ I manage to get up without an alarm.	• Avoid commitments when your energy dips in the afternoon.
____ My friends complain that I'm too chipper early in the morning.	• Consider an afternoon catnap.
____ I tend to run out of steam in the middle of the afternoon.	• Study your hardest coursework before your energy lapses.
____ I prefer intense activity before noon.	• Don't plan to study late at night unless you absolutely must.
____ I can't function without a minimum amount of sleep.	
____ I leave parties early.	

____ I drag myself out of bed, sorry the day has started.	• Schedule your classes in the late morning and early afternoon.
____ I regularly use the snooze button on my alarm clock.	• Try night classes. They may be a perfect match for your energy.
____ My friends complain that I'm too crabby in the morning.	• Buy a good alarm clock (maybe even a backup alarm).
____ I tend to start hitting my stride in the middle of the afternoon.	• Don't study when you're groggy.
____ I prefer intense activity after noon.	• Study late and fall asleep. It may help you retain information.
____ I can function on little or no sleep.	
____ I leave parties late.	

Are you an early bird or a night owl? The category with the most check marks reveals your energy profile, which suggests when study strategies and class scheduling will produce the greatest payoff. Early birds should make their most serious efforts before late afternoon. Night owls should avoid making commitments before late morning.

Am I Ready to Learn and Remember?

Review the elements of effective study strategies below and decide whether each statement is something you already do well or something you need to improve.

	I Do This Well	I Could Improve This
To take advantage of my best energy levels, I purposefully schedule when I will study certain subjects.	_____	_____
I select study environments that have few distractions.	_____	_____
I review course materials regularly to spread my learning out over time.	_____	_____
I try to find some angle in my assignments that will increase my interest.	_____	_____
To ensure my understanding and increase my personal involvement, I question what I read.	_____	_____
I look for ways to add meaning to course ideas during review sessions.	_____	_____
I rehearse key ideas to the point of overlearning.	_____	_____
I use mnemonic strategies for memorization. (List several specific strategies you use):	_____	_____

_____

_____

	I Do This Well	I Could Improve This
When I feel frustrated by partial recall, I divert my attention to recover more details.	_____	_____
I schedule an intensive review session before a test.	_____	_____
I avoid cramming whenever I can.	_____	_____
I use review tests to see whether I need to change my study strategies.	_____	_____

Look over your answers. Could the areas you need to improve mean the difference between a mediocre performance and honor-quality work? What would you need to do to improve? How could you reward yourself for adopting better strategies?

Could I Have a Learning Disability?

You may have a learning disability if you have the following difficulties. Check any that apply to you.

Misunderstand simple printed materials _____

Have a great deal of trouble working with basic math problems _____

Have difficulty writing and speaking _____

Approach studying in a haphazard manner _____

Get easily distracted _____

Confuse *left* and *right* or other spatial words _____

Arrive late often (such as frequent late arrival to class) _____

Struggle with categories and comparisons _____

Have trouble with fine motor skills or finger control _____

Feel awkward in gross motor (body) movements _____

Misinterpret subtle nonverbal cues _____

Have difficulty following instructions _____

Reverse letters in words or words in sentences _____

Hear teachers complain that you "are not living up to your potential" _____

If you feel frustrated in any of these areas, you may want to see if you have a learning disability. First, talk with your advisor about the nature of your difficulties. She or he can recommend changes in your study strategy or refer you to a specialist on campus who can help you with diagnostic testing. On some campuses this evaluation is expensive, but you're likely to get advice that makes the investment worthwhile.

Your Journal

● REFLECT

1. Study-Group Savvy

In which courses would you benefit from forming a study group?

_____

_____

What special talents would you bring that would help the group succeed? Do you have any personality quirks or negative work habits that could adversely affect the group's outcomes? What can you do to address those problems in the study group?

Positive talents: _____

Negative traits: _____

2. Reduce Your Disciplinary Risks

Many people have fears related to disciplines they are required to study to complete their education. In what discipline are you least comfortable? Describe the source of your concern. What might you do to get more comfortable with this discipline? Can you identify any role models who can help you develop a more positive attitude?

Discipline: _____

Issues of concern: _____

Strategies for greater comfort: _____

Potential role models: _____

● DO

1. Thrive Even with Disability

Who is the learning disabilities specialist on campus? Find out and write down the contact information below. If you suspect you might have a problem, make an appointment with this individual to find out about further testing. If you don't think you have a learning disability, talk with a classmate who does. Find out what kinds of compensations seem to be most effective for him or her. Do some of the compensations seem like they might also be useful to you? Which ones?

Learning Disabilities Specialist: _____

Phone #/E-mail address: _____

Information on testing: _____

Helpful compensation strategies: _____

2. Deep Study

Pick a topic area from a subject you're currently studying. Develop a question based on each order level of Bloom's Taxonomy. Now come up with a tentative answer for each question. How much harder do you have to work to come up with a good answer to a higher-order question than a lower-order one? Think about the balance of lower-order and higher-order questions across the courses you are taking. What should this balance suggest about how you study in your courses?

Remember: _____

Understand: _____

Apply: _____

Your Journal

Analyze: _____

Evaluate: _____

Create: _____

● THINK CRITICALLY

1. Call Waiting

You're assigned to a discussion group that will meet throughout the semester, but one of the group members brings her cell phone. The phone usually rings five minutes into the meeting. She excuses herself to take the call and usually misses more than half of each meeting. What strategies could you and your group use to address this challenge?

_____

_____

2. How to Remember

What is something that you frequently forget? It could be an important concept from one of your classes, a particular type of appointment, or where you last left your keys. List a few strategies that might help you address this memory lapse. Try each one. Which strategy worked best and why?

Strategy #1: _____

Strategy #2: _____

Strategy #3: _____

● CREATE

1. What's in a Name?

Select one list of information from any chapter in this book. Develop a mnemonic device for remembering the items in that list. Write it here. Revisit this mnemonic tomorrow and see how well you can remember the items it represents. Did the mnemonic help? Try applying this strategy to other aspects of this course.
Your Mnemonic:

_____

_____

2. Creative Space Management

Identify a place where you have a hard time studying, such as a bus, a noisy dorm room, or a crowded kitchen table. List three strategies that would help you make this place better for studying.

1. _____

2. _____

3. _____

Now try each one. Did they work? Why or why not? What did this teach you about your ideal study location?

_____

_____

Applying the Six Strategies for Success

What did you learn in this chapter that you can apply to the following key strategies to help form the foundation for your success? Write down all of the main points you can remember that support the following strategies:

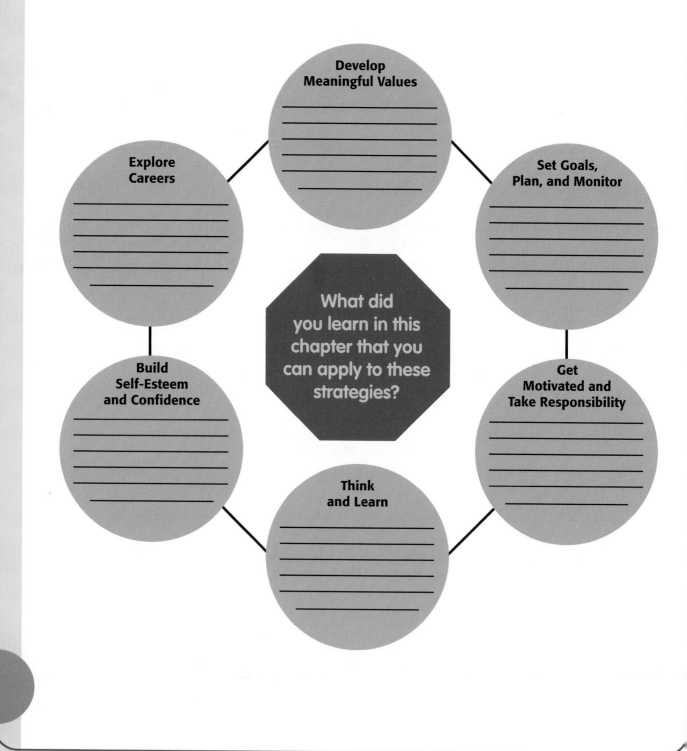

8 Succeed on Tests

© Photodisc/Getty Images

Where Are You? By this point in the term, you've probably already faced one ongoing challenge that all college students encounter—tests! Happily, some tests match how well you've studied and what you've learned. Other exams, however, may have led you to think that you and the instructor weren't on the same planet, let alone in the same classroom.

To evaluate where you stand right now with regard to test-taking, place a check next to only those items that apply to you.

- I pace myself effectively to get ready for a test.
- I figure out ahead of time what will be on the test and try to predict the test questions.
- I control my nervousness about test performance.
- I size up the test to know what I need to do and read all directions carefully before I start.
- I know effective strategies for scoring well on multiple-choice tests.
- I know how to do well on essay questions.
- I regularly complete tests in the allotted time.
- I know how to analyze test results to improve my learning and future test performances.
- I know the consequences of academic dishonesty at my college.

The physicist Albert Einstein was a notoriously poor student and test-taker until the right learning climate helped him to thrive as a learner. Think about how this problem might apply to you as you read his profile on the next page.

217

Images of College Success

Albert Einstein

When he was a small child, no one could have predicted the extraordinary future of Albert Einstein. He was slow in learning to talk and painfully shy. Although he loved science and mathematics, he struggled with the style of his formal education. His teachers at the Luitpold Gymnasium in Munich, Germany, taught by constant drilling, which Einstein found boring. He often skipped classes or was ill-prepared, resulting in punishment for his disobedience and scorn from his classmates.

Although his teachers thought he was dull, Einstein simply hated the persistent drilling he faced in school. When his father's business failed and the family moved to Italy, Einstein purposefully failed so many tests that he was asked to leave his school. One teacher told Einstein that he was glad to see him go, because the teachers thought he encouraged other students to be disrespectful.

When his family later suggested that he needed to prepare for a career, Einstein applied to a technical school in Switzerland. To be admitted, he had to pass rigorous entrance examinations. Although his scores on his math and science exams clearly showed promise, he was a dismal failure in zoology, botany, and language. A remedial year at a relatively creative school, where his questioning was encouraged rather than discouraged, allowed him to catch up. He passed his entrance exams on his second attempt and went on to revolutionize the field of physics. Ironically, the Luitpold Gymnasium, an institution once offended by Albert Einstein's uncooperative and dull academic performance, was renamed in honor of him before he died (Levinger, 1949).

Einstein himself would have been quite amused at the extent to which his own ideas would become the basis for testing millions of physics students struggling to understand his creative conceptualization of energy and matter. When asked to explain the theory of relativity, Einstein once joked, "Put your hand on a hot stove for a minute and it seems like an hour. Sit with a pretty girl for an hour and it seems like a minute. That's relativity!"

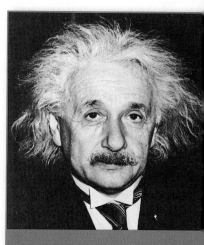

What can we learn from **ALBERT EINSTEIN'S** experiences in testing?

Develop
Meaningful
Values

Set Goals, Plan,
and Monitor

Get
Motivated
and Take
Responsibility

Successed
on Tests

Build
Self-Esteem
and
Confidence

Explore
Careers

Think
and
Learn

As you read, think about the "Six Strategies for Success" listed to the left and how this chapter can help you maximize success in these important areas. For example, preparing for tests may be one of your strongest motivations to learn. Test-taking can sharpen your planning skills, and your test results can clarify your career direction.

Get On with It!

No matter what course of study you pursue, your efforts are going to be evaluated. Believe it or not, tests can benefit you. They can help:

- *Pace your reading.* College reading assignments can feel overwhelming, so it's easy to get behind. Tests throughout the term push you to do the work on time.
- *Consolidate your learning.* Tests encourage you to study the course material more intensively and retain the ideas longer. Your effort in preparing for tests can produce insights you might not have made without the pressure of the exam.
- *Improve your thinking.* Tests sharpen your critical-thinking skills. Whether you're figuring out which multiple-choice alternative to eliminate or determining how to structure an essay, tests give you practice in careful observation, analysis, and judgment.
- *Get feedback.* Test results tell you whether your study strategies have worked. Good results confirm that you're on the right track. A string of poor scores suggests that you need to improve your motivation or study skills.
- *Achieve special status.* As demonstrated in the introductory story about Albert Einstein, test results can confer special status. For example, good results might qualify you for a scholarship or allow you to skip preliminary courses and move on to more advanced ones.

Difficulties, opposition . . . there is a special joy in facing them and in coming out on top.

Vijaya Lakshmi Pandit
20th-century Indian diplomat

Get in Gear

You know that instructors are going to test you. What can you do to show them you've got the right attitude to succeed? First, recognize that there are important differences between

"You're kidding! You count S.A.T.s?"

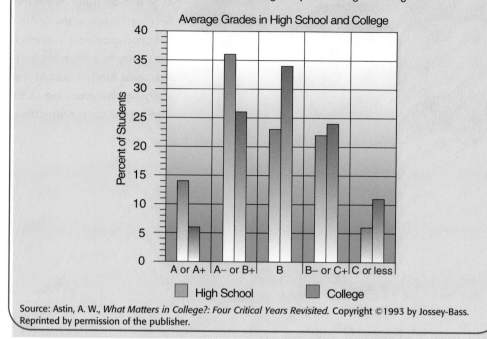

FIGURE 8.1 How Grades Can Change

As you can see in the graph, grades drifted downward from high school to college. This means that you have to study harder to maintain the same grade point average in college.

Average Grades in High School and College

(Percent of Students, by grade category: A or A+, A− or B+, B, B− or C+, C or less — comparing High School and College)

Source: Astin, A. W., *What Matters in College?: Four Critical Years Revisited.* Copyright ©1993 by Jossey-Bass. Reprinted by permission of the publisher.

ON TARGET TIPS

How *Not* to Cram

- **Concentrate on the big picture.** Keep a master calendar for the term. Put all your scheduled tests on it. Post the calendar in your study area.
- **Design your test preparation across courses.** Plan how you'll read, study, and review assigned materials and class notes according to the test demands in all your courses. Wherever possible, distribute your study sessions over time to minimize interference among courses.
- **Keep up with your reading.** If you keep up with your reading, class experiences will reinforce your learning. Avoid massive catchup reading the night before the test—there will probably be too much ground to cover, understand, and remember.
- **Reward yourself for staying on target.** A shiny "A" would be a powerful reward for strong test-preparation habits. However, that reward may come too far in the future to help you sustain better test preparation. Reward yourself on a regular basis for sticking to your study plan. For example, after you've studied hard each evening, watch a tape of a favorite TV show, listen to some music that you really like, or talk with someone you enjoy.
- **Schedule a concentrated review session.** If you've kept up, a solid review session the night before your test should be adequate.

tests in high school and those in college. Most students regularly take more tests and quizzes in high school, but experience tests in college as harder. See Figure 8.1, "How Grades Can Change," to see how grades tend to drift downward as testing difficulties intensify. The Journal activity "Then and Now," on page 244 examines how your high school patterns might predict success. Then, use the following systematic approach to do your best on future tests.

Plan for the Long Term

Successful test-taking requires good long-term and short-term planning. Some good long-term suggestions include the following.

Pace Yourself Don't count on cramming! Eleventh-hour learning is fragile. It may crumble under pressure. The strategies offered in On Target Tips, "How *Not* to Cram," will help you pace yourself so you won't have to go through a last-minute rush to learn.

Meet Your Social Need If you have an extraverted style, studying with others will motivate you to do your reading and help to identify trouble spots. Ask other students who seem to understand the course—at least as well as you do, if not better—to join a study group. Screening helps to ensure that the group will be productive and not slowed down by students who don't reliably do their work. To improve testing success, study group members can compare notes to create the most comprehensive understanding, share hunches about likely test material, develop practice questions, and challenge fuzzy explanations.

By contrast, if the stimulation of a study group is not compatible with your introverted style, find less socially intense support strategies. For example, identify another strong student with a similar style and make a commitment to connect via e-mail to clarify questions or try out test-taking strategies.

Learning is such a very painful business.

May Sarton
20th-century American writer

Protect Your Health If you stay healthy throughout the term, you'll have fewer problems in managing your study schedule and fewer distractions at test time. You can't do your best if you're fighting off the urge to nap, feeling bad from a hangover, or coming down with a cold.

Adopt the Right Attitude Examinations can be emotional events. Nearly everyone feels some test anxiety, but some are overwhelmed by it. Others view testing as doing battle. They cast the instructor as a villain out to trick them and bring them down. This student gets distracted into trying to "outfox" the instructor rather than learning the material. By contrast, to go boldly into a test on hope rather than solid preparation will rarely achieve the outcome you want. Facing the test with the confidence that comes from conscientious planning and systematic study is the best way to overcome unproductive attitudes and emotions.

Plan for the Short Term

Following are some suggestions to improve your short-term planning for taking tests.

Know What to Expect Test conditions vary. In large lecture classes, security issues may be intense. For example, your instructor may require you to sit in alternate seats to reduce cheating. Proctors may roam the aisles and retrieve all materials after the test. Your instructor may not even be present, so you might want to get all of your questions answered before the day of the test. In smaller classes with the instructor present, you may be able to clarify issues as they arise. Either during the class or in the syllabus, most instructors describe the kinds of tests they are planning.

Some instructors even make sample tests from prior semesters available for study purposes. Many welcome questions about how to prepare. On Target Tips, "Will This Be on the Test?," suggests questions you can ask your instructor to clarify the nature of the exam. You may know some students who have completed the course before you. Find out what they did to succeed or what strategies didn't work. Don't be afraid to research your instructor's test-construction practices.

"Psych out" the Teacher Some students seem psychic when guessing what will be on a test. How do they do it? They size up the instructor by identifying what concepts have been stressed enthusiastically during class lectures and discussions. Instructors often use specific cues to identify important and *testable* material (Appleby, 1997). They may be signaling test material when they:

- Repeat or emphasize certain concepts
- Illustrate key ideas with examples
- Stop pacing back and forth behind the lectern
- Intensify eye contact

ON TARGET TIPS

Will This Be on the Test?

Some instructors don't offer many clues about the tests they give. If you have one of these instructors, you might ask these questions:

- How long will the test be?
- What types of questions will be on it?
- Are there any particular aspects of the work we've been doing that you'll emphasize?
- What topics *won't* be on the test?
- Are there penalties for wrong guesses?
- Will this material also be covered on a cumulative exam at the end of the term?

- Use gestures in more dramatic ways
- Change their tone of voice
- Say "in conclusion . . . " or "to summarize . . . "
- Pause to allow you time to write your notes
- Write on the board or point to ideas on an overhead transparency
- Highlight ideas in their introductory remarks or conclusion

Complete the Journal activity "Construct Your Own Exam" on pages 244–245 to help you develop good skills for anticipating test design.

Design Your Study Strategy Your success depends on adapting your learning style to the kind of thinking measured by the test. Take responsibility to find out as much as you can about what the test will involve. Then plan a suitable study strategy. Keep track of your progress as you prepare for the test.

Many tests, especially in introductory-level courses, focus on memorization. Your most effective memorization strategy will use your preferred sensory mode effectively. For example:

- *Visual learners* should use visualization techniques or drawings and diagrams to memorize material.
- *Auditory learners* may prefer to rehearse key ideas aloud or make up songs or rhymes to fix facts in memory.
- *Tactile learners* may try role-play or other hands-on strategies to add cues that help them recall information.

Other types of tests may focus on more sophisticated kinds of thinking. Find out what the format of the test will be ahead of time. Know how points will be distributed across the test. This knowledge may help you decide where to spend your time if it's clear you won't be able to finish. For example, the multiple-choice section may be worth 20 points, and the essay section, 50 points. Even though the multiple-choice comes first, you may want to start with the essay, which counts for more. Find out whether there are penalties for guessing.

Objective Tests.

Memorizing facts is usually a good strategy for answering simple objective test questions. These include tests with multiple-choice, matching, true-false, and fill-in-the-blank items. Successful memorizing strategies include using flash cards, making a concept vocabulary list, reviewing a text's study guide, and reorganizing your notes. Find the memorizing strategy that works best for your learning style.

At the college level, most instructors ask objective questions that require more than just rote memory. When you have to do more than recall facts, your study strategy will also be more complex. Draw organizational charts or diagrams to identify relationships. Design some practice questions that exercise your ability to reason.

Essay Tests.

Digesting a whole term's worth of material for an essay can be a challenge. If you know the specific topics ahead of time, scan the notes you've made and highlight all related ideas in a specific color. This will let you concentrate on those ideas as you think about questions or practice answers. If you don't know the essay topics ahead of time, go back over your course and reading notes and write a paragraph for each text chapter or course lecture. These paragraphs would summarize the key ideas in the passage.

© Bonnie Kamin/PhotoEdit

To succeed on tests, you need to review your notes to think about how the ideas can be incorporated in designated test formats.

Procedural Tests.

Some types of tests ask you to demonstrate specific procedures, such as applying a formula to solve a math problem, conducting an interview in nursing, or solving for an unknown in chemistry. To prepare for procedural tests, perform the target skill until you're comfortable with it. If test time will be limited, build time limits into your practice.

Protect Your Study Time Classmates may request your help at the last minute, especially if you live with them. You may happily accept. Helping others can build your self-esteem and can also help you rehearse material. Or you may need to use the time alone to master the material yourself. If giving help does not work with your study schedule, explain that you've planned out your study strategy and need every minute to concentrate to do your best.

What if a loved one makes demands on your time that interfere with your study schedule? Explain to partners or family members, including children, that you need extra help from them before a test to make it as easy as possible to study. Promise them that you will spend time with them after the test. Then keep your promise. The Journal activity "Find Your Quiet Place" on page 245 provides some additional pointers on ways to envision and manage your study environment to produce the best test preparation conditions.

If you practice good long-term and short-term strategies, your work is much easier as the test gets closer. Figure 8.2, "A Timetable for Sensible Study Strategies," summarizes strategies for pacing yourself for the least stressful test preparation.

> *You have to accept whatever comes and the only important thing is that you meet it with the best you have to give.*
>
> Eleanor Roosevelt
> *20th-century American humanitarian and lecturer*

FIGURE 8.2 A Timetable for Sensible Study Strategies

After each assignment	Write a summary paragraph of what you learned and how it relates to the course objectives.
After each class	Review your notes to consolidate your learning.
During the last class before the test	Find out about the test: 　　What will be and won't be on the test 　　The format of the test 　　The contribution of the test to your grade Clarify any confused ideas from past classes.
After the last class before the test	Plan your final review session.
The night before the test	Organize your notes for systematic review. Study the test material exclusively—or last—to reduce interference. Practice the kind of thinking the test will require: 　　Rehearsal and recital for objective tests 　　Critical analysis for subjective tests Identify any fuzzy areas and confer with classmates to straighten out your confusion. Get a good night's sleep.
The day of the test	Organize your supplies. Eat a good breakfast/lunch/dinner. Review your notes, chapter summaries, course glossary.
The hour before the test	Review your notes. Go to the classroom early and get settled. Practice relaxing and positive thinking.

If You Must, Cram Strategically

It's a bad idea to depend on cramming, but sometimes it can't be helped. You may have too many courses to manage any other way. What are some of the best ideas for last-minute, concentrated study?

- *Clear the decks.* Dedicate your last study session before the test to only that exam. Studying anything else can interfere with the test at hand.
- *Use textbook study aids.* The chapter headings and chapter end-matter can help you organize your last-minute study strategies by identifying key ideas before you begin reading. First, go through and look at the headings—in a good textbook, these will provide you with an outline of the key ideas in the chapter. This practice is especially appropriate in an introductory book. Then read the summary, and look at the key terms and review questions. You will get a pretty good idea of the most important material in the chapter.
- *Skim for main ideas.* Once you know what to look for, skim the chapter with the key ideas in mind. You may even want to skim just to answer the review questions. Scan each paragraph in relevant readings for the key ideas. Topic sentences that capture the central idea of each paragraph are usually the first or the last sentences in the paragraph. Skim the entire assignment to improve your chances of remembering the material.
- *Divide and conquer.* Once you've skimmed the entire body of study materials, size up how much you have to learn in relation to your remaining time. Divide the information into reasonable sections and make your best guess about which will have the largest payoff. Master each section based on whatever time you have left. Even if you don't get to the lower-priority material, your test performance may not suffer much.
- *Stay focused and alert.* Study in good light away from the lure of your bed. Take regular breaks and exercise mildly to stay alert through your session. Caffeine in moderation and regular snacks also may help.
- *Be cautious about professional summaries.* Use professional summaries of great works if you can't complete a full reading. If you rent a film version of a great work of literature, be aware that films and even professional summaries often depart from the original in ways that may reveal your shortcut.
- *Learn from your mistakes.* When you enter a test feeling underprepared, you've undermined your ability to succeed. Even if you luck out and do well, this strategy short-changes what you think and learn over the long term. Consider the factors that left you in such desperate study circumstances. Commit yourself to doing all you can to avoid getting stuck in a situation where you have to cram.

> *Sixty minutes of thinking of any kind is bound to lead to confusion and unhappiness.*
>
> James Thurber
> 20th-century American cartoonist

Set the Stage for Test-Taking Success

It's almost here. Whether you're filled with dread or eager to show what you know, the following last-minute strategies give you the best chance of doing well.

- *Get a good night's sleep.* Research shows that you need **at least** eight hours of sleep to stay alert and do your best thinking, problem solving, and communicating. If you deprive yourself of that dose of sleep, you are already at a disadvantage before you even begin.
- *Bring supplies for your spirit.* A bottle of water or cup of coffee may keep up your spirits (and your caffeine level). Instructors usually specify what comforts you can bring to class. Avoid causing distractions, such as unwrapping noisy candy wrappers; other students are likely to be as nervous and distractible as you are. If you get stress headaches, don't forget to pack your aspirin.

- *Bring required academic supplies—and spares.* You may need to bring a blue book (a standard lined essay book for handwritten responses). Bring a sharpened pencil or pen and a backup, a calculator, scratch paper, or whatever other supplies the instructor allows. Make sure you have a watch or can see a classroom clock so you can pace your work.
- *Organize your resources.* In some cases, instructors may let you bring a summary of notes to jog your memory during the test. They even may let you have open access to your books and notes (a sure sign that the test will be hard). Write your summaries clearly so that you don't lose time trying to decode your own writing. Attach some tabs, use marked index cards, or highlight your resources in other ways that will make them easy to navigate under pressure.
- *Bring reference aids.* If you struggle with writing and spelling, bring a dictionary or a spell-checker if they are permitted. Many instructors will let you use them because it shows your desire to do good work. Some instructors will refuse because of concerns about security and fairness.

Control Your Test Anxiety

Just moments before your instructor hands out an exam, you may feel as if you're in the first car of a roller coaster about to hurtle down the first drop. Your heart pounds. You're sweating. The butterflies just won't go away. A few butterflies are okay. A little anxiety even can be a good sign. It encourages you to prepare for the test and can motivate you to do your very best.

Too many butterflies, though, can cripple your test performance. Nervousness and worry activate the emergency systems in your body. Your pulse increases. Your heart beats faster. Your hands perspire. These responses prepare you to flee or to fight. In stressful circumstances, they help you survive. But in the quiet of the classroom, they interfere with your ability to focus on the test. Self-Assessment 1 "How Serious Is My Test Anxiety?" on page 241 will help you determine if your test anxiety is interfering with your performance.

Sabotaging Success Test-anxious students sabotage their own efforts because they focus on themselves in negative ways (Kaplan & Saccuzzo, 1993). Preoccupied with the certainty of their own failure, they can't free up the energy to perform well. This reaction increases their chances of failure. Text-anxious students interpret even neutral events as further proof of their own inadequacy. For example, if a test proctor looks troubled, the test-anxious student may assume that her or his own behavior somehow caused the troubled look. They are more likely to experience stress-related physical symptoms, such as an upset stomach or a stiff neck, that further hinder performance.

If you have anxiety about tests, you need to do two things:

1. cope with your anxiety
2. improve study skills to build your competence and confidence (Zeidner, 1995).

If you learn to cope with anxiety but don't improve your study skills, you'll feel calmer and more in control but won't improve your performance. By contrast, if you improve your study skills but don't master your anxious feelings, your performance may still erode. It will take some effort to do both things, but consider the long-term rewards.

"Hello, you've reached the office of Professor Arte. If your excuse for not turning your paper in on time is that your computer broke down, press '1.' If your excuse is that you had psychological problems, press '2.' If your excuse is that your grandmother died, press '3.' If your excuse is . . ."

© Harald Bakken

Mastering Anxiety What are some specific things you can do to master test anxiety?

- *Invest your time properly.* Think about it. If you haven't spent as much time preparing for a test as you should, it makes sense to be frightened about performing poorly. Test jitters may only mean that you need to invest more time. If the format your professor will be using doesn't play to your strengths as a test-taker, allocate more time to compensate for this challenge. See the Journal activity "Format Fever" on page 244 to help you think about testing formats that will demand more from you.

- *Neutralize anxiety.* One simple strategy is to neutralize your anxious feelings by learning to breathe in a relaxed manner under stress. See On Target Tips, "Get a Grip," for some pointers on how to achieve greater control.

- *Talk positively to yourself.* Test-anxious students often make their anxieties worse by predicting their own failure. Instead of tormenting yourself with criticism and dire predictions, substitute positive statements, such as "I will overcome this challenge" or "I feel confident I will do well." Practice an optimistic outlook and more positive self-esteem will follow.

- *Exercise regularly.* Many students find relief from their anxieties by building a regular exercise program into their busy schedules. Exercise is a great stress reliever. It also promotes deeper, more restful sleep.

- *Avoid drugs.* Monitor your caffeine intake. Too much can compound agitated feelings. But this is minor compared with problems that result from using harder drugs to ward off anxiety or to stay alert. See Staying Out of the Pits, "Just say 'Whoa'," to learn more about the cost of drug abuse.

> *Anxiety is the interest paid on trouble before it's due.*
>
> William R. Inge
> *20th-century American playwright*

ON TARGET TIPS

Get a Grip

When people are under stress or feel anxious, they may be inclined to overbreathe or hyperventilate (Zuercher-White, 1997). The signs of hyperventilation include shallow, heavy breathing, mouth breathing, gasping for air, yawning, and frequent clearing of the throat. Although it won't hurt you, hyperventilation can make you feel like you are suffocating. Ironically, your sense of smothering is caused by taking in too much air. What can you do to get a grip and breathe more normally during exams?

- **Hold your breath.** If you can devote a minute or two to holding your breath in several 10–15 second spurts, carbon dioxide will build up and counter hyperventilation and feelings of panic.
- **Breathe into a paper bag.** You may look a little funny, but this trick works. Exhale carbon dioxide into a paper bag that covers your mouth and nose. Then rebreathe the carbon dioxide until you feel calmer.
- **Breathe from your diaphragm.** You may have to practice this technique ahead of time to deploy it in the classroom. To learn diaphragm breathing:

1. Find a comfortable place to recline and place a pillow on your stomach. Breathe in slowly through your nose and watch the pillow rise. Breathe out slowly and watch the pillow lower.
2. Once you get the hang of it, remove the pillow but place your hand on your stomach. You will be replacing visual cues with kinesthetic cues that will be helpful when you try breathing in different postures. Concentrate on your stomach as it moves up and down with your measured breathing.
3. Practice diaphragm breathing without your hand on your stomach in different postures. Emphasize rehearsal of the skill while sitting for greatest help during the exam.
4. Slow down your breathing. Pause before inhaling. This practice will give you the greatest sense of control over your feelings of panic.
5. Once you have achieved success, practice twice a day. Maximum success will occur when you can move easily into controlled breathing at the first hint of panic. Practice will facilitate your command.

- **Find support.** Most campuses offer support groups for test anxiety. These groups emphasize study strategies, anxiety management techniques, and moral support.

Handle Emergencies Honestly

What happens if you can't make it to the test? Most instructors have strict regulations about taking scheduled tests on time to ensure fair treatment for all students. However, sick children, car accidents, and deaths in the family can interfere at test time.

If you can't report at the scheduled time, call your instructor *before* the test. Explain your situation. Ask whether you can take a makeup exam. Being courteous encourages your instructor's cooperation. Instructors may ask you to document your absence (for example, with a doctor's excuse) before they'll let you make up a test. Do all you can to take tests on schedule to avoid this kind of complication. See Staying Out of the Pits, "The World's Toughest Test," to see what can happen when you fail to exercise personal responsibility about testing demands.

Meet the Challenge

The test is just moments away. You take your seat. The class quiets down as the instructor hands out the questions. How can you maximize your performance?

Use General Test-Taking Strategies

The following general strategies will help make the most of your studying to succeed on tests.

- *Relax.* Take a deep breath. The calmer you stay during a test, the better you'll do. Take relaxing breaths at the start and continue breathing calmly throughout the test. Concentrate on breathing slowly from your diaphragm. When you do this right, your stomach will move out as you breathe in, and in as you breathe out. "Chest breathing" can make you feel more agitated.
- *Look at the entire test.* Examine the structure. Count the pages. Think about how to divide your time, given your strengths and weaknesses. If the test includes different types of questions (such as multiple-choice and short essay), begin with the type you do best on to build your confidence. As you plan how to allot your time, leave more time for parts that require more effort or that make up more of your total score. Plan some time at the end to review your work.
- *Read the instructions . . . twice!* You'll be very upset if you discover near the end of the exam time that you were supposed to answer only certain questions rather than all the questions on the test. Read the instructions carefully. Then read them again. Read Staying Out of the Pits, "Rush at Your Own Risk," to reinforce why reading carefully pays off.
- *When you get stuck, identify the problem and move on.* You'll be taking most exams under time pressure, so you can't afford to spend too much time probing the depths of your memory. If time is left over after you've finished the parts of the exam that you could answer with confidence, return to the parts you skipped.

- *Concentration despite distractions.* If you start daydreaming, circle the item that got you off task and come back to it later. Avoid getting caught up in competition with any students who complete the test early. Do the test at your pace—don't worry about who gets done first.
- *Ask for clarification.* When you're confused, ask your instructor or proctor for help. Most instructors try to clarify a question if they can without giving away the answer. An instructor may even decide that the question doesn't work and will throw it out.
- *Learn from the test.* The test itself may jog your memory. One area of the test may hold clues that can help you with other areas.
- *Proofread your work.* Whether it's a series of math problems or an extended discussion on Japanese haiku, review your work. Under pressure, it's easy to misspell, miscalculate, and make other errors even on things you know well. Using clear editing marks on your test paper demonstrates that you were being as careful as possible about your work.

Master Multiple-Choice Strategies

You'll probably face many tests that are mainly multiple choice: "question stems" or incomplete statements, followed by possible answers from which to choose. Figure 8.3, "Multiple-Choice Format," provides an example. The following strategies will help improve your scoring on multiple-choice questions.

- *Read the test items carefully and completely.* Cover up the alternatives and read just the stem. See whether you can answer the question in your head before you look at the alternatives. Then read *all* the alternatives before you identify the best one. This is especially important when your instructor includes "All of the above" or "A and C only" types of choices.
- *Strike out wrong answers.* When you can't easily identify the correct answer, eliminate the wrong choices so you can concentrate only on real contenders.
- *Mark answers clearly and consistently.* Use the same method of marking your choices throughout the test. This may be important if questions arise later about an unclear mark. If your test is machine scored, avoid having extra marks on the answer sheet. They can be costly.
- *Change your answers cautiously.* Make sure you have a good reason before you change an answer. For example, change your answer if you mismarked your exam, initially misread the question, or clearly know you're moving to the correct alternative. If you aren't certain, it's best not to change. Your first impulse may be best.
- *Guess!!* Some tests subtract points for incorrect answers. In this case, answer only the questions that you know for certain. However, most multiple-choice tests give credit for correct answers without extra penalty for wrong answers. In this situation, guess. If the question has four alternatives, you have a 25 percent chance of being correct.

FIGURE 8.3 Multiple-Choice Format

The best way to succeed on multiple-choice tests is	[question stem]
A. Read the question carefully	[contender]
B. Check on the weather	[distracter]
C. Look for language cues to throw out choices	[contender]
D. Cry like a baby	[distracter]
E. A & C	[correct contender]

- *Look for structural clues.* When the item involves completing a sentence, look for answers that read well with the sentence stem (see Figure 8.4 for examples). Sometimes instructors don't pay close attention to how the wrong alternatives read. If a choice does not work grammatically with the stem, it's probably not the right choice. In complex questions, the longest alternative may be the best one. The instructor may simply require more words to express a complex answer.

Master True-False Strategies

True-false questions ask you to make judgments about whether propositions about the course content are valid or truthful. For example, consider this item: "True or False: It is always a bad idea to change your answer." This would be a good true-false question to assess your understanding of the last section on multiple-choice questions. (The answer is "False.") To maximize your performance on true-false items:

- *Go with your hunch.* When you don't know the answer on a true-false question, you have a 50 percent chance of being right when you guess. Choose the alternative with the intuitive edge.
- *Don't look for answer patterns.* Instructors generally strive to make the order of true-false answers random. This means there is no particular pattern to the true and false answers. Selecting "False" on question 35 should have no bearing on how you answer question 34 or 36. Focus your energy on the questions themselves rather than on trying to detect nonexistent patterns.
- *Honor exceptions to the rule.* If you can think of exceptions to the statement, even one exception, then the statement is probably false. In the earlier example, if you can think of even one circumstance in which changing your answer is a good idea, then the statement should be marked "False."
- *Analyze qualifying terms.* Words that specify conditions, such as *always, usually,* and *never,* usually identify an item that is false. Those terms suggest an unlikely or unwarranted generalization. Notice in our example, "It is always a bad idea to change your answer," the word *always* makes the statement invalid, because there are some times when changing your answer makes sense.

Master Fill-in-the-Blank Strategies

Like multiple-choice questions, fill-in-the-blank questions test how well you recall information. An example of a fill-in-the-blank format is "Instructors try hard to make a _____ pattern of answers on true-false tests." (The answer is "random.") You probably either know or don't know the answers to these kinds of questions but you may recover some answers that you don't know initially by skipping them and returning to them after you complete the rest of the test. This process may cue you to come up with just the right fill-in.

Master Short-Answer Strategies

Short-answer questions demonstrate how well you can explain concepts briefly. For example, a short essay question might be "Describe some strategies for doing well on true-false questions." To maximize your score on short-answer questions, write clear, logical, and brief answers. Writing a great deal more than asked or including information not asked for suggests that you do not understand the concepts. When you skip a short essay question because it stumps you, look for cues in the rest of the test that may help you go back and answer it later.

Master Essay-Question Strategies

Essay questions evaluate the scope of your knowledge and your ability to think and write. They tend to be much more demanding than objective test questions. What are some steps you can take to do your best on essays?

- *Anticipate possible questions.* If you were in your teacher's shoes, what questions would you ask? If you practice predicting and answering questions, your performance is likely to improve even if your predictions aren't on target. For example, an essay question that you could predict about the material in this section could be "Compare and contrast multiple-choice and essay question strategies as a way of measuring your learning."
- *Read the question carefully.* A well-developed answer won't help you capture points if you don't answer the right question.
- *Highlight the requested action.* For example, in our earlier sample question you could underline compare and contrast to keep you focused on the most successful approach. See Figure 8.5, "Decode Essay Questions," for help. Then turn to the Journal activity "Decode Essay Instructions" on page 245 for practice.
- *Outline the key ideas.* A systematic blueprint can help you capture the most important ideas in your answer (as shown in the following example):
  I. How are multiple-choice and essay questions alike?
      A. They're constructed from the same material.
      B. You start with remembering concepts.
      C. You demonstrate your mastery of material.
  II. How are multiple-choice and essay questions different?
      A. Multiple-choice usually relies more on rote memory—recognition or recall of terms. Essays usually involve higher-order thinking skills.
      B. Multiple-choice questions can be answered more quickly.
      C. Multiple-choice questions usually have crisper right answers.

PEANUTS reprinted by permission of United Feature Syndicate, Inc.

FIGURE 8.5 Decode Essay Questions

Look carefully at the verbs your instructor uses in essay questions. This chart offers some hints about how your instructor wants you to construct your answer.

When your instructor wants you to . . .	Your answer should . . .
ANALYZE	break into smaller parts and interpret importance
APPLY	extend a concept or principle to a new situation
COMPARE	identify similarities between two concepts
CONTRAST	distinguish important differences between two concepts
CRITICIZE	judge the positive and negative features of a concept
DEFINE	offer the essential idea behind a concept
DESCRIBE	provide sufficient details to establish key ideas in a concept
DESIGN	develop a new strategy to accomplish a goal
EXPLAIN	clarify the meaning of a concept through detail or example
EVALUATE	make a well-reasoned judgment about value or worth
GENERALIZE	apply a principle to make predictions about a new problem
HYPOTHESIZE	develop a specific prediction about a complex situation
IDENTIFY	designate the key elements involved
ILLUSTRATE	provide examples or details to clarify
INTERPRET	offer your distinctive point of view about a concept's meaning
LIST	identify factors in a systematic or comprehensive manner
PREDICT	offer your best guess about an outcome
PROVE	create your best argument using examples or reasoning
RECOMMEND	put forward a preferred course of action with a rationale
RELATE	draw connections among ideas
REVIEW	discuss the most important aspects of the concept
SUMMARIZE	briefly identify the most critical ideas

   D. Essay questions are usually harder to answer.
   E. Essay questions are probably harder to grade.
   F. Well-written essays require planning and outlining.
- *Represent the question in your opening sentence.* Don't waste time rewriting the question. Set the stage for the information that will follow such as: "Instructors use multiple-choice and essay questions to evaluate how much you have learned from a course. These strategies share some similarities, but each offers some strategic advantages over the other."
- *Develop the main body of the essay.* Each paragraph should address an element required in the question: "The common characteristics of multiple-choice and essay questions include . . . Multiple-choice and essay questions also differ in what information they impart about a student's learning . . ."
- *Summarize only if you have time.* Write like a reporter; present key ideas first and follow with details. This practice increases the likelihood that you'll cover the

most important and point-scoring information before you run out of time.

- *Write legibly.* If your handwriting gets worse under stress—slow down. Instructors can't give credit for what they can't decipher. For some other pointers about good essay format, see On Target Tips, "Get Your Essay Points."
- *Proofread your work.* Under time pressure, your written language can easily escape your control. Go back over your work and make any corrections the instructor will need in order to understand you clearly. Don't worry about the mess. Your own editing marks show that you care about the quality of your thinking.
- *Don't bluff.* The longer you write and the more you ramble, the more you expose what you really don't know.
- *Use humor carefully.* Unless you have clear cues from your instructors that they would appreciate a light-hearted response, don't substitute humor for an effective answer.

Self-Assessment 2 "How Well Do I Test?" on page 242 reviews many points that we've just covered. Use it to evaluate your current test-taking methods and to identify areas that need improvement.

Make the Grade

Grades don't change what you learned for the test, but grades can affect your self-esteem and motivation to study in the future, two important strategies for success. For example, good grades make you feel proud. They encourage you to stick with the study strategies that worked. Bad grades prompt you to make changes in order to succeed. But bad grades also can harm your self-esteem.

Recover Your Balance

At some point in your college career, you may not perform as well on a test as you hoped you would. Sometimes instructors don't design tests effectively. At other times, you simply may be pushed in too many directions to concentrate and do your best. Or the course may be a bad match to your natural skills and interests.

Don't let yourself become undone by one failure. Frame this disappointment as an opportunity to do some good critical thinking to figure out the causes of poor performance and to craft some new strategies to improve your situation. This approach can start by a careful review of your test results.

> *To talk without thinking is to shoot without aiming.*
>
> English proverb

Review Your Work

Some reviewing of your test results will help you do better on the next test. Review to:

- **consolidate** your learning
- **analyze** what worked and what didn't work in your study strategy, and
- **ensure** that the grade was accurate.

Review all items, not just ones on which you made mistakes. Review and rehearse one more time the material that your instructor thinks you need to learn in the course. This can help you in the long run, especially if you have a cumulative exam at the end of the term.

Your test review should tell you whether your study strategy worked. Did you spend enough time studying for the test? Did you practice the right kinds of thinking to match the particular demands of this teacher? How can you use your study time more efficiently for the next test? Talk with the instructor about better ways to prepare.

What if your instructor doesn't allow extensive time for review of your exam during class—or worse, doesn't return the exams at all but only posts the grades? Visit your instructor during office hours and ask for the chance to review your test results. This visit also allows you to clarify any questions you have about your instructor's testing or grading practices, and shows that you are taking personal responsibility for your learning.

Know When to Challenge

Check the grading. Instructors can easily make errors when applying test keys or counting up point totals. Also identify questions that were not clearly written. Even if your critique of a question does not persuade an instructor to change your grade, your review may give you insight into how the instructor constructs tests, which can help you on the next one. Instructors are unlikely to change a grade without good reason. Most construct tests carefully and grade them as fairly as possible. However, if you believe the instructor misunderstood you or made an actual error in calculating your score that affects your grade, by all means ask for a grade change. Remember, though, that instructors can't give you extra points if it gives you an unfair advantage over others in the class.

If you view grades as a key to the future, you may want to fight for the grade you deserve. Some strategies for getting maximum consideration from your instructor are shown in Take Charge, "Negotiate a Grade Change."

TAKE CHARGE
Negotiate a Grade Change

At some point in your college career, you will disagree with an instructor's evaluation of how well you have performed. If getting your points restored is critical to your grade, by all means, get the points you deserve by conferring with your instructor. You will enhance your success by using the following strategies.

- **Ask for time after class to present your case.** Most instructors will not spend class time on the challenges of one student.
- **Develop your argument.** Point to evidence, such as an interpretation in the book that conflicts with something said in lecture, to support your request.
- **Explain your interpretation.** If you misinterpreted a question, describe your interpretation. Instructors will sometimes grant partial credit for a well-argued but off-base interpretation.
- **Avoid labeling a question as "bad."** Placing blame on the instructor will probably not encourage a helpful response.
- **Be gracious, whether you win or lose.** Most instructors remember and admire students who effectively advocate for themselves.

Understand Grading Systems

What systems of grading do most colleges use?

Traditional Grades Most schools use the traditional A–F grading system. Many also include plus ($+$) and minus ($-$) judgments to make even finer distinctions in quality of work. Schools that use the traditional system convert grades into a grade point average, or GPA. In this system, A = 4 points, B = 3 points, C = 2 points, and D = 1 point. The point values of grades in all your courses are added up, then averaged to create your GPA.

For example,

American history	C	2 points
College algebra	A	4 points
Intro to business	A	4 points
Sociology	B	3 points

GPA = 13 points divided by 4 courses = 3.25

A higher GPA improves your chances of getting a good job after college or being accepted into graduate school. A GPA also has special meaning at some colleges. For example, GPAs over 3.5 may qualify you for the Dean's List, the roster of students

> *Do not on any account attempt to write on both sides of the paper at once.*
> W. C. Sellar
> *20th-century British writer*

Imagine yourself at the end of your college career. How important will your GPA be toward securing the future you have in mind? Not all opportunities following college require a 4.0. However, if you decide to continue your studies in graduate school, you need to start right now building a GPA that gives you the widest options. Write down the GPA range that you think would be most desirable at the conclusion of your career. Be realistic. Keep in mind how willing you are to make the sacrifices that will be required to excel.

Now think about whether you have laid the proper foundation to achieve that outcome. If you have, congratulations! If you haven't, list three things you could do to get on track.

recognized for academic excellence. Some academic honor societies, such as Phi Beta Kappa and Phi Kappa Phi, invite students to join on the basis of GPA.

If your GPA falls below 2.0, you may be placed on academic restrictions or probation. On some campuses, probation limits the number of courses you can take in the next term and slows down your progress in your major. Because GPA is averaged across terms, a bad term's GPA will exert a heavy weight on your overall record, even if your performance improves in later terms. If your GPA remains low, you can flunk out.

Instructors sometimes assign test or course grades by using a curve. The overall results of the test for the class are tied to the strongest performance in the class. Other students' scores are judged in relation to that strongest score. For example, suppose that on a test with 100 points the highest score was 85. An instructor who is grading on a curve might give As to scores of 76–85, Bs to scores 66–75, and so on. Instructors may do this when a test turns out to be much harder than originally intended. However, even when most of the class performs poorly, some instructors don't curve the grades.

Building a satisfying grade point average will help you achieve your goals. See On Target Tips, "Targeting Your GPA," to explore some strategies for achieving the outcomes that will maximize your future options.

Pass-Fail Systems Some schools determine progress on a pass-fail basis, giving only pass (P) and fail (F) grades. When this is the only grading system a college uses, students may get extensive feedback about how well they have met their learning objectives. Instead of a grade point average, students graduate with other indicators of the quality of their work, such as a *narrative transcript.* In this document, their instructors describe their academic work and how well they achieved their goals.

Some colleges use both A–F and pass-fail grading. For example, students might get A–F grades in most of their courses but be allowed to take a certain number of credits outside their majors on a pass-fail basis. This dual system allows students to take some courses that they otherwise might avoid because of a potential mediocre grade.

The presence of grades appeals to externally motivated students who find they can more easily settle down and do the work when they know feedback will help them stay the course. Other students with stronger intrinsic motivation think grades and the pressures that go with them are distracting. Which do you prefer? See the Journal activity "Grades: Carrots or Sticks?" on page 245 to clarify your thinking.

Build Your Character

Each test that you take actually tests you twice, once on the content and once on your character. Every test gives you an opportunity to demonstrate your personal integrity, and integrity matters greatly. Unfortunately, cheating is widespread in college. A comprehensive survey of 6,000 college students showed how big the problem is (S. F. Davis and others, 1992). Although more than 90 percent said that it was wrong to cheat, 75 percent said that they themselves had cheated in college or high school or both. Another survey (McCabe & Trevino, 1993) of over 6,000 undergraduates on over 30 campuses revealed that 78 percent of college students cheat at least once; over half of the respondents claimed that they cheated on tests.

Most students won't report other students' cheating. In one survey, three fourths of the students witnessed cheating by others but only one in a hundred informed the instructor (Jendrick, 1992). Many of the students ignored the situation even though it made them angry or upset. One third of the students said cheating didn't bother them.

Understanding Cheating

Cheating in college has many causes (Whitley & Keith-Spiegel, 2002). Often students who cheat feel pressure to succeed. They feel overwhelmed by the demands of so many deadlines and can't see any other way to get by. Successful cheating gives students better grades with less effort.

Many students and instructors simply expect people to cheat if they have the opportunity. Some students reason that because other students cheat, it's okay for them to cheat, too. Instructors sometimes make it easy to cheat by not monitoring tests closely.

Often students who cheat do not get caught or aren't punished when they are caught. Although most students recognize that cheating involves some risk, they report that they have seen students cheat and get away with it. Many instructors don't feel confident in challenging students who cheat, so they overlook suspicious acts. Inaction by the instructor encourages others to cheat.

Some students who cheat may not recognize when they are cheating (Keith-Spiegel, 1992). Some students "work together" and share answers either before or during a test. They believe that there is nothing wrong with sharing answers as long as both parties agree to collaborate. These students don't recognize that how they arrive at answers is just as important as the answers themselves.

How else do students justify cheating? Figure 8.6, "Excuses for Academic Dishonesty" (from Whitley & Keith-Spiegel, 2002), summarizes explanations that students offer for their behavior. Complete Journal activity "What's the Risk?" on page 245 to explore motivations for maintaining integrity on your own campus.

> *Character is destiny.*
> Heraclitis
> *Greek philosopher, 500 B.C.E.*

Show Integrity and Resist the Impulse

Would you want to be cared for by a physician who cheated her way to a medical license? When the outcome of education involves life-and-death decisions, we clearly want to be cared for by someone with sound knowledge and skills.

Even if you don't plan to become a physician, you'll benefit from direct and accurate measurements of what you know. For example, your survival in more difficult, advanced courses may depend on your learning from an earlier course. By cheating, you increase the likelihood of serious academic problems in the future. Explore your own reasons for choosing responsibly in the Journal activity "Reflect on Cheating" on page 244.

In their mission statements, most colleges pledge to foster moral and ethical behavior. Some colleges have a stringent honor code. These principles, usually described in the student handbook, recognize that students will have plenty of opportunities to cheat. When you exercise integrity, however, you demonstrate not just to your instructor but also to your classmates that you're a trustworthy, moral person.

Denial of Injury:	*Cheating hurts no one.*
	Cheating is only wrong in courses in your major.
Denial of Personal Responsibility:	*I got the flu and couldn't read all the chapters.*
	The course is too hard.
Denial of Personal Risk:	*Professors won't do anything to you.*
	No one ever gets caught.
Selective Morality:	*Friends come first and my friend needed my help.*
	I only did what was necessary at the time.
Minimizing Seriousness:	*It's only busy work.*
	Cheating is meaningless when it has little weight on my grade.
A Necessary Act:	*If I don't do well, my parents will kill me.*
	I'll lose my scholarship if I don't get all B's.
Dishonesty as a Norm:	*Society's leaders do it, so why not me?*
	Everyone does it.

Source: Adapted from Whitley & Keith-Spiegel Copyright ©2002 by Lawrence Erlbaum Associates, Inc. Reprinted by permission of the publisher.

Career Connections

From the beginning of her college career, Sue was quite taken with the whole process of test-taking. She was intrigued to see how a professor's personality shaped the manner in which she would end up being tested. She began to notice that some professors crafted tests with great care whereas others threw their tests together haphazardly. The latter situation made it much easier for Sue to argue adjustments to her score based on her ability to identify flaws in test construction. After four years of test-taking experience, Sue decided to go into a graduate program in educational psychology to learn more about test design and administration. Degree in hand, she applied to a large firm that developed national achievement tests where she could continue to analyze test quality for fun and profit.

Mischa was distressed to find that cheating was rampant in his college classes. He believed that cheating was simply wrong and felt compelled to promote a different standard of character. He pursued and won a position on the committee that reviewed complaints about student integrity. This committee, comprised of students and faculty, had to make judgments about whether students had violated the integrity code and decide on the appropriate consequence. Mischa was surprised at how satisfying this work turned out to be. He decided a future in law would allow him to have a career in which he could put his high standards and analytic skills to work for the common good.

Cheating can have ugly consequences. Even if they get away with cheating, some students struggle with a nagging conscience. The relief they initially feel in escaping a bad grade can be replaced by self-doubt, dissatisfaction, and guilt. These students suffer because they have fallen short of their own ideals, creating long-term harm for their self-esteem and self-confidence. Furthermore, once they cheat and get away with it, they may be tempted to do it again the next time they aren't as prepared as they should be.

When cheaters do get caught, they face multiple risks. Being accused of cheating in front of others is humiliating. Being found guilty of cheating means that they may have to explain this judgment to their friends or parents. Worse, some instructors will turn them over to a student court for punishment, spreading their humiliation even further. Penalties for cheating differ. An instructor may give cheaters a "0" on the exam or an automatic F in the course. On campuses that practice a strict honor code, one episode of cheating leads to expulsion. On some occasions, cheating students have received surprising consequences. See Staying Out of the Pits, "Protecting Your Options," for one example of the long-term consequence to giving in to the temptation to cheat.

What will you do when faced with an opportunity to cheat? If honesty is an important value for you, then you may have already committed yourself to making sure that you take no shortcuts to success. But what if you're not persuaded? Perhaps you've seen dishonest people get away with too much. After all, if 78 percent of students report that they have cheated, how wrong can it be?

Cheating is not a victimless crime. Students who cheat potentially rob themselves of learning that may be useful to them in the future. If you aspire to true excellence, you can't really do so by being a fraud. If you can't be a trustworthy student, how can you be a trustworthy partner or friend? To explore your own perspective about cheating, complete Self-Assessment 3 "Your Personal Honor Code" on page 243. Also see the Journal activity, "Promote Better Test Preparation" on page 245 for a creative way to summarize what you have learned about test preparation.

STAYING OUT OF THE PITS

Protecting Your Options

Randy had a weak moment in his sophomore year. He had not set aside the right time to complete the take-home test assigned in his French class. However, he remembered that his roommate had taken the course the semester before and had done very well. He scanned the hard drive of the computer they shared and found his roommate's exam. "Just this once," he thought as he downloaded the exam, modified parts of the essay, and submitted it as his own work.

His instructor recognized the essay because the work had stood out the first time. Busted, Randy had to take a zero in the course. He lost "face," the tuition, the time, and the course credit. What he didn't expect was that his advisor refused to write letters of recommendation for graduate school based on his lack of integrity. Randy was surprised to learn that one impulsive act had such serious long-term impact on his future.

Summary Strategies for Mastering College

Tests can help you refine your skills in planning and achieving goals as you build your knowledge base and your personal integrity.

Focus on the "Six Strategies for Success" above as you read each chapter to learn how to apply these strategies to your own success.

1 Get On with It!

- Accept that tests are a fact of life in college. They offer feedback for how well you're learning and give you a sense of accomplishment when you succeed.
- Tests also help you pace your reading, consolidate your learning, improve your thinking, and achieve special status.

2 Get in Gear

- Use long-term strategies: pacing yourself, protecting your health, and getting in the right frame of mind.
- Use short-term strategies: knowing what to expect, sizing up the teacher, and designing study strategies that suit your learning style.

- Cramming happens. Concentrate your efforts in the home stretch if you haven't had time to prepare.
- Reduce your test anxiety through positive self-talk, appropriate preparation, and relaxation strategies.
- Handle emergencies immediately and honestly.

3 Meet the Challenge

- Plan how to use your time in each testing challenge.
- Use a variety of general test-taking strategies to improve your performance.
- Look for cues in objective tests to help you determine the best answer.
- Do your best on essay questions by planning, expressing yourself precisely, and writing legibly.

4 Make the Grade

- Review your results to consolidate your learning and to plan better study strategies.
- Use good judgment when you challenge your instructor's judgment about the fairness of a grade.
- Don't waste a semester. A bad semester will have a whopping impact on your cumulative GPA.

5 Build Your Character

- Demonstrate your academic integrity by resisting cheating.
- Set a high personal standard to build your character.
- Avoid the ugly personal outcomes of cheating, including possible expulsion from school if you are caught.

Review Questions

1. How does a positive attitude influence your success on tests? List three other strategies you can implement to improve your test performance in the future.

   1. _____

   2. _____

   3. _____

2. How should your study strategies vary according to the kind of test you'll be facing? List a few specific types of tests followed by a description of an appropriate study strategy.

   Test: _____ Study Strategy: _____

   Test: _____ Study Strategy: _____

   Test: _____ Study Strategy: _____

   _____

   _____

   _____

3. Describe a few specific ways to overcome test anxiety.

   _____

   _____

   _____

4. Why should you review your test results carefully when the instructor returns your work? What else should you do after a test to maximize your overall grade in the course?

   _____

   _____

   _____

5. What advantages follow when you avoid the temptation to cheat on tests? List three disadvantages that can result from cheating.

   1. _____

   2. _____

   3. _____

Learning Portfolio

SELF-ASSESSMENTS

YOUR JOURNAL

STRATEGIES FOR SUCCESS

Develop Meaningful Values

Get Motivated and Take Responsibility

Set Goals, Plan, and Monitor

Succeed on Tests

Build Self-Esteem and Confidence

Explore Careers

Think and Learn

How Serious Is My Test Anxiety?

Check the category that best describes the way you feel when you take tests:

	Never	Occasionally	Regularly
I feel physically ill just before a test.			
I fail to complete tests, because I fret about what will happen when I fail.			
I can't seem to organize my time to prepare well for exams.			
I know I could do better if I could ignore how nervous I feel during tests.			
I struggle with stomach pain and bathroom urges just before a test.			
My mind has gone completely blank during the middle of an exam.			
I fear that I'll end up turning in the worst performance on the test in the entire class.			
I have difficulty getting a good night's sleep before a test.			
I'm very concerned about what my instructor will think of me if I don't do well on a test.			
I get more distracted during the test than other students seem to do.			
I start to panic when other students finish their exams while I'm still working.			
I know the material better than my exam score indicates.			
I know I won't be able to have the kind of future I want unless I can get a better grip on my testing fears.			

These items give you a general idea about how seriously test anxiety may be interfering with your test performance. If you marked any items "regularly" or marked several "occasionally," you might benefit from a more in-depth assessment of your test anxiety. Contact the study skills center on your campus.

After evaluating the nature of your difficulty, the study skills specialists can make specific recommendations to help you master your anxiety. If you're seriously troubled by test anxiety, seek counseling.

How Well Do I Test?

Rate how often you use these skills.

	Always	Usually	Sometimes	Never
As part of my general test-taking strategy				
I stay relaxed during the exam.	_____	_____	_____	_____
I look at the entire test before I start.	_____	_____	_____	_____
I read the instructions carefully.	_____	_____	_____	_____
I concentrate even when distracted.	_____	_____	_____	_____
I ask the instructor for help when I'm confused.	_____	_____	_____	_____
I move on when I get stuck.	_____	_____	_____	_____
I look for clues in other parts of the test.	_____	_____	_____	_____
I proofread my work.	_____	_____	_____	_____
In multiple-choice questions				
I read the test items carefully and completely.	_____	_____	_____	_____
When I'm uncertain which answer is right, I take steps to rule out the alternatives that are wrong.	_____	_____	_____	_____
I mark the correct answer clearly and consistently.	_____	_____	_____	_____
I change my answers only when I'm certain I should do so.	_____	_____	_____	_____
When I don't know an answer, I guess.	_____	_____	_____	_____
When stumped, I look for cues in the question's structure.	_____	_____	_____	_____
On true-false items				
I go with my hunches.	_____	_____	_____	_____
I avoid looking for patterns on the answer sheet.	_____	_____	_____	_____
I analyze qualifying terms (such as *always, never*).	_____	_____	_____	_____
I try to find exceptions to the rule.	_____	_____	_____	_____
On fill-in-the-blank questions				
I don't loiter when stumped.	_____	_____	_____	_____
In short answer questions				
I write brief, logical answers.	_____	_____	_____	_____
In essay questions				
I underline the verbs in the question to help figure out what kind of thinking I need to do.	_____	_____	_____	_____
I think and outline before I write.	_____	_____	_____	_____
I reflect the question in my opening sentence.	_____	_____	_____	_____
I write main ideas first and fill in details and examples later.	_____	_____	_____	_____
I don't bluff when I don't know.	_____	_____	_____	_____
I write for readability.	_____	_____	_____	_____
I'm careful about using humor.	_____	_____	_____	_____

Now go back over the list and circle the test-management skills that you marked "rarely" or "never." Check your calendar for the date of your next exam. Use your goal-setting skills to make improvements for that exam.

Your Personal Honor Code

Check the questions with which you agree.

Under what circumstances do you think most students might be inclined to cheat?

When it's unlikely that they would be caught   _____

When they feel desperate to get a better grade   _____

When a great deal is riding on a particular grade   _____

If they haven't managed their time well enough to study effectively   _____

When they might be teased by their peers if they refused to cheat   _____

Other: _____

If someone is caught cheating, which consequence do you think is the most appropriate?

Expulsion from school   _____

Failure in the course where the cheating occurred   _____

Failure of the assignment on which the cheating occurred   _____

Review by the school's honor board   _____

Public censure   _____

Repeating the assignment without cheating   _____

Depends on the cheater's history   _____

Other: _____

Rank order the things that discourage you from cheating:

I would lose my self-respect.   _____

I would be frightened of getting caught.   _____

I want my test results to reflect my learning accurately.   _____

I consider it my honor to uphold academic integrity.   _____

I don't want to give in to group pressure to do things that I don't believe in.   _____

Other: _____

Will you be able to withstand the temptation to take the easy (but risky) way out of making the grade?

Your Journal

● REFLECT

1. Then and Now

Think about the grades you made in high school. How much time did you put into studies then compared with now?

- Are you managing the same levels of achievement?
- Have you had to increase your effort just to hold your ground?
- Are you now studying harder than you ever have?
- Is that effort resulting in the achievement you're aiming for? If not, what steps should you take to feel more satisfied?

2. Format Fever

Students differ in the preferences they have for the formats in which they are tested. Some students love the challenge of crafting a solid essay response to a well-framed question. They may dislike the crispness of a multiple-choice question. Other students live in stark fear of having to write what they know. Instead they thrive on the opportunity to hammer a set of multiple-choice questions. Rank order the following test formats in the order of your preference:

____ Fill-in-the-blank
____ Multiple-choice
____ True-false
____ Essay

In your journal speculate about why you ordered the formats as you did. How does your achievement history influence your choice? Does your learning style dictate which formats are more appealing?

3. Reflect on Cheating

You've probably experienced a situation in which you could easily have cheated but you resisted the opportunity.

- Describe what would have made the cheating easy.
- Identify the feelings and values that were involved in resolving this problem.
- Were you satisfied with the resolution?
- What actions, if any, did you take to feel comfortable with the outcome?

● DO

1. Construct Your Own Exam

Construct a sample test for the next real test you'll face. If you were the teacher, what would be the most important concepts to test for? How would you go about assessing them? If you think it would be helpful, make an appointment with your instructor to compare your own strategy with the one you have created. What insights can you gain from the conversation that will make you even more effective at predicting test design?

_____

_____

2. What's the Risk?

Locate a copy of your school's honor code or procedures that govern academic integrity. Review it to determine the risks involved in cheating. In most cases, the outcomes of being caught and punished for cheating are fairly severe. How can you reconcile this outcome with the fact that 75 percent of college students report cheating at some point

Your Journal

in high school or college or both? Consider how learning styles and personality factors might influence the decision to cheat.

_____

_____

● THINK CRITICALLY

1. Decode Essay Instructions

Find some examples of essay questions, preferably ones from tests you took this term. Circle the verbs that represent the kind of thinking the instructor has asked you to do in completing the essay. Think about what kind of question is being asked. How will this decoding exercise influence your study strategy for the exams you will face in the future?

_____

_____

2. Grades: Carrots or Sticks?

Many students thrive in graded systems. They like the clearcut messages they get when their efforts are rewarded by good grades. However, other students find grades less rewarding. They think competition for grades undercuts meaningful learning and feel stressed out by the process.
With a group of students, discuss the advantages and disadvantages of using grades to evaluate learning. Which system would most effectively motivate your learning?

_____

_____

● CREATE

1. Promote Better Test Preparation

Create a website for one of your courses in which you explore the hazards of cramming or offering six bits of good advice about how to succeed on tests in this class. Make an appointment with the instructor for feedback. If the feedback is positive, perhaps your website can be incorporated in the planning the next time the course is taught.

_____

_____

2. Find Your Quiet Place

Imagine your favorite peaceful place. Where would it be?
What would you be doing there? Think of this calming refuge to help you ward off anxiety while studying test-taking. What would you need to do to make this image one you can rely on during stress to restore your peace? Also try the exercise "Learn to Relax" on the CD-ROM that comes with this book.

_____

_____

Applying the Six Strategies for Success

What did you learn in this chapter that you can apply to the following key strategies to help form the foundation for your success? Write down all of the main points you can remember that support the following strategies:

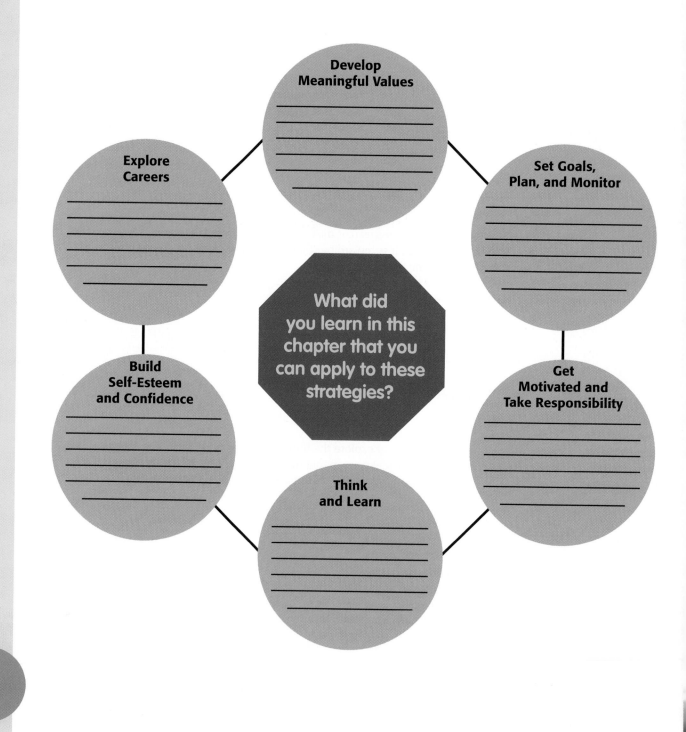

9 Refine Your Expression

Where Are You? One exciting aspect of college is the opportunity to develop confidence in your self-expression. In this chapter, you'll explore ways to improve your writing and speaking skills. You'll also learn some strategies for overcoming common problems involving communication. To evaluate where you stand right now, place a checkmark next to only those items that apply to you.

- ● I pursue opportunities to practice effective communication skills.
- ● I can design and execute projects involving research.
- ● I prepare writing or presentational projects well in advance.
- ● I avoid problems with plagiarism.
- ● I seek criticism from other people to improve the quality of my work.
- ● I use strategies to engage the audience during speeches.
- ● I can control jitters when communicating.
- ● I can rebound when my communicational efforts don't succeed.

Now read how the writer Amy Tan combines rich personal experience with good communication strategies to produce writing and speaking that makes an impact.

247

Images of College Success

Amy Tan

When she won her first essay contest at age eight, Amy Tan knew she wanted to write fiction. However, her mother wanted her to follow a different dream. In the late 1940s, Tan's parents had emigrated from China to Oakland, California. They were eager for their only daughter both to enjoy the advantages of their adopted land and to honor her Chinese heritage. After her father's unexpected death from a brain tumor, Tan decided to major in premed at Linfield College in Oregon. But the lure of the liberal arts proved too strong. Despite her mother's protests that her father would have been disappointed in her decision, she chose English as her major. Tan completed her education at San Jose City College and San Jose State University.

Writing was not easy for Tan. Consistent with the traditions of her ethnic origins, Tan's mother maintained very high expectations for her children's achievement. This intensity about excelling produced a hypercritical atmosphere that undermined Tan's ability to express herself. She was even advised by a former employer to go into accounting because her writing skills were so poor. Despite these obstacles, she began doing freelance writing. This developed into a successful career in business writing, including projects with companies such as IBM. As Tan acquired clients, she struggled with 90-hour work weeks and a growing sense of feeling unfulfilled. She joined a writer's group and began to write fiction.

Tan published her insights as a series of interrelated stories about the struggle between Chinese mothers and Chinese-American daughters. Published in 17 languages, including Chinese, *The Joy Luck Club* has sold more than three million copies and became a successful film. Her most recent work, *The Bonesetter's Daughter*, also became a best-seller. Tan not only achieved her childhood dream of writing fiction professionally but often speaks to enthusiastic audiences on promotional tours.

Tan uses her writing to make sense of her life. "Life is a continual series of bumps and crises. You think you're never going to get over a hurdle, and you get over it. . . . You can look back on what's just happened and you make sense of it and grow, or you stagnate and you go back down. The hurdles and conflicts are really momentary" (Tan, 1996). Learning to express yourself can be an important means of finding your balance in difficult times and making the very best of good times.

Amy Tan's challenging personal life gave her the foundation for an award-winning career as a novelist.

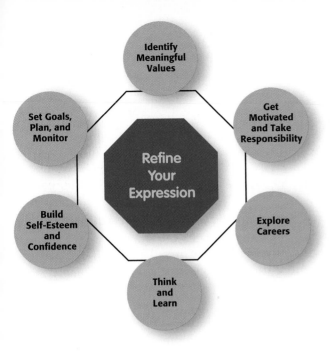

Identify Meaningful Values

Set Goals, Plan, and Monitor

Get Motivated and Take Responsibility

Refine Your Expression

Build Self-Esteem and Confidence

Explore Careers

Think and Learn

As you read, think about the "Six Strategies for Success" listed to the left and how this chapter can help you maximize success in these important areas. For example, motivate yourself to practice your communication skills whenever you can. Setting and achieving communication goals will help you succeed in college and prepare you for any career.

Express Yourself!

If you are not interested in becoming an author like Amy Tan, you may wonder why you need to learn how to write. You may want to go into business or law or medicine. However, in most professional worlds, skilled writing and public speaking can be critical to your success.

If you choose your college opportunities carefully, you'll learn to express yourself in writing and speaking with precision, poise, and polish. Even if you think that you're not a good writer, you can learn. Writing is not an innate skill. If you get discouraged, remember Amy Tan, the best-selling author who was advised to go into accounting because her writing skills were so poor.

Writing essays, lab reports, and papers in college prepare you to write effective memos, proposals, and reports in the work world. Practice in editing and proofreading will improve your attention to detail. Writing projects also encourage the kind of creativity that would be highly valued in fields like advertising, publishing, and marketing. Classroom speaking provides practice for interviewing, supervising, persuading, negotiating, selling, and other aspects of working with the public. Enhance your future career prospects by honing your writing and speaking skills now.

If you connect well with others and can usually think of the right thing to say at the right time, you may be a natural communicator. Most of us need practice and hard work. Bringing personal expression under your control through a variety of projects in college will give you great flexibility for the challenges you'll face after graduation.

Beginning communication assignments by concentrating on writing and speaking about personal experiences. As you progress further into your major, communication performances will become more challenging, tailored to your chosen discipline. With some practice, you can significantly improve your skills by graduation. How much better you become will depend on your making the most of your opportunities. Build your self-confidence as a communicator by exploring Take Charge, "Conquer Your Communication Qualms."

> *Good communication is as stimulating as black coffee, and just as hard to sleep after.*
>
> Anne Morrow Lindbergh
> *20th-century American poet*

Conquer Your Communication Qualms

It's normal to fret a bit about whether you will fare well in the writing and speaking assignments that lie ahead. What kinds of strategies can you use to gain confidence in your ability to get your message across?

- **Seek opportunities.** When something is unsettling, it is human to try to avoid those situations. However, the only way you can improve in this vital skill is through practice, practice, practice. Whenever you are given an opportunity to write or speak in a class, grab it!
- **Build from strength.** Audit what you do well in communication assignments and concentrate on adding one more area of strength with each new assignment. For example, suppose you can write a good sentence but have trouble stringing them together in paragraphs that have impact. Concentrate on coherent paragraph development as the next area to master.
- **Develop an overarching plan.** Feedback on your communication skills is generally helpful regardless of the class in which it originates. For example, one of your instructors may point out that you need to develop your ideas more. Consolidate such feedback from multiple sources. Then set some overall goals for improving those skills in all of your assignments. See the Journal activity "What Are Your Writing Trends?" on page 279 to help you develop a master strategy.
- **Pursue balanced feedback vigorously.** Your skills will grow best when your critics reinforce your strengths as well as point out your deficits. Make certain that you get confirmation on what you did well to build your confidence. Find additional reviewers if you can't get positive feedback from your instructor.
- **Don't crumble if you misfire.** The most talented communicators foul up from time to time. A shaky speech or a less-than-ideal paper should encourage you to prepare or rehearse to improve your control the next time.

Prepare Before You Write

Whether your project involves writing or speaking, the following strategies can help you produce your best effort.

Clarify Your Goal

Make sure you understand the goal of the assignment from the instructor's point of view. Look at the syllabus and try to link the specific assignment to the overall goals of the course. Ask questions to clarify anything that is unclear. Compare your ideas with your classmates' perceptions. Actively evaluate how the goal of the assignment can help you achieve your writing goals. For example, if your assignment is to write a three- to five-page essay, you might opt for the shorter three-page goal to help you work on developing short, coherent arguments. By contrast, if you receive feedback that you need to develop your ideas in greater depth, go for the five-page limit. You also might want to tailor assignments to your career goals. For example, if you are interested in advertising, you might choose to write a persuasive essay.

Define Your Purpose

If you're lucky, you'll have an opportunity to write in a variety of formats that will prepare you for the diverse writing demands in professional life. Strong writing skills are a great asset in virtually every professional career. Before you begin writing, review the directions and make sure you understand the purpose of the assignment. There are basically five reasons for writing:

- *To explain an idea or provide information (expository).* Research papers and essays often have this purpose. Instructors often assign research papers to develop your research skills as well as your writing skills. Essays develop your writing and reasoning skills, and demonstrate your ability to think analytically about the subject you're learning.
- *To persuade or argue a point.* This type of assignment often combines writing and problem-solving skills and can benefit from the following organizational strategy:
  - Define the problem and its impact clearly
  - Describe the origin of the problem
  - Identify any other relevant factors
  - Propose a solution
  - Predict the impact of the solution, including negative outcomes
  - Develop a follow-up strategy
- *To describe an experiment or process or report on lab results.* In science classes, you may work independently or collaborate on a lab report that describes a specific scientific procedure. Lab reports are usually highly structured, based on a set of

conventional headings. For example, a botany instructor might ask you to experiment with how different nutrient levels affect plant growth. The lab report will contain the following sections:

- *Introduction:* The nature of the problem, including relevant research
- *Methods:* The procedure used to investigate the problem
- *Results:* The findings
- *Discussion:* The significance of the results; improvements to the procedure

- *To reflect on your own experience.* Journal writing lets you explore the personal significance of what you are studying. Instructors usually don't grade journals in a traditional way. They will give you feedback about your insights or the seriousness of your effort. Although research may not be required in such projects, it's a good idea to connect with course concepts to show what you have learned.

- *To create an original piece of writing.* Literature instructors may assign creative writing projects, such as poetry and short stories, to foster an appreciation of these genres. Don't rule out doing research in reflective assignments. Locate authors whose style you admire. Do some background reading on a topic that might focus your work.

Select a Topic

Many instructors will select your topic, at least in a general way. However, you still may have to narrow it down. Choosing well can help you take responsibility and embrace the work that lies ahead. What strategies can help?

1. Look through your notes. What concepts stand out as the most interesting to you?
2. Examine your textbook and course readings, explore the encyclopedia, or cruise the Internet to spark your imagination.
3. Explore your personal experience. Think about aspects of the assignment that naturally connect to your own life. For example, Amy Tan's troubled relationship with her mother became the basis of her remarkable fiction. Refer to the Journal activity "Exploiting Your Life" on page 278 to develop a reservoir of good ideas for future projects.
4. Consider what topic would be the most fun or would have the most future value for you. Are there topics that will connect in a meaningful way to your future career plans? Give those ideas top consideration.
5. Carry a small notebook or maintain a separate file in which you can capture ideas that come to you. Think often about your topic to sensitize yourself to ideas that might strengthen the development of your argument. Although popular media resources such as magazines and television programs may not be acceptable resources for a formal research paper, they can suggest interesting directions for more formal research.
6. Consider developing a research stream. Good students see the value of an ongoing focus for their college papers (Hansen & Hansen, 1997). They develop a "research stream" that begins with the first paper they write and builds with each new project. This way they don't have to start from scratch, and can manage greater depth in each new assignment.

For example, Paulo enjoys thinking about environmental issues. He looks for opportunities in his writing assignments to read what he enjoys. He writes about literature with ecological themes, evaluates ecology-related legislation in social science classes, and explores environmental crises in natural science term papers. As a result, Paulo knows his material very well and expands what he knows with each project. His focused writing may serve his job-hunting future better than a hodgepodge of unrelated essays. When you choose topics for papers and other projects, keep your long-term career goals in mind.

Narrow Your Topic

As you explore possible topics, avoid ones that are too large, too obscure, too emotional, or too complicated for you to work with in the allotted time. Do not write or speak about areas where you have little knowledge because it's easier to stay engaged with a project where you have personal interest. Conduct research until you have the knowledge you need to succeed. You may need to redefine the project several times before settling on a topic that speaks to you. Although there are a number of techniques for narrowing your topic once you have a general idea of what you want to write about, most approaches encourage you to "mess around" with the ideas to begin to make them your own (McKowen, 1996).

Free Write   Free writing involves writing without stopping for a set period of time, usually 5–10 minutes, to help get your thoughts on paper. Then review your work to see if any key ideas stand out. When you have identified key concepts in your writing, do another freewrite on these topics until you have a more specific concept for your paper. Spontaneous writing may help you uncover new ideas, questions, and connections. Simply write whatever you think about the topic and save the parts that have potential.

Brainstorm   Concentrate on the assignment and write down all of the concepts or ideas that occur to you. Don't worry about the order, clarity, or meaning of the ideas. Just write down everything that comes to mind. Following your brainstorming session, impose some order on what you have produced. Draw connecting lines. Strike out distracters. Make new concept maps that display the most meaningful connections as the basis for your writing.

Talk It Out   You may find it easier to narrow your topic by pretending that you're talking to a friend. Once you have some ideas to work with, jot down the parts of the conversation you liked and proceed to the formal aspects of writing. Or talk to real friends and colleagues. Use the most interesting parts of that conversation to launch your own perspective.

Ask Questions   Journalists follow a specific protocol that can be helpful to generate good writing. Go after your task with *who?, what?, when?, where?,* and *why?* Answers to those questions can provide new directions to your work.

Begin Reading on the Topic   If the assignment is relatively focused to begin with, you may just be able to start reading, and that will spark ideas and interest.

Develop a Working Thesis

After you have narrowed your topic to an area of specific interest to you, refine it even further by developing a **thesis.** Your *thesis statement* conveys your general position on the topic and guides the direction of your writing, which supports your thesis. The thesis is essential because it focuses your topic and provides a clear direction for your thinking, research, and writing.

A good working thesis:

1. Reduces the topic to a single controlling idea, unifying opinion, or key message
2. Presents your position clearly and concisely, in one sentence
3. Makes a statement that can be supported by statistics, examples, quotes, and references to other sources within the time and space constraints of the assignment
4. Creates interest in the topic
5. Establishes the purpose of the paper
6. Establishes the approach or pattern of organization

Each paragraph should develop a separate but connected point that supports your thesis. For example, your art history instructor might ask you to contrast the work of two impressionist painters. Your thesis statement might read as follows: "Both Manet and Monet are important impressionist artists, but Monet's work has achieved wider popularity." Subsequent paragraphs could address the following elements of the thesis statement:

- What is impressionism?
- Why are the artists considered important?
- What distinguishes the work of each?
- What evidence suggests that one artist is more highly regarded than the other?

To answer each of these questions, include expert opinions found in your research. Don't be afraid to modify your thesis. If your research is not supporting it, restate your thesis to reflect the supporting evidence. Sometimes you will need to do some preliminary research before you can even write your thesis statement.

Do Your Research

Many writing and speaking assignments require research to flesh out facts, figures, and background information about your topic. Good research involves gathering reliable sources of information from a variety of resources such as books, journals, and Internet sites.

Gather Sources

How many research sources should you include in your paper? Sometimes instructors will specify a minimum number; sometimes they won't. You may not have a clear idea about what will work best until you have done some research. Think responsibly about how many sources you will actually need to develop the most effective argument, but plan to look at more materials than you ultimately will refer to in your work. Not every resource you read will be relevant in the end. Choose those that help you develop a sound argument. Quality of evidence, not quantity, will impress your instructor.

Good researchers find and carefully show appropriate, persuasive evidence. For example, you can include statistics in a political science essay because numerical evidence communicates information about voting trends. However, citing statistical evidence in an expressive essay about literary criticism in a humanities class probably won't work. The point of any formal expressive assignment is to demonstrate your knowledge of course-related ideas.

As you do your research, also find sources that argue *against* your assertions. This practice may surprise you. Anticipating criticisms that the reader might have and defending against them in your writing, strengthens your overall argument.

> *Research is to see what everybody has seen, and to think what nobody else has thought.*
>
> Albert Szent-Györgyi
> *20th-century Hungarian biochemist*

Write down the complete reference for each source *as you go*. It's frustrating to assemble a reference list at the end of your work only to discover that you forgot to write down the year a book was published, an important page number, or an Internet address.

Master the Library

Get to know your library's resources so you can locate information quickly. Take a tour if you haven't already done so. If you have trouble locating what you need, ask! Most librarians enjoy helping students. Approach the librarians who appear friendliest or pursue those with the most specialized knowledge on your topic.

Library searches often start in the reference room, which usually houses both paper and electronic databases. From there you may be routed to other areas of the library where you can locate original or *primary* sources (for example, books and journal articles), *secondary* sources (for example, textbooks and other sources that review primary works), or popular press items. References to research or expert opinions that you use in your research are called *citations*.

Your research assignment may specify which types of sources you can use. Most instructors prefer original (primary) sources. They also are more impressed by journal articles that are "peer reviewed." This means that the article was critically analyzed and then approved by other experts in the field. Check with your instructor whether some sources are off-limits, such as popular magazines. Once you've collected several sources, discard the unhelpful ones. Read those with potential carefully, taking notes that will help you represent the author's ideas. It can be helpful to collect pertinent information on 3" × 5" notecards that you can easily reorganize during the writing process.

Use the Internet

Whether you use the library or the Internet, your search will begin with a key word or two that you'll enter into an appropriate database. Do key word searches on several search engines to see what the nature of the discussion might be on the topic you have in mind. For example, if your environmental science class requires a paper on effective recycling strategies, start with the word *recycling*. Using that key word may produce so many "hits" that you could be overwhelmed. Narrow your search to something more specific such as *newspaper recycling* to find more targeted information. If your search produces too few hits, broaden the concept until you find some resources that will help you.

Relying on the Internet, however, can be risky. Most instructors still favor library research that will help you locate printed publications and peer-reviewed sources. The information on the Internet isn't always reliable. Anyone can post anything, making it hard to sift out the gold. Don't assume that an Internet source will be acceptable. However, instructors may be willing to accept Internet citations that are:

1. written by a recognized authority in the field
2. supported by a reputable host group
3. peer reviewed

Good research is important for many types of writing and speaking assignments, providing the basic information you then craft into your final presentation. Gathering your research notes on 3" × 5" cards is a good strategy for both writing and speaking projects. Following are some additional strategies for organizing your work to maximize success.

Get Organized

For some people, coming up with ideas isn't the hard part of good writing. Developing the organization and having the discipline to bring good ideas under control can be difficult aspects of successful writing.

Establish Your Writing Routine

A writing routine can help you get down to business and avoid wasting both time and energy.

Honor Your Writing Rituals Curiously, not all of the activity involved in preparing to write is logical. Some students go through specific writing rituals to bring them good luck. For example, Jim does not feel confident about his writing unless he uses his "lucky" pen, a scratched-up, medium-point Papermate he has had since 10th grade. Alicia must have her beagle resting his head in her lap before she can be creative. Ernest Hemingway sharpened a certain number of pencils before he wrote each morning. As long as they don't take too much time, such rituals are fine. As your abilities and confidence grow, you may not need them to bring out your best.

Stock Your Reference Shelf Good writers rely on expert help. For example, Charmaine likes to embellish her work with well-written quotations that elegantly capture the spirit of whatever topic she is writing about. She has amassed a collection of six quotation sourcebooks to help her with her goal. By contrast, Tony strives to come up with just the right word in his writing so he owns a well-used thesaurus. Invest in references that will help you develop and express your ideas. For example:

- A *Dictionary* can help you with definitions, pronunciation, and spelling.
- A *Thesaurus* provides synonyms and can help expand your vocabulary.
- An *Atlas* provides geographic facts and figures.
- A *Style Manual* can help you with grammar and writing conventions, including the *American Psychological Association* and *Modern Language Association* procedures.
- A *Book of Quotations* provides proverbs and memorable quotations organized by topic, author, or key phrases.

Find a Place to Write Most writers say that they need uninterrupted time to think about their writing. Find a quiet place where you won't be interrupted. Hang a "Do Not Disturb" sign on your door to reduce distraction. Don't answer the phone or e-mail messages.

Develop Your Writing Plan

Many students overconfidently sit down the night before a paper is due and dash off a first draft to submit the next day. In most cases, that plan will guarantee unhappy feedback. Good writing requires time and a plan for how to use that time most effectively. Examine the due date for the assignment and work backward to allow the right amount of time to get the job done. Make sure that you factor in how assignments in other classes must be addressed in your overall timetable. Chapter 3 offers some helpful hints about time management for writing projects. In addition, Figure 9.1, "A Sample Timetable for a Writing Deadline," offers guidance.

> *A #2 pencil and a dream can take you anywhere.*
>
> Joyce A. Myers
> *Contemporary American businesswoman*

FIGURE 9.1 A Sample Timetable for a Writing Deadline

One to two months before the deadline	Select your topic. Map your ideas. Develop your writing plan. Begin to develop a thesis statement. Start your research.
Two weeks before the deadline	Develop individual sections of your paper. Revise with vigor. Complete your research. Finalize your thesis statement.
The week before the deadline	Polish the individual sections of the paper. Create an interesting title. Check your references for accuracy. Obtain some feedback from a friend.
The night before the deadline	Combine the parts of the paper. Print the final draft. Proofread your paper. Assemble the paper.
The morning of the deadline	Proofread your paper one more time.

Prepare Outlines

Generate outlines before you write that allow you to represent the scope of your thoughts, incorporate your research, and make your best argument.

The Informal Outline An informal outline lists the points to be covered in your paper. Putting them down allows you to begin to organize and group them into related clusters. As you find connections and consolidate points, you should revisit your thesis. Does the evidence still support it? Do you need to restate it? If you haven't already written a working thesis, this consolidation of ideas should lead to one. Outlining often reveals areas that require further research.

The Formal Outline A formal outline provides a more structured order to your points, identifying which are the key ideas and which are subordinate. The key ideas become paragraphs with the subordinate ideas providing supportive evidence.

Write with Impact

Over time, writing projects improve your writing skills, develop your confidence as a writer, and build your self-esteem, one of the important steps to success listed at the beginning of this chapter.

Your First Draft

The draft stage is an important first step in the process of actually writing your paper or speech. However, don't confuse a first draft with a final presentation. Following are some important things to keep in mind when first drafting your assignment.

Know Your Audience Strike the right tone for your audience. For example, some tasks require objective and precise presentation of the facts. In other projects you must be exploratory and imaginative. Some projects work best with a casual tone; others may require a polished professional presentation. Knowing your audience can help you make the right decisions.

Keep It Casual, and Keep It Moving In your first draft, you should try not to get bogged down. Write quickly. If you've done your research, and have given yourself enough time to think about the project, you'll be surprised at how much you know without referring to your note cards. Much of what you write comes from thinking that is done without you even knowing it.

You don't have to write in a particular order. Develop the points first that you know best and end with those that require more thinking or references to research. Consider writing your introduction last, and your conclusion first. This way you will know where you're going and all paragraphs must lead to that ending. Set subgoals for how much writing you want to accomplish in any given sitting. For example, it may help to draft the conclusion one day and key paragraphs on other days.

Organize Your Argument Formal papers usually have three parts: an introduction, a body, and a conclusion.

- *Introduction.* The introduction, which contains the thesis statement, lays a foundation for the rest of the piece. Good writers establish the *context* or the purpose for writing, even when the instructor is the audience. They state their intentions early and anticipate the kinds of information readers might want to know to help them understand the motive in writing. Throughout the paper, keep in mind what your audience already knows and what they need to know. See On Target Tips, "A Winning Introduction," for some pointers.
- *The body.* The body of the paper should include your opinions and the evidence that supports your argument. Each paragraph in the body should introduce a separate idea, and support it with details such as quotes, examples, statistics, and references to other sources. Each paragraph should follow logically from the one before, and all paragraphs must relate to the thesis of the paper. The body should use a clear pattern of organization such as listing patterns, comparison patterns, sequencing patterns, cycle patterns, problem-solving patterns, cause/effect patterns, definition/example patterns, and topical/categorical patterns, as discussed earlier in the text.
- *The conclusion.* In a long paper, your conclusion should summarize your argument or review your main points. Make sure that your conclusions fit with the thesis statement you established at the beginning. You can say more

ON TARGET TIPS
A Winning Introduction

Writing a strong first paragraph or introduction is essential in developing a successful paper. What elements should an introductory paragraph contain to succeed in setting the stage for the paper to follow? What characteristics limit success? A good introduction should:

- **provide a hook:** engage the reader with an interesting fact, a powerful statistic, or an amusing anecdote that will make the reader want to finish reading your work.
- **establish point of view:** convey your interest in the topic and your ownership of the ideas that follow.
- **provide context:** help the reader understand why your writing is important, including the purpose or the background.
- **set up the thesis:** provide sufficient detail in the introduction that the thesis statement becomes the natural consequence of the information you provide.
- **define key terms:** offer basic definitions of the terminology or concepts that will be critical to the development of your ideas.
- **create atmosphere:** establish the right emotional tone (for example, playful, analytic, persuasive) to get the job done.

A good introduction should not:

- **be too general:** plan on losing your reader if you can't make an interesting point.
- **state intention in an uninspired way:** avoid openings such as "In this essay I will . . ." or "The instructor assigned me to write . . ."
- **make statements that can't be substantiated:** avoid making claims that don't have clear support in the body of your paper.

Blot out, correct, insert, refine,
Enlarge, diminish, underline,
Be mindful, when invention fails,
To scratch your head, and bite
your nails.

Jonathan Swift
18th-century English satirist

about its implications for action or further study. In a short essay, the conclusion may just refer to the thesis or introduction. The conclusion represents your last opportunity to win over your reader. See Staying Out of the Pits, "Finishing Touches," for some additional suggestions.

Revise and Revise Again

Always leave plenty of time for revision. It is the single most important part of the writing process. In fact, you should plan to spend at least 50 percent of your time on this part of the writing process. You may have four or five working drafts before you reach the final draft.

Assess It After you have finished the first draft, put it aside for a couple of days. Each draft should be separated by at least a day of time away from the paper. This "away time" gives your brain a chance to process the material at a subconscious level, and allows you to come back to it with a fresh perspective.

Reread It Before you begin your revision, read it aloud to yourself or someone else. How does it sound? Does it flow? Does it make sense? Is it too long or too short? You may find you need to do more research to expand on certain points that don't seem adequately supported. You should go through and put a check next to the passages that are fine and a question mark next to any that require work. Check out the Journal activity "One More Go-Around" on page 278 to help you practice your revision skills.

Give It to Others to Read Writers can lead solitary lives, but that stereotype isn't necessarily accurate. Most writers benefit from reviews by others. When your draft is almost finished, get feedback from others who write well. Ask them to point out places where you're not clear or identify points that need further development. For example, despite her successful publishing record, Amy Tan still uses her writing support group to help her refine her work. Find a writing partner and exchange services. Avoid getting feedback from friends who may be struggling with their own writing or you could pick up their bad habits. Your campus may have a writing center where experts can help you improve your writing or recommend a writing tutor. Your instructor also may be willing to read an early draft of a paper.

Write the Appropriate Length Beginning writers sometimes struggle with knowing how much to write. Typically, they write too little rather than too much. Check your writing to see that you explained your intentions to the reader. Provide good examples. Make sure that the parts connect to each other with good transition sentences. All writing elements should follow logically from your original thesis statement.

Some writers have the opposite problem. Their long-winded sentences contain nonessential elements. For example, phrases such as "It is well known that" or "There are many things that" are usually unnecessary; they flatten good writing. Using too many adjectives and adverbs also slows down the reader and reduces your writing's impact. In good writing, "less is more." What if the instructor doesn't specify how long

PEANUTS reprinted by permission of United Feature Syndicate, Inc.

a paper should be? See Staying Out of the Pits, "As Long as It Takes," to help decipher what your instructor may want.

Edit

Editing involves stylistic changes, as well as modifying sentence structure and correcting spelling, punctuation, and grammatical errors.

Refine Your Style Your communication should provide a showcase for your distinctive point-of-view. When it captures exactly what you think and feel, the thrill can be comparable to a hole-in-one or taking a first prize. What are some strategies to achieve a memorable style in your writing and speaking? McKowan (1996) offers the following suggestions:

- Add more words only when it will enhance your impact.
- Remove words, brutally if necessary, to clarify your meaning.
- Replace words when you know there's something not quite right about your choice.
- Shorten sentences to make your writing crisper.
- Rearrange sentences until you find what works best.

Write with an active voice, using action verbs. Be specific, using descriptive language that: draws on the senses; uses specific, concrete nouns; and avoids too many adverbs and adjectives. "It was a beautiful warm summer day" versus "I sauntered out into a brilliant May morning, smiling at the lilting song of the diminutive sparrow and the sweet smell of my neighbor's manicured lawn." Notice how the simplicity of the first sentence makes it more appealing.

Resist the urge to use overblown language just because you are in college. Journalist Edwin Newman (1976), in *A Civil Tongue*, suggested that we embellish language to appear smarter than we really are. He cites as examples these gems from his personal experience:

- "After ingesting alcohol, exclude vehicle use." (Don't drink and drive.)
- "In order to improve security, it is requested that, effective immediately, no employees use the above subject doors for ingress or egress to the building." (Don't use these doors.)
- "I don't wish to defray, but I'll particularize that with more specificity at a later date." (I'll give you more details later.)

You don't want your readers to scratch their heads in wonder because they can't decode your message. Strive to use precise, clear language to the best effect. Limit your use of extreme adjectives

STAYING OUT OF THE PITS — As Long as It Takes

You've probably heard this unhappy exchange at least some time in your academic career.

Student: "How long should this paper be?"
Teacher: "As long as it takes."

The student feels exasperated by the teacher's answer, and the teacher feels discouraged by the student's question.

The student wants a straightforward answer, such as "five pages," so that she can plan how to go after the right number of resources to fit the assignment length. In effect, the desired length of the assignment will dictate the intensity of the effort that will go into her final product.

The teacher's response comes from another perspective. The teacher developed the assignment to encourage the student to explore an interesting idea. The teacher would much rather give free reign to the student's exploration than constrain the process with an artificial boundary.

What strategy would work better to get the help that you need? Communicate your interest in the topic you have chosen and express the concern that you may be tempted to write too much. Ask if there are upper limits that will stress the patience of the teacher. You may be able to ask to see some successful past models on similar assignments if you establish your intention to invest yourself in the assignment's central ideas rather than unintentionally communicating that you will be striving to meet the teacher's minimum expectations.

and superlatives. Think of how often we hear "amazing," "fantastic," "incredible," "awesome," and so on. Overuse of such words can have adverse long-term effects on how people interpret your experience. For example, if you are "desolate" at missing a dinner date, how would you describe your feelings when someone close to you dies? If your new computer game is "awesome," how would you describe the Grand Canyon? Which actually fills you with awe? Invest some time in selecting just the right word to get your point across. The English language is rich with options.

Will the time you spend on refining your style pay off? This principle is illustrated nicely by a sign posted on the office door of a writing teacher:

First draft:

"*I think about you all the time and admire you for all your many qualities. I probably even love you. I could go on and on. . . .*"

Final draft:

"*How do I love thee? Let me count the ways.*"

—*Elizabeth Barrett Browning, 19th-century poet*

Follow the Rules Effective writers are careful about following the rules or *conventions* (for example, grammar and spelling) of good writing. As you get closer to your final draft, you should make sure your writing has followed these rules. Specific *style manuals* will also help you adjust to different disciplinary conventions. The American Psychological Association (APA) offers the standard for writing in the natural and social science disciplines; online tips for using APA style can be found at http://www.apastyle.org. The Modern Language Association (MLA) publishes another common set of guidelines and helpful pointers for this approach are posted online at http://webster.commnet.edu/mla/index.shtml. Ask your instructor which style manual is best for your purpose.

Instructors vary in how much they care about such conventions. Some simply reject papers that include substantial problems with spelling, grammar, and sentence structure. Others overlook these matters if the ideas expressed in the paper are good. Some are sticklers about learning and implementing APA or MLA format. They may provide a *style sheet* that states how the paper must be written. Others may not specify guidelines but expect you to observe general principles of good writing that you've learned in composition class.

Grammar. Even seasoned writers have questions about grammar in their writing. Have a reference manual handy during polishing and proofreading. Consult Staying Out of the Pits, "Top Ten Grammar Violations in College," to help your papers get the most enthusiastic reception.

Punctuation. Punctuation marks pace how the audience reads your writing. Here are some general rules for the most challenging punctuation uses:

- Semicolons: Use to connect thoughts that are closely related; use these sparingly. Semicolons go well with "however," "therefore," "for instance," and so on. They also should be used to separate items in a series that contain commas.
- Dashes and exclamation marks: Use these in informal projects or in limited ways in formal work.
- Quotation marks: Quotes longer than three lines require special indentation and marking. In shorter uses, punctuation marks belong *inside* quotation marks.
- Apostrophes: Use for contractions (for example, can't, don't, wouldn't) and possessive indicators (Ted's, the child's, the women's). Good writers generally avoid using contractions in formal work. Take note that "its" and "it's" are not the same. "Its" is the possessive form of the pronoun "it." "It's" is a contraction of "it is" and does not indicate possession. (Example: *It's* a good thing that working hard is *its* own reward.)

Spelling. Some lucky people are naturally good spellers. They imagine how the word looks, sound words out, and memorize spelling conventions (for example, "*i* before *e* except after *c*"). However, even good spellers use the dictionary or the computer's spell-checker to help polish their papers. A spell-checker won't catch all errors. Be vigilant about the challenges of *homonyms*, words that sound alike but mean something different. They can easily slip into writing and elude even careful proofreaders. For example:

- *two* versus *too* or *to*
- *their* versus *there*
- *hear* versus *here*

Finish in Style

Before you submit your final paper, there are a still a few more steps you can take that will help it stand out in the pile your instructor will be evaluating.

Pick a Compelling Title Many assignments require a title. Some writers wait until the project is almost completed before creating a title that captures the appeal of the work. Strive to create one that compels the reader to read further. Which paper would you rather read?

> An Analysis of the Poetry of the Beat Generation
>
> OR
>
> The Poet's Place in the Beat Generation
>
> OR
>
> Where Has All the Rhyming Gone? Poetry from the Beat Generation

STAYING OUT OF THE PITS

Top Ten Grammar Violations in College

What are some of the most frequent grammar violations that trigger a negative mindset in your instructors when they grade your writing? Teachers tend to recoil when they see grammar errors like these:

- "Me and Todd went to the store."
  - → Todd and *I* went to the store. (proper pronoun use)
- "A person should follow their own dream."
  - → "*People* should follow *their* own *dreams*. (noun-pronoun agreement)
- "The football was thrown by the quarterback."
  - → "The quarterback *throws* the football. (active voice)
- "Do you know where you're going to?"
  - → "Do you know where you are *going*? (excess prepositions; avoid using "where at" and "where to")
- "I need to go get orientated."
  - → "I will get *oriented* instead. (proper use of orient as a verb)
- "I except your apology."
  - → "I *accept* your apology if I want to make up.
  - → "I *take exception* to your apology if I'm still angry. (proper use of *accept*, meaning to go along with, versus *except*, meaning to set aside)
- "My homework effects my mood."
  - → "My homework *affects* my mood. (affect means to influence; effect means to create, but is used more rarely)
- "I plan to win irregardless of what you do."
  - → "I plan to win *regardless* of what you do. (irregardless is not a proper word)
- "I could care less."
  - → "I *couldn't* care less. (if you could care less, it means you are still bothered)
- "I can't hardly finish my work."
  - → "I *can* hardly finish my work. ("can't hardly" is a double negative)

ON TARGET TIPS

The Saving Grace

Using a word processor can help your writing, but some precautions are in order.

1. **Save your writing as you go.** Nothing is more frustrating than having the power go down after you've been working on your computer for hours. In this situation you'll lose everything that has not been saved. Develop a habit of frequently saving as you write. For example, save your work every time you complete a section or a page of writing. Or, turn on the automatic save function so you won't have to think about doing it manually.

2. **Make a backup copy—just in case.** Computer viruses can wreak havoc with your hard drive. By making a backup copy on a floppy disk, Zip drive, or CD, you'll still have your complete work if your hard drive crashes. Label your disks so you don't have to waste time searching multiple disks to find your paper.

3. **Avoid eating and drinking around your computer.** A spilled soda can foul up your computer and lead to expensive repairs. Move away from your computer when you eat and drink.

4. **Have a backup plan.** Even the most reliable computer can fail when you need it most. If you've duplicated your work on a portable medium, make sure you know where you can find a compatible system to use in a pinch. Your campus computer center may provide some backup machines.

©Paul Thomas/Getty Images

Word processing programs offer many features such as spell check, grammar help, and word count to enhance the quality of your work.

Both the second and third options are likely to engage the reader more successfully than the flat approach in the first title. Refer to the Journal activity "Entitlement" on page 279 to further explore how creative titles can enhance reader interest.

Produce a Professional Product Your writing is an extension of your self. Your final product not only reveals your ability to construct an argument but also communicates your pride about your own work. Smudge-free, easy-to-read writing says a great deal about your high standards and professionalism. Most instructors expect you to use word processing to produce your paper. That way you can revise easily. Although word processors can save time, they can also frustrate you if you overlook some simple precautions. See OnTarget Tips, "The Saving Grace," for some good advice.

Include a cover page with the title of the paper, your name, your instructor's name, the course, and the date unless your instructor requires a different format. Be sure to number the pages. Ask your instructors for other format preferences, including whether they like fancy covers. Many instructors disdain plastic folders or binders as a waste of money and resource. By contrast, some think a cover gives a more professional look.

Proofread the Final Draft Proofreading can be tricky. You may be so close to what you've created that you can't spot errors easily. A break can help. For example, Bret likes to get a good night's sleep before he proofreads and prints his final draft. By returning to the paper later, he feels more confident about catching the subtle errors that he might miss when he is tired. Proofreading your paper aloud may help you catch more errors. Some experts recommend reading your paper sentence by sentence from back to front (Axelrod & Cooper, 1996). Altering your usual method of reading may help you see weak sentence structure. When you think that you've caught all errors, proofread one more time. If the errors are minor, you won't need to print another copy. Making last-minute proof marks on your paper signals to your instructor that you made a final pass to ensure the work is your best effort.

Evaluate Your Work Once a paper is finished, good writers assess the quality of their work. Complete Self-Assessment 1 "What Are My Writing Strengths and Weaknesses?" on page 275 to explore reviewing skills that will lead to better papers. If you formally evaluate the quality of your work early enough, you still may have time to revise it and earn a better grade.

Meet Deadlines Turn projects in on time or negotiate an exception with an instructor *before* the deadline. Even if you've written the best paper in the history of the class, many instructors penalize late submissions. Some even refuse to accept them.

Solve Writing Problems

Even the best writers sometimes run into problems that can keep them from achieving their goals. The first problem may be that they only look at the grade that comes back on a paper, never taking the time to read and carefully consider the instructor's comments. Other common problems include difficulty developing a distinctive voice, procrastination, and writer's block.

Learn from Feedback

Instructors vary in the methods they use to evaluate papers. Some simply assign a grade that captures the overall quality of your work. This approach is sometimes referred to as *holistic grading*. Others provide detailed feedback, often relying on a *rubric*, or formal set of criteria, to detail your strengths and weaknesses. When you get detailed feedback, read it carefully so you can learn something that will help in future assignments.

A river of red ink can be hard to take. Read extensive criticisms quickly, then take some time to recover before you try to learn from the feedback. Let yourself be disappointed. Maybe even mope a little. Then return with the intention of learning what to do to improve your writing. Remember, we all often learn more from mistakes than from successes.

Ask for feedback if you don't understand your grade. Many instructors believe students are willing to settle for a summary judgment—a grade—with little or no justification. However, when you don't understand how your instructor derived your grade, ask. Specific feedback on your strengths and weaknesses is essential to becoming a good writer.

Watch your growth as a writer by keeping track of how your papers are improving. Review your collection of papers now and then, especially when you're disappointed by an evaluation. In some college programs, you may be asked to construct a portfolio of your work to track your progress. Establishing a portfolio (a folder or binder of past papers, organized chronologically) will also help you establish a research stream, as discussed earlier in this chapter. Also complete the Journal activity "What Are Your Writing Trends?" on page 279 for some ideas on using past writing assignments to improve your future performance.

> *I love criticism just so long as it's unqualified praise.*
> Noel Coward
> *20th-century English playwright*

Find Your Unique Voice

Some college students struggle with self-esteem issues, and expressive projects expose personal uncertainty. From past experience, some worry that their ideas will be poorly received. Communication projects provide a way to discover, express, and polish your thoughts. Your instructors don't expect perfection. In fact, projects that are too well crafted can generate concern and suspicion. Most instructors enjoy working with you to find your voice. Your self-esteem as a communicator will grow with your serious effort.

Although most instructors favor logical and uncluttered writing, many respond enthusiastically to work that has a creative flair. Consider what it must be like for the instructor to grade one essay after another that strives merely to meet a narrow set of criteria. Like most other people, instructors generally appreciate variety, unusual insights, and even some humor in their students' assignments. You can build a distinctive approach in various ways. Find out what other students typically do, then do something different. Consider a unique slant for the project. Create an engaging title. Use a thesaurus to expand your word choice. Add interesting quotations. See the Journal activity "The Liberal Arts Flair," on page 279 for some practice.

Stop Procrastinating

Like many writers, you also may struggle with getting down to business. Sometimes other more pressing projects intrude or distract. Or the project may be one in which you have little interest. In any case, you may suddenly find yourself with a deadline looming before you and end up submitting an assignment that you dashed off at the last minute. Submitting a rough draft may make your instructor think that you weren't taking the task seriously. To combat procrastination, plan a reasonable schedule that breaks your research and writing into manageable parts, like the one outlined in Figure 9.1. Then stick to it. Reward yourself for completing each phase. For some other strategies to help reduce procrastination, see Staying Out of the Pits, "Good Intentions."

Unlock Writer's Block

Sometimes you have nothing to say. Don't panic. All writers face times when inspiration fails and words don't come easily. Interestingly, one good response is to write about your writer's block. Write about how it feels to be empty. Describe the nature of your blocks. You may gain insight into your resistance and find ideas that will get you moving. Another good step is asking for a conference with your instructor. By talking about the assignment, your instructor can offer tips or hints that can unleash your creativity. Ask whether your instructor has any model student papers. By observing how others tackled related problems, you may be able to spark some ideas of your own.

You also can try a creativity-generating computer program that provides a systematic approach to helping you plumb your ideas. *IdeaFisher* and *Inspiration* are two popular programs. Explore some other options by visiting this Internet site: http://members. ozemail.com.au/~caveman/Creative/ Software/swindex.htm.

Build Your Integrity

Communication projects can be both exciting and challenging. Sometimes this challenge encourages students to cut corners, presenting others' work as their own. Make this an opportunity to practice honest, appropriate behavior and build your integrity.

Understand Plagiarism *Plagiarism* means presenting someone else's words or ideas as your own. This is a serious academic offense. Most campuses specify harsh outcomes for those found guilty. Ironically, Amy Tan reports a miserable experience related to plagiarism. Her brother was caught and punished for allowing a friend to copy a paper in college. He later developed a terminal illness that their mother swore was caused by the shame of committing this dishonorable act. Although no one has proven that plagiarism is fatal, it can shortchange your learning and severely risk your academic health.

Types of Plagiarism Experts suggest that students who plagiarize generally fall into one of two categories: those who inadvertently plagiarize and those who do it on purpose (Harris, 2001). The penalties for inadvertent plagiarism can be just as severe as for those who intentionally misrepresent their work, so make sure you understand the rules.

Accidental Plagiarism Inadvertent plagiarizers can fall into the trap by not knowing the rules that govern appropriate citation. For example, some students erroneously believe that they can lift words from a source if they simply cite it. Wrong! Importing an author's words directly into your own work requires quotation marks and proper citation. Some students believe if you change a word or two in a sentence, that's good enough. It's not. Both strategies can make you vulnerable to charges of plagiarism by alert instructors. See Figure 9.2, "From Original Source to Proper Citation," for some examples that will help you avoid plagiarism by accident. Then check out your understanding of the rules by taking Self-Assessment 2 "Are You at Risk for Plagiarism?" on page 276.

Purposeful Plagiarism Why would anyone plagiarize on purpose? Harris (2001) offers many reasons. Some students may have been trained in a different tradition. For example, some foreign students have learned to cite a source word-for-word to "honor the writer" (Harris, p. 12). However, others may be looking for a shortcut to produce a project that they can submit for a grade. They may feel swamped by too many deadlines or insecure in their own writing skills. They may believe their instructors don't really read the papers so that justifies not going to the trouble of writing it. Unfortunately, some students also enjoy defying authority. They relish the opportunity

FIGURE 9.2 From Original Source to Proper Citation

Suppose you are writing a paper for psychology class about the meaning of body piercing in contemporary culture.

From your literature review imagine that you have found a great resource in a recent article published in a peer-reviewed journal by Lydia Gray.

How do you incorporate Gray's ideas to support your argument? You have two options:

Appropriate Citation with Quote:

Gray (2001, p. 55) stated, "Body piercing represents a teenager's attempt to shock her parents and distance herself from their values."

Your citation gives full credit to the person who originated the idea. The quote marks tell the reader that the author stated the argument in these words on a specific page in the original resource. Use quotations sparingly, but do so when the author has used especially vivid words or examples and their impact would be lost by paraphrasing.

Appropriate Citation with Paraphrase:

Gray (2001) speculated that adolescents may alienate their parents on purpose by certain behaviors, such as body piercing, that don't fit with their parents' value system.

Your citation gives credit to the original author, but you translate the original idea into your own words. This approach is the preferred way to cite evidence in most cases. It honors the author and the idea but relies on your ability to translate the idea into your own words.

When do you run the risk of being accused of plagiarism?

Overt Plagiarism: Direct Use of Author's Words, No Paraphrase, No Citation

Gray originally stated,

"Body piercing represents a teenager's attempt to shock her parents and distance herself from their values."

You write in your paper:

Body piercing represents a teenager's attempt to shock her parents.

Using this line, word-for-word, in your paper misrepresents the idea as your own. Merely leaving off the last half of the sentence does not protect you from the accusation of stealing the author's words.

Overt Plagiarism: Direct Use of Author's Ideas, Insufficient Paraphrase, No Citation

Gray originally stated,

"Body piercing represents a teenager's attempt to shock her parents and distance herself from their values."

You write in your paper:

Body piercing can be a girl's attempt to upset her parents and distance herself from their values.

Substituting a few words in the author's original sentence and not giving credit to the author for the original idea counts as plagiarism.

Prevent Plagiarism

Following are some strategies to help you avoid being accused of plagiarism during your college career.

- **Paraphrase when you do research.** As you take notes from various resources, translate the ideas of others into your own words. Compare what you have written with the original source to make sure that your paraphrase captures the spirit of the ideas written, not the actual words and phrases themselves.
- **Give proper credit.** When you directly quote or refer to the ideas of another writer, provide source information in the format required by your instructor.
- **Make your own observations stand out in your notes.** Put your own ideas in the margin or print them so that they look physically different from the ideas you received from others. Later you can use your own observations without fear of committing plagiarism.
- **Use quotations sparingly.** Rely on the words of experts only when their writing is so elegant that your paraphrase will not do it justice. Using many or long quotations is a sign that you're uncomfortable expressing your own ideas.
- **Don't help others plagiarize.** Lending others your papers when you suspect the borrowers plan to submit something based closely on your work implicates you in plagiarism. If the borrower's submission is questioned, you may find yourself in the unpleasant situation of explaining why you lent your paper for an unethical purpose.
- **Guard against others plagiarizing your work.** If you use a community-based computer, do not store your work on the computer's hard drive. Others who use the computer can easily download your writing and submit it as their own without your knowledge or permission.

to outsmart the professor by not getting caught when submitting the work of others as their own.

Think about examples you have seen of students who plagiarize to meet their course requirements. Consider the Journal activity "The Cost of Plagiarism" on page 279 to determine if there are other explanations. How do they do it? They may borrow a paper from a friend, download a paper from the Internet, build a paper from multiple cut-and-pasted resources, "recycle" a paper from a prior class, or even buy a term paper through the Internet.

How do they get caught? According to Harris, not all faculty members pay careful attention, but the ones who do have well-developed strategies that can identify plagiarism. Among obvious factors, instructors look for

- inconsistent "voice" throughout the paper
- vocabulary that doesn't fit with what the student should know
- sentence structure that is too complex for the student's level
- content that doesn't quite fit with the topic
- parts of the paper don't fit together well
- missing important recent references
- inconsistent format throughout the paper

In addition, some students plagiarize sloppily. They whiteout the names of the real author or leave other clues for a careful reader that will lead to their downfall. Instructors can also test drive portions of papers through electronic databases to identify whether a project is original.

Protect Yourself Being accused of plagiarism can be extremely stressful, both for you and your instructor. How can you avoid the complications of being involved with a plagiarism accusation? Staying Out of the Pits, "Prevent Plagiarism," offers a few good ideas.

If you end up getting drawn into a plagiarism inquiry, cooperate with your instructor. You have the right to due process. Be prepared to bring your resources, to share what you know about the information in the project, and describe how you completed your work. You may be able to resolve the problem with a sound explanation. If that approach is unsuccessful, familiarize yourself with your campus procedures and batten down the hatches. It's going to be a stormy sea ahead.

Speak!

Although both speaking and writing provide an opportunity to express yourself, speaking differs from writing in significant ways. When you write, you can refine your work until it says exactly what you want. However, when you speak, even though you can practice to a fine point, the reality of live performance adds a whole new communication challenge.

Pursue the Spotlight

College should offer several opportunities for you to improve your speaking skills in the contexts of working individually and collaborating with others. For instance, you may be asked to address the class formally by delivering a carefully researched position or give an extemporaneous speech on a topic given just moments beforehand. Some courses promote expressive reading of dramatic works. These opportunities will refine your public-speaking skills, including pacing, voice quality, and connecting to the audience.

Group speaking projects include case presentations, panel discussions, and debates. These projects are most successful when group members can coordinate their individual pieces and practice together. However, the addition of group effort can sometimes make these assignments even more challenging.

You also can learn about speaking by observing good speakers. College campuses often host dynamic speakers who can show you how it's done. In addition, you can get experience in the spotlight by asking questions at the end of the speech. If that option feels overwhelming at first, approach the speaker with your questions or comments when the speech is over. Most speakers want your feedback. By being an active audience member, you can learn a great deal about good speaking skills.

Videotape has captured a variety of brilliant speeches that showcase masterful communication. Some of these may also be available on DVD or over the Internet. Take advantage of lessons from speakers at the height of their persuasive skills. Such a review can inspire you to do your best.

Write a Good Speech

All famous speeches were written before they were delivered and became memorable. Keep in mind that the skills involved in preparing good papers also apply to good speeches. For example, you will want to develop a thesis statement, research your topic, create an outline, and organize your points into an introduction, main body, and conclusion. What additional strategies can you apply?

Define Your Purpose Know your goal. Are you supposed to persuade? Inform? Entertain? Debate? Your purpose will determine how to use resources and structure your speech so you can achieve success. It also will help you avoid running too short or too long. To enhance your success, talk with your instructor about your intentions. Submit a thesis statement, outline, or concept map before your scheduled presentation time. Ask for comments to help you stay close to the goal of the assignment.

Engage Your Audience Most college audiences will be sympathetic. After all, your peers will be in your shoes before the term is over. This usually provides a uniquely supportive learning environment in which to give a speech. If you assume that your audience is supportive, you may feel less apprehensive about giving the speech. Identify your purpose early in your speech. Keep in mind what your audience knows already and what they need to know. However, never omit your purpose, even if the audience already knows it. It's best to be brief but clear.

Effective speakers address the audience members on their level. For example, if your college recruits you to talk to high school students about college life, your vocabulary and examples might be different than those in the same kind of speech given to their parents. Good speakers also try to understand the values of their audience so they appeal to them more effectively.

> *The best impromptu speeches are the ones written well in advance.*
>
> Ruth Gordon
> *20th-century American actress and writer*

Build Your Message An anonymous speech instructor once recommended the perfect structure for public presentations, "Tell 'em what you are going to tell 'em, tell 'em, then tell 'em what you told 'em." Although this approach might sound boring, repeating the key ideas of a speech really counts. As in good writing, the main point of the speech serves as the backbone, and each portion of the speech must support it. Many speakers hand out a printed outline of a speech so the audience can follow it better.

As you construct the body of your talk, pay attention to the kinds of support that appeal most to the audience. You don't have to overwhelm your audience with statistics and stories to make your point. Choose your evidence carefully to create both emotional and logical appeal. Class speeches should reflect what you've learned from the course. You can draw ideas from the textbook, class notes, or other readings that relate to what you're studying. However, if you give a speech that shows no evidence of what you've learned from the course, your grade will probably suffer as much as your audience.

Deliver a Good Speech

If you have invested time wisely in getting your ideas together, a speech gives you the opportunity to shine. How can you get the most out of these opportunities?

Rehearse The time put into rehearsal often makes or breaks a speech. If you know your speech well enough, you should need your note cards only for cues about what you intend to say. Otherwise, you may be tempted to read what you've written, which disconnects you from the audience. Because effective speakers know their own intentions and order of ideas, they don't need to rely heavily on their notes or a memorized script. They give the impression of connecting with the audience by talking with them rather than reciting from memory or reading directly from a prepared text.

> *If you have an important point to make, don't try to be subtle or clever. Use a pile driver. Hit the point once. Then come back and hit it again. Then hit it a third time—a tremendous whack!*
>
> Winston Churchill
> *20th-century British prime minister*

Look the Part How you look will influence your speaking success (Hillman, 1999). Dress to meet the expectations of the audience. For example, some formal speeches may work better if you dress less casually. How you dress should not distract from your message. Your clothes should be comfortable without being distracting. Make sure your shoes match. Avoid playing with your hair and jewelry. You will want the audience to pay attention to your message, not your fashion sense.

Start your speech with a personal experience or a joke. Introduce an interesting news item, quotation, or event that the audience will remember. In all cases, conclude your opening with a statement of your objective and a description of where you intend to go.

Polish Your Delivery Stand straight and breathe in a controlled manner. Speak clearly and confidently. Make gestures that are purposeful, directing attention to underscore what you are saying. Look your audience in the eye. And don't forget to smile or frown appropriately to express the emotion you feel about your topic. Even casual speeches benefit from the polish that comes from practice. Minimize the number of pauses, "ums" and "ahs," or other interruptions that invite your audience to stop listening. Effective speakers also project their voices to reach people at the back of the room and put life in their voices to keep people's attention. A monotone delivery can be deadly. Nothing can harm good ideas more than bad grammar and sloppy sentence structure. When you practice giving your speech to a friend, ask for specific feedback on grammar and language.

Use Media Effectively Good speakers use a variety of means to make their ideas believable, including stories, video clips, quotations, statistics, charts, and graphs. Every element should play a meaningful role in the development of the speaker's position.

If you use an overhead projector, computer-generated images, or PowerPoint slides, practice with the equipment before the speech since its use can be tricky. Make the lettering large and easy to read. (To test the size of your lettering, put the transparency on the floor and stand over it or walk a few feet away from your computer screen. If you can read from this position, the font is probably large enough.) Prepare typed overheads; handwritten ones suggest a lack of pride in your work. If you use audiotapes or videotapes to support your presentation, be sure to wind the tape to the appropriate starting point ahead of time. For other suggestions to deliver great presentations with Power Point, see On Target Tips, "All Power, No Point." Also complete the Journal activity "PowerPointers" on page 278.

Finish Gracefully When you conclude your speech, return to your key themes. Summarize what you've covered and identify any actions the audience should take as a result of your speech. If you've given a long speech, repeat your objectives. Then smile and prepare to receive your applause. Many instructors include a question-and-answer period following a student's speech. Such activity encourages you to think on your feet and to learn how to manage unexpected events. See On Target Tips, "Winning in the Home Stretch," for how to manage the question-and-answer period.

Improve Your Speaking Skills

Good speaking skills don't just develop overnight. By revisiting your performances after the fact you can improve for the future.

Evaluate Your Work Good speakers check the quality of their speaking as they rehearse, as well as during and after the actual performance. Complete Self-Assessment 3 "What Are My Speaking Strengths and Weaknesses?" on page 277 to examine your speaking skills in detail.

Solve Delivery Problems You will be experiencing a variety of speeches throughout your college career. Some will dazzle you. Others will be painful to watch. Many students choke, tear up, or show other obvious signs of nervousness when they speak to a group. See the Journal activity "The View from the Audience" on page 278 to explore some lessons offered by problematic speeches from your classmates. Delivery problems can undermine your effectiveness. However, there are several strategies that can put you at ease.

- *Diagnose your problem carefully.* If you routinely choke during oral presentations, identify when the problem occurs and whether there are any consistent causes. Contrast those situations with other performances that have been more satisfying. This analysis will help you find ways to improve your delivery.

ON TARGET TIPS

All Power, No Point

The use of PowerPoint for presenting visual support in lectures and speeches has become rampant but many presentations violate good communication standards, leading one pundit to suggest that a PowerPoint presentation was "all power, no point." What are some other pointers for making PowerPoint work?

- Don't use PowerPoint if the light conditions will make it hard to see your visuals.
- Use bullets, not complete text.
- Limit content to four to five ideas per slide.
- Use colors that complement each other.
- Use sound effects sparingly, if at all.
- Don't turn your back on the audience to read your slides.
- Rehearse on the system that will deliver your presentation.

ON TARGET TIPS

Winning in the Home Stretch

When your classmates ask questions that stump you after you've given a speech, consider these strategies for coping with the strain:

- **Ask for a restatement of the question.** This can give you clues to help you answer the question or provide extra time to think through your response.
- **Say "I don't know."** Sometimes it's best to admit that the questioner poses a new topic for you, then move on. No one expects a speaker to have all the answers.
- **Ask the questioner for an opinion.** Many people who ask questions have their own ideas about what constitutes a satisfying answer. Your willingness to share the stage will be seen as gracious, and the gesture gives you more time to respond.

"I could have been a big celebrity but for my fear of public speaking."

Career Connections

Myra loved to write. She had always received great feedback from her instructors throughout high school. She was tempted to major in English in college but was surprised to discover how much she liked her science classes. The lectures offered answers to the questions she had entertained about how the universe worked. She seemed especially drawn to mysteries about the functioning of the human body. Although she enjoyed the labs that usually accompanied her courses, what she most enjoyed was writing about science. Her biology instructor made a comment on one of her papers that became a turning point in her life decisions: "You write so well. You should write about science!" Before that comment, she had never really considered that there might be a career that would combine her two loves. With the help of a career counselor, she discovered a variety of interesting career opportunities, including science fiction writing, grant development, magazine writing, and science journalism.

Todd hated public speaking in high school. His knees used to knock and he would feel nauseous at the thought of having to share his ideas. When he took a required public speaking course, the practice involved in having to design and deliver four speeches in the course of a semester got him past the "willies." He began to relax and enjoy the challenge of presenting his ideas. He discovered that he enjoyed persuasive opportunities the most. By the time he graduated, he targeted a career in pharmaceutical sales, a choice that was effectively supported by a major in communications and a minor in chemistry.

- *Anticipate what your body needs.* Breathe deeply and stretch your muscles to give your body signals about your intention to control your nervousness. Take a bathroom break before your talk begins. Have a glass of water handy to relieve parched lips and give you time to regain your composure.
- *Organize yourself to maintain control.* Prevent losing your place by using well-organized, easy-to-read note cards. Number the cards so that you can restore their order quickly if you drop the stack. It happens!
- *Use technology strategically.* A tape or video recorder during rehearsal can provide clues about where your delivery suffers. If you use technology during your presentation, rehearse blending these elements with your talk. A graceful pause to review a slide can focus audience attention on your content and away from your own anxiety.
- *Note any mannerisms or gestures that may distract your audience.* Practice reducing these problems until you're satisfied that you can perform smoothly.
- *Enlist audience support.* If you announce that your hands are shaking or your knees are knocking, your audience will think about your hands or knees and not your ideas. If you lose your place, however, admit the problem to the audience, then stop and regain your control. If you lose your composure because you feel overwhelmed, tell the audience that this topic is hard for you. They'll appreciate your candor and support you.

Seek a Second Chance All great speakers suffer an occasional bad performance. Recognize your potential to learn from experiences that don't go well. Commit yourself to better preparation, goal setting, and improved performances in the future. See if you can work out a second chance with your instructor. Sometimes your speech can be videotaped in the college media facilities so the instructor can review it at a convenient time. Whether this second chance improves your grade or not, your positive practice will help you turn in a performance in which you have greater pride.

> *It is no sin to attempt and fail. The only sin is not to make the attempt.*
>
> SuEllen Fried
> *Contemporary American social activist*

Summary Strategies for Mastering College

Refine your expressive skills by seizing every opportunity to practice communicating, prepare properly, and evaluate how well you met your goals.

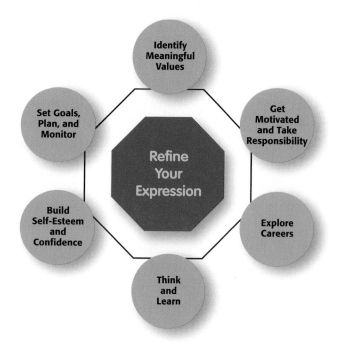

Focus on the "Six Strategies for Success" above as you read each chapter to learn how to apply these strategies to your own success.

1 Express Yourself!

- Recognize why future employers place great value on communication skills.
- Seek opportunities for practice and feedback.

2 Prepare Before You Write

- Clarify your goals for improving your writing.
- Use strategies to generate ideas and refine your topic.
- Develop a thesis statement to organize your research.

3 Do Your Research

- Know how to gather the best sources.
- Become familiar with the library.
- Select the best evidence to support the positions you'll develop.

4 Get Organized

- Consider developing a research stream to improve efficiency.
- Use reference books, a time table, and an outline to aid your writing.

5 Write with Impact

- Start early, revise regularly, and meet deadlines.
- Know and meet your audience's expectations.
- Organize your argument with an introduction, main body, and conclusion.

6 Solve Writing Problems

- Learn from your instructors' feedback.
- Develop your distinctive voice and writing flair.
- Avoid plagiarism through careful note taking and proper citation practices.
- Avoid procrastination and writer's block.

7 Speak!

- Explore all the speaking opportunities you can find.
- Use technology and multimedia to produce professional results.
- Overcome speaking jitters and delivery problems through self-control and practice.

Review Questions

1. Why are communication skills important for life after graduation? List a few ways that good writing and speaking skills can improve your job performance.

    1. _____
    2. _____
    3. _____

2. Describe at least three things you might want to accomplish in writing and speaking assignments.

    1. _____
    2. _____
    3. _____

3. What is a thesis statement?

    _____
    _____
    _____

    Why is it important?

    _____
    _____
    _____

4. Why should students avoid plagiarism? List a few strategies for making sure this doesn't happen to you.

    _____
    _____
    _____

5. What are some typical problems faced in giving formal speeches and how can these be overcome?

    _____
    _____
    _____

6. What are some ways to recover from disappointing performances in communication?

    _____
    _____
    _____

Learning Portfolio

SELF-ASSESSMENTS

YOUR JOURNAL

STRATEGIES FOR SUCCESS

Identify Meaningful Values

Get Motivated and Take Responsibility

Set Goals, Plan, and Monitor

Refine Your Expression

Explore Careers

Build Self-Esteem and Confidence

Think and Learn

What Are My Writing Strengths and Weaknesses?

Once you've completed at least one formal college writing assignment, examine your work using the guidelines here (based on Alverno College, 1995). The feedback or grade you received from your instructor may provide some clues about areas that you need to improve. Keep the writing criteria handy to help guide your future writing projects.

Writing Criteria	Completely	Partially	Barely or Not At All
I followed the instructions.			
	Effectively	**Partially**	**Barely or Not At All**
I established *appropriate context* and kept this focus throughout.			
I crafted the *style* of the paper and selected *words* carefully to suit the purpose.			
I showed conscientious use of appropriate *conventions*, including spelling and grammar.			
I *structured* the paper, including an introduction, main body, and conclusion.			
I included *evidence* to support my thesis.			
I added *content* that reflected learning specific to the course.			

Now review your responses to these criteria and answer the following:

- *What are your writing strengths?*

- *What do you need to improve?*

- *Is this pattern typical of your writing projects?*

- *What strategies will help you improve?*

- *Would it be useful to consult with the campus writing center?*

Source: Adapted from *Criteria for Effective Writing*. Reprinted with permission of Alverno College Productions.

Are You at Risk for Plagiarism?

Which of the following are acceptable ways to acknowledge the ideas of others in your own writing?

_____ Reproducing the writer's original words—with quotation marks

_____ Reproducing the writer's original words—without quotation marks

_____ Leaving out a portion of the writer's original sentence

_____ Rearranging the words in the writer's original sentence

_____ Substituting a few words in the writer's original sentence

_____ Identifying the writer, but putting the original sentence in your own words

_____ Without identifying the writer, putting the original sentence in your own words

There are only a few appropriate strategies you can use to acknowledge the work of others: These include:

- *Reproducing the writer's original words—with quotation marks*

- *Identifying the writer, but putting the original sentence in your own words.*

Keep this in mind when preparing all of your writing assignments, regardless of the discipline area.

What Are My Speaking Strengths and Weaknesses?

Even if you haven't already had a speaking assignment in college, you've probably developed a sense of your strengths and weaknesses in giving presentations. Review the following, based on Alverno College's *Writing and Speaking Criteria* (1995), to determine how effective you are as a public speaker. Keep these speaking criteria available to help you in future speaking assignments.

Speaking Criteria	Routinely	Often	Rarely
I connect with the audience by talking directly to them rather than reading my notes or delivering a memorized script.			
I state my purpose and keep this focus throughout.			
I craft the style of the speech and select words carefully to suit the purpose.			
I effectively deliver the speech, using eye contact, supportive gestures, and effective voice control.			
I follow appropriate conventions, including grammar.			
I organize the speech well, including the introduction, main body, and conclusions.			
I include evidence that supports and develops my ideas.			
I use media effectively to help the audience grasp key ideas.			
I include content that reflects my learning from the course.			

Now review your accomplishments in speaking.

- *What are your strengths?*

- *What criteria show that you need to improve?*

- *Is this pattern typical of your speaking projects?*

- *What strategies should you pursue?*

Your Journal

● REFLECT

1. The View from the Audience

Recall a time when you observed someone making a bad speech.

- At what point did you recognize the speech would be unsatisfying?

_____

- Did the speaker make any attempts to correct the failing outcome during the speech?

_____

- How did you feel as you watched the speech flop?

_____

- What advice could you have offered the speaker to turn the speech around?

_____

- How should these observations influence your preparation for future speaking challenges?

_____

2. Exploiting Your Life

Amy Tan explored a turbulent theme in her personal life—the challenging relationship between mother and daughter—that resonated with her audience. Make a list of important events in your own life that might become a resource for future expressive writing projects. Keep the list in your dayplanner or somewhere else that you can refer to easily throughout your college career.

● DO

1. PowerPointers

You have probably already been exposed to many PowerPoint lectures that vary in their quality. Select a lecture and think about ways that the delivery of information could be improved. Make some notes about what worked and what didn't work. How might your critique influence your own strategies when it is your turn?

2. One More Go-Around

Commit yourself ahead on the next writing assignment to leaving extra time at the end of the process. Finish your work one week ahead of the deadline. Try several different revision strategies:

- Sleep on it
- Read it aloud to friends
- Work your way backward through the paper paragraph by paragraph
- Scrutinize word choice to see if you have chosen the right word for the right effect
- Use computer editing to verify spell checking and grammar
- Proofread two hours before the deadline to catch any final errors

Which of these strategies seem to work best to help you produce your most effective writing?

_____

Your Journal

● THINK CRITICALLY

1. The Cost of Plagiarism

List some reasons why students you have known resorted to plagiarism to satisfy their course requirements. After each reason, list a potential justification for this act. Finally, list all of the consequences of plagiarism, whether the student is caught or not.

1. Reason: _____ Justification: _____

2. Reason: _____ Justification: _____

3. Reason: _____ Justification: _____

Consequences: _____

How does this exercise influence your own resilience in resisting taking the easy way out on writing assignments?

_____

2. What Are Your Writing Trends?

Begin a collection of papers from your courses to establish your writing portfolio. Arrange them in chronological order in a file folder or binder. What trends are apparent in the feedback that you are receiving?

_____

Is the positive feedback you are getting consistent with your own self-image as a writer?

_____

Is the negative feedback you are getting a clue about where you should concentrate your efforts to improve?

_____

Do you see a potential "research stream" that you can capitalize on in future writing projects?

_____

● CREATE

1. Entitlement

Think about a writing assignment you are working on now or look over your course syllabi for one that is due later in the semester. List the course below, along with the topic you are or will be studying when the writing project is assigned.

Course: _____ Topic: _____

Now start brainstorming about potential titles, based on that topic area. Don't be afraid to be creative or silly—this is just an exercise. Revisit this list of ideas once you actually sit down and start working on the assignment. You are already ahead of the game.

2. The Liberal Arts Flair

Many expert communicators find that the well-placed quotation can be an effective way to craft elegant writing. Quotations can be used to open or close a speech or a paper with some drama. Examine your upcoming work assignments to identify some possibilities to cruise for quotes to elevate the stature of your writing. Use either print quotation sources or go online to exploit any of the great quotation sites that will help you find just the right embellishment. Locate at least five quotes that would produce your intended effect.

Source: Alverno College. Writing and Speaking Criteria 1995.

Applying the Six Strategies for Success

What did you learn in this chapter that you can apply to the following key strategies to help form the foundation for your success? Write down all of the main points you can remember that support the following strategies:

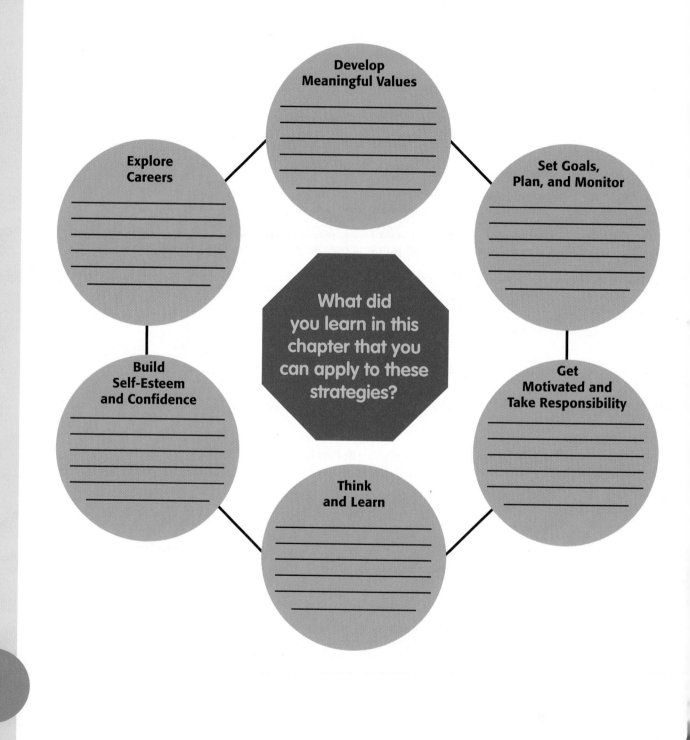

Develop Meaningful Values

Explore Careers

Set Goals, Plan, and Monitor

What did you learn in this chapter that you can apply to these strategies?

Build Self-Esteem and Confidence

Get Motivated and Take Responsibility

Think and Learn

Communicate, Build Relationships, and Appreciate Diversity

Where Are You? Success in college isn't just about grades. Total college success involves mastering communication and developing positive relationships with many different kinds of people. Being skilled in these areas will make your college years more enjoyable and productive. To see where you stand right now, place a checkmark next to only those items that apply to you.

- I am a good listener.
- I am a good communicator.
- I have strategies for resolving conflicts.
- I get along with my instructors.
- I have good relationships with my family.
- I have one or more good friends.
- If I get lonely, I can usually find ways to remedy this.
- I get along well with people from other cultural and ethnic groups.
- I get along well with the opposite sex.

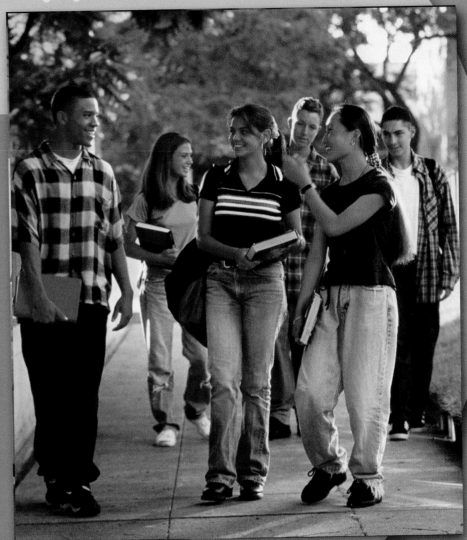

As you read about Oprah Winfrey, think about how good communication skills have been central to her life and career.

Images of College Success

Oprah Winfrey

Oprah Winfrey hosts one of the most watched TV shows in America. She also received an Oscar for her role in *The Color Purple*, in which she played a proud, assertive woman. Oprah was born on a Mississippi farm and spent her early years there, reared by her grandmother. When Oprah was six, she was sent to live with her mother in a Milwaukee ghetto. From the age of nine, she was sexually abused by a series of men she trusted. She began committing delinquent acts as a young adolescent, until her father had her come live with him in Nashville. At that point, her life improved dramatically.

As a high school senior, when raising money for charity, Oprah visited a local radio station and talked her way into a part-time job broadcasting the news. On a scholarship at Tennessee State University, she started a major in speech and drama. At age 19, she switched from radio to local television and became the youngest person and first African-American woman to anchor the evening news at Nashville's WTVF-TV. Still, she continued college until a Baltimore TV station lured her away in her senior year. A few years later, she moved to Chicago to host a local talk show that eventually became *The Oprah Winfrey Show*, now the highest-rated talk show in television history.

The billions of dollars Oprah has earned have not decreased her motivation to achieve. She continues to seek new ways to use her tremendous energy and talent productively. As Oprah says, "I have been blessed, but I create the blessings." Success has not spoiled her. Oprah spends many nights lecturing, often for free, at churches, shelters, and youth organizations. She established the Little Sisters program in a poverty-stricken area of Chicago. She continues to spend some of her Saturdays working with young girls to improve their lives.

When she finally finished college, Oprah was a multimillionaire. In 1987, when invited to speak at TSU's commencement, she insisted on finishing the last bit of coursework for her degree. Then, because her father had always urged her to finish college, she endowed 10 scholarships in his name.

What are some of Oprah Winfrey's effective communication skills?

©Albert Ferreira/Reuters/Landov

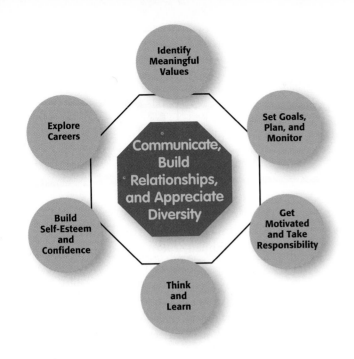

When employers are asked what they seek most in college graduates, the consistent answer is "communication skills." Thus, mastering communication skills will benefit you not only in college, but in future careers and many other aspects of your life. So will building good relationships with many different kinds of people and appreciating their diversity. As you read, think about the "Six Points to Success" listed to the left and how this chapter can help you maximize success in these important areas.

Communicate Effectively

Oprah Winfrey's communication skills are admirable. She listens attentively, shows interest, and asks appropriate questions. She also knows how to get people to open up, talk, and feel good about themselves.

It's hard to do much in life without communicating. We communicate when we ask an instructor a question and listen to a student give an explanation of a concept. We communicate in the warmth of an intimate exchange, the heat of an intense conflict, even the chill of a faded relationship.

Communication skills are powerful. For example, asking good questions and listening carefully can stimulate thinking and advanced learning. When you communicate well, other people tend to like you, which can increase your self-esteem. By being a supporting communicator, you can also help others feel good about themselves. Good communication skills also can help you reach your goals and attain career success. As mentioned, employers rate communication skills as the most important skills they look for in potential employees. Let's explore some of the characteristics of communication.

Communication involves a *sender* delivering a *message* to a *receiver*. Senders are speakers who produce or *encode* messages; receivers are listeners who attempt to understand or *decode* messages. Messages can be delivered verbally or nonverbally and much of interpersonal communication is not a one-time brief interaction that lasts for several seconds. In contrast, most interpersonal communication involves an ongoing volley of verbal and nonverbal actions between the sender and receiver. Initially, person A may be the sender, whereas person B is the receiver; then, after 15 seconds or so, person A may become the receiver, whereas person B is the sender; and so on, back and forth, over a period of time. At the same time person A is sending a message verbally, person B may be sending a nonverbal message.

In the back and forth exchanges of communication, messages can easily become garbled and misunderstood (DeVito, 2004; Tannen, 1986). Consider the communication between two college students—Latisha and Alex. Latisha feels Alex doesn't really listen to her, asking her questions and then answering them himself, before she has a chance to respond. She complains that he talks *to* her rather than *with* her. When they get together with his friends, the conversation moves so fast, Latisha can hardly get a word in edgewise. Afterward, Alex complains that Latisha is too quiet, although she is certainly not like that with her own friends. Alex thinks it is because she doesn't like his friends, whereas Latisha feels they ignore her. Let's now explore some ways you can become a better listener and speaker when you are communicating with someone.

Develop Good Listening Skills

In the third century B.C.E., the Greek philosopher Zeno of Citum said that the reason people have two ears and one mouth is so they can listen more and talk less. But you can hear what another person is saying without really listening.

As one college student put it, "My friends *listen* but my parents only *hear* me talk." Listening is a critical skill for making and keeping relationships. If you're a good listener, others will be drawn to you. Bad listeners hog conversations. They talk *to* rather than *with* someone. Good listeners actively listen rather than passively absorbing information. On Target Tips, "Develop Active-Listening Skills," provides some good advice.

Avoid Barriers to Effective Verbal Communication

Messages are conveyed more effectively when you speak in a simple rather than a complex way, a concrete rather than an abstract way, and a specific rather than a general way. When you do need to convey ideas that are abstract, general, or complex, use appropriate examples to illustrate the ideas. Often the best examples are those that listeners can relate to their own personal experiences. For instance, if Margaret is trying to explain to some friends what feminism is and what it is like to be a feminist, it will help if she provides examples such as favoring equal opportunities regardless of gender, and then asks her friends to think about others they know who are feminists.

Good speakers also make their verbal and nonverbal messages consistent. If you say one thing and nonverbally communicate

---

ON TARGET TIPS

Develop Active-Listening Skills

- **Pay careful attention to the person who is talking.** This shows you're interested in what he or she has to say. Maintain good eye contact and lean forward slightly, at least in U.S. culture.
- **Paraphrase.** State in your own words what someone just said such as "Let me see, what I hear you saying is . . . " or "Do you mean . . . ?" Paraphrasing is particularly useful when someone says something important.
- **Synthesize themes and patterns.** Conversations can become strewn with bits and pieces of disconnected information. A good active listener summarizes the main themes and feelings the speaker has expressed in a long conversation such as: "One theme you seem to be coming back to is . . . " or "Let's go over the ground we've been covering so far . . . "
- **Give good feedback.** Verbal or nonverbal feedback gives the speaker an idea of how well he or she is getting a point across. Good listeners give feedback quickly, honestly, clearly, and informatively such as: "I understand what you mean . . . " or "I am not sure I am following all of your points . . . "

the opposite, you are likely to create confusion and distrust. For example, if you are trying to explain to an instructor why you didn't turn a paper in on time and you look down at the floor rather than maintaining eye contact, the teacher may be less likely to believe you, even if your excuse is legitimate.

Good speakers also avoid barriers to effective communication. Consider Mike, who says, "I blew it again. When I went home last weekend, I vowed I wouldn't let my older brother get to me. We were only with each other for about ten minutes when he started in and I couldn't take his criticism any more. I started yelling and calling him names." Like Mike, we all too often want to communicate better with others but run into barriers we just can't seem to get around. Barriers to good communication include (Gordon, 1970):

- *Criticizing* (making negative evaluations): "It's your own fault—you should have studied."
- *Name-calling and labeling* (putting down the other person): "You're such an idiot for not planning better."
- *Advising* (talking down to the other person while giving a solution to a problem): "That's so easy to solve. Why don't you just . . . ?"
- *Ordering* (commanding the other person to do what you want): "Get off the phone, right now!"
- *Threatening* (trying to control the other person): "If you don't listen to me, I'm going to make your life miserable."
- *Moralizing* (preaching to the other person what he or she should do): "You know you shouldn't have gone there tonight. You ought to be sorry."
- *Diverting* (pushing the other person's problems aside): "You think *you* have it bad. Let me tell you about my midterms."
- *Logical arguing* (trying to convince the other person with logical facts without considering the person's feelings): "Look at the reasons why you failed. Here they are. . . . So, you have to admit I'm right." It's good to use logic to try to persuade someone, but if you lose sight of the person's feelings, no matter how right you are, the other person won't be persuaded and may be hurt. To evaluation some of your own barriers to good communication, complete the Journal activity "Overcome Your Barriers" on page 309.

Tune in to Nonverbal Communication

How do you behave when talking with others? Does the way you fold your arms, cast your eyes, move your mouth, cross your legs, or touch someone send a message? Communications experts believe it does. You might:

- lift an eyebrow for disbelief
- clasp your arms to isolate or protect yourself
- shrug your shoulders for indifference
- wink one eye for intimacy
- tap your fingers for impatience
- slap your forehead for forgetfulness

These are conscious, deliberate gestures people make in the course of communicating. Are there also unconscious nonverbal behaviors that offer clues about what a person is feeling? Hard-to-control facial muscles especially tend to reveal emotions that people are trying to conceal. Lifting only the inner part of your eyebrow may reveal stress and worry. Eyebrows raised together may signal fear. Fidgeting may reveal anxiety or boredom.

Many communications experts believe that most interpersonal communication is nonverbal. Even if you're sitting in a corner silently reading a book, your nonverbal

What you are speaks so loudly I cannot hear what you say.

Ralph Waldo Emerson
19th-century American poet and essayist

behavior communicates something—perhaps that you want to be left alone. It might also communicate that you're intellectually oriented.

You'll have a hard time trying to mask or control your nonverbal messages. True feelings usually express themselves, no matter how hard we try to conceal them so it's good to recognize the power of nonverbal behavior (DeFleur et al., 2005). To think about how touch can communicate information, complete the Journal activity "What Does Touch Communicate?" on page 309.

TAKE CHARGE: Of Your Anger

Everyone gets angry at one time or another. These strategies can help you take responsibility for controlling your anger (American Psychological Association, 2002; Tavris, 1989):

- When your anger starts to boil and your body is getting aroused, work on lowering your arousal by waiting. Your anger will usually simmer down if you just wait long enough.
- Slowly repeat a calm word or phrase, such as "relax," or "take it easy." Repeat it to yourself while breathing deeply.
- Change the way you think. Angry people tend to curse, swear, or speak in highly colorful terms that reflect their inner thoughts. When you are angry, you can exaggerate and become overly dramatic. Try replacing these thoughts with more rational ones. For example, instead of telling yourself, "Oh, it's awful, it's terrible, everything is ruined," say something to yourself like, "It's frustrating and it's understandable that I'm upset about it but it's not the end of the world and getting angry isn't going to fix it anyway."
- Don't say the first thing that comes into your head when you get angry, but slow down and think carefully about what you want to communicate. At the same time, listen carefully to what the other person is saying and take your time before answering.
- Work on not being chronically angry over every little bothersome annoyance. Also, avoid passively sulking, which simply reinforces your reasons for being angry.
- Take the perspective of others and think about how you look to them when you get angry. Is this how you want others to think of you?

Use Communication to Resolve Conflict with Others

Conflicts are inevitable in our everyday interactions, especially in an intense college environment. Developing skills to resolve these conflicts can make your life calmer and more enjoyable. Strategies for reducing interpersonal conflict include assertiveness and effective negotiation. Four main ways to deal with conflict include:

- *Aggression.* People who respond aggressively to conflict run roughshod over others. They communicate in demanding, abrasive, and hostile ways often characterized by anger. Aggressive people often are insensitive to the rights and feelings of others. See Take Charge, "Of Your Anger," for some ideas about being more responsible for controlling your anger.
- *Manipulation.* Manipulative people try to get what they want by making others feel sorry for them or feel guilty. They don't take responsibility for meeting their own needs. Instead, manipulative people play the role of the victim or martyr to get others to do things for them, working indirectly to get their needs met.
- *Passivity.* Passive people act in nonassertive, submissive ways. They let others run roughshod over them. Passive people don't express their feelings or let others know what they want or need.
- *Assertion.* Assertive people act in their own best interests. They stand up for their legitimate rights and express their views openly and directly. Assertiveness also builds equal relationships (Alberti & Emmons, 1995).

- *Assertion.* Of the four styles of dealing with conflict, acting assertively is clearly the most appropriate. Assertiveness is an attitude as well as a way of acting. Be assertive in any situation in which you need to express your feelings, ask for what you want, or say "no" to something you don't want.

To determine your dominant style of dealing with conflict, complete Self-Assessment 1 "Do You Blow Up, Get Down and Get Dirty, or Speak Up?" on page 305. In addition, some helpful strategies advocated by behavioral expert Edmund Bourne (1995) are described in On Target Tips, "Become More Assertive."

Negotiate Effectively Everybody negotiates. You negotiate when you apply for a job, dispute a grade with a teacher, buy a car, ask your landlord to paint your apartment, or try to get your roommate or partner to do something. Whenever you want something from someone whose interests are at odds with your own, you can choose to negotiate.

Some negotiation strategies are better than others. Negotiating effectively helps you to get what you want from others without alienating them. Negotiation experts often describe three main ways of solving problems with others: win–lose, lose–lose, and win–win.

- *Win–lose strategy.* In this type of negotiating, one party gets what he or she wants and the other comes up short such as: "Either I get my way or you get your way." For example, a couple has a specific amount of money they can spend, but they totally disagree on how to spend it. Most of the time a win–lose strategy is not wise. Why? Because the loser may harbor bad feelings and one person is always dissatisfied with the outcome.
- *Lose–lose strategy.* This usually unfolds when both parties initially try a win–lose strategy that does not work. As a result of the struggle, both end up unsatisfied with the outcome. In the money example, both individuals could end up spending too much and go deeply in debt.
- *Win–win strategy.* The goal in this strategy is to find a solution that satisfies both parties and avoid winning at the other person's expense. By working together, they can find a solution that satisfies everyone. For example, after considerable discussion and negotiation, each member of the couple agrees to some concessions and they arrive at an agreeable spending plan.

Some compromises are often necessary in this win–win ideal. You and the seller settle on a price for a used car. The price is between what the seller was asking and what you wanted to pay. Neither of you got exactly what you wanted, but the outcome left each of you happy. Similarly, you and your companion each want to see a different movie. In order to spend the evening together, you might choose another movie that you both agree on.

The best solutions of all, though, are not compromises. Rather, they are solutions in which all parties get what they want. For example, Andrea and Carmen are roommates with different study habits. Andrea likes to study in the evening. This leaves most of her day free for other activities. Carmen thinks that evenings should be for relaxation and fun. They arrived at the following solution. On Monday through Wednesday, Andrea studies at her boyfriend's; Carmen does anything she wants. On Thursday and Sunday, Carmen agrees to keep things quiet where she and Andrea live. On Friday and Saturday they both have fun together.

ON TARGET TIPS

Become More Assertive

- **Evaluate your rights.** Determine your rights in the situation at hand. Act assertively if you feel these rights are being violated.
- **Designate a time for discussing what you want.** Unless you need to be assertive on the spot, find a mutually convenient time to discuss the problem with the other person involved.
- **State the problem in terms of its consequences for you.** Clearly outline your point of view, even if it seems obvious to you. This allows the other person to get a better sense of your position. Describe the problem as objectively as you can without blaming or judging. For example, you might tell someone you live with, "I'm having a problem with your music playing so loud. I need to study for a test tomorrow, but the stereo is so loud I can't concentrate."
- **Express your feelings about the particular situation.** When you express your feelings, even others who completely disagree with you can tell how strongly you feel about the circumstance.
- **Make your request.** This is an important aspect of being assertive. Make sure to ask for what you want (or don't want) in a straightforward way.

> *Be fair with others, but then keep after them until they are fair with you.*
>
> Alan Alda
> *Contemporary American actor*

John felt lucky to have landed his part-time campus job working in the admissions office. Although he spent a good deal of time filing applications and doing data entry, he also answered phones and helped greet parents and prospective students when they arrived for interviews. He needed to listen closely to help address their questions and communicate effectively about the strengths of the school. The campus had a very diverse student body, providing him with the chance to meet a lot of different types of people. He did his best to establish relationships with prospective students from a variety of backgrounds to help them feel comfortable during their visit. While he had always planned on becoming an accountant, this experience made him think more about ensuring that his future career included enough interpersonal interaction. He was surprised by how much he enjoyed it—and how much his communication skills had improved already.

Elise had majored in Communications, so was thrilled to land a job as an associate events planner her first year out of college. She assisted in the planning of corporate events from the negotiation of contracts with caterers and hotels to the ordering of food and flowers. It was important to listen to all of the client's needs and communicate effectively about the status of the event throughout the process. She also was working on building relationships with clients to help ensure repeat business in the future. It was a very challenging job, but she loved all of the interaction and felt that her communication skills were being utilized every day.

The win–win strategy gives you a creative way of finding the best solution for a problem between two or more parties. You can use it to solve conflicts with others and make everyone involved feel better.

Develop Good Relationships

Relationships play a powerful role in college. As you think about your relationships with family members, partners, roommates, friends, and dates, keep in mind that the strategies for communication, assertiveness, and negotiation we just discussed will serve you well.

In Chapter 1, "Commit to College Success," we discussed that college students who have positive close relationships are much happier than those who do not. One recent study found that very happy college students rated their relationships with their friends, family, and romantic partners more positively than college students who were average in happiness or very unhappy (Diener & Seligman, 2002). In this study, the very happy college students were more likely than the other two groups to spend considerably less time alone and more time with family, friends, and a romantic partner (see Figure 10.1).

As social creatures, human beings are motivated to bond or be attached to others and do so in different ways. These attachment styles develop in infancy and may affect the ease with which you make and maintain relationships with friends and romantic partners. Three types of attachment that characterize adults are (Shaver, Belsky, & Brennan, 2000):

- *Secure attachment.* Secure adults find it easy to get close to others and don't worry much about becoming too dependent or being abandoned. They tend to have satisfying and enduring close relationships (Scott & Cordova, 2002).
- *Avoidant attachment.* Adults with this type of insecure attachment tend to avoid closeness, be less invested in close relationships, and more likely to leave them. They tend to be either *fearful* ("I'm uncomfortable getting close to others") or *dismissing* ("It is very important for me to feel independent and self-sufficient"). About 20 percent of adults have an avoidant attachment style.
- *Ambivalent attachment.* Adults with an ambivalent attachment style are less trusting and thus more possessive and jealous. They may break up repeatedly with the same person. When discussing conflicts, they tend to become very emotional and angry. About 10 percent of adults have an ambivalent attachment style.

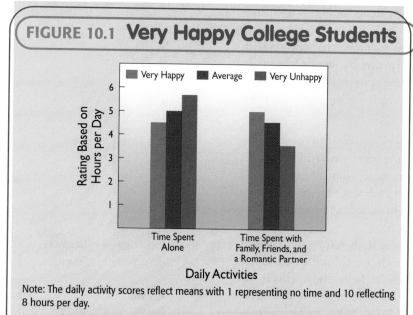

FIGURE 10.1 Very Happy College Students

Note: The daily activity scores reflect means with 1 representing no time and 10 reflecting 8 hours per day.

Source: *After data presented by Diener & Seligman. "Very Happy People,"* Psychological Science, *13, 81–84.* Copyright © 2002 by Blackwell Publishing. Reprinted by permission of the publisher.

If your attachments tend to be avoidant or ambivalent, you may find that your relationships with friends and romantic partners are difficult and this is an area that you can work to improve. Self-Assessment 2 on page 306 will help you evaluate your current attachment style.

Get Along with Instructors

An important, but often overlooked, aspect of relationships in college is being able to get along with instructors. Many students never talk with an instructor in or out of class. One student remarked that he had no idea what kind of people his instructors were and for all he knew, they were all locked in a vault each evening and then unleashed on Monday to feed on poor students during the day. Of course, that's not so.

Instructors have personality styles and social relationships just as students do. Some are shy, others are gregarious. Some have great social relationships, others miserable ones. For the most part, to get along with instructors you are going to have to adjust to their styles because they are unlikely to adjust to yours. On Target Tips, "Getting Along with Instructors," provides some good suggestions.

Connect with Parents

For college students who still depend on their parents financially and in other ways, relationships can vary considerably. Some parents treat their first-year students as if they are still completely under their wing. Some college students remain too dependent on the security of their parents and don't tackle enough new challenges on their own. Some parents have little contact and provide little support for first-year students while some students break off communication with their parents. Recall from Chapter 1, "Commit to College Success," that there is a link between college success and student/parent relationships (Halberg & others, 2000).

Let Your Parents Know You Haven't Fallen off the Planet No matter how much independence you want, it is not a good idea to break off communication with your parents. You'll likely need them at some point, possibly for money, a place to live, or emotional support.

Maintaining communication doesn't mean you have to write them a letter three times a week, e-mail daily, or call every night. You don't have to tell them everything you do. However, if they don't hear from you for a couple of weeks, they may fear that something really bad has happened to you. In most cases parents want to know regularly how you are getting along.

What is regular contact? If you're away from home, a phone conversation or informative e-mail once a week should do. One first-year student didn't want his roommates to kid him about calling home regularly, so he wrote a coded reminder on his calendar once a week, "E.T.," from the movie where E.T. phones home. E-mail is cheap, convenient, and easy—another great way to keep in touch.

If you're a young adult student in your first year, your parents are probably concerned about your increased independence. They may ask questions that seem intrusive. "How much are you studying?" "How come you didn't get an A on your English test?" "What's your roommate like?" "Are you dating anyone?" "Have you been going to religious

---

Getting Along with Instructors

Here are some good strategies for developing a positive relationship with an instructor (www. academictips.org):

1. *Assume that all instructors are human.* This may sound a little ridiculous, but too many students see instructors as aloof and not of this world. However, like you, they are human and they have families, learning and personality styles, likes and dislikes, and good and bad days. Understanding that they are human may help you to demystify beliefs that you won't be able to get along with them or get to know them no matter how hard you try.

2. *Evaluate your learning and personality styles and your instructor's.* In Chapter 4, "Diversify Your Learning Style," you spent considerable time examining your learning and personality styles. You probably will like and get along better with an instructor whose learning and personality styles are similar to yours. Don't let this restrict your opportunity to get along with an instructor. Just being aware of such differences may help you to think about ways to interact more positively.

3. *Talk with other students who have previously taken classes from the instructor.* Interview them about what the instructor is like. Ask them about his or her style over an entire course, how easy or hard it was to get to know and get along with the instructor, and any strategies that might have worked in developing a positive relationship.

4. *Establish rapport with an instructor early in the course.* You can ask questions after class and/or visit an instructor during his or her office hours. It is a good idea to begin this process early so that you will feel more comfortable talking with the instructor later when you don't understand a topic or might be having difficulty in the course.

"If you can hear me, give me a sign."

©The New Yorker Collection, 1993 Frank Cotham, from cartoonbank.com. All Rights Reserved.

services?" Try to listen politely to their questions. Realize that they have your best interests at heart. You don't have to tell them all the details of your life. They usually will accept your answers if you tell them a few general things and contact them weekly.

What Your Parents Can't Find Out without Your Approval Your parents know only what you choose to tell them about your college experiences. According to the Family Education Responsibility and Privacy Act, the college cannot release your records to anyone but you. Instructors can discuss your progress or problems only in your presence or with your permission. This legal constraint encourages your family members to let you resolve your own problems. Use this control responsibly and wisely.

Relate to Spouse or Partner

Students who are married or have a partner face special challenges. Some strategies for keeping relationships with a partner positive include (Sternberg, 1988):

- *Don't take your relationship for granted.* The seeds of a relationship's destruction are planted if you or your partner take each other for granted. Continue to nourish the relationship, giving it high priority along with your studies. You don't want to get a degree and lose your partner. Schedule time with your partner just as you do for classes and studying. Don't expect your partner to take over all of the household duties or pamper you.
- *Develop self-esteem and confidence.* Don't seek in your partner what you lack in yourself. Feel good about your pursuit of education—it will enhance your confidence. When both partners have high self-esteem, their relationship benefits. This is an important strategy in your "Six Points to Success."
- *Share your college life.* Let your partner know what you're doing in college. Discuss your schedule, what you're learning, and what your day is like. Look for campus activities or events—such as lectures, sporting events, and plays—that you can attend together. To avoid being too self-focused, remember to ask about your partner's activities.
- *Be open with your partner.* Sometimes it seems easier in the short run to lie or hold back the painful truth. The problem is that once omissions, distortions, and flat-out lies start, they tend to spread and ultimately can destroy a relationship. Talk becomes empty because the relationship has lost its depth and trust.
- *See things from your partner's point of view.* Ask yourself how your partner perceives you. This helps you to develop the empathy and understanding that fuel a satisfying, successful relationship.
- *Be a friend.* Researchers have found that one of the most successful factors in a successful marriage is the extent to which the partners are good friends (Gottman & Silver, 1999). Friendship acts as a powerful shield against conflict.
- *Understand differences in communication style between men and women.* Men tend to view talk in a relationship as an opportunity to give information (Tannen, 1990). By contrast, women are more likely to view it as a way of exploring a relationship. Understanding this difference in perception can help you conquer this gender communication gap. To think further about differences in males and females, complete the Journal activity "Are Men Really from Mars and Women Really from Venus?" on page 309.

Care for Children

If you're a parent as well as a student, you also face special challenges. Some helpful strategies include:

- *Be authoritative.* The psychologist Diana Baumrind (1991) wanted to know whether one type of parenting style is linked with having a child who is well-adjusted and competent. She found that the best parenting style is authoritative, which involves being nurturing, engaging in verbal give-and-take with the child, and exercising some control but not in a punishing way. That is, authoritative parents don't let children run wild and give them feedback to help develop self-control. By contrast, being either permissive and uninvolved or punitive and cold are ineffective parenting styles. Children reared by these types of parents often have trouble controlling their behavior.

- *Communicate.* If your children are old enough, talk with them about how important they are to you as well as the importance of your education. Each day set aside time to listen to your children.

- *Be a good time manager.* At times, you may feel overwhelmed with juggling a family and school. Planning can be an important asset in your effort to balance your academic and family time. Check into child-care facilities and community agencies for services and activities for your children before and after school. Chapter 3 also offers many helpful time management strategies.

- *Set aside time for your children and yourself.* It's not going to be easy, but be sure to block out at least some time each week for activities you enjoy or for relaxation. You might have a hobby, like exercise or going to movies. Set aside time every day for your children's interests as well.

Develop Responsible Dating Behavior

Dating can involve wonderful, happy times. It also can be a source of unhappiness, anxiety, and even violence.

The Dating Scene Some first-year students date frequently, others very little or not at all. Some students view dating as a way to find a spouse. Others see it as an important part of fitting into the social scene. Some students date for romantic reasons, others for friendship or companionship.

Dating can detract from or enhance your college success. It's clearly not a good idea to get so head-over-heels in passionate love that all you can think about is your romantic partner. If that happens to you, you'll probably spend too little time studying. On the other hand, some people who date someone regularly or live with a partner feel more settled down and freer to work.

It's not unusual for many first-year students to have a relationship back home. Also, many commuter students have a romantic partner who does not go college or attends

DILBERT reprinted by permission of United Feature Syndicate.

Strategies for Avoiding Settings in Which Rape Most Often Occurs

Things to do:

- Go places with other people.
- If you go alone, tell someone your plans.
- Walk briskly, with purpose.
- Stay in well-lighted, populated areas.
- Limit your drug and alcohol intake; these can make you vulnerable.
- Exercise good judgment about sharing your private information.
- Have your keys ready when going to your car or residence.
- Lock all doors and windows in your car and residence.
- Do not open doors for strangers.
- Carry a whistle or other alarm.
- If someone is following you or you feel threatened, go to a public place, call the police, run, scream, or blow a whistle.

Things to Remember:

- No one has the right to rape you.
- Rape is never the fault of the victim.
- Rape is a criminal act of violence for the purpose of power.
- Date or acquaintance rape is still rape.
- Rape is a sexual assault. Assault is a crime.

From WIN—Women's Issues Network, Dallas Working Against Rape brochure.

college somewhere else. You do not necessarily have to give up this romance. However, it's important to evaluate how much time you think about it at the expense of your academic work and relationships on your campus.

Too many first-year students get caught up in wanting to date an ideal rather than real person. They search for the stereotypical jock, person with movie-star looks, or punk rocker. Some first-year students also look at every date as a potential girlfriend or boyfriend, someone they eventually might marry. College counselors say that such students would probably be better adjusted and happier if they broadened their perspective. Don't look at every date as a potential Mr. or Mrs. Perfect. Dates can be potential friends as well as romantic partners.

Rape and Unwanted Sexual Acts Rape is sexual intercourse that is forced on a person. A special concern in college is date or acquaintance rape. One third to one half of college men admit that they have forced sexual activity on women (Bachar & Koss, 2001).

Rape is a traumatic experience for victims. They initially feel shocked and numb. Recovery is easier with the support of parents and friends and professional counseling also can help. See On Target Tips, "Strategies for Avoiding Settings in Which Rape Most Often Occurs," for some safety precautions.

Some people engage in unwanted sexual acts when not physically forced to do so. Why would they do this? They might be:

- turned on by their partner's actions and later regret it
- fearful that the relationship will end if they don't have sex
- intoxicated or high on drugs
- obligated because of the time and money spent by a partner

In sum, monitor your sexual feelings and make good sexual decisions. As in other aspects of communication and relationships, being aware of people's motives and acting assertively rather than aggressively, manipulatively, or passively are good strategies.

Get Along with Roommates

If you live on campus, you will find that relationships with roommates vary. You might become best friends or you might grow to hate each other. You might be indifferent and simply live in the same place. In many cases, a first-year student's roommate is a total stranger. You're asked to live in close quarters for nine months with someone you know little or nothing about. That's enough to cause apprehension in anyone.

Some good strategies for getting along with this total stranger are described in On Target Tips, "Getting Along with a Roommate." Then do the Journal activity "Reflect on Your Relationship with Your Roommate" on page 308 to explore how to deal with roommate problems. But what if, after trying hard to reconcile problems, you still hate your roommate? What if your roommate difficulties are lowering your grades? What can you do?

If you live in a college dorm, you probably have an RA (resident advisor) with whom you can discuss your roommate problems. Take the initiative. Go to the RA and ask for advice about what to do. Try out the advice and give it a chance to work. Then, if things are still intolerable, go to the campus housing office. Courteously and clearly state your roommate problems and explore your options there.

Value Friends

Having friends can reduce loneliness, be a source of self-esteem, and provide emotional support, especially in times of stress both for women and men. However, women tend to have more close friends and their friendships involve more self-disclosure and exchange of mutual support than men's friendships. Women are more likely to listen at length to what a friend has to say and be sympathetic (Garner & Estep, 2001).

Regardless of whether you are a man or a woman and are seeking a man or a woman as a friend, some strategies are likely to benefit your efforts. These strategies include:

- *Be nice, kind, and considerate.* Compliment others.
- *Be honest and trustworthy.* Tell the truth, keep promises, share, and cooperate.
- *Respect others.* Have good manners, be polite and courteous. Listen to what others have to say. Have a positive attitude.
- *Provide emotional support.* Be supportive, help, give advice, and show that you care. Engage in activities together.

The following strategies not only are inappropriate for making friends but can also end a friendship:

- *Be disrespectful and inconsiderate.* Show disrespect, have bad manners. Be inconsiderate and uncooperative. Ignore, don't share. Hurt their reputation or feelings. Gossip, spread rumors, embarrass and criticize them.
- *Present yourself negatively.* Be self-centered, snobby, conceited, and jealous. Show off, care only about yourself, and be bossy. Be mean, have a bad attitude, be a grouch, be a slob, throw temper tantrums, start trouble, and be overly critical.
- *Be untrustworthy.* Be dishonest, disloyal, tell lies, tell secrets, and break promises.

Network

Success in college not only is enhanced by good friendships but also by your ability to network effectively with people in general. Networking involves connecting with others to enhance your opportunities. Successful networking takes practice. Some strategies include (Mrosko, 2002):

- *Commit, be patient, and follow up.* In many instances, it takes time to develop a relationship. Effective networking doesn't happen overnight or all at once. Follow up initial contacts. Consistent, focused contacts build relationships.
- *Give and get.* Both sides need to receive a benefit, either now or in the future. In many instances, a good strategy is to give before receiving. For example, be the first to share new information.
- *Listen.* Take notes and really hear what others are saying.
- *Ask for help.* Be specific about what you need.
- *Become involved.* Become active in support groups and campus organizations. Volunteer to be on a committee.

Networking is especially beneficial in finding a job or learning more about a career. Networking skills, as well as friendship skills, can help college students keep from being lonely. Let's now explore loneliness in college students.

ON TARGET TIPS

Getting Along with a Roommate

1. **Address problems early.** Whenever two people live together, problems appear. Don't let them fester. Detect and resolve them early.
2. **Use good communication skills.** This includes being an active listener and avoiding barriers to communication. If you have a roommate problem, review the strategies presented on pages 284 and use them with your roommate.
3. **Be responsible.** You may have gotten into the habit of not keeping your room clean before you came to college. Old habits are hard to break. Do your share of picking up. Make your bed. Keep your area clean and neat.
4. **Show respect.** You can learn a lot about the importance of give-and-take in relationships by living with a roommate. To get along, you have to show respect for each other. It's not a good idea to come in at 2 A.M., flip the lights on, and wake up your roommate. It's also not a good idea to rev up the stereo when your roommate is trying to study.
5. **Be assertive.** If you think that you're doing more than your fair share of the giving in your roommate relationship, be more assertive. Stand up for your rights. Use the strategies for being assertive outlined earlier in the chapter.

"We live to have relationships with other people."

Albert Camus
20th-century French-Algerian philosopher

Deal with Loneliness

Loneliness can be a dark cloud over your everyday life. Researchers have found that loneliness is linked with impaired physical and mental health (Cacioppo, 2002). Don't confuse loneliness with being alone. Time spent alone can be meaningful and satisfying. However, when we feel isolated and long to be with others, we need to do something to become more connected.

Leaving Home When young college students leave the unfamiliar world of their hometown and family to go to college, they often face loneliness. Many first-year students feel anxious about meeting new people and developing new social lives. One student comments,

> My first year here at the university has been pretty lonely. I wasn't lonely at all in high school. I lived in a fairly small town. I knew everyone and they knew me. I was a member of several clubs and played on the basketball team. It's not that way here. It is a big place. I've felt like a stranger so many times. It has taken a while but I'm finally adapting better. In the past few months I've been making a special effort to meet people and get to know them. It has not been easy.

As the passage indicates, first-year students rarely carry their high school popularity and social standing into college. Especially when students attend college away from home, they face the challenge of forming new social relationships. In one study, two weeks after the college year began, 75 percent of the first-year students felt lonely at least part of the time after arriving on campus (Cutrona, 1982). Loneliness is not reserved for first-year students just out of high school. Older first-year students can be lonely as well. The demands of school, work, and family may leave little time to feel replenished through contacts with friends.

Are You Lonely? If you feel like you aren't in tune with the people around you and can't find companionship when you want it, you're probably lonely. If you've recently left an important relationship, you'll likely feel lonely until you rebuild your social network. To evaluate the extent to which you are lonely, complete the Self-Assessment 3 "Loneliness" on page 307.

Strategies for Reducing Loneliness How can you become better connected with others? Here are some ideas:

- Get involved in activities with others through college, work, community announcements, or religious organizations. Join and volunteer time with an organization you believe in. You'll probably meet others who share your views. One social gathering can lead to new social contacts. This is especially true if you introduce yourself to others and start conversations.
- Consider joining a new group at dinner, sitting with new people in class, or finding a study or exercise partner. Meeting new people and developing new social ties always involves risk, but the benefits are worth it.
- Recognize the warning signs of loneliness. People often become bored or alienated before loneliness sinks in. Take action to head it off. Planning new activities is easier than struggling to escape loneliness once it has set in.
- Practice certain qualities when interacting with friends or potential friends. Be kind and considerate. Be honest and trustworthy. Share and cooperate. Use active-listening skills. Have a positive attitude. Be supportive. Comment on something special about the other person.
- If you can't shed your loneliness and make friends on your own, contact the student counseling center at your college. A counselor can show you ways to connect with others on your campus and reduce your loneliness.

Where you used to be, there is a hole in the world, which I find myself constantly walking around in the daytime, and falling into at night.

Edna St. Vincent Millay
20th-century American poet

To practice interacting with new people, complete the Journal activity "Combat Loneliness" on page 308. Also, see the resources section on this book's website at http://success.wadsworth.com/santrock/4e. So far we have explored ways to communicate more effectively, improve relationships, and reduce loneliness. As we'll see next, relationships with diverse others can also contribute positively to college life.

Appreciate Diversity

Ana Bolado de Espino came to Dallas, Texas, from Mexico in 1980. She did not speak a word of English, but she did have a dream. Ana wanted to become a medical doctor. She worked as a maid, scrubbing floors and doing laundry for 15 years to earn enough money to get through college. Divorced, she raised two children while attending college and working.

She feared that she would never make it to medical school. She also hit a major snag. As a young teen, her daughter began to hang out with a gang, ran away, and became pregnant. Ana thought about dropping out of college to spend more time with her daughter, but her daughter told her to stay in college and, at age 15, started to turn her own life around.

Ana was 38 years old when she obtained her college degree with a GPA of almost 4.0. She worked as an outreach AIDS counselor for a year after graduating from college. Recently she was accepted into medical school.

Ana Bolado de Espino represents the increased diversity in U.S. college campuses. Diversity can come into our lives in many ways, both in terms of our own characteristics and the diverse others we interact with. In some cases, the diversity is very welcome; in others, it may involve conflict and uneasy feelings. Let's explore some aspects of the diversity you may encounter in your college life and some strategies for improving relationships with diverse others.

> *We need every human gift and cannot afford to neglect any gift because of artificial barriers of sex or race or class or national origin.*
>
> Margaret Mead
> *20th-century American anthropologist*

Respect Culture and Diversity

We should be accustomed to thinking of the United States as a country with many different cultures. Our population is diverse and originates from many different places and college campuses are among the most diverse settings in this country. Some smaller colleges tend to be more homogeneous, with most students and faculty sharing a predominant ethnic or religious heritage, whereas larger campuses tend to be more diverse; most have international students and U.S. students, as well as faculty and staff, from many ethnic backgrounds.

Despite the opportunities to mix, people often associate with their "own kind." Think about where you eat lunch. Commuters often hang out with other commuters. Fraternity and sorority members sit off by themselves. Faculty and students tend not to mix. Our fear of the unknown may keep us close to those whose background we share. This can prevent us from taking advantage of the rich opportunities on campus to meet and learn about people who differ from us. Let's explore some factors that can help us understand cultural diversity better.

Ethnicity, Stereotypes, and Prejudice on Campus College campuses present many issues and concerns related to diversity. According to a survey of students at 390 colleges and universities, ethnic conflict is common on many campuses (Hurtado, Dey, & Trevino, 1994). More than half of the African Americans and almost one fourth of the Asian Americans said that they felt excluded from college activities. Only

An increasing number of college students are from ethnic minority groups. It's important to keep in mind that each ethnic group is diverse. Not taking this diversity and individual variation into account leads to stereotyping. A good strategy is to think of other students as individuals, not as members of a majority or minority group.

©Rob Gage

6 percent of Anglo Americans said that they felt excluded. Other research continues to show that a higher percentage of minority students experience discrimination (Biasco & others, 2001; Marcus & others, 2003).

Many of us sincerely think that we are not prejudiced. However, experts on prejudice believe that every person harbors some prejudices (Sears, Peplau, & Taylor, 2003). Why? Because we are naturally disposed to do it. We tend to identify with others who are like us. We tend to be *ethnocentric*, favoring the groups we belong to and tending to think of them as superior. We also tend to fear people who differ from us. All of these human inclinations contribute to prejudice, so we need to monitor ourselves in an effort to reduce such harmful attitudes.

Reduce Prejudice and Stereotyping To explore prejudice on campus, think about these stereotypes: the blonde cheerleader; the computer nerd; the absent-minded professor; the Asian math whiz; the rigid, snarly librarian; the female basketball star; and the class clown. Notice that with merely a simple label we can conjure up an image and expectations about what a person will be like.

Now imagine that you get to know these people. You discover that

- The "blonde" cheerleader has a 4.0 average.
- The computer "nerd" plays in a hot new jazz band at a local club on weekends.
- The "absent-minded professor" never misses a class.
- The "Asian math whiz" is only an average math student but is a campus leader who is very popular with her peers.
- The "rigid, snarly" librarian gives freely of her time to local charities to help improve the lives of children.
- The "female basketball star" is dating a man in his second year of law school.
- The "class clown" recently organized a campuswide initiative to decrease the pollution coming from a nearby chemical plant.

Clearly, stereotypes lead us to view others in limited and limiting ways. There's so much more to people than the social roles they play or the groups to which they belong (Jandt, 2004).

Prejudice is ugly and socially damaging and many people believe that college campuses should demonstrate leadership in reducing it. Recently, various diversity initiatives have been enacted to work toward this goal: on-campus celebrations of ethnic achievements, festivals that highlight different traditions or beliefs, required coursework to promote the explorations of traditions other than one's own, and inclusion of examples from a broader range of human experience in required readings. In spite of diversity

How unpleasing to the eye if all the flowers and plants, the leaves and blossoms, the fruits, the branches, and the trees were all the same shape and color. Diversity of hues, forms, and shape enriches and adorns the garden.

Allah Baha'
19th-century Persian founder of the Baha'i faith

initiatives, we still have a long way to go to reduce discrimination and prejudice. Examine your experiences with discrimination and prejudice by completing the Journal activity "Your Own Experience with Discrimination and Prejudice" on page 308.

International Students Some colleges have students from a wide range of countries. These students bring with them customs, values, and behaviors that may be quite different from those of U.S. students (Lin & Yi, 1997). If you're a U.S.–born student, consider getting to know one or more international students. It will expand your education. If you're an international student, even if you were well-adjusted at home, adapting to college in the United States may bring confusion and problems. You now have to cope with a whole new set of customs and values. In some cases, you have to learn a new language and new rules for special conduct. On Target Tips, "International SOS," provides some advice.

ON TARGET TIPS

"International SOS"

- **Be patient.** Give yourself time to adapt to your new life. Things may not be easy at the beginning. Over time, you will develop greater comfort with U.S. culture.
- **Create or join a support system.** Most campuses have international student clubs where you can meet and get to know other international students.
- **Make new friends.** Get the most out of your international experience by reaching out to others to learn about their cultures.
- **Share your culture.** Look for opportunities to share your background so your teachers and classmates can learn about your culture.
- **Keep your own goals in mind.** Don't let cultural barriers get in the way of a great education.

Understand Gender Issues

Gender refers to our social and cultural experiences as a female or a male person. We live in a world in which gender roles are changing, and these changes have affected campus life. For example, first-year student Gina is the first woman in her family to attend college. Her grandmother did not go, because it was not an option. Neither did her mother, who still believed that her place was in the home. However, her mother supported Gina's desire for a different kind of life.

Women now attend college and seek careers outside the home in greater numbers than ever before. In 1966, 57 percent of first-year college students agreed that a married woman should be confined to the home and family; in 2003, that figure had dropped to 22 percent (Sax & others, 2003).

The Controversy Not long ago, virtually all American boys were expected to grow up to be "masculine" and girls to be "feminine." The gender blueprints seemed clear-cut. The well-adjusted man should be independent, assertive, and dominant. The well-adjusted woman should be dependent, nurturing, and submissive. These beliefs and stereotypes led to *sexism*, the negative treatment of females because of their sex. Some examples are:

- thinking that women are not as smart as men
- not being equally comfortable with a woman or man as a boss
- thinking that a woman's only place is in the home

©Bill Losh/Getty Images

If you're a student from the United States, respect the differences between yourself and international students. Value diversity. If you're from another country, create a support system and get involved in campus life. Be patient in adjusting to this new culture.

"So according to the stereotype, you can put two and two together, but I can read the handwriting on the wall."

Consider also these stereotypes about males:

- thinking that men can't be nurses
- believing that men can't cook
- thinking it's not okay for men to cry

Today's society is generally more flexible than before, but this flexibility produces confusion and uncertainty for many people. Although they have gained greater influence in several professional spheres, many women still experience "glass ceilings" that limit their access to the most powerful positions. In contrast, women who choose more traditional roles sometimes think that other women criticize them unfairly for "selling out." Some men are confused by the changes in gender expectations. They struggle to grasp what life is really like for women. Some women are angry at men in general for their historic abuse of privilege. The glass ceiling is still real. Females' share of executive management positions dropped from 32 percent in 1998 to 19 percent in 2000 (U.S. Bureau of Labor Statistics, 2003).

Improving the Lives of Women College offers many opportunities for women to explore their lives and set out on a course to improve their opportunities.

Examine Competencies and Needs. In her study of women's lives, Jean Baker Miller (1986) concluded that a large part of what women do is active participation in the development of others. Women help others emotionally, intellectually, and socially. For example, Ana Bolado de Espino supported her daughter while pursuing her dream of going to medical school, and her daughter supported her. Miller argues that women need to retain their relationship skills but become more self-motivated as well by focusing more on themselves and their own needs.

Another gender expert, Harriet Lerner (1989), echoes these beliefs. She states that competent women can stay emotionally connected with others ("YOU-ness"). They also need to focus on improving themselves ("I-ness").

In *The Mismeasure of Woman*, Carol Tavris (1992) wrote that no matter how hard women try, they can't measure up. They are criticized for being too female or not female enough. Tavris argues that women are judged by how well they fit into a man's world, which tends to fixate on the beauty of a woman's body. Tavris said that we need more emphasis on a woman's *soul* as the key indicator of competence and worth.

The message to women is this. Women are certainly not inferior to men. Start evaluating yourself in terms of female competencies, not male ones. For example, women (and society) need to place a higher value on relationship skills. To be leaders, women do not need to stop caring for others. Developing positive relationships with others and developing ourselves are important for both sexes.

Don't Put Up with Sexual Harassment. Improving women's lives also requires reducing and eventually eliminating sexual harassment. Sexual harassment in colleges and the workplace is a major barrier to women's progress. Two million women currently enrolled in college will experience some form of sexual harassment in their student lives (Paludi, 1998). This includes:

- *Gender harassment.* Sexist remarks and behavior that insult and degrade women, a problem apart from harassment for sex.
- *Seductive behavior.* Unwanted, inappropriate, and offensive advances toward women.
- *Sexual bribery.* Harassment for sex, with the threat of punishment for refusal. For example, a woman might be threatened with a lower or failing grade if she does not go along with a professor's advances, or if she reports him to the school authorities.

Every college is required by law to take action against sexual harassment and many have resources to protect women from this harassment. If you are sexually harassed, report it to your school's administration.

Improving the Lives of Men What can men do to improve their lives? Should they become more masculine and virile? Do they need to become more sensitive and tuned in to relationships?

Have Today's Men Become Too Wimpy? Some believe that men today have become soft and vulnerable, letting women run their lives. One such man is Robert Bly (1990), the author of *Iron John*. Iron John is a mythological creature with a deep masculine identity. He is spontaneous, sexual, and aggressive. He has untamed impulses and thoughtful self-discipline. Will Bly's proposal of a return to the virile, forceful man of yesterday make today's world a better place to live in? Many critics say that Bly's strategy only creates more turmoil between men and women rather than promoting cooperation between them.

Be in Tune with Your Emotions and Build Good Relationships. If heightened masculinity isn't the answer for men, what is? One gender expert, Herb Goldberg (1980), says that a huge gulf separates the sexes: women sense and articulate feelings; men tend not to because of their masculine conditioning. Men's defensive armor causes them to maintain self-destructive patterns. They become effective work machines, but suffer emotionally. As a result men live about eight years less than women, have higher hospitalization rates, and more behavior problems. Goldberg believes that men are killing themselves when they strive to be "true" men like Iron John. That is a heavy price to pay for masculine "privilege" and power.

How can men live more physically and psychologically satisfying lives? Goldberg argues that they need to become better attuned to their emotional makeup and relationships with others. He believes that men can retain their self-assertiveness while doing this. For more recommendations on how women and men can lead more competent lives, see On Target Tips, "Gender-Based Strategies for Self-Improvement."

Respect Sexual Orientation

A large majority of people are heterosexual. Although for many years it was estimated that about 10 percent of the U.S. population is homosexual (attracted to people of the same sex), more recent surveys put the figure at about 2–5 percent (Michael & others, 1994). About 1 percent is bisexual (attracted to both men and women).

Issues Related to Homosexuality and Bisexuality In most ways, the college goals of homosexual and bisexual students are similar to those of heterosexual students. However, their minority status does bring some difficulties. Many heterosexual students still consider them as abnormal rather than simply different. Even the American Psychiatric Association once labeled homosexuality as abnormal behavior and a mental disorder. That is no longer the case, but the stigma remains, along with discrimination. Homosexual and bisexual students often encounter physical abuse, hostile comments, and demeaning jokes. Heterosexuals may feel

ON TARGET TIPS

Gender-Based Strategies for Self-Improvement

Women:

- Don't use male standards to judge your competence.
- Retain strengths in building relationships and staying in touch with emotions. Be proud of them.
- Improve your self-motivation. Focus on knowing your own needs and meeting them. Go beyond the idea that this is selfish. It is self-assertive.
- Know what qualifies as sexual harassment. Report it when it happens.

Men:

- Retain your strengths. Be self-motivated and achievement-oriented.
- Do a better job of understanding your emotions and self. Explore yourself. Ask what kind of person you want to be. Think more about how you want others to perceive you.
- Work on your relationship skills. Give more consideration to the feelings of others. Make relationships a higher priority in your life.
- If you're aggressive and hostile, tone down your anger. Be self-assertive but not overly aggressive. That is, control yourself and your emotions. Work toward better understanding of your own emotions and the feelings of other people.

Be tolerant of others' sexual orientations.

uncomfortable around them. For example, when he found out that one of his fraternity brothers, Bob, was gay, Jim said he felt uncomfortable and increasingly avoided him. Several years later, Jim said that he regrets treating Bob the way he did. He realized that nothing prevented a heterosexual from being friends with a homosexual. Explore your own attitudes toward homosexuality and bisexuality by completing the Journal activity "Evaluate Your Own Attitudes Toward Sexual Diversity" on page 309.

Improving the Lives of Gay, Lesbian, and Bisexual College Students How can gays, lesbians, and bisexual students have a better college experience? What positive role can heterosexuals play in this?

- Many campuses have organizations for gays, lesbians, and bisexuals that you may want to join. Some of them include friends and family, as well as other students with questions, regardless of sexual orientation. These organizations provide a safe place for students to voice their thoughts and feelings about sexual orientation.
- If you are homosexual or bisexual and your campus does not have a related organization, consider starting one. This may require following procedures that your student activities office has established for establishing a campus organization. If you feel uncomfortable on your own campus, consider joining an organization on a nearby campus or in the local community.
- Some good books written by and for homosexual and bisexual people cover many practical issues. See the list in the resources on the website for this book at http://success.wadsworth.com/santrok/4e.
- Be tolerant of the sexual orientation of others. If you are a heterosexual and harbor negative feelings toward homosexuals, consider taking a course on human sexuality. You'll learn not only about homosexuality but about yourself as well. Researchers have found that college students who take such a course gain positive views of homosexual and bisexual people (Walters, 1994).

Improve Your Relationships with Diverse Others

How can you get along better with people who differ from you? Here are some helpful strategies.

Assess Your Attitudes One of the first steps is to understand your own attitudes better. Most of us sincerely think that we are not prejudiced. Are there people you don't like because of the group they belong to? Honestly evaluate your attitudes toward people who:

- are from different cultures
- are from different ethnic groups
- are of the opposite sex
- have a different sexual orientation

Take the Perspective of Others You can improve your attitude toward others by clarifying your perspective and trying to better understand that of others. Ask yourself,

- "What is this person feeling and thinking?"
- "What is it about their background and experiences that makes them different from me?"
- "In what ways might we be similar?"
- "What kinds of stress and obstacles are they facing?"
- "Is the fact that they are different reason enough for me not to like them or to be angry with them?"
- "How much do I really know about the other person? How can I learn more?"

Seek Personal Contact Martin Luther King once said, "I have a dream that my four little children will one day live in a nation where they will not be judged by the color of their skin but by the content of their character." How can we reach the world Martin Luther King envisioned, a world beyond prejudice and discrimination? Mere contact with people from other ethnic groups won't do it. However, a particular type of contact—personal contact—often is effective in improving relations with others (Brislin, 1993).

Personal contact here means sharing one's worries, troubles, successes, failures, personal ambitions, and coping strategies. When we reveal information about ourselves, we are more likely to be perceived as individuals than as stereotyped members of a group. When we share personal information with people we used to regard as "them," we begin to see that they are more like "us" than we thought.

Respect Differences but Don't Overlook Similarities Think how boring our lives would be if we were all the same. Respecting others with different traditions, backgrounds, and abilities improves communication and cooperation. When we perceive people as different from us, we often do so on the basis of one or two limited characteristics such as skin color, sex, age, or a disability. When someone seems different, do you ever try to see how the two of you might be similar? Think about the many similarities between you and someone you regard as totally different.

- You might both be shy and anxious, fearful of speaking in public.
- You might both feel overwhelmed by all the demands you need to juggle.
- If you've both chosen the same campus to pursue your education, you might have similar achievement standards like making the Dean's List.
- You may share an interest in a certain sport, type of movies, computer games, or food.

You probably have much more in common than you imagine. Complete the Journal activity "Seek Common Ground" on page 308 to explore similarities between you and someone from a different cultural or ethnic background.

Search for More Knowledge In many instances, the more you know about people who are different from you, the better you can interact with them. Learn more about the customs, values, interests, and historical background of such people. Take a course on cultures around the world, for example.

Treat People as Individuals In our culture, we want to be treated as individuals. We each want to be unique. You will get along much better with others who seem different if you keep in mind that they are individuals than if you think of them as members of a group. Talk with them about their concerns, interests, worries, hopes, and daily lives. Avoid stereotypes.

Master Communication Skills and Build Relationships

1 Communicate Effectively

- Develop active-listening skills. Pay attention to the person who is talking. Paraphrase.
- Speak in simple, concrete, and specific ways. Make your verbal and nonverbal messages consistent.
- Avoid barriers to effective verbal communication.
- Tune in to nonverbal communication and think about your own nonverbal messages.
- Resolve conflicts with others by being assertive and negotiating effectively rather than relying on aggression, manipulation, or passivity.

2 Develop Good Relationships

- Understand that instructors are human. Evaluate their learning and personality styles, and establish rapport with them.
- Keep in touch with your parents to ease any concerns about your independence.
- If you have a partner or spouse, use good communication skills to have a positive relationship with him or her during your college years.
- If you have children, be an authoritative parent, communicate well and be a good time manager.

- Remember that dates can be potential friends as well as romantic partners and show respect.
- Avoid settings in which rape occurs most often, limit alcohol and drug use, and use good judgment. Make good sexual decisions.
- If you have a roommate, address any problems early and use good communication skills.
- Value friends. They can reduce loneliness, be a source of self-esteem, and provide emotional support. Learn about strategies for making and keeping friends.
- Network to enhance your opportunities.
- If you're lonely, recognize it early on. Get involved in activities with others.

3 Appreciate Diversity

- Appreciate cultural and ethnic diversity.
- Recognize and reduce any prejudice and stereotyping you might engage in or encounter.
- If you're an international student, be patient, create or join a support system and make new friends.
- Appreciate diversity in gender. If you're a woman, examine your competencies and needs. Retain your strengths in building relationships and emotional skills. Improve your self-motivation. Don't put up with sexual harassment. If you're a man, retain your strengths related to self-motivation and achievement. Do a better job of understanding your emotions and self. Work on your relationship skills. If you're aggressive and hostile, tone down your anger.
- Appreciate diversity in sexual orientation. Homosexual and bisexual individuals can join supportive campus organizations. Be tolerant of the sexual orientation of others.
- To improve your relationships with diverse others, assess your attitudes, take the perspective of others, seek personal contact, and share information. Respect differences but don't overlook similarities. Seek more knowledge about people who differ from you. Treat people as individuals rather than stereotyping them.

Review Questions

1. List three basic strategies for improving your communication skills. Now list at least one situation in which you can practice each strategy.

   1. Strategy: _____ Situation: _____

   2. Strategy: _____ Situation: _____

   3. Strategy: _____ Situation: _____

2. Describe a conflict you are currently experiencing or anticipate in the near future. What are some strategies you can apply to this problem?

   _____

   _____

   _____

   _____

   _____

3. List a few common problems with relationships among roommates or other individuals with whom you might live. What are some positive ways of addressing these issues?

   _____

   _____

   _____

   _____

   _____

4. Describe at least three strategies for combating loneliness. How can these strategies also help you build relationships and network on campus?

   _____

   _____

   _____

   _____

   _____

5. What types of diversity do you encounter on a regular basis? How can the strategies described in this chapter help you improve your relationships with diverse others?

   _____

   _____

   _____

   _____

   _____

Learning Portfolio

Identify Meaningful Values

Explore Careers

Set Goals, Plan, and Monitor

Communicate, Build Relationships, and Appreciate Diversity

Build Self-Esteem and Confidence

Get Motivated and Take Responsibility

Think and Learn

Do You Blow Up, Get Down and Get Dirty, or Speak Up?

Think about each of the following situations. Check which style you tend to use in each.

	Assertive	Aggressive	Manipulative	Passive
You're being kept on the phone by a salesperson trying to sell you something you don't want.	✓			
You want to break off a relationship that no longer works for you.	✓			✓
You're sitting in a movie and the people behind you are talking.			✓	⊘
Your doctor keeps you waiting more than 20 minutes.				✓
You're standing in line and someone moves in front of you.			✓	⊘
Your friend has owed you money for a long time and it's money you could use.	✓			
You receive food at a restaurant that is over- or undercooked.	✓			✓
You want to ask your friend, romantic partner, or roommate for a major favor.	✓			
Your friends ask you to do something that you don't feel like doing.				✓
You're at a large lecture. The instructor is speaking too softly and you know other students are also having trouble hearing her.	✓			
You're sitting next to someone who is smoking, and the smoke bothers you.			✓	
You're talking to someone about something important to you, but they don't seem to be listening.	✓			
You're speaking and someone interrupts you.	✓	✓		
You receive an unjust criticism from someone.	✓			

Total up the number of your aggressive, manipulative, passive, and assertive marks. Whichever style has the most marks is your dominant personal style of interacting with others in conflicts. If you did not mark the assertive category 10 or more times, you would benefit from working on your assertiveness.

Source: *After E. J. Bourne,* The Anxiety and Phobia Workbook, *Revised Second Edition. Copyright © 1995 by New Harbinger Publications, Inc., Oakland, CA, www.newharbinger.com.*

Your Attachment Style

Instructions

Which of the following paragraphs best describes your feelings about being emotionally close to other people? Place a check mark in front of the one paragraph that best describes you.

Items

_____ I find it relatively easy to get close to others and am comfortable depending on them and having them depend on me. I don't often worry about being abandoned or about someone getting too close to me.

_____ I am somewhat uncomfortable being close to others. I find it difficult to trust them completely, difficult to allow myself to depend on them. I am nervous when anyone gets too close, and often, love partners want me to be more intimate than I feel comfortable with.

_____ I find that others are reluctant to get as close as I would like. I often worry that my partner doesn't really love me or won't want to stay with me. I want to merge completely with another person, and this desire sometimes scares people away.

Scoring and Interpretation

Checking the first item indicates that you likely have a secure attachment style. Checking the second item suggests that you likely have an avoidant attachment style. And checking the third item indicates that you likely have an ambivalent attachment style. Researchers have found that a secure attachment style is often linked with positive aspects of romantic and social relationships. If you feel that you have an avoidant or an ambivalent attachment style, you might want to consider talking with a counselor or psychologist at your college or university's counseling office to explore ways to change your attachment style to a more secure attachment style.

Source: Hazan, C., & Shaver, P. "Romantic love conceptualized as an attachment process." Journal of Personality and Social Psychology, 52, 511–524. Copyright © 1984 with permission from the American Psychological Association.

Loneliness

Read each of the following statements and describe the extent to which they characterize you as:

1 = Never   2 = Rarely   3 = Sometimes   4 = Often

_____   1. I feel in tune with the people around me.

_____   2. I lack companionship.

_____   3. There is no one I can turn to.

_____   4. I do not feel alone.

_____   5. I feel part of a group of friends.

_____   6. I have a lot in common with the people around me.

_____   7. I am no longer close to anyone.

_____   8. My interests and ideas are not shared by those around me.

_____   9. I am an outgoing person.

_____ 10. There are people I feel close to.

_____ 11. I feel left out.

_____ 12. My social relationships are superficial.

_____ 13. No one really knows me well.

_____ 14. I feel isolated from others.

_____ 15. I can find companionship when I want it.

_____ 16. There are people who really understand me.

_____ 17. I am unhappy being so withdrawn.

_____ 18. People are around me but not with me.

_____ 19. There are people I can talk to.

_____ 20. There are people I can turn to.

Total your score for these 10 items 1, 4, 5, 6, 9, 10, 15, 16, 19, 20. Next, reverse your score for items 2, 3, 7, 8, 11, 12, 13, 14, 17, and 18 (For example, if your score was a 1 on item 2, change it to a 4 for scoring purposes) and add up your total for these 10 items. Add the two subtotals (subtotal 1: plus subtotal 2:) to arrive at your overall loneliness score:

If you scored 70 or above, you likely have good social connections and experience little loneliness.

If you scored 60–69, you likely experience quite a bit of loneliness. If you scored 59 or below, you likely experience a great deal of loneliness. If you are a lonely individual, a counselor at your college can likely help you develop some good strategies for reducing your loneliness and becoming more socially connected.

Source: *From D. Russell, et al., "The revised UCLA Loneliness Scale: Concurrent and discriminant validity evidence."* Journal of Personality and Social Psychology, 39, 472–480. *Copyright © 1980 by the American Psychological Association. Adapted with permission.*

Your Journal

● REFLECT

1. Reflect on Your Relationship with Your Roommate

Think about your relationship with your roommate. Are there ways you could make it better? Write down everything that you don't like about your roommate. Cross out those issues you can live with. Then write down strategies for dealing with those behaviors you can't tolerate and plan a time to talk about these issues.

_____

_____

_____

2. Your Own Experience with Discrimination and Prejudice

What life experiences have you had with discrimination and prejudice? The discrimination might have been directed at you, or someone else. What were the consequences? If the discrimination took place in school, did anyone do anything about it? The discrimination doesn't have to be about race or gender. You might have been discriminated against because of the part of the country you're from, the way you dress, or how you style your hair. If you were discriminated against, how did you feel? If it was someone else, how did you respond?

_____

_____

_____

● DO

1. Seek Common Ground

Identify someone who comes from a different cultural and ethnic background from yours. It might be a classmate, someone who lives in your neighborhood, or someone in an interest group you attend. Ask him or her to sit down and talk with you for 15 minutes. Tell them this involves a requirement for a college class you're taking. Your conversation objective: Establish how similar you are in as many ways as you can. Describe the identity of the person and list these similarities below. Were you surprised by anything that you learned?

_____

_____

_____

2. Combat Loneliness

Choose a club meeting or another social activity to attend. At this activity, strike up a conversation with one person in the room. Take some time to observe and listen, picking a person with whom you might like to have a relationship. Then come back to your room and write about the conversation. Write down other things that you would like to know about this person and make a plan for getting together again in the near future.

_____

_____

_____

_____

Your Journal

● THINK CRITICALLY

1. What Does Touch Communicate?

Touch and posture can be important forms of communication. What are some different ways they can communicate information? How might the same touch or posture be interpreted differently depending on the identity of the person being touched—a friend, a romantic partner, a teacher, a person of a different age, or a stranger, for example?

_____

_____

_____

2. Evaluate Your Own Attitudes Toward Sexual Diversity

No matter how well intentioned we are, life circumstances produce some negative attitudes toward others. Think about people with a sexual orientation different from yours.

● Do you have any negative attitudes toward these people? Explain.

_____

● Did the attitude come from a bad encounter with someone you decided was representative of the group?

_____

● Have you learned any prejudices by modeling the attitudes of others you admire?

_____

● What will it take for you to eliminate your negative attitudes toward this group or person?

_____

● CREATE

1. Overcome Your Barriers

For one week, make a note of every situation in which you feel you could have communicated better with someone. This could be an instructor, friend, family member, or even your doctor or a store clerk. At the end of the week, revisit this list and write down some strategies for improving similar conversations in the future. What barriers do you think you encountered and how can you address them better next time?

_____

_____

_____

2. Are Men Really from Mars and Women Really from Venus?

In the popular book, _Men Are from Mars, Women Are from Venus_, the differences between men and women were described as being so extensive that the two sexes are from different planets. Get together with three or four male and three or four female college students and brainstorm about whether men and women are as different as this book suggests or whether they actually have more in common. Write down some of your conclusions here.

_____

_____

_____

Applying the Six Strategies for Success

What did you learn in this chapter that you can apply to the following key strategies to help form the foundation for your success? Write down all of the main points you can remember that support the following strategies:

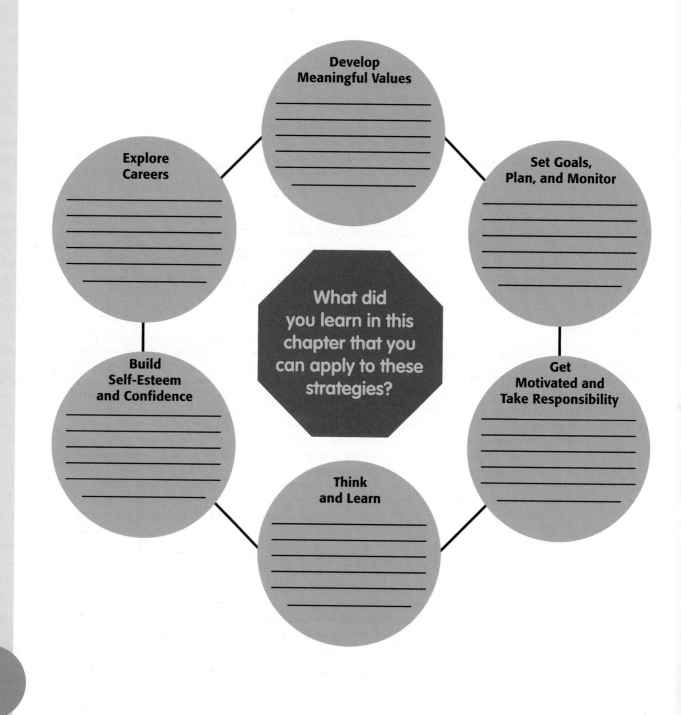

11

Take Charge of Your Physical and Mental Health

Where Are You? There is no getting around it—college has many stressful moments. Cherish your physical and mental health. Motivating yourself to be physically and mentally healthy will help you stay on track as you pursue your academic goals. To evaluate how well you take care of your health, place a checkmark next to only those items that apply to you.

- I live a healthy lifestyle.
- I exercise regularly.
- I get enough sleep.
- I eat right.
- I don't smoke.
- I don't take harmful drugs.
- I make good sexual decisions.
- I cope effectively with stress.
- I am not depressed.
- I know where to seek help for mental health problems.

©Dennis MacDonald/PhotoEdit

As you read about Brooke Ellison, think about the physical challenges she overcame in her college career. What can you learn from this?

Images of College Success

Brooke Ellison

Brooke Ellison's life took an unexpected turn as she passed the fire station walking to school on her first day in the seventh grade. A car struck her, paralyzing her from the neck down and rendering her unable to breathe. She credits the prompt response of emergency workers and police for saving her life. However, the accident left Ellison a quadriplegic.

A tragedy of this magnitude would prompt many people to throw in the towel, but Ellison claims that the accident inspired a deeper faith: "My situation has given me a different perspective on life. I see things with different eyes. I see the value in things that are sometimes overlooked by other people—having family and friends, being able to appreciate a beautiful, sunny day. These are things I came so close to losing" (Gewertz, 2000).

When Ellison gained entry into Harvard, the challenges of college life for a student with such substantial physical limitations were daunting. Ellison's mother moved into her dorm at Harvard to help her with everything from her health care needs to turning pages of her college texts.

Ellison graduated from Harvard with a degree in cognitive neuroscience. She is drawn to research on regenerating spinal tissue, because she is optimistic about her prospects for recovery. Her own studies on resilience suggest that people can learn how to be hopeful in the face of extraordinary obstacles to success.

Since her graduation, Ellison has co-written a book with her mother, *Miracles Happen*, and worked as a motivational speaker. She plans to attend graduate school at Harvard's Kennedy School for Government and hopes this experience will prepare her to help shape policies and issues that directly impact lives. In addition, the late Christopher Reeve directed a TV movie based on her story.

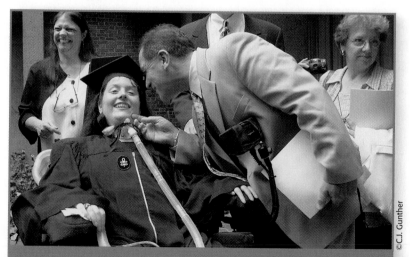

© C.J. Gunther

CONGRATULATED HERE BY HER FATHER, Brooke Ellison graduates from Harvard with a degree in cognitive neuroscience. Her mother (left) helped her overcome tremendous physical obstacles in reaching her academic goals.

Develop Meaningful Values

Explore Careers

Set Goals, Plan, and Monitor

Take Charge of Your Physical and Mental Health

Build Self-Esteem and Confidence

Get Motivated and Take Responsibility

Think and Learn

As you read, think about the "Six Strategies for Success" listed to the left and how this chapter can help you maximize success in these important areas. For example, maintaining good physical and mental health gets you in shape to reach your academic goals. Your self-esteem is also closely linked to your health.

Value Health and Adopt a Healthy Lifestyle

Your health is influenced by many factors—heredity, the environment, health education, the availability of health care, and lifestyle. Most of these factors are out of your personal control, but the one factor that is probably the most important, and entirely in your control, is lifestyle. Lifestyle is your way of living—your attitudes, habits, choices, and behavior. To evaluate your lifestyle now, complete Self-Assessment 1 "Is Your Lifestyle Good for Your Health?" on page 335.

What did you find out from this assessment? Are your lifestyle choices promoting good health or are they placing you at risk for developing serious health problems?

Value Your Health

How much do you value your physical and mental health? Like other achievements, strong physical and mental health are supported by setting goals, planning how to achieve them, and monitoring progress. Like everything worthwhile, your vigor and health depend on your values and motivation. Self-esteem also follows from physical and mental health, and vice versa. If you have high self-esteem you're more likely to embark on a program of improvement than if you have low self-esteem. If you're fit, you'll tend to have higher self-esteem. As you can see, your health is closely linked with many of the strategies for success listed above.

Consider having a healthy body weight. Individuals who place a high value on this are more likely to be motivated to eat balanced, healthy meals and to exercise. If they begin to become overweight, they are likely to set goals, plan, and monitor their progress toward the goal of returning to a healthy weight. Further, setting and reaching weight goals, getting motivated, and valuing a healthy weight tend to increase self-esteem. Conversely, high self-esteem increases the likelihood that people will actually put forth the effort to reach a more healthy level of weight.

Good health requires good health habits. By making some lifestyle changes, you may be able to live a much longer, healthier, happier life. In fact, as many as seven of the ten leading causes of death (such as heart disease, stroke, and cancer) can be reduced by lifestyle changes, yet most of us tend to deny that the changes we think *other* people need to make also apply to us. For example, in one study most college students said that they never would have a heart attack or a drinking problem but that other college students would (Weinstein, 1984).

Risks to College Students

If you are like many college students, you're not nearly as healthy as you could be. In a recent national survey of first-year students, half said their health could be improved (Sax & others, 2001). Male college students engage in riskier health habits than females. For example, they are less likely to consult a physician or health care provider when they have unfamiliar physical symptoms, less likely to go to scheduled health checkups, and more likely to be substance abusers (Courtenay, McCreary, and Merighi, 2002).

Young adults have some hidden health risks. Ironically, one risk stems from the fact that they often bounce back quickly from physical stress and abuse. This can lead them to abuse their bodies and neglect their health. The negative effects of abusing one's body do not always show up immediately. However, at some point later one may pay a stiff price.

The following lifestyle patterns have been linked with poor health in college students: Skipping breakfast or regular meals, relying on snacks as a main food source, overeating, smoking, abusing alcohol and drugs, avoiding exercise, and not getting enough sleep. Do any of these habits apply to you?

Pursue and Maintain Physical Health

Are you as healthy as you can be? What did Self-Assessment 1 reveal about your current lifestyle choices?

Develop Healthy Behaviors and Address Problems

Let's look at specific aspects of your health. To further evaluate behaviors that contribute to your physical health, complete the Self-Assessment "My Health Habits," on your CD-ROM. Are you putting your health knowledge to work by developing good health habits? If you had low scores on the self-assessments, ask yourself some frank questions. You're probably not doing all that you can to be healthy.

However well or poorly you scored, be sure to seek medical help promptly when you have a detectable problem. For example, seek medical attention without delay if you experience any of the following (Vickery & Fries, 2000):

- develop a lump in your breast
- have unexplained weight loss
- experience a fever for more than a week

- cough up blood
- encounter persistent or severe headaches
- have fainting spells
- develop unexplained shortness of breath

In some circumstances, these symptoms can signal a cancer or other serious problems. In many cases, though, a thorough medical exam will confirm that nothing serious is wrong. Either way, it is always best to be well informed about your health.

After 30, a body has a mind of its own.

Bette Midler
Contemporary American actress

Exercise Regularly

In a national survey of first-year college students, regular exercise was linked with good health, and heavy TV viewing was related to poor health (Astin, 1993). In recent research, exercise has been shown to actually generate new brain cells (Holmes & others, 2004).

Additional health benefits associated with exercise include:

- improved cardiovascular fitness
- greater lean body mass and less body fat
- improved strength and muscular endurance
- improved flexibility
- greater life expectancy
- fewer stress symptoms
- improved mood and less depression
- higher self-esteem

Clearly, exercise alone is not going to ensure that you reach your academic goals. However, the fact that it can help you generate new brain cells is linked with thinking and learning. What are some other ways the benefits listed above might help improve academic performance?

Exercise is certainly good for you and includes both aerobic or anaerobic activities.

- *Aerobic exercise* is moderately intense, sustained exercise that stimulates your heart and lungs, while increasing your heart rate and the flow of oxygen through your body. Jogging, cycling, and swimming are examples of aerobic activities.
- *Anaerobic exercise* requires more oxygen than your body can take in, so it can only be done at short intervals. It often involves quick or intense movement such as doing pushups or running a 100-yard dash. In contrast, running a long distance is mainly aerobic.

Aerobic exercise has significant cardiovascular benefits and burns fat (what you want for weight loss). Anaerobic exercise builds muscle tissue but does not help you lose weight as much. Many exercise activities are both aerobic and anaerobic, such as tennis, basketball, and circuit training (circulating among different exercise machines and stations).

If you don't exercise now, how can you motivate yourself to get going? On Target Tips, "Motivate Yourself to Exercise," provides some good hints.

Get Enough Sleep

Most of us have occasional sleepless nights. Maybe we are stressed out and can't sleep soundly. In this case, we don't deliberately lose

ON TARGET TIPS

Motivate Yourself to Exercise

- **Make exercise a high priority in your life.** Give exercise a regular place in your schedule. Don't let unimportant things interfere with your exercise routine. Don't make excuses.
- **Chart your progress.** Record each of your exercise sessions in a systematic way. Use a notebook or a calendar, for example. This practice can help you to maintain the momentum you need to work out regularly.
- **Make time for exercise.** It's easy to sabotage your own commitment to exercise with excuses. If your excuse is, "I don't have time," find it. Ask yourself, "Am I too busy to take care of my health? What do I lose if I lose my health?"
- **Learn more about exercise.** The more you know about exercise, the more you're likely to continue it. Examine the resources on the website for this book to read more about exercise.

sleep. However, many college students deliberately pull all-nighters now and then to cram for a test. In a national survey, more than 80 percent of first-year college students said they stayed up all night at least once during the year (Sax & others, 1995). More common than all-nighters are successive nights with significantly reduced sleep because of parties, talking late with friends, and studying late. Just living with other students can produce irregular sleep patterns.

The dorm might be noisy or your roommate might not have a class until noon and stays up late while you have a class at 8 A.M. How might you deal with these situations? In many instances, college students don't get adequate sleep as a result of their own choices. Take the responsibility of saying no to staying late at parties, going out late when you have an early class, or staying up late when some friends just want to talk. You can set aside a time during the next day to talk with them if it is not an emergency. Many students think that sleeping late on the weekends makes up for lost sleep, but research recently has shown that this is not the case (Voelker, 2004). College students have twice as many sleep problems as the general population (Brown, Buboltz, & Soper, 2001).

How Much Sleep Do You Need? The amount of sleep needed varies from person to person. Most students need at least eight hours of sleep to function competently the next day (Maas, 1998). Researchers have found that many college students do not get this much sleep and, therefore, do not function at optimal levels the following day (Dement & Vaughan, 2000).

One study found that college students average only about 6½ hours of sleep per night (Hicks & Pellegrini, 1991). Many are unaware that their academic difficulties may be related to their sleep habits (Brown & Buboltz, 2002). In addition to academic problems, sleep deprivation is associated with higher levels of stress, headaches, inability to concentrate, less effective memory, irritability, and possibly increased susceptibility to illness (Insel & Roth, 2002).

Why Might You Be Having Sleep Problems? As many as one in five students have *insomnia*, a sleep disorder that involves an inability to sleep. Although insomnia itself is not a result of lifestyle choices, alcohol, nicotine, and caffeine can interfere with your sleep and contribute to such problems. For example, drinking before you go to sleep keeps you from getting a full night of restful sleep, because it dehydrates you. Stress also can cause sleep problems. For more information on good sleep, see On Target Tips, "How to Sleep Better." The Journal activity "Evaluate Your Sleep" on page 339 also provides an opportunity to critically evaluate your current sleep habits.

Eat Right

Many college students have poor eating habits. A recent study of 1,800 college students found that 60 percent eat too much artery-clogging saturated fat and 50 percent don't get enough fiber in their diet (Economos, 2001). Almost 60 percent said that they know their diet has gone downhill since they went to college.

Obesity has become a major health risk in the United States and in many countries around the world. Strong evidence of the environment's influence on weight is the doubling of the rate of obesity in the United States since 1900. More than 60 percent of U.S. adults are currently either overweight or obese (U.S. Center for Health Statistics, 2004). This dramatic increase is likely

ON TARGET TIPS

How to Sleep Better

- **Get into a regular daily routine.** This lets you go to sleep and wake up at approximately the same time each day.
- **Do something relaxing before you go to bed.** Maybe listen to some soft music.
- **Avoid discussing stressful problems before you go to bed.** This includes money or dating problems.
- **Make sure your sleeping area is good for sleeping.** It should have minimum light, minimum sound, and a comfortable temperature.
- **Cut out naps.** It is okay to take a brief nap after lunch but do not take naps that last more than an hour and are no later than 3 P.M. Napping during the day can interfere with night sleeping.
- **Engage in regular exercise.** However, don't exercise just before going to bed, because exercise increases your energy and alertness.
- **Manage your time effectively.** You should get 7–8 hours of sleep every night.
- **Manage your stress.** Learn how to relax and cope with stress effectively.
- **Contact your college health center.** If the above strategies don't work, get some help from health professionals.

because of greater availability of food (especially food high in fat), energy-saving devices, and declining physical activity. One recent study found that in 2000, U.S. women ate 335 calories more a day and men 168 more a day than they did in the early 1970s (National Center for Health Statistics, 2004). Obesity is linked to increased risk of hypertension, diabetes, cardiovascular disease, and early death (International Obesity Task Force, 2004).

The "freshman 15" refers to the approximately 15 pounds that many first-year students gain. The weight often shows up in the hips, thighs, and midsection. Why do first-year students gain this weight? During high school many students' eating habits are monitored by their parents, so they eat more balanced meals. Once in college, students select their own diets, which often consist of chips, chips, and more chips, fast food, ice cream, late-night pizza, and beer. Once the extra 15 pounds arrive, what do first-year students do? They diet. Dieting is a way of life for many college students.

The current hot diet trend is low-carbohydrate, such as the Atkins diet and the South Beach diet. The Atkins diet restricts carbohydrates to less than 10 percent of total calories eaten, whereas people in the United States typically get more than 50 percent of their total calories from carbohydrates such as bread, processed foods, starch in vegetables, and sugar in fruits. On the Atkins diet you can eat as much protein and fat as you want. Short-term studies show that individuals who follow this diet do lose weight (Noakes & Clifton, 2004; Stern & others, 2004).

However, critics argue that long-term studies have yet to be carried out and that the Atkins diet may pose health risks, especially for the heart, over the long term (Mayo Clinic, 2004). It is well-documented that foods promoted in the low-carbohydrate diets—for example, foods high in saturated fats such as meat, butter, or cream—increase the risk of heart disease and some types of cancer. And foods restricted on these diets—such as whole grains, vegetables, and fruits—have vitamins, minerals, and other nutrients that reduce the risk of heart disease, cancer, and other diseases.

Be wary of diets that promise quick fixes or that sound too good to be true. Aim for a long-term plan that involves eating a variety of vegetables, fruits, and grains, and being physically active on a daily basis. This plan may produce slower results, but it works far better over the long term and is much healthier for you (Mayo Clinic, 2004). To think more about your own diet, complete the Journal activity "Think About Your Diet," on page 338.

One of the best sources of nutritional advice, the *Dietary Guidelines for Americans*, is issued by the U.S. Department of Health and Human Services. These guidelines are revised every five years. The most recent ones support these six principles:

1. *Eat a variety of foods.* Use the four basic food groups to evaluate your diet:
   - The milk group (cheese, yogurt, milk)
   - The fruit and vegetable group
   - The grain group (cereals, bread, noodles)
   - The meat group (poultry, fish, red meat, and nuts)

   Healthy adults need to eat at least three servings of vegetables, two of fruit, and six of grain products every day. Megadose supplements of vitamins are no substitute for a healthful diet, and they can be harmful. Avoid them.

2. *Maintain a healthy weight.* Some college students are overweight, others underweight. Preoccupation with dieting can lead to dangerous loss/gain cycles that are hard on your body. Strive to maintain a reasonable, manageable weight.

3. *Follow a diet low in fat, saturated fat, and cholesterol.* Unfortunately, many of the best-tasting foods are the worst for you. Fat is found in large quantities in fried foods (fried chicken, doughnuts), rich foods (ice cream, pastries), greasy foods (spare ribs, bacon), and many spreads (butter, mayonnaise). In contrast, yogurt is low in saturated fat. Cholesterol, a key contributor to heart disease, is found only in animal products.

Fitness expert Covert Bailey (1991) says that if you throw a pound of butter in a swimming pool, it will float just like a cork. The fat in your body will float in the same way, so the fatter you are, the more you'll float. Bailey says that he once had a friend who floated so well he could read a book while coasting along on top of the water in a swimming pool.

If you have more than 25 percent body fat, you'll float easily. At 13 percent or lower, you'll sink quickly. Healthy body fat percentages vary for women and men. The highest healthy body fat content is 22 percent for women, 15 percent for men. Unfortunately, the average woman has 32 percent body fat, the average man 23 percent.

4. *Substitute plenty of vegetables, fruits, and grain products for unhealthful foods.* Replace fatty foods with more healthful sources of starch and fiber. This involves eating grain products, legumes (dried beans, peas), fruits, and vegetables not cooked in fat.

5. *Use sugar only in moderation.* In addition to table sugar, other common sugar products include brown sugar, syrups, honey, jams, jellies, ice cream, cookies, cakes, and most other desserts. If you eat dessert, try eating fresh fruit instead of foods with added sugar. Replace soft drinks with water.

6. *Use sodium in moderation.* Some people are sensitive to sodium and are at risk for hypertension (persistent high blood pressure). To reduce the sodium in your diet, eat less salt. Flavor your food with lemon, spices, herbs, or pepper.

Anorexia Nervosa and Bulimia Nineteen-year-old Andrea gradually eliminated foods from her diet to the point at which she lived on jello and yogurt. She spent hours observing her body. She wrapped her hands around her waist to see whether it was getting any thinner. She fantasized about becoming a fashion model. Even when her weight dropped to 80 pounds, Andrea still felt fat. She continued to lose weight and was hospitalized for *anorexia nervosa*, an eating disorder that involves the relentless pursuit of thinness through starvation (Polivy & others, 2003). Anorexia nervosa can eventually lead to death.

Most anorexics are white female adolescents or young adults from well-educated middle- and upper-income families. They have a distorted body image, perceiving themselves as overweight even when they become skeletal. Numerous causes of anorexia nervosa have been proposed (Smolak & Striegel-Moore, 2002). One is the current fashion image of thinness, reflected in the saying, "You can't be too rich or too thin." Many anorexics grow up in families with high demands for academic achievement. Unable to meet these high expectations and control their grades, they turn to something they can control: their weight.

Bulimia is a disorder that involves binging and purging. Bulimics go on an eating binge then purge by vomiting or using a laxative. Sometimes the binges alternate with fasting. However, they can also alternate with normal eating. Anorexics can control their eating; bulimics cannot. Bulimia can produce gastric and chemical imbalances in the body, as well as long-term dental damage. Depression is common in bulimics. If you have anorexic or bulimic characteristics, go to your college health center for help.

Don't Smoke

Some stark figures reveal why smoking is called suicide in slow motion:

- Smoking accounts for more than one fifth of all deaths in the United States.
- It causes 32 percent of coronary heart disease cases in the United States.
- It causes 30 percent of all cancer deaths in the United States.
- It causes 82 percent of all lung cancer deaths in the United States.
- Passive smoke causes as many as 8,000 lung cancer deaths a year in the United States.

TABLE 11.1 Psychoactive Drugs: Depressants, Stimulants, and Hallucinogens

Drug Classification	Medical Uses	Short-Term Effects	Overdose	Health Risks	Risk of Physical/Psychological Dependence
Depressants					
Alcohol	Pain relief	Relaxation, depressed brain activity, slowed behavior, reduced inhibitions	Disorientation, loss of consciousness, even death at high blood-alcohol levels	Accidents, brain damage, liver disease, heart disease, ulcers, birth defects	Physical: moderate; psychological: moderate
Barbiturates	Sleeping pill	Relaxation, sleep	Breathing difficulty, coma, possible death	Accidents, coma, possible death	Physical and psychological: moderate to high
Tranquilizers	Anxiety reduction	Relaxation, slowed behavior	Breathing difficulty, coma, possible death	Accidents, coma, possible death	Physical: low to moderate; psychological: moderate to high
Opiates (narcotics)	Pain relief	Euphoric feelings, drowsiness, nausea	Convulsions, coma, possible death	Accidents, infectious diseases such as AIDS (when the drug is injected)	Physical: high; psychological: moderate to high
Stimulants					
Amphetamines	Weight control	Increased alertness, excitability; decreased fatigue, irritability	Extreme irritability, feelings of persecution, convulsions	Insomnia, hypertension, malnutrition, possible death	Physical: possible; psychological: moderate to high
Cocaine	Local anesthetic	Increased alertness, excitability, euphoric feelings; decreased fatigue, irritability	Extreme irritability, feelings of persecution, convulsions, cardiac arrest, possible death	Insomnia, hypertension, malnutrition, possible death	Physical: possible; psychological: moderate (oral) to very high (injected or smoked)
Hallucinogens					
LSD	None	Strong hallucinations, distorted time perception	Severe mental disturbance, loss of contact with reality	Accidents	Physical: none; psychological: low
Marijuana	Treatment of the eye disorder glaucoma	Euphoric feelings, relaxation, mild hallucinations, time distortion, attention and memory impairment	Fatigue, disoriented behavior	Accidents, respiratory disease	Physical: very low; psychological: moderate

Source: *From John Santrock, Adolescence, Ninth Edition. Copyright © 2003 McGraw-Hill Companies, Inc. Reprinted by permission of the publisher.*

FIGURE 11.1 The Hazardous Consequences of Binge Drinking in College

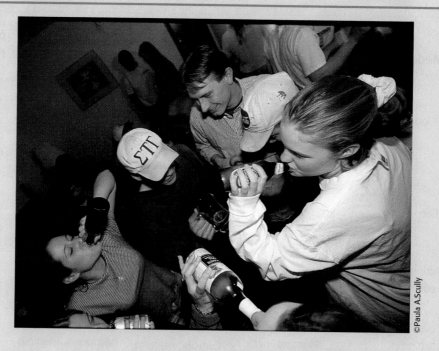

©Paula A.Scully

The Troubles Frequent Binge Drinkers Create for . . .

Themselves[1]		and Others[2]	
(% of those surveyed who admitted having had the problem)		(% of those surveyed who had been affected)	
Missed a class	61	Had study or sleep interrupted	68
Forgot where they were or what they did	54	Had to care for drunken student	54
Engaged in unplanned sex	41	Were insulted or humiliated	34
Got hurt	23	Experienced unwanted sexual advances	26
Had unprotected sex	22	Had serious argument	20
Damaged property	22	Had property damaged	15
Got into trouble with campus or local police	11	Were pushed or assaulted	13
Had five or more alcohol-related problems in a school year	47	Had at least one of the above problems	87

[1]Frequent binge drinkers were defined as those who had had at least four or five drinks at one time on at least three occasions in the previous two weeks.
[2]These figures are from colleges where at least 50% of students are binge drinkers.

Source: "The Trouble That 'Frequent Binge Drinkers' Create for Themselves and Others" from Journal of the American Medical Association (November/December 1994). Copyright © 1994 by the American Medical Association. Reprinted by permission of the publisher.

- *Listen to what others are saying to you.* Chances are that your roommate, a friend, or someone you've dated has told you that you have a substance abuse problem. You probably denied it. They are trying to help you. Listen to them.
- *Seek help for your problem.* There are numerous resources for students who have a substance abuse problem. These include Alcoholics Anonymous, Cocaine Anonymous (CA), Al-Anon, and Rational Recovery Systems. Most towns have one

or more of these organizations, which are confidential and are led by people who have successfully combatted their substance abuse problem. They can help you a great deal. Also, the health center at your college can provide help.

- *Use the resources on this book's website.* Examine the resources for reducing drug use. They include phone numbers, information about organizations that can help you overcome your problem, and links to other relevant websites.

Make the Right Sexual Decisions

Making smart sexual decisions has never been more important than today. AIDS, other sexually transmitted diseases, and unwanted pregnancy pose life-altering challenges (Crooks & Bauer, 2004). Individuals vary in the extent to which they believe it is acceptable to engage in various sexual behaviors. To evaluate your sexual attitudes, complete Self-Assessment 3 "My Sexual Attitudes" on page 337.

Avoid Sexually Transmitted Infections *Sexually transmitted infections (STIs)* are diseases contracted primarily through sex. This includes intercourse as well as oral-genital and anal-genital sex. STIs affect about one of every six adults.

Symptoms. With certain STIs, you may be showing no immediate symptoms and yet still pass the infection on to someone else who will suffer. Following are some symptoms for which you should certainly see a doctor or visit a clinic as soon as you can.

Men:

- Foul-smelling, cloudy discharge from the penis
- Burning sensation when urinating
- Painless sore on the penis
- Painful red bumps in the genital region, usually on the penis, turning into tiny blisters containing clear fluid
- Warts in the genital area, either pink/red and soft or hard and yellow/gray

Women:

- Yellow-green discharge from the vagina
- Painful sore on the inner vaginal wall or cervix
- Burning sensation during urination
- Painful red bumps on the labia, turning into tiny blisters containing clear fluid
- Warts in the genital area, either pink/red and soft or hard and yellow/gray

No single STI has had a greater impact on sexual behavior or created more fear in the last decade than HIV-AIDS. Experts say that AIDS can be transmitted by sexual contact, sharing hypodermic needles, blood transfusion, or other direct contact of cuts or mucous membranes with blood or sexual fluids (Hyde & DeLamater, 2005). It's not who you are but what you do that puts you at risk for getting AIDS. *Anyone* who is sexually active or uses intravenous drugs is at risk. No one is immune.

Reduce Your Chances. What can you do to reduce the likelihood of contracting an STI? First, recognize that the only completely effective

©Bill Bachman/PhotoEdit

If you have sex, be proactive rather than reactive. Use effective contraception and protect yourself against STIs. Promiscuity greatly increases your chances of contracting AIDS and other STIs. Think before you act. Too often enchanted evenings are followed by disenchanted mornings.

strategy is abstinence. But if you do choose to have sex, here are some ways to reduce your chances of being infected (Crooks & Bauer, 2005):

1. *Assess your and your partner's risk status.* If you've had previous sexual activity with others, you may have contracted an STI without knowing it. Have you been tested for STIs in general? Remember that many STIs don't produce detectable symptoms. If you care enough to be sexually intimate with a new partner, you should be willing to be open with him or her about your own physical sexual health.

   Spend time getting to know a prospective sexual partner before you have sex with him or her. Ideally, this time frame is at least 2–3 months. Use this time to convey your STI status and inquire about your partner's. Keep in mind that many people are not honest about their sexual history.

2. *Obtain prior medical examinations.* Many experts on sexuality now recommend that couples who want to begin a sexual relationship abstain from sexual activity until both undergo medical and laboratory testing to rule out the presence of STIs. If cost is an issue, contact your campus health service or a public health clinic in your area.

3. *Use condoms.* When correctly used, condoms help to prevent the transmission of many STIs. Condoms are most effective in preventing chlamydia, gonorrhea, syphilis, and AIDS. They are less effective against the spread of genital herpes and genital warts. Recommendations for the effective use of condoms include the following:

   • put on a condom before any genital contact has occurred
   • make sure the condom is adequately lubricated
   • don't blow up the condom or fill it with water to test it for leaks (this stretching weakens the latex)
   • don't unroll the condom first like a sock and then put it on but instead unroll it directly onto the erect penis
   • twist the end of the condom as it is rolled onto the penis to leave space at the tip
   • if the condom breaks, immediately replace it; never reuse a condom.

4. *Avoid having sex with multiple partners.* One of the strongest predictors of getting AIDS, chlamydia, genital herpes, and other STIs is having sex with multiple partners.

Protect Against Unwanted Pregnancy Most college students want to control whether and when they have children. That means either abstaining from sex or using effective contraception. Students who feel guilty and have negative attitudes about sexuality are less likely to use contraception than are students who have positive attitudes about sexuality.

Following are the main contraceptive choices:

• *Abstinence.* This is the only strategy that is 100 percent effective in preventing unwanted pregnancy.
• *Oral contraceptives.* Advantages of birth control pills are a high rate of effectiveness and low interference with sexual activity. However, the pill can have adverse side effects for some women, such as blood clots, nausea, and moodiness.
• *Condoms.* A main advantage is protection against STIs. A small proportion of condoms break. Improve protection by using a spermicide with condoms.
• *Diaphragm.* This consists of a latex dome on a flexible spring rim that is inserted into the vagina with contraceptive cream or jelly. The diaphragm must be fitted by a skilled medical practitioner. The diaphragm has few negative side effects and a high effectiveness rate when used properly. A cervical cap is like a miniature diaphragm that fits over the cervix.

- *Spermicides.* These include foam, suppositories, creams, and jellies that contain a chemical that kills sperm. Advantages include a lack of serious side effects. Disadvantages include potential irritation of genital tissues and interruption of sexual activity. Most experts on sexuality say not to rely on spermicide alone for contraception.
- *IUD.* The intrauterine device (IUD) is a small, plastic device that is inserted into the vagina. The IUD's advantages include uninterrupted sexual activity and simplicity of use. Possible disadvantages include pelvic inflammation and pregnancy complications.
- *Norplant.* Norplant consists of six thin capsules filled with a synthetic hormone that are implanted under the skin of a woman's upper arm. The implanted capsules gradually release the hormone into the bloodstream over a five-year period to prevent conception. Working like a mini birth control pill, Norplant provides highly effective contraception. Its negatives include potential bleeding and hormone-related side effects.
- *Depo-Provera.* Depo-Provera is an injectable contraceptive that lasts three months. Users have to get a shot every 12 weeks. Depo-Provera is a very effective contraceptive method but can cause menstrual irregularities.
- *Tubal ligation.* This is the most common sterilization procedure done for women. It involves severing or tying the fallopian tubes.
- *Vasectomy.* This is a male sterilization procedure that involves cutting the sperm-carrying ducts.

Figure 11.2 summarizes the effectiveness of these contraceptive methods and lists some other, ineffective choices. As it indicates, using no contraceptive method, trying to withdraw the penis just before ejaculation, and periodic abstinence are not wise strategies. If you're sexually active, compare the various contraceptive methods and choose the method that is the safest and most effective for you.

As you have learned in this section, maintaining good physical health is important for your success in college and beyond. For some additional strategies for improving your health, see Take Charge, "Of Your Physical Health." The Journal activity "Promoting Safe Sex" on page 339 also provides an opportunity for you to think more about ways to promote safe sex on your campus.

Safeguard Your Mental Health

As we said at the beginning of the chapter, an important factor in being mentally healthy is having high self-esteem. This section describes several strategies for improving mental health, all of which are linked with building self-esteem.

FIGURE 11.2 Effectiveness of Contraceptive Methods

The following are birth control methods and their failure rates in one year of average use.

Method	Unintended-pregnancy rate*
No Method (Chance)	85.0
Spermicides	30.0
Withdrawal	24.0
Periodic Abstinence	19.0
Cervical Cap	18.0
Diaphragm	18.0
Condom	16.0
Pill	6.0
IUD	4.0
Tubal Ligation	0.5
Depo-Provera	0.4
Vasectomy	0.2
Norplant	0.05

*Figures are based on women of reproductive age, 15 to 44. Rates vary with age. Failure rates with perfect use are lower, but people rarely use methods perfectly.

Source: *From Susan Harlap, et al, Preventing Pregnancy, Protecting Health: A New Look at Birth Control Choices in the United States, Table 8.1. Reprinted with the permission of the Alan Guttmacher Institute, New York and Washington, DC.*

TAKE CHARGE   Of Your Physical Health

Throughout this book, we have emphasized how important it is for you to take responsibility for your behavior. Your physical health is no exception. Exercising regularly, getting enough sleep, eating right, not smoking, avoiding drugs, and making the right sexual decisions all require you to consistently take charge of your life and not let yourself slide into bad habits.

Five steps in developing a self-control program to improve your health are (Pear & Martin, 2003):

1. Define the problem.
2. Commit to change.
3. Collect data about yourself.
4. Design a self-control program.
5. Make the program last–maintenance.

(continued)

1. *Define the problem* What would you like to change? Which aspect of your health would you like to more effectively control? For one person, this might be "lose 30 pounds," for another it might be "quit smoking," and for yet another person it might be "engage in aerobic exercise for 30 minutes, four days a week." What aspect of your health do you want to change?

2. *Commit to change.* When college students commit to change, they become better self managers of their smoking, eating, exercise, and other aspects of their lives. Some good strategies for committing to change are:
   - Tell others about your commitment to change—they will remind you of your commitment.
   - Rearrange your environment to provide frequent reminders of your goal, making sure the reminders are associated with positive benefits of reaching your goal.
   - Plan ahead for ways that you can deal with temptation, tailoring these plans to your program.

3. *Collect data about yourself.* This is especially important in decreasing excessive behaviors such as overeating and frequent smoking. Make up a chart and monitor what you do everyday in regard to what you want to change.

4. *Design a self-control program.* A good self-control program usually includes both long-term and short-term goals and developing a plan for how to reach those goals.

5. *Make the program last.* Establish specific dates for postchecks. Establish a buddy system by finding a friend with a similar problem. The two of you can set maintenance goals and once a month check each other's progress.

Cope with Stress

There is no doubt that stress is a factor in your mental health. However, do you know how important it is? According to the American Academy of Family Physicians, two thirds of all medical office visits are for stress-related symptoms. Stress is also a major contributor to heart disease, accidental injuries, and suicide. There are a number of life events that have been identified as stressful enough to significantly impact one's physical health. To evaluate your own chances of becoming ill due to stressful events, complete the Self-Assessment "Life Events and My Chance of Significant Illness in the Coming Year" on your CD-ROM.

What are the most common stressors for college students? In one study (Murphy, 1996), the academic circumstances creating the most stress for students were tests and finals, grades and competition, professors and class environment, too many demands, papers and essay exams, career and future success, and studying. Do any of these apply to you?

In this same study, the personal circumstances that created the most stress for students were intimate relationships, finances, parental conflicts and expectations, and roommate conflicts. Another study showed that the first year of college was by far the most stressful for students (Sher, Wood, & Gotham, 1996).

Coping with stress is essential to making your life more productive and enjoyable (Blonna, 2005). Coping means managing difficult circumstances, solving personal problems, and reducing stress and conflict. Not everyone responds the same way to stress; some of us have better strategies than others. The Journal activity "Examine Your Coping Style" on page 338 provides an opportunity for you to analyze how well you cope.

The good news is that if you don't currently cope with stress effectively you can learn to do so (Folkman & Moskowitz, 2004). Before we talk about the positive ways to cope with stress, let's look at some typically unsuccessful ways of dealing with a stressful problem:

- Repress it so you won't have to think about it.
- Take it out on other people when you feel angry or depressed.
- Keep your feelings to yourself.
- Tell yourself the problem will go away.

DILBERT reprinted by permission of United Features Syndicate, Inc.

- Refuse to believe what is happening.
- Try to reduce tension by drinking and eating more.

Fortunately, there are successful coping strategies as well.

See Stress As a Challenge Rather Than a Threat Consider how first-year students view stress differently. Antonio sees an upcoming test as stressful; Anna sees it as a challenge. Greta views a D on a paper as a disaster; Dion views the same grade as a challenge to improve his writing. To some extent, stress depends on how we interpret events.

To cope successfully, it helps to (1) see the circumstances as a challenge to overcome rather than an overwhelming, threatening stress and (2) have good coping resources such as friends, family, a mentor, and the counseling center at your college (Lazarus, 1998).

Develop an Optimistic Outlook and Think Positively Do you look on the positive side of things, or the negative? To find out, complete the Self-Assessment "Am I an Optimist or a Pessimist?" on your CD-ROM. How important is it to be optimistic? In one study, college students were initially identified as optimists or pessimists (Peterson & Stunkard, 1986). Then their health was monitored over the next year. The pessimists had twice as many infections and doctors' visits as the optimists did. A recent study also found that students who were optimistic at the beginning of their first semester of college had less stress and depression and more social support over the course of the semester (Brissette, Scheier, & Carver, 2002).

How can you develop a more optimistic outlook? One way is to use positive thinking to challenge self-defeating thoughts (Roth, Eng, & Heimberg, 2002). This strategy helps you avoid ruminating and wallowing in self-pity when bad things happen. Another good strategy is to dispute your negative thoughts (Ellis, 2002). Pessimists tend to use absolute, all-encompassing terms to describe their defeats. They often use words like *never* and *always*. If this sounds like you, talk back to these negative thoughts in a self-confident, positive way that will get rid of self-blame and negative feelings.

Thinking positively helps to put you in a good mood and improves your self-esteem. It also gives you the sense that you're controlling your environment rather than letting it control you. Thinking positively improves your ability to learn. A negative outlook increases your chances of getting angry, feeling guilty, and magnifying your mistakes.

Talk positively to yourself. It can help you reach your full potential. Monitor your self-talk, because unchallenged negative thinking has a way of becoming a self-fulfilling prophecy. That is, if you tell yourself you can't do something well, you won't. How can you monitor your self-talk? At random times during the day, ask yourself, "What am I saying to myself right now?" Potentially stressful moments are excellent times to examine your self-talk. You also can ask friends to give you feedback on your negative or positive attitudes.

Seek Emotional Support In stressful times, family members, friends, classmates, and coworkers can help by reassuring you that you're a valuable person who is loved. Knowing that others care about you can give you the confidence to tackle stressful circumstances.

Consider Juan, who was laid off from three jobs in three years. By all accounts he should be depressed. Yet he says he is a happy person. When asked his secret in the face of adversity and stress, Juan says it stems from the support of a wonderful family and great friends.

Recognize the potential support in your own life. Learn how to draw on these resources in times of stress. Sometimes you can improve your

ability to cope by joining community groups, interest groups, or informal social groups that meet regularly (Taylor, 2003).

Relax We usually think of relaxation as unwinding in front of the TV, taking a quiet walk in the evening, and so forth. These activities can be relaxing. However, a different form of relaxation can also help college students cope with anxiety and stress. It's called *deep relaxation*.

Try the following to attain a deeply relaxed state (Davis, Eshelman, & McKay, 1995):

1. In a quiet place, either lie down on a couch or bed or sit in a comfortable chair with your head supported.

2. Get into a comfortable position and relax. Clench your right fist tighter and tighter for about five seconds. Now relax it. Feel the looseness in your right hand. Repeat the procedure with your left hand. Then do it with both hands. When you release the tension, let it go instantly. Allow your muscles to become limp.

3. Bend your elbows and tense your biceps as hard as you can. After a few seconds, relax and straighten out your arms. Go through the procedure again. Tighten your biceps as hard as you can for a few seconds and then relax them. As with your biceps, do each of the following procedures twice.

4. Turn your attention to your head. Wrinkle your forehead as tightly as you can, then relax it. Next, frown and notice the strain it produces. Close your eyes now. Squint them as hard as you can. Notice the tension. Now relax your eyes. Let them stay closed gently and comfortably. Now clench your jaw and bite hard. Notice the tension throughout your jaw. Relax your jaw.

5. Shrug your shoulders. Keep the tension as you hunch your head down between your shoulders. Then relax your shoulders.

6. Breathe in and fill your lungs completely. Hold your breath for a few seconds. Now exhale and let your chest become loose. Repeat this four or five times. Tighten your stomach for several seconds. Now relax it.

7. Tighten your buttocks and thighs. Flex your thighs by pressing your heels down as hard as you can. Relax and feel the difference. Next, curl your toes downward, making your calf muscles tight. Then relax. Now bend your toes toward your face, creating tension in your shins. Relax again. To avoid muscle cramping, don't overtighten your toes.

Some students have limited success when they first try deep relaxation. With practice, though, it usually works. Initially you may need 20–30 minutes to reach a deeply relaxed state, but eventually many students can become deeply relaxed in two to three

CATHY ©Cathy Guisewite. Reprinted with permission of Universal Press Syndicate.

minutes. The resources section on this book's website provides further information about deep relaxation. *Note:* If you have high blood pressure and are taking medication for it, do not try the deep relaxation exercise, because it could lower your blood pressure too far.

Write about Your Stress   In Chapter 1 we described James Pennebaker's research that found that first-year students who wrote about their stress in a journal were healthier than those who did not. Writing about your stress not only provides a release of pent-up tension but also can stimulate you to think about ways to cope more effectively with the stress (Pennebaker, 2001). Some further strategies for writing about your stress appear in On Target Tips, "Writing about Stress." Also, the Journal activity "Write about Your Stress" on page 338 gives you an opportunity to use writing as a coping strategy.

Tackle Depression

Depression is all too common among college students. In one study, depression was linked with poor academic performance (Haines, Norris, & Kashy, 1996). Consider Sally, who was depressed for several months. Nothing seemed to cheer her up. Sally's depression began when the person she planned to marry broke off their relationship. Her emotional state worsened until she didn't feel like getting out of bed most mornings. She started missing many classes and got behind in all of them. One of her friends noticed how sad she was and got Sally to go to the counseling center at her college.

Each of us feels blue or down in the dumps some of the time. These brief bouts of sad feelings or discontent with the way our life is going are normal. If sad feelings last for only a few hours, a few days, or a few weeks, you won't be classified as depressed. But if the sad feelings linger for a month or more, and you feel deeply unhappy and demoralized, you probably are in a state of depression. A person with depression often has the following symptoms:

- changes in sleep patterns
- changes in appetite
- decreased energy
- feelings of worthlessness
- difficulty concentrating
- feelings of guilt

Depression is so widespread that it's called the "common cold" of mental disorders (Nolen-Hoeksema, 2004). More than 250,000 people in the United States are hospitalized every year for depression. Students, professors, and laborers get depressed. No one is immune to it, not even great writers such as Ann Sexton and Ernest Hemingway, or famous statesmen such as Abraham Lincoln and Winston Churchill.

A man's lifetime risk of having depression is 10 percent. A woman's lifetime risk is much greater—almost 25 percent. Many people with depression suffer unnecessarily, because depression can be treated effectively. To evaluate whether you may be depressed, complete Self-Assessment "Am I Depressed?" on your CD-ROM.

Increasing numbers of college students are taking antidepressants, drugs that are designed to reduce depression. Researchers have found that antidepressant drugs work best when combined with psychotherapy (Beck, 2002). Furthermore, nondrug

---

ON TARGET TIPS

Writing about Stress

Here are some recommended strategies for writing about stress (Pennebaker, 1997):

- *What to Write.* You don't need to write about the biggest trauma in your life. Write about issues that currently bother you and preoccupy your thinking. Write about things that you may not be telling others out of fear of embarrassment or punishment. Write as objectively as you can about an experience that troubled you. Express your emotions and write as deeply as you can about your feelings.
- *How to Write.* Just start and keep writing. If you get stuck, go back and repeat what you were writing before you got stuck.
- *When and Where to Write.* Write when you feel like it. Write when you feel ready to pursue writing on an emotional level. Find a place where you won't be interrupted or distracted.
- *What to Expect.* Writing about your stress is not a cure-all. It is not a substitute for tackling problems that may keep you sad, angry, or frustrated. However, writing about stress can help you see things from a better perspective. You may feel sad or depressed for several hours after writing about your stress but most people report that they feel relieved, happier, and more content over time when they write about their stress.

treatments, such as regular exercise, also have shown positive benefits in reducing depression (Lane, Crone-Grant, & Lane, 2002). To think further about depression and other health issues, complete the Journal activity "Become a Movie Producer" on page 339.

Understand Suicide

The rate of suicide in the United States has tripled since the 1950s. Each year about 25,000 people in this country take their own lives. As many as two out of every three college students say they have thought about suicide on at least one occasion. Immediate and highly stressful circumstances can produce suicidal thoughts. These include the loss of a partner, a spouse, or a job; flunking out of school; and unwanted pregnancy. In many cases, suicide or its attempt has multiple causes (Eggert & others, 2002).

Consider Brian, who just flunked two of his college courses. When the grades came in, his father harshly criticized Brian and told him he had not put enough effort into his classes. This past week, Brian's girlfriend broke off their long-standing relationship. He became depressed and began to think about putting an end to his life. If you know someone like Brian, what can you do? Some guidelines are offered in On-Target Tips, "What to Do When Someone Is Thinking about Suicide."

Seek Help for Mental Health Problems

When should you seek professional help? There is no easy answer to this question. However, as a rule, seek psychological help:

- if you're psychologically distressed
- when you feel helpless and overwhelmed
- if your life is seriously disrupted by your problems

Various mental health professionals can help students. They include clinical psychologists, counselors, social workers, and psychiatrists. Clinical psychologists, counselors, and social workers use psychotherapeutic strategies to help students, but they do not prescribe drugs. Psychiatrists are medical doctors who often prescribe drugs in treating students' emotional problems. They also can conduct psychotherapy.

The counseling or health center at your college is a good place to go if you think that you have a mental health problem. The center will probably have staff to help you or will refer you to a mental health professional in the community. Figure 11.3 shows some reasons college students have sought counseling. In addition, the Journal activity "Visit the Health and Counseling Centers" on page 338 will help you prepare in advance in case you ever need these services.

Some students may not admit their problems or seek help for them because they fear others will think they are weak. It takes courage to face your problems. Instead of a weakness, consider it a strength to admit that you have a problem and are willing to seek help for it. You'll be doing something about a problem that stands between you and your goals.

Making changes can be hard. Be patient and allow some time for professional help to work. Part of the success of therapy involves developing a positive relationship with the therapist, so it

---

ON TARGET TIPS

What to Do When Someone Is Thinking about Suicide

- **Stay calm.** In most cases, there is no rush. Sit and listen, *really* listen, to what the person is saying. Be understanding, and emotionally support the person's feelings.
- **Deal directly with the topic of suicide.** Most people have mixed feelings about death and are open to help. Don't be afraid to ask or talk directly about suicide.
- **Encourage problem solving and positive actions.** Remember that the person in the crisis is not thinking clearly. Encourage the person to refrain from making any serious, irreversible decisions while in the crisis. Talk about the alternatives that might create hope for the future.
- **Get help.** Although you want to help, don't take full responsibility by being the sole counselor. Seek out resources, such as your college counseling center, for help. Do this even if it means breaking confidence. Let the troubled person know that you're so concerned that you're willing to get help beyond what you can offer.
- **Emphasize getting through it.** Say that the suicide crisis is temporary. Unbearable pain can be survived.

FIGURE 11.3 College Students' Main Reasons for Seeking Counseling

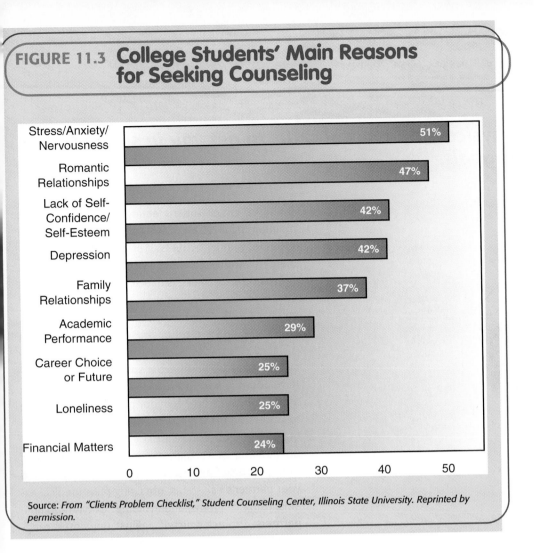

Source: *From "Clients Problem Checklist," Student Counseling Center, Illinois State University. Reprinted by permission.*

may take several sessions for you to notice a change. Also, if you do seek professional help, continue to evaluate how much it is benefiting you. Not all therapists and therapies are alike. If you become dissatisfied, ask to be referred to someone else.

More information about mental health professionals is provided in the resource section on the website for this book. Also, the Journal activity "Increase Awareness of Your Health Behaviors" on page 339 will help you further assess the status of your physical and mental health.

Summary Strategies for Mastering College

Value and practice physical and mental skills to get you in shape to reach your academic goals.

Focus on the "Six Strategies for Success" above as you read each chapter to learn how to apply these strategies to your own success.

1 Value Health and Adopt a Healthy Lifestyle

- Learn to control an important aspect of your health—your lifestyle.
- Evaluate your health habits to improve them.
- Avoid common risks to college students.

2 Pursue and Maintain Physical Health

- Develop healthy behaviors and address problems.
- Exercise regularly. It will help your physical and mental health.
- Get enough sleep, which for most college students means eight hours or more each night to maximize alertness and productivity the next day.

- Eat right, which means eating a variety of foods, maintaining a healthy weight, and not going on extreme, unhealthy diets. Watch out for the "freshman 15," and avoid anorexia nervosa and bulimia.
- Don't smoke. Smoking is difficult to quit once started. Seek help from the health center of your college if you have a smoking problem.
- Don't take drugs. Alcohol abuse is a major problem on college campuses, and it can seriously undermine success. If you have a substance abuse problem, admit it and listen to what others are saying about you. Seek help for your problem, and use the resources on the website for this book.
- Make the right sexual decisions. Increase your understanding of sexually transmitted diseases and protect yourself against them by assessing your and your partner's risk status, obtaining prior medical exams, using condoms, and avoiding sex with multiple partners. Protect yourself against unwanted pregnancy by abstaining from sex or by using effective contraceptive methods.

3 Safeguard Your Mental Health

- Cope with stress. Some strategies include perceiving stress as a challenge rather than a threat, establishing an optimistic outlook and thinking positively, seeking emotional support, and learning how to engage in deep relaxation.
- Know if you are experiencing depression and your resources for help.
- Know what to do when someone is contemplating suicide.
- Seek help for mental health problems at the counseling or health center at your college. Know that making changes can be hard. Be patient and allow some time for professional help to work.

Review Questions

1. List three strategies you can implement to exercise, sleep, and eat better.

   Exercise strategies:

   1. _____
   2. _____
   3. _____

   Sleep strategies:

   1. _____
   2. _____
   3. _____

   Nutrition strategies:

   1. _____
   2. _____
   3. _____

2. If a person has a drug problem, what are some effective strategies for kicking the habit? List a few ways drug use can negatively impact your success in college.

   Strategies: _____

   _____

   _____

   Negative effects: _____

   _____

   _____

3. What can you do to protect yourself from sexually transmitted diseases and unwanted pregnancy?

   Strategies for avoiding STDs: _____

   _____

   _____

   Strategies for avoiding pregnancy: _____

   _____

   _____

4. List three effective ways of coping with stress.

   1. _____
   2. _____
   3. _____

5. How can you tell if you have a mental health problem? If you think you have one, what should you do?

   _____

   _____

   _____

Learning Portfolio

SELF-ASSESSMENTS

YOUR JOURNAL

STRATEGIES FOR SUCCESS

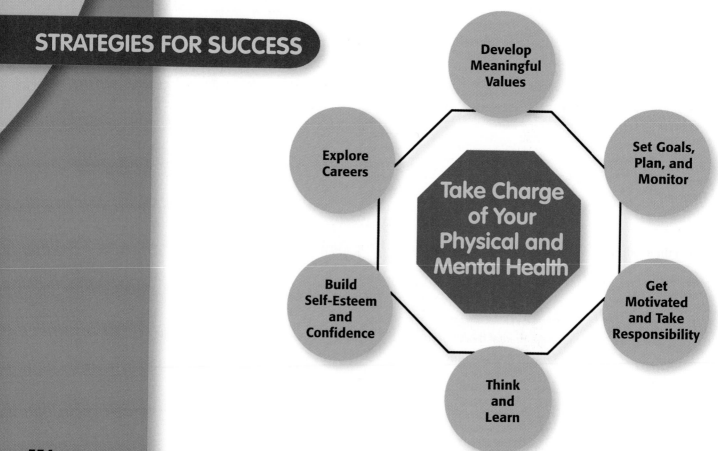

Take Charge of Your Physical and Mental Health

- Develop Meaningful Values
- Set Goals, Plan, and Monitor
- Get Motivated and Take Responsibility
- Think and Learn
- Build Self-Esteem and Confidence
- Explore Careers

Is Your Lifestyle Good for Your Health?

Your lifestyle includes many components: the ways you work, relax, communicate, and perform other activities. The following assessment is designed to help you explore your lifestyle choices and determine whether they are affecting you positively or negatively. Your responses will help you understand the impact of your lifestyle on your health.

Directions: Respond to each of the statements with one of the following designations:
5—definitely true; 4—mostly true; 3—not sure; 2—mostly false; 1—definitely false.

Write the number that corresponds to your answer in the blank at the left.

____ I am doing well in school.
____ I am enjoying myself, not feeling bored or angry.
____ I have satisfying relationships with other people.
____ I express my emotions when I want to.
____ I use my leisure time well and enjoy it.
____ I am satisfied with my sexual relationships.
____ I am satisfied with what I accomplish during the day.
____ I am having fun.
____ I am making use of the talents I have.
____ I feel physically well and full of vitality.
____ I am developing my skills and abilities.
____ I am contributing to society.
____ I am helpful to other people.
____ I have a sense of freedom and adventure in my life.
____ I feel joy or pleasure on most days.
____ I feel that my body is fit enough to meet the demands made upon it.
____ I feel rested and full of energy.
____ I am able to relax most of the day.
____ I enjoy a good night's sleep most nights.
____ I usually go to bed feeling happy and satisfied about the day.

Scoring: Add up the numbers in your answers.

If your score was 90 to 100, you are making lifestyle choices that promote good health. Your lifestyle is making a very positive contribution to your health.

If your score was 80 to 89, you are doing well in many areas. Many of your lifestyle choices are healthful ones. Look at the statements that you marked with a 1, 2, or 3 for areas that need improvement.

If your score was 61 to 79, there are a number of aspects of your lifestyle that could use improvement. Statements to which you responded 1, 2, or 3 indicate areas where you could do better. Your lifestyle choices may be negatively affecting your physical, emotional, intellectual, social, or spiritual health.

If your score was 60 or below, your lifestyle puts your health at high risk. Carefully review your responses, focusing on statements that you marked with a 1 or 2, and decide what you can do now to make better lifestyle choices. Altering your lifestyle will help you preserve your health.

Adapted from R. Allen & S. linde, Lifeagain, p. 25–26. Copyright © 1981 by Human Resources Institute. Reprinted by permission.

Do I Abuse Drugs?

Check Yes or No to the right of each question below.

	Yes	No
I have gotten into financial problems because of using drugs.		
Using alcohol or other drugs has made my college life unhappy at times.		
Drinking alcohol or taking other drugs has been a factor in my losing a job.		
Drinking alcohol or taking other drugs has interfered with my preparation for exams.		
Drinking alcohol or taking drugs is jeopardizing my academic performance.		
My ambition is not as strong since I started drinking a lot or taking drugs.		
Drinking or taking other drugs has caused me to have difficulty sleeping.		
I have felt remorse after drinking or using other drugs.		
I crave a drink or other drugs at a definite time of the day.		
I want a drink or another drug the next morning.		
I have had a complete or partial loss of memory as a result of drinking or using other drugs.		
Drinking or using other drugs is affecting my reputation.		
I have been in a hospital or institution because of drinking or taking other drugs.		

College students who responded Yes to these items from the Rutgers Collegiate Abuse Screening Test were more likely to be substance abusers than those who answer No. If you responded Yes even to just one of the thirteen items on this drug-abuse screening test, you're probably a substance abuser. If you responded Yes to any items, go to your college health or counseling center for help with your problem.

Source: *From M. E. Bennett, et al., "Identifying Young Substance-Abusers: The Rutgers Collegiate Substance Abuse Screening Test," from* Journal of Studies on Alcohol, 54, *pp. 522–527. Copyright © 1993 by Alcohol Research Documentation, Inc.*
Reprinted with the permission of the publisher. The RCSAST is to be used only as a part of a complete assessment battery since more research needs to be done with this instrument.

My Sexual Attitudes

Indicate your reaction to each statement below by choosing a number from 1 to 5 according to the following scale. (The letters to the left of each question will help you interpret your responses.)

Agree Strongly	Agree Somewhat	Cannot Decide	Disagree Somewhat	Disagree Strongly
5	4	3	2	1

(P)	_____	Premarital intercourse between consenting adults is acceptable.
(C)	_____	Sexual intercourse is a kind of communication.
(O)	_____	Oral sex can provide more effective sexual stimulation than does intercourse.
(H)	_____	Homosexuals should be eligible for jobs where they may serve as role models for children.
(M)	_____	Masturbation is acceptable when the objective is simply to attain sensory enjoyment.
(O)	_____	Oral sex should be viewed as an acceptable form of sex play.
(C)	_____	Communication barriers are the key factors in sexual problems.
(H)	_____	Homosexuality should be regarded as a personal inclination or choice.
(M)	_____	Relieving tension by masturbating is healthy.
(O)	_____	Women should be as willing as men to participate in oral sex.
(P)	_____	Women should experience sexual intercourse before marriage.
(P)	_____	Many couples live together because the partners have a strong sexual need for each other.
(C)	_____	The basis of sexual communication is touching.
(P)	_____	Men should experience sexual intercourse before marriage.
(M)	_____	Masturbation should be encouraged in certain circumstances.
(H)	_____	Homosexual practices are acceptable between consenting adults.

Now total your responses for each letter category listed to the left of each question and find your grand total.

	Total	Category	Liberal	Undecided	Traditional
(C)	_____	Sexual communication	15–12	11–7	6–3
(H)	_____	Homosexuality	15–12	11–7	6–3
(M)	_____	Masturbation	15–12	11–7	6–3
(O)	_____	Oral sex	15–12	11–7	6–3
(P)	_____	Premarital intercourse	20–12	15–9	6–4
	_____	Grand total	80–60	59–37	36–16

Questions:
In which categories do you have the most extreme opinions, positive or negative?
Do any of your scores reveal an attitude that you might not have expected in yourself?
Would you be able to cope with sexual matters better if any of your expressed attitudes changed? Which ones?

Think about your sexual *behaviors* and sexual *attitudes*:
   Do you consciously make decisions about your sexual behaviors?
   Would it be better if you did?
   Are your decisions about sexual behaviors ever inconsistent with your attitudes?

Source: *M. Levy et al. Life and Health: Targeting Wellness. p. 11. Adapted from R. F. Valois. "The effects of a human sexuality program on the attitudes of university residence hall students" (Master's thesis, University of Illinois at Urbana-Champaign, 1980). In S. G. Cox et al (Eds.), Wellness. pp. 9–65 Copyright © 1992 by Benjamin/Cummings. Reprinted by permission of the publisher.*

Your Journal

● REFLECT

1. Think about Your Diet

Do you think you have a healthy diet? Let's find out. For one week, keep track of everything you eat, and the times you eat meals and snack. Record this information in a food journal. At the end of the week, review your data. How healthy was your diet? Were there particular days or times when you tended to eat more sweets? List your healthy eating habits and your unhealthy habits below. Then think of ways you can replace unhealthy habits with healthy ones.

Healthy Habits: _____

Unhealthy Habits: _____

Replacement Strategies: _____

2. Examine Your Coping Style

This is good time to take stock of your coping style. Think about how you tend to cope with stress. Examine your life in the last few months. When stressful circumstances have come up, how have you handled them in general?

● Did you appraise them as harmful, threatening, or challenging?

_____

● Did you repress the stress or did you consciously make an effort to solve your problems?

_____

● Did you refuse to believe what was happening or accept the circumstances?

_____

● Did you try to reduce the stress by eating and drinking more?

_____

● DO

1. Visit the Health and Counseling Centers

Where are the health and counseling centers at your college? Record their addresses below. Stop by and find out what services and materials are available. Describe these services below. Ask for copies of any health or mental health brochures that interest you.

Health Center address: _____ Phone#/E-mail address: _____

Counseling Center address: _____ Phone#/E-mail address: _____

Available services: _____

_____

Available materials: _____

_____

2. Write about Your Stress

Follow the advice given in On-Target Tips, "Writing about Stress," and, over the next four days, write about your deepest emotions and thoughts pertaining to the most upsetting experience in your life. Did this writing exercise make you feel better or worse about this experience? Why?

_____

_____

Your Journal

● THINK CRITICALLY

1. Evaluate Your Sleep

Critically evaluate your sleep habits. Do you have trouble falling asleep or remaining asleep for the entire night? How often do you feel well rested when you wake up? Keep a sleep journal for one week. Record your eating and drinking habits each evening, the time you go to bed, any difficulties sleeping throughout the night, and the time you wake. Do you see any patterns that might be impacting your ability to get a good night's sleep?

_____

_____

_____

2. Increase Awareness of Your Health Behaviors

Go back and review all of the self-assessments you completed for this chapter. What did you learn about your own health behaviors? Did you make any resolutions regarding changing any unhealthy behaviors? Too many people are not aware that they engage in unhealthy behaviors and that these behaviors can have serious consequences. For example, they may not be aware that they are stressed or depressed. How can we help people become more aware of the behaviors that are particularly unhealthy, or their problems that they don't seem to acknowledge? What thinking strategies would you recommend to someone for becoming more aware of these behaviors and problems?

_____

_____

_____

_____

● CREATE

1. Become a Movie Producer

Imagine that you're a screenwriter with a major studio. Your task is to create a movie on a college student's health problems, such as drug abuse, anorexia nervosa, or depression. Describe the movie by writing a short treatment of it. Give it a title.

Health Issue: _____

Your Movie Concept: _____

_____

Your Movie Title: _____

_____

2. Promoting Safe Sex

What type of campaign do you think would be most effective in promoting safer sex on your campus? How do you think you could best reach the most students who are at risk? Come up with a slogan for your campaign and write it down below.

Your Safe Sex Slogan: _____

Campaign Strategy: _____

_____

_____

_____

Applying the Six Strategies for Success

What did you learn in this chapter that you can apply to the following key strategies to help form the foundation for your success? Write down all of the main points you can remember that support the following strategies:

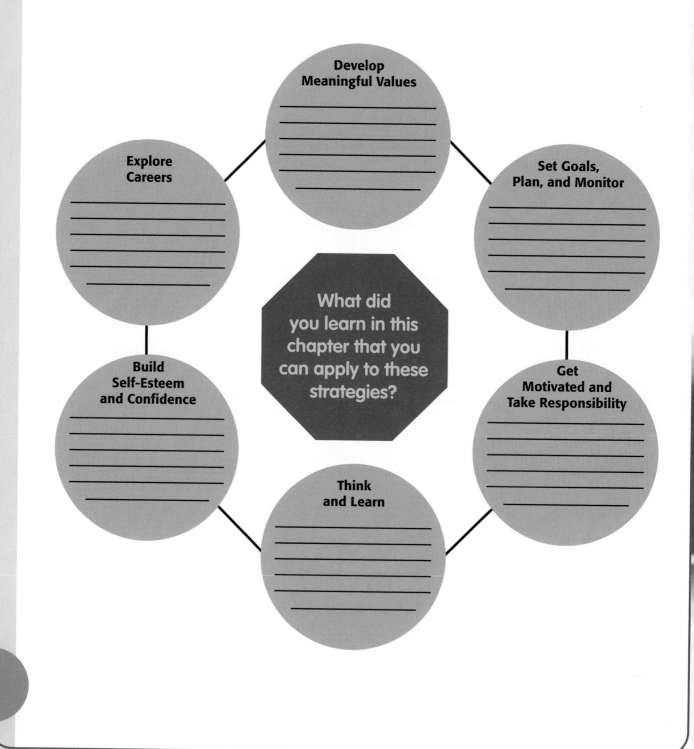

12 Be a Great Money Manager

© Marc Romanelli/Alamy

As you read about Marc Andreessen, think about how he used campus financial resources to support his college success and how he used technology to embark on a remarkable career. His entrepreneurial approach provides one interesting model that illustrates how you don't have to wait until your college degree is in hand to chart your course, take some risks, and manage your funds effectively.

Images of College Success

Marc Andreessen

During his senior year at the University of Illinois, Marc Andreessen supported himself as a lab technician on campus, making $6.85 per hour. Within two years, he was worth more than $50 million. This change in finances resulted from the public offering of stock in Netscape Communications, the company he co-founded in 1994.

Obviously not all on-campus employment leads to making a fortune. But Andreessen's story is a great example of making the best of campus resources. The Internet has been around for a long time, but in the past it was a troublesome array of disorganized information that was difficult for most users to navigate. In his senior year, Andreessen worked with six other students to create *Mosaic* software, the first browser that facilitated access to the Web.

A subsequent partnership with Jim Clark produced *Netscape*, a browser that could search the Web ten times faster than *Mosaic*. When the company offered *Netscape* shares to the public, the stock price zoomed from $28 to $75 per share. In 18 short months *Netscape* grew to 1,100 employees. By 1996, 80 million users were visiting the *Netscape* website daily.

Some computer experts suggested that Andreessen's *Netscape* was like David going up against the Goliath of Bill Gates's Microsoft. When *Netscape* was bought out by AOL in the late 1990s, Andreessen stayed with AOL for a few months then quit. Now, in the 21st century, he has ventured out on his own again, seeking new challenges in the world of technology.

MARC ANDREESSEN'S taming of the Internet demonstrated powerful problem-solving skills.

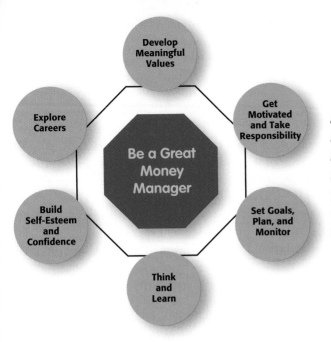

Develop Meaningful Values

Explore Careers

Get Motivated and Take Responsibility

Be a Great Money Manager

Build Self-Esteem and Confidence

Set Goals, Plan, and Monitor

Think and Learn

As you read, think about the "Six Strategies for Success" listed to the left and how this chapter can help you maximize success in these important areas For example, when you take control of your finances, you not only give yourself peace of mind freeing you up to focus on your academic goals, but you lay the foundation for a financially successful future.

Take Control of Your Finances

Money is a concern for many college students. In a recent national survey of first-year college students, more than half were concerned about financing college and one in five students had major concerns (Sax & others, 2000). Nothing will disconnect you from college faster than running out of money. How do people get into debt? They simply spend more money than they have.

Look to the Future

You've probably already thought about your earning potential after graduation. Having your degree will give you the opportunity to get a good-paying job, most likely making more money than you ever have before. But what are you going to do with your money? What will you spend it on? How much will you save? Will you have significant debts? Certainly you can't answer all of these questions now, but your values regarding money will help guide you in your planning. Self-Assessment 1 "Where Does the Money Rank?" on page 367 can help you identify and prioritize these values.

Your Financial Values Remember from Chapter 1 that being aware of what's important to you is the foundation that guides your motivation and directs your goals. You may also realize that while your fundamental values will remain the same, your financial circumstances will not. Depending on whether you have more or less money to work with, your opportunities for experiencing life as you value it, may change. Thus you not only want to consider how to be financially savvy now, but for the future. To explore how you might need and want to spend your money over the next several years, complete the Self-Assessment "Your Future Financial Focus" on your CD-ROM. Developing the habit of using your values to guide your financial plans will make you a better money manager, which could mean the difference between financial security and difficulty.

Where to Start As you come to understand the significance money has in your life and learn ways in which to manage it, keep in mind that this is only the beginning. For many

> *You cannot prevent the birds of sorrow from flying over your head, but you can prevent them from building nests in your hair.*
> —Chinese Proverb

"And this is Daniel, who is busy working toward his degree in money."

Career Connections

Jose had always been careful with his money. His mom worked two jobs to make ends meet and he had chipped in whatever he could from part-time and summer jobs for as long as he could remember. College was a stretch, but with loans and a part-time job at the local pub he was making it work. His roommate was a different story. Alan never seemed to worry about money, eating out, buying expensive computer and stereo equipment, and practically living on his cell phone, until the day his credit card was rejected and he realized he had overdrawn his bank account. How could this have happened?

Alan panicked, having no idea how to deal with his debt. Jose on the other hand, had lots of good ideas. He helped Alan pick up some shifts at the bar where he worked and arrange a plan to pay off his bank and credit card company in small monthly installments that would leave enough to live on—in a much less luxurious manner. This experience and his business major led Jose to consider a career in financial planning. He researched internships at the career counseling office and landed a position with Morgan Stanley for the summer. It was mainly clerical, but allowed him to continue bartending at night and get his foot in the door toward a full-time position after graduation.

Meanwhile, Alan's experience made him realize the importance of finding a career that would allow for the standard of living he preferred, and avoiding the debt problems he encountered in college. It was a good lesson to learn now while his debt was manageable, rather than later when it could more negatively impact his long-term credit history.

students, college marks the start of financial independence and the first time they are faced with their own decisions regarding money. Hopefully you came prepared to take on this responsibility. Using the Journal activity "The Money in My Past" on page 370, think back to the money lessons you learned at home. This will help you identify what you still need to learn about basic money management.

It also is important to think about your future. Your career exploration has probably included consideration of potential salaries. This may motivate you in the pursuit of your degree, but it can also serve as a motivator for becoming financially savvy. If you can't manage your money now, it is not likely you'll do any better when you have more to spend. As you work toward the goal of earning your degree, you also should work toward a financial goal for after graduation as well. Take some time to explore your vision of financial success with the Journal activity "Define Financial Success" on page 371.

One other future issue that requires consideration is postgraduation debt. If you take advantage of any loans during your college years, you will be expected to begin paying them back after graduation. Being aware that you will have to incorporate this into your financial planning can help direct your budgeting efforts now.

Recognize Income and Acknowledge Expenses

The place to start when managing money is to create a budget—a record of how much is coming in versus how much is going out.

Count It All Most of your income is obvious, such as work paychecks and family money or other sources. But be sure not to overlook additional resources such as predictable special occasion checks, money from selling textbooks back at the end of the semester, and additional income from summer jobs. Accurately predicting your annual income stream is a very important aspect of financial planning.

Know Where It Goes Some expenses are easy to anticipate and track. Regular payments for goods and services such as rent, car payments, and your cable bill generally have concrete records for easy reference and tallying. These are considered fixed expenses because the amount is fairly predictable (or "fixed") each month.

Anticipating and tracking variable expenses is more difficult. For example, "entertainment" costs such as attending a rock concert, going out to dinner with friends, or buying a CD are more elusive and vary from month to month. You may experience a month or two in which you do more socializing and go out to various functions quite a bit. When school demands increase, you may find yourself eating at home and watching television for an occasional diversion. Check out On Target Tips, "Following the Money Trail," for ideas on how to keep track of multiple and varied expenditures.

Be Honest with Yourself The important thing when managing money is to begin by acknowledging all the ways in which you spend it, and how much you spend. Not owning up to your bad money habits will result in nagging feelings of guilt, frustration, and the sense you are doing less than your best. Recognizing your spending tendencies will enable you to better understand where your money is going and where it will likely go in the future. It will also enable you to recognize your power in taking control of the situation. Take Self-Assessment 2 "Are You a Compulsive Spender?" on page 368 to see if you show signs of problematic spending.

Budget for Success

Once you have identified all your sources of income and are prepared to acknowledge your expenses, you can create a budget. This is not simply a static presentation of income versus expenses, but rather a *tool* for assessing where you stand financially. More important, it can help you recognize where you need to make changes in order to meet your monetary goals. For example, if you discover a great deal of your money is going toward eating out, you can plan to start eating in more often. Or, if you are spending money regularly to repair your car, you might decide to look into riding the bus or joining a car pool. In an extreme case of costly car maintenance, it may be worthwhile to put your money into a newer, more reliable vehicle.

Financial success is defined differently depending on who is defining it. In college, however, financial success should be marked by your ability to take the course load you want, have enough time to study and do well in your classes, and have as little stress stemming from money worries as possible. In Self-Assessment 3 "Your Money and You," on page 369, you can assess your current financial functioning and whether or not you should be concerned. Also see On-Target Tips, Regulate Your Phone Use, for good suggestions on cutting down a major expense area for many college students.

Choosing a Budget Time Frame There are many ways to approach budgeting. One consideration is the time frame of the budget. Do you want to manage your money on a monthly basis, look ahead six months, or plan for an entire year? When you first begin to make a budget or when you have a major financial change in your life, you may want to work on a monthly basis. This will enable you to focus in more closely on the short-term flow of your money and make adjustments accordingly. Once you've established a routine income and expense cycle, setting goals and planning for longer periods may be more efficient.

The Proactive Budget You also can choose to approach budgeting proactively or reactively. Proactive budgeting involves anticipating your upcoming expenses and making sure they do not exceed your projected income. In this case, you set limits on what you will spend in each expense category in order to stay within your budget.

The Reactive Budget Reactive budgeting involves looking back at what you have earned and what you have spent over a period of time. You already know whether your expenses exceed your income and you can see exactly where your money went. You can

ON TARGET TIPS

Following the Money Trail

A budget is only useful if it is accurate. Keeping track of all that you spend can be challenging, particularly when you are spending cash. Here are a few suggestions to help you identify where your money is going.

- **Use your checkbook register.** When depositing money and writing checks, make it a habit to immediately record the date and transaction in the register.
- **Record the source of deposit.** When making a deposit, note in your checkbook register the source of the income, such as scholarship money, work paycheck, allowance from parents, and so on.
- **Categorize check purchases.** Along with the amount spent and where, record in your checkbook register the *type* of expense, such as food, entertainment, toiletries, gifts, and so on.
- **Keep ATM receipts.** After making a cash withdrawal from an ATM, save the receipt in your wallet or purse and transfer it to a special envelope at home. Use the receipts to identify cash flow from your account.
- **Keep a receipt envelope in your purse or car.** When spending cash for *anything,* keep your receipts. Make it easy by keeping an envelope handy so that you can collect them in one place to use later when budgeting.
- **Note expense category on receipts.** Not all receipts clearly identify the purchases. Quickly jot down what kind of expense it was prior to filing it in your envelope.
- **Keep a categorized file.** Once you get a few minutes at home, transfer the receipts you've collected to an accordian file labeled with your expense categories.
- **File all bills.** When you receive any kind of bill in the mail from utilities to credit cards, file the statements for future reference.

When you are ready to do your budget, you will find you have clear records of all of your income and, particularly, all of your expenses. Keeping receipts allows you to account for cash purchases, which are hardest to track.

The person who doesn't know where his next dollar is coming from usually doesn't know where his last dollar went.

—Anonymous

Regulate Your Phone Use

If you have friends and family who live far away, chances are your phone bill is quite large. Also, it is likely to be a variable expense—different from month to month and difficult to budget. There are ways to both limit long-distance costs *and* establish your phone bill as a fixed expense.

Prepaid phone cards are available for purchase in numerous drug and grocery stores.

- Phone cards can cost as little as $1 or as much as $50 and higher.
- Each price has a set amount of calling minutes.
- Phone cards offer some of the cheapest phone charges per minute available.
- Consider buying one card per month for your long distance calls. When you have used up the time, no more calls from your end until the next month.

Cell phones are continuing to grow in popularity, thus a variety of monthly plans are available.

- Choose a plan which has a set monthly charge that is within your budget.
- Shop around for the best deal, offering the most free minutes per monthly charge.
- If you find a good deal, consider using a cell phone exclusively and eliminating the monthly payment for a land line.
- Be sure to find out if long-distance calls are included in the free minutes or if they involve an additional charge.
- Cell phones inform you of the length of each call. Use this to keep track of your free minutes used.
- If you can't get a good deal with free long-distance calls, reconsider whether or not you really need a cell phone. Don't have one simply to be trendy or slightly easier to reach if it is not in your budget.

> *Money talks . . . but all mine ever says is good-bye.*
> —Anonymous

then decide what to do with any extra money (save, invest, add it to next month's income) or decide how to offset a negative balance (where to cut back in next month's expenditures). Effective budgeting will actually involve a combination of both planning ahead and looking back. The most important task is recognizing your spending limit and sticking to it!

Your Debt-to-Income Ratio An important figure to be aware of is your debt-to-income ratio. This number can give you an idea of whether you should be concerned about your level of expenditures relative to your level of income. Figure 12.1 provides an example of an actual budget you can use to practice what you have learned. It also demonstrates how to calculate your debt-to-income ratio, and indicates what each result means. Take some time to evaluate your current budget and figure your debt-to-income percentage to have a greater awareness of your risk for future debt.

Plan to Save

In addition to your monthly expenses, you should budget to save at least a little money each month. There will be both planned and unplanned reasons for you to use money from savings. When you commit to saving money regularly, you will be better equipped to deal with unforseen circumstances, as well as enable yourself to enjoy unexpected opportunities in the future. In addition, starting good habits about saving now will produce satisfying long-term gains because your savings will have a longer time frame in which to accrue interest.

Expect Emergencies Everyone encounters unexpected events that involve unanticipated expenditures. Given the inevitability of such emergencies, it is important for you to figure out, in advance, how you plan to deal with them. Keep in mind that the last concert of your favorite rock group's "Farewell Tour" may feel like an unexpected must, but you may be the only one who considers it an emergency. Is being the only one not going on the spring break road trip due to lack of funds an emergency? Probably not. These kinds of expenses should serve as a motivator for you to establish a savings plan, but don't plan to use "emergency" funds. The Journal activity "In Case of Emergency" on page 370 will help you prepare in advance for unexpected expenditures.

Anticipate Enjoyment One wise move toward becoming a great money manager is identifying something you want in the future and taking steps to afford it. Whether you want to take your date to the fanciest restaurant in town, sign up to study abroad, or own a new car, putting money away in order to accomplish personal goals shows signs of a mature financial thinker. It also puts a positive spin on saving. When you have enjoyable experiences to look forward to, it is much easier to allot money for savings.

Of course, don't plan on using all of your savings at once—you still need to have an emergency reserve. However, if you can anticipate the cost of your future goals, you can determine how long it will take to reach them based on how much you budget for savings each month. You may even be surprised at what you are willing to cut back on in order to reach your goal sooner!

FIGURE 12.1 **My Monthly Budget**

Fill in your budget plan for the next month in the **Planning** column. Then monitor your income and expenses in the next month. A good monitoring strategy is to keep track of all your expenses in a small notebook each day. Keep a running tab of all your expenses for the next month. At the end of the month, write down your actual income and expenses in the **Actual** column.

	Planning	Actual
Income and expenses for the next month		
Family	$ _____	$ _____
Savings	$ _____	$ _____
Financial Aid	$ _____	$ _____
Work	$ _____	$ _____
Total Income for the next month:	$ _____	$ _____
Fixed expenses for the next month		
Tuition and fees	$ _____	$ _____
Books	$ _____	$ _____
Supplies	$ _____	$ _____
Housing	$ _____	$ _____
Child Care	$ _____	$ _____
Total fixed expenses for the next month:	$ _____	$ _____
Variable expenses for the next month		
Food (at home or prepaid at university cafeteria)	$ _____	$ _____
Food (snacks, lunches, and other meals out)	$ _____	$ _____
Transportation	$ _____	$ _____
Utilities	$ _____	$ _____
Clothing	$ _____	$ _____
Laundry/dry cleaning	$ _____	$ _____
Entertainment	$ _____	$ _____
Hair care/beauty treatments	$ _____	$ _____
Miscellaneous	$ _____	$ _____
Total variable expenses for the next month:	$ _____	$ _____

Add up your total fixed and variable monthly expenses, then subtract this total from your total monthly income. This determines whether your balance at the end of the next month will be positive or negative.

How to Calculate Your Debt-to-Income Ratio

Step One

Add up your total monthly expenditures:

- Rent — $150.00
- Car Payment — $165.00
- Insurance — $105.00
- Credit Card — $ 80.00

Total Monthly Payments: $500.00

Step Two

Divide the total by your income*

$$\frac{\$500.00}{\$2500.00} = 20\%$$

Result

Under 15%	Relax
15–20%	Be cautious
Over 20%	Danger

* Use net pay, after taxes, for income from work paychecks.

If an emergency occurs, are you financially prepared for it? Make a plan now in case you find yourself facing unexpected expenses.

© Owaki-Kulla/CORBIS

Learn Ways to Save Saving money is all about making choices. How you choose to spend your money ultimately determines how much you have to save. While it is often a difficult process, saving plays a big role in successful financial planning. There are things you can do on a large scale to save money, such as having additional roommates to share the rent, foregoing cable television, and using public transportation or a bike instead of having a car. These small daily sacrifices will lead to a huge payoff in the future. Think about what you might be willing to give up in order to save money by completing the Journal activity "Simplifying My Life" on page 370.

Smaller-scale options for saving money abound. At first glance such things as clipping coupons and shopping at discount stores may seem trivial, but the money you save can add up quickly. Check out On-Target Tips, "Beyond Coupons," for many great ideas to get you started. Be an entrepreneur. Similar to the strategies employed by Marc Andreesen, there may be some opportunities that you can exploit to expand available funds. For example, faculty may recruit "house sitters" for specific periods of time or look for competent students to perform child care. Or you may look to other avenues to be entrepreneurial. For example, some clever college students have established a thriving cookie delivery business that delivers treats to studying students as late as 3 A.M. Consider how you might be able to solve some needs of your peers on a larger scale and you may be able to generate some interesting opportunities. Next, consider how your entrepreneurial success might shape your future by completing the Journal activity "My Money Making Dream" on page 371.

ON TARGET TIPS

Beyond Coupons

Clipping coupons is a great way to save money, but there are many other savings opportunities that are available to students. To help you save money, consider the following:

- **Seek out and take advantage of good deals.**
  - Pay attention to on-campus events offering free food and entertainment.
  - Look in the local newspaper for restaurants offering "two-for-one" dinners or student bargain meals. Movie theaters may also have discounted movie times or student discounts.
  - Take advantage of campus resources that are free: tutoring, computer labs with printers, seminars on job opportunities on campus.
  - For leisure reading, don't forget about the campus or public library. Read their books, magazines, and newspapers instead of buying them yourself. They also offer computer use and Internet access if campus facilities are busy or servers are down.
  - Use the college gym rather than joining a health club.
  - Use grocery store coupons to stock up on easy to make meals, rather than ordering out. All of those pizzas add up.

- **Create a "Savings File."** Coupons and fliers for discounts and bargains are useless if you forget about them.
  - Keep an accordian envelope labeled with categories, such as "food," "drug store," "school supplies," "entertainment," and so on.
  - Keep the file in a highly visible, easily accessible place in your dorm or apartment.
  - When you find coupons or receive fliers, file them, highlighting the expiration date.
  - Discard those that have expired so that your file doesn't overflow and become neglected.
  - Check the file each time you're ready to walk out the door.

- **Other sources of discounts:**
  - Your campus newspaper
  - Fliers posted around the dorm or the student union
  - Signs posted on stores, theaters, and restaurants
  - Entertainment coupon books (some must be purchased, but it might be worthwhile to go in on one with your friends or roommates)

Find the Right Place for Your Money

Most people don't hide their money under their mattresses anymore. With so many financial institutions available for you to choose from, it is important to be aware of what they offer and how they work.

Open a Bank Account

The first step in opening a bank account is to research the various banks in your area. Banks vary widely in the services they provide and the deals that they offer. Most banks have a website so that you may gather the information online. Some will even enable you to apply for an account online, without having to visit the actual bank. Specifically check for student banking services. There are often reduced and waived fees for student accounts, and the minimum amount required to open the account, as well as the minimum daily balance, may be significantly lower for students. See On Target Tips, "Banking Basics," for a list of things you should inquire about before opening an account.

Choose Checking, Savings, or Both   The two primary types of bank accounts are checking and savings accounts. Checking accounts enable you to draw money regularly through the use of checks. One of the primary issues you need to research prior to choosing a bank and opening a checking account are the fees. There can be monthly maintenance fees, a charge for your checks, and a fee for processing each check you write. Some banks do waive some or all of these fees if you open a saving account in addition to your checking account, or if you are a student.

A savings account exists for the primary purpose of putting money in, and rarely, if ever, taking it out. Establishing a savings account gives you a safe place to put away money where you won't be tempted to touch it. It can also earn a small amount of interest and grow over time.

Money market accounts are a more sophisticated type of savings account. You will have to keep a higher balance, but some of these accounts offer the benefit of overdraft protection. This means that should you write more checks than you have money for in your checking account, the bank will cover it without charging you a fee or returning the check to the recipient.

Whichever type of account you choose to open, there is likely to be a minimum initial amount required for deposit. This is typically lower for checking accounts, with some student accounts requiring as little as a $10 to $25 deposit. Savings accounts tend to require at least a $100 initial deposit and money market accounts usually require around $1,000. You should plan to bring cash, a check, or a money order with you when you go to open your accounts.

Take Advantage of Additional Services   It is very common for banks to offer additional services to their customers. Most accounts entitle you to an ATM (automatic teller machine) card, which enables you to withdraw cash at numerous locations. Any branch of your bank will have one, as will branches of other banks. ATMs also are located in grocery stores, convenience stores, some movie theaters, and even fast food restaurants! You

> *Finance is the art of passing currency hand to hand until it disappears.*
> —Robert W. Sarnoff
> 20th-Century American businessman

ON TARGET TIPS

Banking Basics

When opening a bank account of any kind, inquire about the following:

- Is there a minimum amount required to open the account?
- Must you keep a minimum balance in the account? If so, what are the penalties for going below the minimum balance?
- Do they offer any special deals for college students?
- What do they charge for a box of checks?
- What is their fee for processing each check you write?
- What happens if you bounce a check? Do they cover it and charge you a fee or do they return it to whom it was written?
- Do they offer an ATM card? What are the fees for using it at your bank and its branches? What is your bank's fee for using it at other bank's ATMs?
- Do they offer a debit card? What fees and conditions apply?
- Do they offer online banking? Can you conduct transactions or just check your balance?

want to inquire about the fees associated with making withdrawals, however. In some cases, banks will charge you to take out cash, if not from their branch locations, at other banks and additional locations. On top of your bank fees, you may be charged a fee from the location of the ATM as well. Research this before you open your account, as some banks offer free ATM use for students.

Another option is a debit card, sometimes called a "check card." It looks like a credit card, but functions like a check. When you make a purchase, the amount is automatically deducted from your checking account. Some check cards double as an ATM card. The benefits of a debit or check card include the fact that they offer a safer means to make purchases than carrying around lots of cash. They also may be used for automatic bill payment, which allows you simply to have your monthly bills deducted from your checking account automatically.

The drawback of a check card is that you need to be very diligent in recording your purchases and cash withdrawals as you make them. These items will be noted on your bank statement, but if you don't keep track of how much is deducted on a regular basis, you may spend more money than you have in your account.

Manage Your Accounts

Once you've placed your money in the bank, it is important that you remain organized in your records and stay on top of managing where the money goes.

Balance Your Checkbook A major benefit of having a checking account is that it makes keeping track of your money quite easy. With each checkbook comes a check register—a table for you to fill in all of your deposits and expenditures. Get in the habit of using your check register at the time you make deposits and write checks. Don't wait to record the information when you get home, since you are quite likely to forget. As soon as you sign and hand over a check, note the date, amount, recipient, and purchase in your register. Keeping a current record will enable you to always know how much money is available to you in your account.

Once a month you will receive a statement from your financial institution. It will note any deposits with the date and amount, along with a list of checks, and the date you wrote them, to whom, and for how much. Also included will be any fees you've incurred or payment for new checks, as well as ATM withdrawals and payments with your check card. You can then reconcile this information with your check register.

The total amount indicated in your register should match with that shown on your statement, with the exception of outstanding checks. Sometimes you will have written checks that are not listed on your bank statement. This is because either you wrote them after the ending date on your statement (too late for the bank to include them on that month's record), or the recipient of the check has not yet cashed it— (it is still *outstanding*). Each item on your statement is listed by the check number; thus, you can go through your register and mark off those checks that have cleared (been cashed and the funds taken from your account).

Also, be sure and note which deposits have been recorded by the bank on your statement. If you just put money into your account, it, too, will not be reflected on your statement.

© Photodisc/Getty Images

Although it can be tedious, it's important to reconcile your checkbook records with your bank statement to maximize financial security.

As you note the items shown on your statement in your register, you can then add the outstanding deposits and checks to the total to know exactly how much money exists in your account.

Remember, banks make mistakes! This is why it is crucial that you keep careful records of your income and expenditures. If you can't seem to reconcile your account after a couple of tries, call to speak with someone at your bank. If you don't resolve discrepancies as soon as you discover them, you are at risk for bouncing checks and being overdrawn.

Keeping Track of Savings If you are serious about saving, you will want to open a separate savings account. This way, you will be less tempted to dip into that money for regular monthly expenses. The best plan for saving is to commit to doing it on a regular basis. Some banks even offer the option of having a certain dollar amount automatically transferred from your checking account to your savings account each month. As it is deducted monthly from checking, you simply note it in your budget and it becomes part of your financial plan. And, because you don't have to make the effort to deposit it each month, you are more likely to see your savings grow.

Just like your checking account, you will note transactions in your savings account in a register. (Hopefully your withdrawals are few and far between.) Your savings account statements will list both deposits and withdrawals along with any interest you have earned. Most savings accounts accrue interest. The rate is generally fairly low but the income is there nevertheless. Be sure and note it in your register.

Invest for the Future If you have some substantial savings and would like the opportunity for your money to actually grow beyond your monthly deposits, consider investing it. There are numerous investment options and certain ones, such as mutual funds, can enable a small regular investment in savings to yield dramatic results over a long period of time. For example, a $100 per month investment started in 1982 is now worth approximately $200,000! A 20-year investment of $100 each month would yield $113,000 at the end of that period. Thirty years of only $100 per month can net you $416,000, and if you continue with that simple investment until retirement in 40 years, you will have earned almost $900,000! (This is based on investments in the Dow Jones Industrial since 1962.)

These are investments designed for long-term financial gain. If you would like to get a head start on saving for a house, starting your own business, or early retirement, consider contacting a financial planner to find out what it takes.

Explore Financial Resources

Many of you have been working closely with your parents to structure your financial aid package. Others may know you are on financial aid, but don't know anything about it. Still others may feel you don't need to worry about financial planning because your family pays for everything. Whatever your situation, it makes good financial sense to research your financial aid opportunities. There are many types of financial aid; you simply need to know where to look and what to look for. The best place to start is at your campus' financial aid office. The Journal activity "It Can't Hurt" on page 371 will get you thinking about how financial aid might benefit you and what steps you can take to obtain some extra money.

Before you go, make an appointment to meet with one of the staff financial aid advisors. Don't consider it a one-time visit. Map out a plan for funding your education in its entirety and expect to meet with your financial aid advisor prior to each semester. By

Work for the fun of it, and the money will arrive someday.

—Ronnie Milsap
Contemporary American
musician

FIGURE 12.2 **Relation of Hours Worked Per Week in College to Grades**

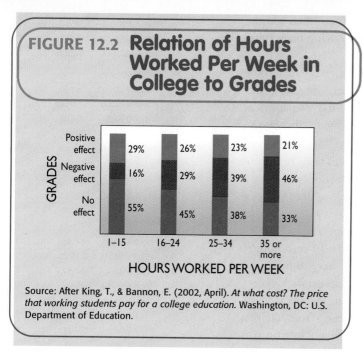

Source: After King, T., & Bannon, E. (2002, April). *At what cost? The price that working students pay for a college education.* Washington, DC: U.S. Department of Education.

developing this relationship, your advisor will be more likely to keep abreast of your situation and alert you to any new options that arise, and you can feel good knowing someone is always working on your behalf.

Get a Job

A recent national study found that 74 percent of full-time college students worked while attending college (King & Bannon, 2002), and 84 percent of those students said that they work simply to meet college expenses. In that same national survey, students who worked more than 25 hours a week said that it interfered with their academic achievement (King & Bannon, 2002). Sixty-three percent of those students, however, reported having no choice but to work that much in order to pay for their education (see Figure 12.2).

It's true that it takes a lot of money to get a college education, but it also takes a lot of studying and hard work. Although many students find it necessary to work in order to pay for college, that same effort to earn the required fees may hinder one's progress toward actually earning the degree itself.

This can lead to very difficult and frustrating circumstances. Students who work long hours are more at risk for failing and dropping courses, at which point it is too late to get their money back. In addition to having lost those fees, they will most likely have to register—and pay for—those courses *again* in order to graduate. Thus, although working more hours earns you more money, you actually end up losing both money and time when work interferes with your success in school.

It makes much more sense to work less and pass your courses the first time around. However, if working means the difference between staying in school and dropping out completely, by all means, get a job. There are many options available for you to pursue, so take the time to investigate what will work best with your needs and goals. See On-Target Tips, "Work and School: Finding a Balance," for things to consider when working during college.

Investigate Work-Study Programs and Internships Work-study programs offer opportunities to work either on campus or in the community, earning at least minimum wage or more depending on the kind of work and required skills for the job. These programs are funded by either the federal government, your academic institution or both, and are based on financial need. Your income is monthly, paid *after* work is completed, and the number of hours you work each week is limited, in recognition of the fact that substantial time is required for schoolwork in order for you to be successful.

Work-study programs focus on employing students either in community service positions or on campus, often in areas related to your course of study. Students who work on campus have the opportunity to become more connected with school, as they frequently see and interact with faculty and staff, meet more peers, and sometimes have additional access to campus resources. They also benefit from having no commute time between going to class and going to work.

You can find out about work-study positions through your campus financial aid office or career services center. If you do not qualify for work-study, there still may be part-time employment opportunities on campus. Check career services, the campus newspaper, or your institution's website for listings.

Work and School: Finding a Balance

If you need or choose to work during your college career, it is important to strike a balance between time spent at your job and the necessary commitment to succeed academically.

Find the Right Job

- Try to get a part-time job on campus. This way you can be close to your classes, obtain easy access to on-campus resources, and have regular contact with faculty, staff, and peers.
- Seek out a job that allows flexibility in scheduling to work around times of greater academic demands.
- Submit your midterm and final exam dates along with other important due dates to your employer as soon as possible.
- Talk to people on and around campus to find an employer who is sympathetic to students' needs and offers flexible scheduling.
- Look for a job in which you have periods of time for reading and studying, such as baby-sitting, manning a switchboard, and so on; or market your skills and be your own boss.

Master Time Management

- Get your monthly work schedule as soon as possible, then plan your classes and study time around work times. Be sure and schedule some down time for rest and leisure activities.
- Break down assignments, papers, and studying into small tasks to do between classes, breaks at work, and shorter periods of time available at home.
- Make the best use of your time at school. If classes are spread out, use the time in between to review, read, study, visit the library, or work in the computer lab.
- Use your commute time between home, school, and work to listen to recordings of lectures or notes you've put on tape.
- If you must have a heavier workload, take fewer classes and get good grades.

Choose the Right Classes

- Talk to other students or research instructor evaluations to find courses that fit your learning needs. For example, classes that have fewer regular assignment demands, or those offering more frequent, but less intensive exams; or more reading as opposed to writing.
- Identify professors who understand about students who work and are willing to be flexible with assignment deadlines and demands.

If you have declared a major, you may want to find out if there are any paying internships or coops available in your related field. Often local companies will hire students on a part-time basis to help them learn about their future career, and to connect the company with potential future employees. Internships can be a great choice of jobs, not only due to the valuable experience that you will gain working in your chosen field, but because company employers are often sensitive to the needs of students. Because they want you to do well in school, they are likely to work around exam and paper due dates, midterms and finals. Summer internships are also a great opportunity to work more hours, gain experience, and make more money to put away for the upcoming semester. You will learn more about internships and coop opportunities in the next chapter.

Look for Jobs with Light Work Loads Some jobs require that you be physically present, but they don't necessarily involve constant effort, and may allow time to do some schoolwork. If you enjoy children, you might consider offering your services as a baby-sitter or part-time nanny. Although child care involves a high degree of responsibility and attentiveness to the children, they may nap or play in their rooms by themselves, giving you the chance to read, review, or outline ideas for a paper.

© Mo Wilson/Photofusion Picture Library/Alamy

Choose a job that allows flexibility in scheduling to accommodate periods in the semester where your academic load will be heavy.

Working a switchboard or in the library reference room also may provide the same study opportunities. Whereas your focus on the responsibilities of your work must be first and foremost, some jobs offer limited "breaks" from the flow of demands, freeing you up to spend some time on school tasks.

Be Your Own Boss If you have a talent to share with others, use it to your advantage to make money. If you play a musical instrument, competitive tennis, or have an artistic flair, consider giving private lessons. You may be an excellent typist or have a great deal of computer know-how. These are also skills that are highly in demand.

If you wish to pursue your own "business," make sure you research competitive fees for your time and expertise (for example, are music lessons going for $10 or $20 an hour? Do typists charge by the page or the hour?). You will also need to advertise. It doesn't require a great deal of money to do this, and in many cases you can do it for free. Check out the local bargain newspaper, campus newspaper, or student union bulletin boards to find out what it takes to present your service. You may even consider creating a website highlighting your skills, work availability, and fees. Not only can you make good money from your own knowledge and skills, but when you are your own boss, you can pick and choose when and how much you work.

Be Assertive in Seeking Your Ideal Job Jobs will not just come to you; you must seek them out, especially if you are looking for something different from traditional food service or retail store employment. Those jobs are popular, but may not allow you the freedom and time to succeed in school. Many jobs, and particularly internships, are not advertised publicly.

Internships are often secured through speaking with professors in your major and declaring your need and interest. Job availability around campus may simply travel by word of mouth, so if you are interested, talk to people in different positions in various departments. If you have other ideas of where you might like to work, pick up the phone and call or visit the location in person. You will learn more about the power of networking in Chapter 13.

Communicate your sincerity in finding a job that fits with your schedule as a student. Often employers respect and appreciate students, and feel they are responsible and reliable workers. Use your motivation to find a balance between earning the money you need and doing well in school to discover and land the right job for you.

Pursue Financial Aid

Numerous types of financial aid exist for students of all nationalities, religions, majors, ages, and talents. There is aid money specifically designated for women, disabled students, international students, students planning to attend law school, business school, and graduate school, even gay and lesbian students. Understanding the different options available is important in order for you to find the right match for you.

Scholarships Scholarships are a form of *gift aid*—monetary awards that the student does not need to pay back. Money for scholarships can be provided by any number of groups, organizations, or schools. They are usually awarded on the basis of academic merit or particular talent or skill, such as athletics or music, but not always. Some take into account financial need, others do not. Many are awarded to the most qualified students meeting certain eligibility requirements, such as membership in a particular organization (Future Business Leaders of America, Debate Club, Girl Scouts/Boy Scouts), participation in a group (church, band, thespians), or children of parents who work for a certain business or are members of a civic group (Kiwanis, Shriners).

Scholarships may be awarded on a one-time basis, or may be available for renewal each semester based on performance in school and continued participation in a designated group or major. The application process may be highly involved with many requiring students to write an essay about themselves, obtaining letters of recommendation, and even going through a personal interview. Although somewhat time-consuming, putting together scholarship applications can be very rewarding. See On Target Tips, "Be Scholarship Savvy," for pointers on putting together a winning scholarship application. Keep in mind that even if you don't receive a scholarship the first time you apply, you may be chosen the next time around. Be persistent.

Grants Another form of gift aid is grants. Unlike many scholarships, grants are awarded on the basis of financial need. The most common grant is the Federal Pell Grant, and the amount available to students each year is based on the funding allotted by Congress. For example, the awards for 2002–2003 range from $400 to $4,000.

The amount given to each student is determined by a combination of factors including whether the student is full-time or part-time (both are eligible for aid), the cost of attending school, and how much money the student's family is able to contribute to his or her education. The government uses a specific formula to calculate this figure, based on information the student provides in the *Free Application for Federal Student Aid* (FAFSA). There are no academic requirements or GPA minimums necessary to receive a Pell Grant; however, certain schools are not considered eligible.

For students with exceptional financial need (as determined by the federal government's lowest Expected Family Contribution calculation) there is the *Federal Supplemental Education Opportunity Grant* (FSEOG). Students awarded a Federal Pell Grant have priority to receive an FSEOG but are not guaranteed the aid. Contributing factors in determining funding from this grant are the level of need, funding and financial aid policies of the school the student attends, and the date the student applies for the grant. Applications and information regarding both grants can be found in your institution's financial aid office.

ON TARGET TIPS — Be Scholarship Savvy

- **Plan ahead.** The scholarship application process can take some time, especially if you apply for more than one, and put the effort into creating an effective set of application materials. Don't rush through your applications—you may pay the price—literally!

- **Research.** There are more scholarships available than most students are aware. Spending time investigating a variety of scholarship websites and publications will increase your chances of finding a list of scholarships that are a good match for you.

- **Organize.** Scholarship applications have numerous parts and requirements for documents. Create a separate folder for each application, attach a checklist of steps required, and file by the deadline date.

- **Prepare to supply:**
  Transcript
  Standardized test scores
  Financial aid forms such as the FAFSA
  Parents' financial information, including tax returns
  One or more essays
  One or more letters of recommendation
  Proof of eligibility (such as group membership credentials)

- **Follow instructions.** One extremely easy way for scholarship screeners to eliminate potential recipients is to discover errors in their application. Be honest in your responses and make sure that you are actually eligible. Include all required documents but no additional items. Also follow the specified length requirements for any essays. Do not exceed them as more is *not* better in scholarship applications.

- **Proofread.** All applications should be completed in ink or typed. Regardless of using your computer's *spell check* option, visually proofread your answers and essays to insure accurate presentation of information.

- **Make copies.** Prior to sending in your application, make a copy of the completed application, along with any accompanying documents, essays, and letters.

- **Beat the deadline.** If at all possible, send your application in well ahead of the deadline. It will not make you more eligible for the scholarship, but you are assured that it will make it there on time. Consider sending it by certified mail.

- **Follow-up.** After allowing ample time for your application to arrive at its destination, follow up with a phone call to confirm its receipt. Also consider writing a thank-you note for considering you as a scholarship recipient.

Loans In addition to gift aid, loans are available to help pay for your college education. The largest source of loan money comes from the federal government. Government loans are very appealing because they offer many ideal conditions for borrowing money. The interest rates are low, there are less stringent credit requirements, and repayment may be deferred, and/or spread over a longer period of time.

The first step in acquiring a federal loan is to fill out a FAFSA form, mentioned in the previous section. As is stated in its name, obtaining the form and submitting it is *free*, and it can even be done on the Internet. States and schools also may use the information on your FAFSA form to determine eligibility for other aid programs such as grants and scholarships. The FAFSA requires that students and their parents provide extensive information on family occupations and income, as well as tax return materials. An online copy of the FAFSA can be obtained at www.fafsa.ed.gov and information to help you fill out the form along with frequently asked questions can be found at <http://www.ed.gov/studentaid>.

The Stafford Loan is the name of the federal loan for students and takes two forms. The *Federal Family Education Loan Program* (FFELP) involves obtaining the loan through private lenders, but with a guarantee against default by the federal government. The *Federal Direct Student Loan Program* (FDSLP) involves loans provided directly from the government, but administered by "Direct Lending Schools," which give the money directly to students and their parents. A Stafford Loan may be either subsidized or unsubsidized.

The former involves the government paying the interest for the duration of your time in school, and requires demonstration of financial need. Unsubsidized Stafford Loans require you to pay the interest; however, they allow you to defer payments until after graduation. Financial need is not a qualifying factor in obtaining an unsubsidized loan, but the amount you may borrow will vary depending on whether you are still a dependent of your parents or are financially independent.

The Perkins Loan is designated for students with exceptional financial need. It is a campus-based program, thus the amount awarded is determined by your school's financial aid office. Perkins Loans have extremely favorable terms if you qualify. They are subsidized by the federal government while you are in school, as well as during a nine-month grace period; the interest rate is then 5 percent and they allow you 10 years to repay them. Perkins Loans also may be used to supplement other loan-based income that does not completely meet your financial needs.

Another loan option is the PLUS program (*Parental Loans for Undergraduate Students*) which is federally sponsored and enables parents to borrow up to the full cost of their child's education (less the amount of other aid received). Private loans are also available through banks, credit unions, and savings and loans. The conditions of eligibility, interest, and repayment for private loans vary by institution, so you need to research these carefully before pursuing any particular one.

Under certain circumstances, the federal government may cancel all or part of your loan repayment. Known as *loan forgiveness programs*, participation in AmeriCorps, Peace Corps, VISTA (Volunteers in Service to America), the National Defense Education Act, and others, will qualify you for partial or complete loan forgiveness. To find out more about these programs and the financial potential they offer, talk with a financial aid advisor, or contact each organization directly.

Understand Credit

> *The surest way to establish your credit is to work yourself into the position of not needing any.*
>
> —Maurice Switzer
> 20th-century Canadian journalist

Our society provides tremendous opportunities for spending money that we don't have. With credit, we can buy a house, a car, go shopping, and even get an education. Credit can be a wonderful option when used correctly, but it also can be the cause of serious, long-lasting problems if abused and misunderstood. When weighing your financial options, you need to consider credit carefully.

Know the Basics

Before you can determine if credit is the right option for you, and in order to implement it correctly, you need to be familiar with the basic terms and concepts. Figure 12.3 provides a list of important definitions.

Establish Good Credit Establishing a good credit history is important for most college students. Many utility companies require a credit check before assigning an account. Further in the future, you might need to lease a car, or get a mortgage. These and another installment plan buying options are all dependent on a good credit history. There are several things you should know to establish credit.

1. Successfully handling a checking or savings account at a bank or credit union is a good means of establishing credit.
2. Creditors look for stability. If possible, remain with the same employer and maintain your place of residence for at least a year prior to applying for any major form of credit.
3. Utilities such as your electric, cable, and phone bill are considered part of your credit history, particularly when you are just beginning to establish credit. Pay them on time!
4. Having someone cosign on a loan may help, but be sure they themselves have a good credit history. If your partner defaults on his or her payments, you will be responsible for the remaining balance.

FIGURE 12.3 Common Credit Terms

Character = The willingness of a potential borrower to repay the debt as determined by his credit history.

Cosigner = A person who, by his signature on a contract, guarantees payment of a debt and is liable for the debt if the original signer defaults.

Credit = A trust that goods and services received now will be paid for in the future.

Credit History = A continuing record of a borrower's debt commitments and how well these have been honored.

Credit Rating = A record of an individual's past credit behavior; rating system assigned by the credit grantor to reflect past credit behavior. Each credit grantor establishes its own criteria for extending credit.

Debtor = A person who receives credit and promises to repay.

Default = Failure to meet payment or to fulfill an obligation.

Finance Charge = The amount charged for the use of the credit services.

Interest = Amount paid for the use of credit over a period of time, expressed as a percentage.

Line of Credit = The dollar amount a lender is making available to a borrower, which may or may not be borrowed.

Overdraft = A check written for an amount exceeding the balance in the signer's account.

Principle = The amount to be paid on the original amount borrowed, not on the interest amount added to the loan.

Repossession = Act of reclaiming property pledged as collateral purchased on credit; for payment that is past due.

5. If you do take out a small loan, be sure to make regular, timely payments.
6. Application for credit of any kind will be noted on your credit report as an *inquiry*. Numerous inquiries may cause denial of future credit.
7. If you do use a credit card, pay all your bills on time and in full if possible.
8. Prospective employers and current employers both have the right to look at your credit report. Consider what it might tell them if it is problematic.

Remember that using credit comes with a great deal of responsibility. It is important that before you take on any major financial obligation you are fully aware of the terms and conditions under which you must operate.

Avoid Problems with Credit Cards

College students are a major draw for credit card companies. You may find you have already been preapproved for several credit cards, and can begin charging purchases at any time. Although you shouldn't be discouraged from having a credit card, they need to be accompanied by words of caution. Keep in mind that the average credit card debt for college students is $2,748! (Tyler, 2001). Surely you don't want this to be you.

Calculate the Costs of Credit Credit cards are often offered to students along with several "perks." These may include everything from free hats and T-shirts to very low interest rates and deferred annual fees. What may look enticing in the beginning can catch up with you very quickly.

How many inquiries do you want to have on your credit report simply to collect some free stuff with bank logos on it? If you decide that you need a credit card, make sure you shop around. Interest rates (APRs) can range from as little as 8.99 percent to more than 20 percent! And annual fees are also variable. They also may vary based on the balance on your card—the less you owe, the higher the interest rate and vice versa. Even if the company offers a low introductory rate, these usually only last six months, at which point the interest rate can skyrocket.

Many companies have credit cards designed specifically for students. They often have no annual fee, but tend to have higher interest rates (15 percent to 20.9 percent). Some cards offer additional benefits, such as frequent flyer miles, systems for earning points toward free merchandise and dining, annual rebates of 1 to 2 percent of your total yearly expenditures, access to low-interest student loans, and consumer protection so that you won't be responsible for unauthorized purchases.

No matter what "good deal" you may find on a credit card, don't assume it will keep you out of trouble. You are still responsible for charging only what you can afford and making timely payments.

Pay the Balance Every Month Although most credit cards enable you to keep a balance on your card (called *revolving* credit) and only require that you pay a minimum balance each month, the best and safest way to use a credit card is to charge only what you know you can completely pay off when the bill arrives (*open* credit accounts, such as American Express, require that you do this) (CCCS, 2000).

STAYING OUT OF THE PITS The $2000 Afternoon

Susan was so excited when her new credit card arrived in the mail! This was her first one and she had a credit limit of $1,000. Susan and her roommate decided to go shopping and break in her card. She "took advantage" of numerous sales, but, with all the new clothes she bought (along with the fancy lunch she treated her roommate to), Susan reached her credit limit by the end of the afternoon.

Susan was shocked at how quick and easy it had been to spend so much money, and vowed never to use the card again.

She wasn't really worried about affording all her purchases though, because she knew she could easily make the $20 minimum payment each month. Susan might have thought twice about her shopping spree however, if she realized that with her 19.9 percent annual interest rate and paying only the minimum payment, it was going to take her eight and a half *years* to pay off her afternoon of fun! Not only that, her original expense of $1,000 will have doubled and those same (now outdated) clothes will have cost her $2,000 in extra interest!

Of course, this is assuming Susan never charged with the card again. If she had made additional purchases even after paying her first bill, she would have incurred an over-the-limit fee, because, out of her $20 payment, only $3.50 would have gone toward paying off her principal balance ($16.50 was required to cover the interest). Thus begins a cycle that becomes increasingly harder to break. See below.

Balance	$1,000.00	New Balance	$ 996.50
Interest	+ 16.50	New Charge	30.00
Payment	− 20.00	Over-the-Limit Fee	+ 25.00
New Balance	$ 996.50	Adjusted Balance	$1,051.50

When you pay your bill in its entirety, you know you are not incurring any debt with your card. Despite the initial appeal of simply paying the minimum, this approach to paying credit card bills will cost you significantly more money. If you continually pay only the minimum, it will take years to completely clear your debt. As one student put it, "Who wants to pay interest on a meal eaten a month ago?" (Tyler, 2001). For an eye-opening analysis of this phenomenon, read Staying Out of the Pits, "The $2,000 Afternoon."

Only pay less than the entire balance if you know that you'll be able to cover your current expense *and* the remaining balance next month. Or you should commit to not using the card at all for the next month in order to only have the remaining balance to pay. However, don't forget to calculate the interest that will accrue on the amount that's not yet paid off—you'll owe that, too. For a look at the effects of compounded interest, see Figure 12.4.

Be sure and make your payments on time. Having a credit card is a fundamental means of establishing credit, so use it in such a way as to ensure you are establishing *good* credit. Mail your payments in order to allow plenty of time for them to reach their destination, and try not to take advantage of the grace period if you are given one. Late payments are one more way of spending more money than is necessary, and in some cases they are noted on your credit report.

FIGURE 12.4 Be Cautious about Compounding

Before you take on the responsibilities of choosing and using a credit card, it is important for you to be aware of the significant impact the interest will have on the price you ultimately pay for things. Investigate the rate at which your interest *compounds*—monthly, weekly, or daily. There is a big difference between interest added to your existing balance once at the end of the year, and interest that is calculated monthly based on your remaining balance, and *added to that balance* each month.

Take a look at the following scenario in which the individual charged $500 and is only paying the minimum requirement of $10 a month. If the individual never charges another thing for the rest of the year, despite putting $120 toward paying off the principal balance, hardly a dent was made. The calculations are based on a 17 percent APR—a very common interest rate for student credit cards—which has a monthly rate of 1.42 percent.

	Month 1	Month 2	Month 3	Month 4	Month 5	Month 6	Month 7	Month 8	Month 9	Month 10	Month 11	Month 12
Unpaid Balance	$500.00	$497.10	$494.16	$491.18	$488.15	$485.08	$481.97	$478.81	$475.61	$472.36	$469.07	$465.73
Interest	$ 7.10	$ 7.06	$ 7.02	$ 6.97	$ 6.93	$ 6.89	$ 6.84	$ 6.80	$ 6.75	$ 6.71	$ 6.66	$ 6.61
Minimum Monthly Payment	$ 10.00	$ 10.00	$ 10.00	$ 10.00	$ 10.00	$ 10.00	$ 10.00	$ 10.00	$ 10.00	$ 10.00	$ 10.00	$ 10.00
Balance Due	$ 497.10	$494.16	$491.18	$488.15	$485.08	$481.97	$478.81	$475.61	$472.36	$469.07	$465.73	$472.34

After an entire year, $472.34 is still owed on the initial $500 charge! Out of the $120 paid, only $27.66 went toward paying the principal, while $92.34 was spent on the interest alone.

Imagine if you had charged that money for a spring break trip—the memories might be fading, but you can't afford to go this year, since you're still paying for *last* year. Maybe you purchased new clothes, but they don't fit anymore. You'll still be paying for them whether or not you're still wearing them.

You can continue to calculate this scenario and others at http://www.bankrate.com.

One of the benefits of using a credit card is that it provides itemized records of your purchases. Your monthly statements will be very useful for assessing your budget and categorizing your expenditures. Also, keep them on file for future reference for tax purposes and budget planning.

Use Credit Only in Emergencies If you decide you need a credit card for emergency situations only, remember that all of this information still applies. First, be sure to define what a true emergency is, as discussed earlier in this chapter. If you begin to define "emergency" as any situation in which you are without cash or your checkbook, you'd better be careful. All that using the card does is relieve you of having to pay the full cash amount at the time of the emergency. You will still receive a bill within a month for anything charged on your card, and you will be responsible for making the payments. Of course, you can pay off the bill in monthly increments if you need to, but you will be charged interest; and if you have any other purchases on the card, you will have a larger balance on which the finance charges will be based.

For financial safety's sake, an emergency should be defined as a circumstance in which you do not have the cash for something you *absolutely cannot do without.* These would be such things as medical assistance, safe, reliable transportation, food, and required school supplies. In a true emergency, you will have *no other means* for obtaining what it is that you need. Always consider your options in situations—have you been to the health center to see a doctor? Can you use public transportation? Are there computers available to you on campus? Do they have printers? Are there articles or books on reserve at the library?

Define your needs stringently and be willing to use other resources if you want to limit credit card use. Assess your credit card characteristics by completing the Journal activity "A Question of Credit" on page 371.

Say Goodbye to Debt

Sometimes debt is unavoidable. What's important to understand is how to get out of debt as quickly as possible. When you recover from a negative balance, you can get your budget back on track and begin repairing your credit history. In some cases, creditors actually applaud your documented recuperation from being in debt.

Reduce Your Expenses

The first place to start when you discover that you're in debt is to reduce your expenses. Most of us live fairly luxurious lives—even in college. It is the norm now for college students to have their own personal computers, elaborate entertainment systems, cars, and money for first-rate entertainment, such as sporting events and rock concerts. If you find yourself in financial trouble, you need to look at ways to cut your spending.

I make myself rich by making my wants few.
–Henry David Thoreau
American author

Spending less can take many forms. Certainly eliminating true luxuries like expensive concert tickets and frequent dining out is one way to save money. But to really get serious about cutting costs, you need to review your basic living expenses.

- *Where you live.* Could you move to a cheaper place? Get an additional roommate (or two)? Move home?
- *Utilities.* Do you like to take long, hot showers? Crank the air-conditioning up in the summer? Leave lights on when you go out? Pay attention to your utility use.

What are your spending habits like?

Shower quickly, turn off all the lights, and spend much of the summer indoors—somewhere else, like the library.

- *Transportation.* Could you sell your car and take the bus? Ride a bike? Carpool with someone and pay for their gas? Not owning a car will also eliminate your insurance bill.
- *Food.* Do you eat out a lot? Even fast food costs add up. Start grocery shopping and find quick and easy recipes in the library or online. Don't forget to cut coupons.
- *Television.* Are you paying for cable or a satellite dish? Do you have premium channels? This is a big luxury, particularly if you're a student and watching TV should be kept to a minimum. Stick with the basic channels and rent an occasional movie.
- *Telephone.* Monthly landlines can be expensive with multiple surcharges and taxes. Consider looking for a good cell phone deal and *only* using that.
- *Computer.* Does your school have computer labs? Can you get a school computer account giving you access to email and the Internet? If so, you don't need your own. If you have one, sell it and cancel your account with your Internet service provider.
- *Entertainment.* Redefine what you do for fun. Check out books from the campus or public library to read (or use their Internet service). Go to the park for a picnic. Hike. Ride a bike. Play board games and card games with friends. Go to free on-campus events.

Getting out of debt requires a number of sacrifices, but who knows? You may find you actually enjoy your new, simplified lifestyle.

When Disaster Strikes: Don't Drop Out

If at any point you realize that your financial problems have reached a serious level, consider all of your options before you consider leaving school.

- **Specify your problems.** Begin by mapping out all of your debts, and to whom they're owed. By visualizing your financial demands, you can create a plan to begin eliminating them.
- **Tally your resources.** Now make a list of your income possibilities that you can put toward your debts. Also note any ideas for increasing your income, such as financial aid options or working extra hours.
- **Identify ways to cut back.** List all of the ways that you could reduce the expenses in your life. Don't hold back. Consider all the things that contribute to your living and entertainment expenses. Add up the money you will save if you cut out cable TV, stop eating out, and get a roommate. Now act on your options.
- **Approach your creditors.** Go down your list of who you owe money to and begin to speak with each one. Be honest in telling them your circumstances and see if they are willing to work with you to defer your payments over a longer period of time. Go to them with a specific plan and amount of money which you are certain you could pay on a weekly or monthly basis. An earnest approach and sincerity about wanting to remain in school will help.
- **Seek credit counseling.** Credit counseling services can be found in most major cities, but your school's financial aid office also may provide this service. They can help you put together a workable plan for paying off your debts, and may serve as a liaison between you and your creditors.
- **Talk to your family.** It is likely that your family members want to see you succeed and graduate. You may want to be independent, and your parents may have told you that you're on your own, but in times of crisis they may be the key to staying in school. They may simply give you money to help out, or they may offer you a no interest, or low interest loan. It doesn't hurt to ask. That's what families are for.
- **Reduce your course load.** If your situation requires that you either spend less on school or work significantly more hours in order to catch up financially, consider the cost of at least some classes as a necessity.
- **Commit to recovery.** Once you have devised your plan and put it in motion, commit to seeing it through. Know that it is possible to get yourself out of debt, even if it takes awhile.
- **Keep your goals in sight.** Nothing should motivate you more than realizing you are making progress toward your future goals. As long as you remain in school, you are getting closer to graduation with every semester.

If you find yourself in debt, there are several options to consider. First, investigate your financial aid options. If you can secure a student loan, or even qualify for some scholarships or grants, that will free up your tuition and book money so that you can apply it to paying off your debts. Remember, student loans won't have to be paid off until you have a permanent job, and they typically have very low interest rates.

Pay It Off Sooner

To get a handle on outstanding accounts, try to make even slightly larger payments on your smallest bills. This will help you pay them off at a faster rate, at which point you can then do the same thing with your larger ones. When you make a larger than required payment, the extra money is applied to the principal balance rather than the interest (CCCS, 2000). Once your principal sum is paid, your balance is zero.

Begin making purchases with cash only. This will force you to reduce your buying to things you really need, as opposed to unnecessary luxuries. You also can keep immediate track of where your money is going, and when it's gone, it's gone.

Consider Friends and Family

Seek other resources. You may really want to be independent and make it on your own, but it's wiser to ask for help before you get yourself in too much debt. Ask your parents or a close relative to loan you some money to get your finances under control. They may be willing to do so for a low interest rate or none at all. You may want to make it official by drawing up a contract for repayment terms and conditions. Although you will still owe money, family and friends want to see you reach your goals, thus they are likely to be supportive and understanding.

Recognize the Incredible Value of School

The majority of students who drop out of college have a GPA of 2.5 or above! (Boyer Commission Report, 2002). Obviously they aren't leaving because they can't do the work, rather because they feel they can't afford it. This demonstrates how critical it is to learn to budget effectively, understand credit, and take advantage of financial aid resources. See Take Charge, "When Disaster Strikes, Don't Drop Out," for some important considerations.

When you become a great money manager, you free yourself up to focus on your education. Earning your degree is one of the most valuable things you can do for yourself. It is a guaranteed investment of both time and money. What you learn throughout your college experience—knowledge in a particular field of study, skills of time management, effective listening, writing, and speaking, dedication, commitment, and responsibility—you will have forever. Your academic accomplishments are only the beginning, as they will propel you toward growth in all areas of your life. It is this growth and your multitude of abilities that will open the door of opportunity, enabling you to reach your goals.

The sacrifices you may be required to make when you are in college will be difficult, and for most students, a lack of money is one of the main reasons that sacrifices must be made. But talk to anyone who has graduated and landed a professional job, and they will tell you it was all worth it. Careful budgeting and money management may seem tiresome and unnecessary, but doing so will insure your education, and guarantee increased earning power after college. Now complete the Journal activity "Imagine That!" to explore your values regarding money.

Summary Strategies for Mastering College

Understand your financial values to manage your money for college and future success.

Focus on the "Six Strategies for Success" above as you read each chapter to learn how to apply these strategies to your own success.

1 Take Control of Your Finances

- Recognize the importance of learning effective money management now.
- Count all your income, know where it goes, and be honest with yourself.
- Create and use a budget to manage your money.
- Establish a source of money for unexpected expenses.

2 Find the Right Place for Your Money

- Open a bank account for either checking, savings, or both.
- Learn how to balance your checkbook, keep track of savings, and even invest money for your future.

3 Explore Financial Resources

- Get a job, but work with caution so as not to disrupt your school success.
- Pursue financial aid with the assistance of an on-campus financial aid advisor.
- Learn about the various scholarship, grant, and loan options available to you.

4 Understand Credit

- Establish good credit by learning what's important in a good credit history.
- Avoid problems with credit cards by knowing how credit cards work and your financial responsibilities when you charge.

5 Say Good-Bye to Debt

- Reassess what you spend each month.
- Pay bills off sooner by allotting more money for smaller accounts.
- Use cash only to keep spending in check.
- Consider friends and family to help you through difficult times.
- Recognize the incredible value of school and that your education is the best investment.

Review Questions

1. Why is it important to look to the future for motivation to become a good money manager *now*? List three actions you can take now to improve your financial future.

    1. _____

    2. _____

    3. _____

2. Describe a few of the different factors to consider when creating a budget and how can it be considered a *tool* for assessing your finances.

    _____

    _____

    _____

    _____

    _____

3. What are some different types of financial aid, and why might everyone benefit from exploring these options?

    _____

    _____

    _____

    _____

    _____

4. What are some advantages of checking and savings accounts? Can you think of any disadvantages?

    _____

    _____

    _____

    _____

    _____

5. Describe at least three important things to know in order to establish good credit.

    1. _____

    2. _____

    3. _____

6. Explain debt-to-income ratio and why is it important. How should you use this information to evaluate your budget on a regular basis?

    _____

    _____

    _____

    _____

    _____

Learning Portfolio

SELF-ASSESSMENTS

YOUR JOURNAL

STRATEGIES FOR SUCCESS

Develop Meaningful Values

Get Motivated and Take Responsibility

Explore Careers

Be a Great Money Manager

Set Goals, Plan, and Monitor

Build Self-Esteem and Confidence

Think and Learn

Where Does the Money Rank?

Rank the following life values in order of importance to you.

_____ comfortable life

_____ job success

_____ community service/volunteer activities

_____ large investment portfolio

_____ culture (movies, theater, and so on)

_____ new home or condo

_____ earning a lot of money

_____ prestige/social recognition

_____ education/knowledge

_____ recreation

_____ excitement/stimulation

_____ reducing or eliminating debt

_____ family activities

_____ religion

_____ family vacation

_____ security

_____ friends

_____ sense of accomplishment

_____ happiness/contentment

_____ shopping/spending money

_____ health

_____ starting/maintaining own business

_____ image/personal appearance

_____ top-of-the-line products and services

_____ independence/autonomy

Evaluate your priorities. What aspects of life do you value the most? How much money is required to obtain the things you value? How might you manage your money in order to live your life according to what you value the most? For a more in-depth look at your specific financial goals, also complete Self-Assessment 2 on your CD-ROM.

Source: Barbara O'Neill, *Saving on a Shoestring.* Copyright © 1995 Dearborn Financial Publishing.

Are You a Compulsive Spender?

Place a checkmark by those statements that apply to you.

_____ It takes 20 percent or more of my income to pay my debts.

_____ I spend more when I am depressed and/or angry.

_____ I am nearing (or at) the limit on lines of credit.

_____ I make only minimum payments on revolving charges and loans.

_____ I am charging food/groceries because I lack cash.

_____ I frequently pay late charges on bills.

_____ I tap into my savings to pay current bills.

_____ I have an insufficient or nonexistent savings cushion.

_____ I would be in immediate financial difficulty if I lost my job.

_____ I am being threatened with repossession or having earnings garnished.

_____ I work overtime to make ends meet.

_____ I have no idea how much I owe.

_____ I worry about money frequently and feel hopeless and depressed.

If you have checked five or more of the statements, your problem may be due to your spending habits. Begin by examining exactly what you are spending money on, and for those things that are not absolute necessities, be honest with yourself as to why you are spending the money. In some cases, low self-esteem can not only result from poor money management but also may be the cause of it, resulting in problematic spending tendencies.

Source: © 2002 Baptist OnLine, www.baptistonline.org.

Your Money and You

Check the column that best represents you for each statement.

	Never	Sometimes	Often	Always
I tend to be late in paying bills; I shuffle them around, paying some this month and others next month.				
I am unsure where my money goes.				
I am at the maximum limit on my bank credit cards.				
I pay only the minimum amount due each month on my charge accounts.				
Some of the creditors have started sending reminders about overdue payments.				
I frequently have checks bounce or frequently use the overdraft loan feature on my checking account.				
I don't discuss money with my family because I feel uncomfortable or am afraid it will start an argument.				
I've had to borrow money from parents or other close relatives just to meet basic living expenses.				
My financial situation makes me feel depressed and/or affects my performance at school.				

Give yourself one point for each "Never" answer, two points for each "Sometimes" answer, 3 points for each "Often" answer, and 4 points for each "Always" answer. Add up your total number of points and divide by 9. The higher your score, the more concerned you should be about your situation.

Total:

Source: From http://www.answerdesk.orst.edu. Reprinted with permission.

Your Journal

● REFLECT

1. The Money in My Past

Think about your experiences with money in the past—earning it, spending it, getting an allowance.

- What lessons did you learn from your family about money? What did you learn from observing their financial management?

_____

- What lessons from your past do you think will be helpful as you become increasingly financially independent?

_____

2. Simplifying My Life

List some examples of things have you become accustomed to having that you really don't need, but simply enjoy having as a convenience or little "extra"? How much could you save if you didn't have them?

_____

_____

● DO

1. In Case of Emergency

Brainstorm about some emergency situations you might encounter in the coming year such as car problems, doctor visits during flu season, or a family emergency requiring a trip home. List these situations below. Then talk with family members, friends, or your boss to find out to what extent they are willing to help you out in an emergency situation. Adjust your resources above accordingly.

_____

_____

2. It Can't Hurt

With all of the different kinds of financial aid available to students, you may be surprised to find that there are options that appeal to you, and would alleviate some of your money concerns. Visit your school's financial aid office and speak with a financial aid advisor to investigate. What are some questions you should prepare?

_____

_____

_____

Your Journal

● THINK CRITICALLY

1. Define Financial Success
Financial success means something different to everyone. By examining your values, you will be able to define financial success for yourself. Begin with your dreams (and dream big!). What is your financial ideal for the future? Don't feel like you have to use a dollar amount; however, identify what it is you would like to be able to do and use your money for. Do you see those dreams as a reality based on your career path? If not, what might you more realistically be able to expect in terms of "financial success"?

_____

_____

2. A Question of Credit
You've heard many warnings about credit cards for college students, but they also can offer several benefits. Using them appropriately and responsibly is truly a matter of awareness and self-control. What do you find challenging or tempting about having the card? What have you done to overcome these challenges and temptations?

_____

_____

● CREATE

1. My Money-Making Dream

- If you could be an entrepreneur doing anything you want, what would it be?

_____

- Does it relate to your current career goals? If so, how?

_____

- What can you do now to help make this dream a reality?

_____

2. Imagine That!
Suppose you are one of those very rare individuals who manages to win the lottery. (The odds are not very favorable. It has sometimes been estimated that it is more likely you will be struck by lightning twice when on horseback!). However, if you inherited sudden wealth, what would you do with that resource? Describe five actions you would take if you didn't have to worry about money. Then examine what those actions communicate about your values. How does your imaginary wealthy existence compare to the real values you express in your routine financial decisions?

Applying the Six Strategies for Success

What did you learn in this chapter that you can apply to the following key strategies to help form the foundation for your success? Write down all of the major points you can remember that support the following strategies:

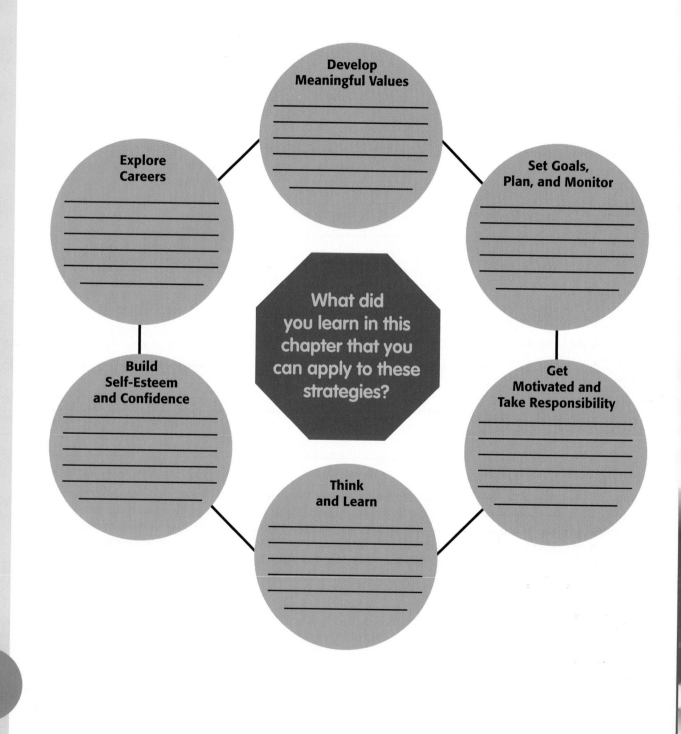

13 Explore Careers

©Amy Etra/Photo Edit

Where Are You? Concentrate on identifying careers that fit with your values and interests. The time you spend exploring careers will help anchor your college work and your success after college. To evaluate where you are now in your career exploration, place a checkmark next to only those items that apply to you.

- I have begun to explore career options and know of at least one that matches up with my values.
- I know what my skills are and how they will help me in a career.
- I know my personality and how it might connect with careers.
- I have ideas about work experiences during college that might help me with my long-term goals.
- I have studied the *Occupational Outlook Handbook*.
- I have talked with a career counselor.
- I have set career goals and planned how to reach them.
- I have networked about careers and job possibilities.
- I know how to land a great job after college.

As you read about Giselle Fernandez, think about how her part-time work in college provided her with an important context for deciding what career path she wanted to follow.

Images of College Success

Giselle Fernandez

Born in Mexico, raised and educated mainly in California, Giselle Fernandez pursues a genuine passion for journalism. She currently is coanchor of Los Angeles television station KTLA's morning news show and has earned five Emmy awards for her journalistic efforts. She was the first reporter in 20 years to interview Cuban dictator Fidel Castro in English. Giselle also has her own interview program on the Si TV cable network titled *Café Ole* and heads up her own production company, *Skinny Hippo Productions*, at which she develops programs for cable network TV.

When Giselle decided on a career in politics, she wanted to be near the nation's capitol so she applied to Goucher College in Baltimore and received a partial scholarship. She enrolled there and chose a major in international relations. When she was at Goucher, she was awarded an internship to work with a U.S. senator. This experience led her to become disillusioned with Washington politics and motivated her to look for a different career path.

Giselle transferred to Sacramento State University and changed her major to journalism. There she worked for the college newspaper, the *Sacramento Hornet*, and for a magazine, *Executive Place.* She covered news events at the California state capitol in Sacramento. When Giselle went to the state capitol to cover a story, she remembers seeing TV reporters seeming to have more fun than she was as a newspaper reporter and magazine writer. After graduating from Sacramento State University with a major in journalism and a minor in international relations, she embarked on a career as a TV reporter.

Giselle made a videotape to send out to prospective employers. She knew she needed an expensive outfit to look good on the videotape but did not have enough money to purchase one. She went to a department store and convinced the manager to let her borrow an expensive suit for a few hours to make her videotape. She sent about 100 copies to TV stations all across the United States and was hired for her first TV job as a reporter and photographer for the Pueblo bureau of the Colorado Springs station, KRDO-TV.

Today, Giselle Fernandez is one of the leading Latinas in broadcast journalism. She also actively lectures on subjects of Latina empowerment, health, and fitness, and is active in raising money and awareness for breast cancer research, education, and treatment.

GISELLE FERNANDEZ, a leading Latina broadcast journalist, whose internship and part-time jobs during college helped to shape her career path.

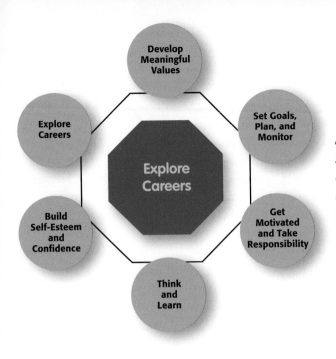

As you read, think about the "Six Strategies for Success" listed to the left and how this chapter can help you maximize success in these important areas. For example, linking your values with your career goals will help motivate your through college.

Evaluate Yourself

Making the right career choice is a critical step in the journey of life. This is a good time to get motivated to consider several different career paths and evaluate your values, interests, abilities, and skills. As you read this chapter, think about how your career interests and goals align with the courses you are taking and your college major, as well as your general interests. The Journal activity "Collect Inspirations," on page 394 can also help with this process.

Choose Career Options That Match Your Values

An important first step in choosing career options is to know your values. Knowing what you value most—what is important to you in life—will help you refine your career search and choice.

Some people want to pursue a career in which they help others. Some desire a career that is prestigious. Others seek one in which they will make a lot of money. Yet others want one that will give them plenty of time for leisure and family interests. Complete Self-Assessment 1 "My Values and My Career Pursuits" on page 391 to examine your values in relation to your career pursuits.

Clarifying your values helps you zero in on the careers that will likely be the most meaningful and rewarding to you. Once you've decided on a career, you need to set goals, plan how to reach them, and monitor your progress, one of the important strategies for success listed above. When your values, career choice, and career goals are established and aligned, your internal motivation to think and learn will be strengthened.

> *Whatever you can do, or dream you can, begin it. Boldness has genius, power, and magic.*
>
> Johann Wolfgang von Goethe
> *19th-century German playwright and novelist*

Source: *Copyright by David Killeen. Used by permission.*

Assess Your Skills

Skills include both your academic and personal strengths. We develop some skills easily while others are more difficult to learn. Honestly evaluating your areas of strength and weakness will help you a great deal in realistically appraising majors and careers.

SCANS Skills The U.S. Department of Labor issues reports created by the Secretary's Commission on Achieving Necessary Skills (SCANS). The SCANS reports describe skills and personal qualities that will benefit individuals as they enter the workforce. It focuses on four types of skills and personal qualities (basic, thinking, personal, and people). You have already studied about and completed exercises related to many of these skills and personal qualities in this book. As you read, consider which skills represent areas of strength or weakness for you.

Basic Skills. Basic skills include:

- *Reading*
    Identify basic facts
    Locate information in books/manuals
    Find meanings of unknown words
    Judge accuracy of reports
    Use computers to find information
- *Writing*
    Write ideas completely and accurately in letters and reports with proper grammar, spelling, and punctuation
    Use computers to communicate information
- *Mathematics*
    Use numbers, fractions, and percentages to solve problems
    Use tables, graphs, and charts
    Use computers to enter, retrieve, change, and compute numerical information
- *Speaking*
    Speak clearly
    Select language, tone of voice, and gestures appropriate to an audience
- *Listening*
    Listen carefully to what a person says, noting tone of voice and body language
    Respond in a way that indicates an understanding of what is said

Thinking Skills. Thinking skills include:

- ***Creative Thinking***
  Use imagination freely, combining information in innovative ways
  Make connections between ideas that seem unrelated
- ***Problem Solving***
  Recognize problems
  Identify why a problem is a problem
  Create and implement solutions to problems
  Observe to see how effective a solution is
  Revise as necessary
- ***Decision Making***
  Identify goals
  Generate alternatives and gather information about them
  Weigh pros and cons
  Choose the best alternative
  Plan how to carry out your choice
- ***Visualization***
  Imagine building an object or system by studying a blueprint or drawing

Personal Qualities. Personal qualities include:

- ***Self-Esteem***
  Understand how beliefs affect how a person feels and acts
  Listen and identify irrational or harmful beliefs that you may have
  Know how to change these negative beliefs when they occur
- ***Self-Management***
  Assess one's own knowledge and skills accurately
  Set specific and realistic personal goals
  Monitor progress toward goals
- ***Responsibility***
  Work hard to reach goals, even if a task is unpleasant
  Do quality work
  Have a high standard of attendance, honesty, energy, and optimism

People Skills. People skills include:

- ***Social***
  Show understanding, friendliness, and respect for others' feelings
  Be assertive when appropriate
  Take an interest in what people say and why they think and behave the way
  they do
- ***Negotiation***
  Identify common goals among different people
  Clearly present your position
  Understand your group's position and the other group's position
  Examine possible options
  Make reasonable compromises
- ***Leadership***
  Communicate thoughts and feelings to justify a position
  Encourage or convince
  Make positive use of rules or values
  Demonstrate the ability to get others to believe in and trust you because of your
  competence and honesty

- *Teamwork*
  - Contribute your ideas to the group in a positive manner
  - Do your own share of the work
  - Encourage team members
  - Resolve differences for the benefit of the team
  - Responsibly challenge existing procedures, policies, or authorities

Additional Skills The National Association of College Employers conducted a survey of its members. The employers ranked oral communication, interpersonal relations, and teamwork as the three most important skills of a prospective job candidate (Collins, 1996). All of these skills involve communicating effectively. Complete the Journal activity "How Good Are Your Communication Skills?" on page 394 to evaluate your skills in this area. Employers also value candidates with the following abilities:

- Speaking Skills
- Leadership Skills
- Interpersonal Skills
- Proficiency in Field of Study
- Analytical Skills
- Writing Skills
- Teamwork Skills
- Computer Skills
- Flexibility

Self-Management Skills Self-management skills were described above as important personal qualities. Many people think of work-related skills as engineering, writing, speaking, and computer skills, to name a few. These skills are important in many jobs. However, self-management skills are also extremely important to career success (Farr, 1999). By completing Self-Assessment 2 "My Self- Management Skills" on page 392 you can evaluate your strengths in this area.

The skills and qualities you checked off in Self-Assessment 2 are among the most important things a prospective employer should learn about you. They have to do with your ability to be a competent worker in many different situations and adapt to challenging tasks. Even so, most job seekers don't understand how important they are and don't mention them during interviews. Don't make this mistake.

Link Your Personality and Career Choice

Recall that we introduced two personality scales in Chapter 4, The Myers-Briggs Type Indicator (MBTI) and the Big Five Personality Theory. These two approaches to evaluating personality styles are especially relevant to learning styles. The MBTI was not designed as a career assessment tool but it is often used alongside interest and aptitude assessments to provide career direction. If you are interested in taking the Myers-Briggs test as part of determining your fit with various careers, contact the career counseling center at your college.

The Big Five personality traits (openness, conscientiousness, extraversion, agreeableness, and neuroticism/emotional instability) have not been widely used to direct career choice. However, the Big Five typology has been used to assess work and nonwork environments that affect career change, work performance, and job satisfaction.

One of the most commonly used systems for examining the link between personality style and career choice was developed by John Holland (1997). Holland believes that there are six basic personality types: realistic, investigative, artistic, social, enterprising, and conventional. Following is a description of each, linked with some appropriate careers.

- *Realistic.* People who have athletic or mechanical ability, prefer to work with objects, machines, tools, plants or animals, or to be outdoors. They often are less social, have difficulty in demanding situations, and prefer to work alone. This personality type matches up best with jobs in labor, farming, truck driving, construction, engineering, and being a pilot.
- *Investigative.* People who like to observe, learn, investigate, analyze, evaluate, or solve problems. They are interested in ideas more than people, are rather indifferent to social relationships, are troubled by emotional situations, and are often aloof and intelligent. This personality type matches up with scientific, intellectually oriented professions.
- *Artistic.* People who have artistic, innovative, or intuitional abilities and like to work in unstructured situations using their imagination and creativity. They enjoy working with ideas and materials that allow them to express themselves in innovative ways. They value nonconformity, freedom, and ambiguity. Sometimes they have difficulty in social relationships. Not many jobs match up with the artistic type. Consequently, some artistic individuals work in jobs that are second and third choices and express their artistic interests through hobbies and leisure.
- *Social.* People who like to work with other people to enlighten, inform, help, train, or cure them, or are skilled with words. They tend to have a helping orientation and like doing social things more than engaging in intellectual tasks. This personality type matches up with jobs in teaching, social work, and counseling.
- *Enterprising.* People who like to work with people, influencing, persuading, performing, leading or managing for organizational goals or economic gain. They may try to dominate others to reach their goals and are often good at persuading others to do tasks. The enterprising type matches up with jobs in sales, management, and politics.
- *Conventional.* People who like to work with data, have clerical or numerical ability, carry out tasks in detail or follow through on others' instructions. They function best in well-structured situations and are skilled at working with details. The conventional type matches up with jobs in accounting, banking, and secretarial work.

From *Making Vocational Choices*, 3rd Edition. Copyright ©1973, 1985, 1992, 1997, by Psychological Assessment Resources, Inc. Reproduced by special permission of the Publisher.

Most people are a combination of two or three types and this is taken into account in matching up a person's type with careers in Holland's system. Be sure to do the Self-Assessment "Matching Your Personality Type to Careers" on this book's website that is based on Holland's ideas.

When taking a test to find out the best careers for you, there are some cautions you should note, described in On Target Tips, "Rules about Taking Career Tests."

ON TARGET TIPS

Rules about Taking Career Tests

Richard Bolles (2002), author of the popular book *What Color Is Your Parachute?*, offered these rules for taking career tests:

1. *There is no one career test that always gives better results than others.* One career test may work well for you, another one for your best friend.
2. *You should take several tests, not just one.* You likely will obtain a better picture of your career interests from as many as three or more tests rather than just one.
3. *Consult your intuition.* You likely know more about yourself than a test does. Treat no test outcome as "gospel." If the test results seem just dead wrong to you, evaluate yourself apart from the test and use your intuition as part of figuring out your career interests.
4. *You are never finished with a test until you have done some good, hard thinking about yourself.* Career tests can be fun but just reading the results is not enough. You also need to think deeply about what makes you different from everyone else, what makes you (like your fingerprints) unique. This deeper inquiry about yourself can help you to find the careers that are likely best for you.

Acquire Positive Work Experiences During College

As discussed in Chapter 12, students can participate in part-time or summer work, internships, and cooperative education (co-op) programs relevant to their field of study. This experience can be critical in helping students obtain the job they want when they graduate. Many of today's employers expect job candidates to have this type of experience.

Explore Relevant Part-Time and Summer Jobs

College students benefit more when their jobs are on campus rather than off. This apparently keeps students more in touch with campus life and it takes them less time to commute to their job. Also, on-campus jobs are more likely to be linked with academic pursuits. A good strategy for finding out about on-campus jobs is to go to the financial aid office at your college and ask for a list of available part-time positions. See if any of them will help you develop skills for a future career.

Most departments on a college campus hire student assistants, usually to perform specialized duties such as website design, data input, or clerical work. If you are interested in a major and career in psychology or biology, you might want to go to these departments and ask if any student assistant jobs are available.

With advanced planning, summer jobs can provide good opportunities not only to earn money but also to obtain experiences relevant to your major and career interests. Obtaining this type of summer job can give you a glimpse of the day-to-day workings of a career you might be interested in and provide a better sense of whether this is the type of life work you want to do. Even if you don't find a part-time or summer position that is relevant to your career interests, most jobs allow you to demonstrate work-related skills and a work ethic that any prospective employer will find attractive.

Do an Internship or a Co-op

Many college students wonder: How do I figure out what I want to do? How do I get a job without experience? How do I get experience without a job? What if I spend four years studying in a particular major and it turns out I don't like it? Internships and co-op experiences can help you answer these questions. These are jobs in the real world that are linked to your academic and career interests.

Internships Most internships are part-time jobs that last for about three to six months, although some last longer. The only time that they might be full time is in the summer and you aren't taking summer classes. Some internships pay a little money but most don't include a salary. Nonetheless, they can significantly help you down the road when you begin looking for full-time employment and a career after college. One study found that students who served in internships during college were 15 percent more likely to find employment after graduation and 70 percent said that they were better prepared for the workplace because of this internship experience (Knouse, Tanner, & Harris, 1999).

Co-ops Co-ops pay a salary and typically last more than a year. Many co-op programs offer academic credit and a typical student makes $7,000 a year. In four-year colleges, you may not be able to pursue a co-op experience until your junior year, whereas in two-year colleges the co-op experience may be available to both first- and second-year students.

In a national survey of employers, almost 60 percent said their entry-level college hires had co-op or internship experience (Collins, 1996). More than 1,000 colleges in the United States offer co-op (cooperative education) programs.

Co-ops and internships let you test your career objectives, can help you identify your talents, and acquire valuable skills that you may need in a future career. Before seeking a particular co-op or internship, ask yourself these questions:

- What type of work do I want to do?
- In what field?
- In what type of organization do I want to work?
- What skills do I want to gain from the work experience?

For some strategies in obtaining an internship experience, see Take Charge, "Of Getting an Internship Experience."

Engage in Service Learning

A wide range of life experiences during college may also help you explore your values related to careers. One example is *service learning*, which involves engaging in activities that promote social responsibility and service to the community (Sherrod & Brabeck, 2002). In service learning, you might tutor, help older adults, volunteer in a hospital, assist in a day care center, or clean up a vacant lot to make a play area.

Why should you participate in service learning during your college years? Researchers have found that when students participate in service learning,

- Their grades improve, they become more motivated, and they set more goals (Johnson & others, 1998).
- Their self-esteem improves (Giles & Eyler, 1998).
- They become less self-centered (Santilli, Falbo, & Harris, 2002).
- They increasingly reflect on society's moral order and social concerns (Metz & McLellan, 2000).

To think further about your work experiences and skills, complete the Journal activity "My Work Skills" on page 393.

TAKE CHARGE — Of Getting an Internship Experience

Here are some recommendations for internship opportunities:

- Check with your academic advisor or the campus career center to find out about the internship opportunities that are available.
- Attend job fairs. Employers often use job fairs to identify students for coop or internship experiences.
- Contact the Chamber of Commerce in the city where you are attending college or in the city where you will be living next summer.
- Network. Talk with friends, family, instructors, professionals in the field in which you are interested, and others. Let them know that you want to obtain an internship experience.
- If a particular company interests you, contact them to see if they have internships that are available.
- The Internet has sites that can be helpful. The following site lists internships (and co-op opportunities) across the United States: http://www.careerplanit.com. The following site also lists many internships: http://www.internjobs.com.
- Explore *Peterson's Internships*, a book that lists more than 40,000 internships. If it is not available on your campus, call 1-800-338-3282 to find out where it can be located.

Become Knowledgeable about Careers

Career exploration involves investigating the world of work and becoming knowledgeable about different careers. Think about what type of work you are likely to find rewarding and satisfying. This involves exploring different job opportunities while still in college as well as conducting research to gather information from many sources about different fields, industries, and companies.

Explore the *Occupational Outlook Handbook*

As you explore the type of work you are likely to enjoy and in which you can succeed, it is important to be knowledgeable about different fields and companies. Occupations

Karen was shocked when her first semester books and supplies wiped out her spending money for the entire term. She checked the college newspaper for part-time jobs, thinking that a position on campus would be more convenient and maybe even provide a chance to get some studying done. She lucked into a job at the college library based on her experience using the Internet and her organizational skills—she had done some filing and clerical work in high school.

Although she was able to get some studying done while things were quiet, she was generally busy helping students do Internet searches for research materials and find journals and articles online. This helped build on her skills in this area and motivated her to take some courses in Web design. When the time came to think about a long-term career, she began researching technology opportunities at some of the larger companies in the area, eventually landing a job as an assistant in the Internet support group of a local healthcare firm. Her hands-on experience and a solid reference from her supervisor in the campus library were instrumental to her success.

Tamika was an English major who loved her courses and writing assignments, but had no idea how this could lead to any type of career. She approached the chair of the English department who suggested she consider the area of publishing. She then went to the campus career resource center, which had a list of alumni who were involved in this industry. With phone numbers and e-mail addresses in hand, she contacted a half dozen resources and lined up a few informational interviews.

Most of this networking was conducted over the phone, as her contacts lived and worked all over the country, but they were still incredibly helpful in teaching Tamika about the publishing industry and suggesting various entry level career paths. Most important, she learned about an internship program with an educational publisher in her general geographic area and secured a nonpaying internship in their marketing department for the summer before her senior year. Although she had to waitress at night to make ends meet, it was worth it for the experience she gained and the contacts she made in the office. She felt confident that she would be seriously considered for a full-time position after graduation and knew what it would take to make herself a top candidate.

may have many job openings one year but few another year, as economic conditions change. Thus, it is critical to keep up with the occupational outlook in various fields. An excellent source for doing this is the *Occupational Outlook Handbook*, which is revised every two years. Based on the 2004–2005 edition, service industries are expected to provide the most new jobs with professional and related occupations projected to increase the most.

Approximately three fourths of the job growth will come from three groups of professional occupations: computer and mathematical occupations, health practitioners and technical occupations, and education, training, and library occupations (*Occupational Outlook Handbook*, 2004–2005).

Projected job growth varies widely by educational requirements. Jobs that require a college degree are expected to grow the fastest. Education is essential to getting a high-paying job. All but one of the 50 highest paying occupations require a college degree (*Occupational Outlook Handbook*, 2004–2005).

You can access the *Occupational Outlook Handbook* online at http://www.bls.gov/oco/home.htm. The handbook provides excellent information about what workers do on the job, working conditions, training and education needed for various jobs, and expected job prospects in a wide range of occupations. Libraries are also good sources for finding more about careers. You might want to ask a librarian at your college or university to help you with your career information search.

Select Several Careers, Not Just One

When initially seeking the right career, it's good to have several in mind rather than just one. In a recent national survey of first-year college students, only 14 percent believed that they were likely to change their major field of interest (Sax & others, 2003). In reality, far more than this will. Thus, it pays to be knowledgeable about more than just one career field. It also pays to develop a wide variety of general skills, such as communication, that will serve you well in various fields.

Network

Networking involves making contact and exchanging information with other people. Check with people you know—your family, friends, people in the community, and alumni—about career information. They might be able to answer your questions themselves or put you in touch with people who can. For example, most college career centers have the names of alumni on file who are willing to talk with students about careers and their work. Networking can lead to meeting someone who can answer your questions about a specific career or company. This is an effective way to learn about the type of training necessary for a particular position, how to enter the field, and what employees like and don't like about their jobs. See the Journal activity "Your Network" on page 394.

See a Career Counselor

You might want to talk with a career counselor at your college. This professional is trained to help you discover your strengths and weaknesses, evaluate your values and goals, and help you figure out what type of career is best for you. The counselor will not tell you what to do. You might be asked to take an interest inventory, which the counselor can interpret to help you explore various career options. To think further about seeing a career counselor, complete the Journal activity "Visit Your College's Career Center" on page 393.

Scope Out Internet Resources

The dramatic growth of websites has made instantly available almost countless resources for job possibilities and careers. Most companies, professional societies, academic institutions, and government agencies maintain Internet sites that highlight their latest information and activities.

The range of career information on the Internet tends to overlap with what is available through libraries, career centers, and guidance offices. However, no single network or resource is likely to contain all of the information you're searching for, so explore different sources. As in a library search, look through various lists by field or discipline or by using keywords. Table 13.1 describes some of the leading computer-aided occupation searches. For example, Guidance Information System (GIS) contains information that links careers with interests, physical demands, work conditions, lifestyle, salary, employment potential, and education/training.

Be sure to scan the resources on the website for this book. You'll find some helpful books and web links that explore many aspects of careers. To think further about careers, complete the Journal activity "Why Do People Choose Particular Careers?" on page 394.

TABLE 13.1 Widely Used Computer-Guided Career Systems

System	Publisher
Career Information System	Career Information System National Office, Eugene, Oregon
Career Visions	Wisconsin Career Information System, Madison, WI
Career Ways	Wisconsin Career Information System, Madison, WI
Choices	Careerware: ISM Systems Corp., Ottawa, Ontario (Canada)
Modular C-Lect	Chronicle Press, Moravia, NY
COIN	COIN Educational Products, Toledo, OH
Discover	American College Testing, Hunt Valley, MD
Guidance Information System	Riverside Publishing, Chicago, IL
SIGI Plus	Educational Testing Service, Princeton, NJ

Note: To learn more about any of these systems, type in the title of the system or the publisher on an Internet search engine like Google.

Source: *From Lee E. Isaacson & Duane Brown. Career Information, Career Counseling, and Career Development, 7th Ed. Published by Allyn & Bacon, Boston, MA. Copyright ©2000 by Pearson Education. Reprinted by permission of the publisher.*

Set Career Goals

From your self-evaluation and increased knowledge of careers, a picture should begin to emerge about the kind of work you would like to do and where you want to do it. Once you have decided on one or more careers that you would like to pursue, it is helpful to think about some long-term and short-term goals. It is important that you be able to articulate these goals to employers and interviewers. The kind of information you should think about incorporating in your career goal setting includes (OCS Basics, 2002):

- major career field target
- preferred type of work, including the ideas or issues you would like to pursue
- income requirements
- geographical requirements (city, rural, mobility, near home, climate, and so on)
- special needs (training, management development, advancement opportunities, career flexibility, entrepreneurial opportunity, and so on)

- industry preferences (manufacturing, government, communications, nonprofit, high tech, products, services, and so on)

You can think further about your career goals by completing the Journal activity "My Ideal Job," on page 393.

Land a Great Job

A career-oriented position may not be the only job you are thinking about for the future. You also might be looking for a part-time campus job, a job between terms, or one for next summer. As with exploring potential careers, finding the right job involves doing your homework and becoming as knowledgeable as you can about jobs in which you have an interest. Among the most important things for you to do in your job search are:

1. know what employers want
2. research the job
3. network
4. create a resume and write various letters
5. prepare for a job interview

Know What Employers Want

In the national survey of employers of college students mentioned earlier in the chapter, employers said that first-year students need to be already thinking about the career they want to pursue (Collins, 1996). Graduation and job hunting are only a few years away. Much of what employers look for in top job candidates (such as relevant experience) takes time to acquire. The employers especially recommend that first-year students focus on obtaining:

- work-related experience
- good grades
- computer skills
- leadership positions
- participation in campus or extracurricular activities

Research the Job

Research the type of job that you want, identifying the skills and experience necessary to perform it. Determine both the general requirements of the job and the day-to-day tasks and responsibilities. Brainstorm about a potential employer's needs, attitudes, and goals. Also research the company or employer in general. If you can determine the company's philosophy, you will be able to determine more accurately how you might contribute to the company and whether it is a good match for you.

The more you know about the job, the stronger a candidate you will become. Check out ads in newspapers and use web resources related to your interests and skills. If you are looking outside of your geographic area, arrange to receive any newspapers that include job listings in your area of interest, or read them on the Web. Two websites stand out for their benefits in a job search. *The Riley Guide* (http://www.rileyguide.com) has an online tutorial that takes you through a series of steps on how to use the Internet in a job search. *The Job Hunter's Bible* (http://www.jobhuntersbible.com) is also a valuable job-hunting resource (Bolles, 2005).

Network Some More

Earlier in the chapter, we described networking as a valuable tool for learning more about careers. It also is valuable in a job search and is especially helpful in finding out about nonpublicized job openings. When you network, you can ask for suggestions of people that you might contact for information about job or internship possibilities. The personal contact gained through networking can enhance your chance of getting a job compared to an anonymous application. On Target Tips, "Networking Strategies," provides some strategies for effective networking.

Create a Resume and Write Letters

To land a great job, you are going to need a good resume. You also need to know how to write a variety of letters.

Resume A resume is a clear and concise description of your interests, skills, experiences, and responsibilities in work, service, extracurricular, and academic settings. There are a number of different styles for resumes and no particular one is considered universally the best. Use white paper, a 10–12 font size, and black type. There should be no errors—misspelled words, grammatical errors, typos—whatsoever in your resume. Also, your resume must be an accurate reflection of your job history and accomplishments. Lies on your resume will catch up with you.

Three types of resumes are most commonly used (OCS Basics, 2002):

1. *Chronological.* This is the most common format, which describes your experiences in reverse chronological order, beginning with your most recent experiences.
2. *Functional.* This highlights your marketable skills by organizing your accomplishments by skill or career area. This format may be the best choice if you have limited work experience related to the job for which you are applying.
3. *Achievement.* This format highlights prior work or academic accomplishments. It can be used as an alternative to the first two formats when your accomplishments are centered on a particular skill or experience category.

Most resumes include the following parts (Writers Workshop, 2002):

- NAME: Centered and boldface font
- ADDRESS: Present and permanent. May include your phone number and/or e-mail address.
- JOB OBJECTIVE: This likely will be different for each job you apply for. It summarizes your reason for submitting a resume (the position you desire) and your qualifications. The rest of your resume should relate to and support your job objective.
- EDUCATIONAL RECORD: Begin with your most recent education (college you are now attending) and list all schools attended and degrees earned since high school. Indicate your major and areas of specialization. You may want to include your GPA if you have a "B" average or better. You might list distinctions and honors, such as the Dean's list or scholarships, or you can save these for a separate category, "Awards and Honors."

"I threw in a couple of paragraphs about my love life to make my resume interesting."

©Engleman/Rothco Cartoons.

- EMPLOYMENT HISTORY: List the dates, job title, and organization involved in each job you have held. Do not disclose salary information. This section is organized in reverse chronological order, that is, you begin with the most recent job and conclude with your first.

  Remember that you can include volunteer jobs or working with a professor on a project in this section if they are relevant. Alternatively, these types of work experiences could be placed under "Educational Record" if they are academic or "Special Skills" or "Activities." Be sure to include a brief description of your work on each job, the tasks you performed, the skills you acquired, any special responsibilities or projects, and promotions or achievements.

- SPECIAL SKILLS: List any skills that are relevant to the job you want but are not mentioned elsewhere on the resume. For example, expertise with specific software packages or fluency in foreign languages.

- PROFESSIONAL AFFILIATIONS/ACTIVITIES: List your membership in any professional organizations and any active role or office you have held. Do not include personal interests or leisure activities.

- HONORS AND AWARDS: List any honors you have earned or awards you have received since high school. If you have two honors or less, delete this section and include the information with the "Professional Affiliations" section or under an "Honors and Activities" heading.

- REFERENCES: Don't include references on your resume unless they are specifically requested. State "References available upon request" and take a typed list of two to four references with you to any job interview (name, title, organization, relationship, address, and phone number).

For further strategies in writing resumes, see On Target Tips, "Resume Writing Guidelines." To think further about your esume, also complete the Journal activity "Current and Future Resume" on page 393.

Letters Letters provide a great opportunity to communicate in a personal and professional manner. They give you an opportunity to stand out in a crowd. One important rule of thumb is to never use a form letter. Always tailor each letter individually to the person you are writing. Letters should always be addressed to an individual by name and include the person's title and address. If you don't know this information, call or consult the company's website. Among the different types of letters that you might need to write are employment inquiry letters, cover letters, and thank-you letters (OCS Basics, 2002).

Employment Inquiry Letter. You can write an employment inquiry letter if you have identified a specific organization for which you would like to work. You are not asking for a job but for advice and information.

Introduce yourself and concisely explain why you are writing. Then, demonstrate that you have researched the company, highlight your relevant experience, and clarify why you think you are well qualified for this type of work. Finally, express your interest in obtaining advice from this person and state that you will call at a specific time, usually in about one week, to arrange a time to meet.

ON TARGET TIPS

Resume Writing Guidelines

Some good strategies for writing good resumes include (Writers Workshop, 2002):

- *Do a self-evaluation.* Jot down all of your significant experiences, including jobs, course projects, internships, volunteer work, or extracurricular activities. Analyze your experiences in terms of skills that most resemble those needed in your desired career.

- *Write.* After you have determined which experiences are most relevant to the job you want, write short descriptive phrases for each job activity. Use action verbs such as *prepared, monitored, organized, directed*, and *developed*. Emphasize skills, such as "designed new techniques for . . ." Use bullets with short sentences rather than lengthy paragraphs. Whenever possible, give specific evidence to illustrate your skills, such as "Designed new techniques for computer processing, saving the company $50,000 over a one-year period." Decide which of the three resume styles that we described best suits your needs, then write a draft of your resume on a word processor.

- *Revise.* Let your draft sit for a day or two, then critically reexamine it. Get other people to look at your resume and see what they think about it. Based on these critical analyses, revise the resume.

- *Print.* When you have written a draft you like, print out an error-free copy on a quality printer and have it photocopied onto good paper. Your final resume should be only one or two pages. If it is longer, be suspicious of irrelevant or unnecessary material. If your resume is two pages, make sure the most important information is on the front page.

Cover Letter. A second type of important job letter is a cover letter that introduces you to a potential employer. You should never send a resume to a potential employer without a cover letter. The cover letter briefly describes your qualifications, motivation, and interest in the job. Don't just repeat information in the resume but come up with fresh phrases and sentences related to your experiences, skills, and the job you want.

Thank You Letters. Also get in the habit of writing thank you letters to the people related to your job search within 24 hours of meeting them. This might be done after an informational meeting with someone you have networked with and should always follow a job interview. It might be tempting to follow up with an e-mail as it tends to be more efficient. However, a more formal letter sent through "snail mail" is much more impressive and memorable. Don't cut corners here.

"Uh-huh. Uh-huh. And for precisely how long were you a hunter-gatherer at I.B.M.?"

Knock 'em Dead in a Job Interview

A key step in getting the job you want is to perform well in an interview. Following are some strategies for success (Yate, 2005):

- *Be prepared.* Interviewers ask for detailed examples of your past experience. They figure you'll do as well on the new job as the old one, so the examples you give can seal your fate.
- *Know your resume.* Resumes are important. Employers use them to decide whether they want to interview you in the first place and will often ask questions about what they contain. Organize your resume, write it clearly, and avoid jargon.
- *Don't wing the interview.* Do your homework. Find out as much about your prospective employer as possible. What does the company do? How successful is it? Employers are impressed by applicants who have taken the time to learn about their organization. This is true whether you are interviewing for a part-time job at your college library or for a full-time job in a large company after you graduate.
- *Anticipate what questions you'll be asked.* Do some practice interviews. Typical interview questions include "What is your greatest strength?" "What interests you the most about this job?" "Why should I hire you?" Also be prepared for some zingers. For example, how would you respond to "Tell me something you're not very proud of." "Describe a situation where your idea was criticized." These are examples of questions some interviewers ask to catch you off guard and see how you handle the situation.
- *Ask appropriate job-related questions.* Review the job's requirements with the interviewer.
- *Keep your cool.* Always leave in the same polite way you entered.
- *Decide whether you want the job.* If so, ask for it. Tell the interviewer that you're excited about the job and that you can do it competently. If it isn't offered on the spot, ask when the two of you can talk again.
- *Follow-up.* Immediately after the interview, send your follow-up letter. Keep it short, less than one page. Mail it within 24 hours of the interview. If the decision is going to be made in the next few days, consider hand-delivering the letter. If you do not hear anything within five days, call the organization to ask about the status of the job.

Summary Strategies for Mastering College

Explore careers and jobs and link them to your values to motivate yourself through college.

Focus on the "Six Strategies for Success" above as you read each chapter to learn how to apply these strategies to your own success.

1 Evaluate Yourself

- Choose career options that match your values.
- Assess your academic and personal strengths as well as your communication skills.
- Evaluate your self-management skills.
- Link your personality and career choice, considering Holland's system.

2 Acquire Positive Work Experiences During College

- Explore relevant part-time and summer jobs to make money and obtain relevant work experience.
- Consider an internship or a co-op position to gain valuable experience and explore different careers.
- Engage in service learning to improve your motivation, grades, and self-esteem.

3 Become Knowledgeable about Careers

- Explore the *Occupational Outlook Handbook* to assess career opportunities.
- Consider several careers and develop general skills.
- Network to learn more about career options.
- See a career counselor to explore your strengths and weaknesses and assess your interests.
- Scope out Internet resources to learn more about various companies and positions.

4 Set Career Goals

- Know your short- and long-term goals for a career.
- Understand how to articulate your goals to a potential employer.

5 Land a Great Job

- Know what employers want and focus on obtaining those skills.
- Research the type of job you want.
- Network some more to find out about all possible job opportunities.
- Learn how to create a resume organized chronologically, functionally, or based on achievements.
- Know how to write an appropriate employment inquiry letter, cover letter, and thank you letter.
- Knock 'em dead in a job interview by being prepared, anticipating questions, asking appropriate questions, and following up.

Review Questions

1. List a few important aspects of evaluating the career(s) you want to pursue.

_____

_____

_____

_____

_____

_____

_____

_____

2. What are some of the most effective ways to acquire work experience while you are still in college?

_____

_____

_____

_____

_____

_____

_____

_____

3. Describe some advantages of networking and using the Internet to explore career opportunities.

_____

_____

_____

_____

_____

_____

_____

_____

4. List three different strategies for creating a strong resume. Which one do you think will work best for you?

   1. _____

   2. _____

   3. _____

5. Describe three different types of letters that are part of the career-exploration process. List a few aspects of each.

   1. _____

   2. _____

   3. _____

Learning Portfolio

SELF-ASSESSMENTS

YOUR JOURNAL

STRATEGIES FOR SUCCESS

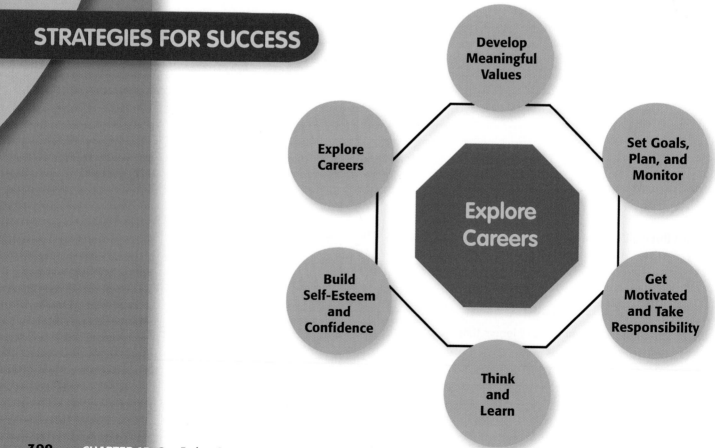

Develop Meaningful Values

Set Goals, Plan, and Monitor

Explore Careers

Get Motivated and Take Responsibility

Think and Learn

Build Self-Esteem and Confidence

Explore Careers

My Values and My Career Pursuits

Place a checkmark next to those values you consider important in a career.

_✓_ Work with people I like.

_____ Feel powerful.

_✓_ Have peace of mind.

_✓_ Make a lot of money.

_✓_ Be happy.

_____ Have self-respect.

_____ Contribute to the welfare of others.

_____ Not have to work long hours.

_____ Be mentally challenged.

_____ Be self-fulfilled.

_____ Have opportunities for advancement.

_____ Work in a setting where moral values are emphasized.

_____ Have plenty of time for leisure pursuits.

_✓_ Have plenty of time to spend with family.

_____ Work in a good geographical location.

_____ Be creative.

_____ Work where physical and mental health are important.

_____ Other: _____

_____ Other: _____

_____ Other: _____

As you explore careers, keep the values you checked off in mind. How do those values match the careers you've thought about pursuing? Explain.

My Self-Management Skills

To explore your self-management skills, place a checkmark next to any skills and qualities that you believe you have.

_____ accept supervision

_____ complete assignments

_____ get along with co-workers

_____ learn quickly

_____ get things done on time

_____ take pride in work

_____ good attendance

_____ sense of humor

_____ hard working

_____ honest

_____ productive

_____ punctual

_____ able to coordinate

_____ ambitious

_____ assertive

_____ cheerful

_____ conscientious

_____ creative

_____ dependable

_____ eager

_____ energetic

_____ flexible

_____ well-organized

_____ friendly

_____ helpful

_____ humble

_____ imaginative

_____ intelligent

_____ loyal

_____ mature

_____ motivated

_____ open-minded

_____ optimistic

_____ patient

_____ persistent

_____ responsible

_____ self-confident

_____ sincere

_____ trustworthy

_____ other _____

_____ other _____

_____ other _____

Now go back through the list and select your five strongest self-management skills. Number them 1–5. Are there any items you did not place a check mark next to that you think would help you in the careers you might pursue? If so, what can you do to develop these self-management skills and qualities? Make sure to mention these strengths in future interviews.

Source: *From J. M. Farr, (1999). America's Top Jobs for College Graduates, 3rd Ed., pp. 365–366. Indianapolis, IN: JIST Works.*

Your Journal

● REFLECT

1. My Ideal Job

If you have not done so yet, complete **Self-Assessments 1** and **2** before you do this exercise.

- Write down your ideal occupation choice.

_____

- Describe the degree you'll need for your ideal job, such as an AA, BA, MA, or PhD. How many years will this take?

_____

- On a scale of 1 to 10, estimate your chances of obtaining your ideal job.

Poor 1 2 3 4 5 6 7 8 9 10 Excellent

- What can you do now to increase your chances of obtaining this career?

_____

2. My Work Skills

List all of the work experiences you have had so far.

_____

Are any of these related to any careers that might interest you? Why or why not?

_____

What kind of career-related or general work skills have you demonstrated in these jobs that might be attractive to a potential employer?

_____

● DO

1. Current and Future Resume

Based on what you have read in this chapter, begin creating or updating your resume. List your education, work experience, high school or college campus organizations, and extracurricular activities. List any honors or awards you have achieved. Then write down what you would like your resume to look like when you apply for your first job after college. How do the two differ?

_____

2. Visit Your College's Career Center

Visit the career center at your college. Write down the relevant contact information for future reference:

_____

What materials and services are available for your career search?

_____

Consider making an appointment with a career counselor. List a few questions you would like to discuss.

_____

Your Journal

● THINK CRITICALLY

1. Why Do People Choose Particular Careers?

Consider your opinions about different careers. For example:

- Are some people born to be engineers or nurses? Why or why not?
- Did your parents shape your career interests?
- Do your teachers influence your career interests?
- What kind of an impact can mentors have on a career choice?
- Are economic factors important to you?
- What values are most important and why?

_____

_____

_____

2. How Good Are Your Communication Skills?

Among the skills that employers want college graduates to have, communication skills are the most important. Honestly examine your communication skills. Rate yourself from 1 to 5 on the following:

	Weak				Strong
Speaking skills	1	2	3	4	5
Interpersonal skills	1	2	3	4	5
Teamwork skills	1	2	3	4	5
Writing skills	1	2	3	4	5
Listening skills	1	2	3	4	5

- What are your strengths and weaknesses? _____
- Find out how important each of these skills is for the job you want to pursue when you graduate from college.
- What can you do now to start improving your areas of weakness?

_____

● CREATE

1. Collect Inspirations

Many creative people write down daily impressions, events, and feelings on index cards or in notebooks. These notes can be the raw material from which creative ideas spring.

Some artists tear out dozens of interesting images from magazines and newspapers, put them in boxes, and then return to them for creative inspirations. Start keeping a special box to store your impressions, feelings, and images related to your career interests and dreams. Come back to them from time to time for inspiration.

2. Your Network

Brainstorm for 10 minutes about all of the individuals you know who could serve as a career network. This includes family, friends, employers, teachers, and mentors. Write down each name, followed by a sentence or two about how they might be able to aid your job search. Then write down contact information for each individual. Try to talk with one of these people each week to start building your network now.

Applying the Six Strategies for Success

What did you learn in this chapter that you can apply to the following key strategies to help form the foundation for your success? Write down all of the major points you can remember that support the following strategies:

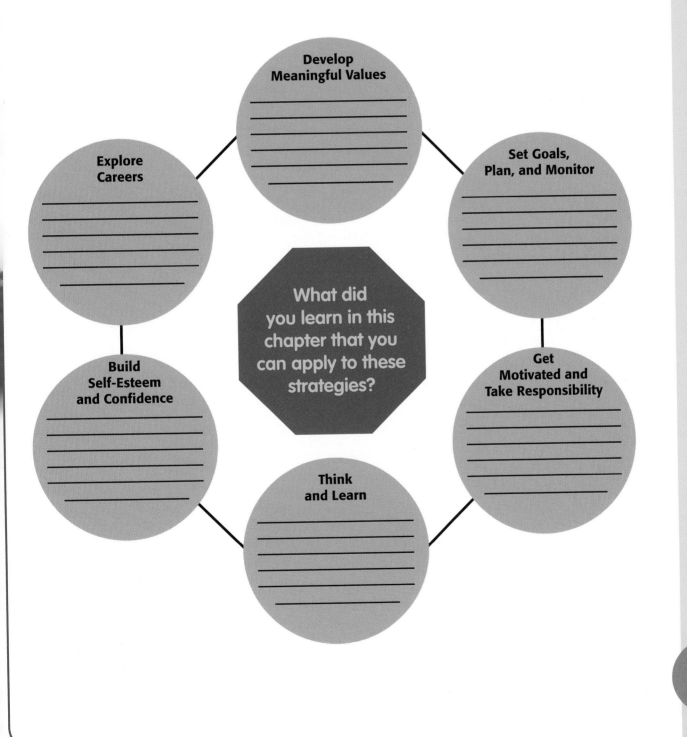

Develop Meaningful Values

Explore Careers

Set Goals, Plan, and Monitor

What did you learn in this chapter that you can apply to these strategies?

Build Self-Esteem and Confidence

Get Motivated and Take Responsibility

Think and Learn

Putting It All Together

How has the term or year gone so far? Are you mastering college? Have you put to good use many of the strategies we have described? It's always good to take stock periodically of where you are now, how things have gone, and where you're headed. This is a good time to reflect on the six strategies for success that form the backbone of this book and your success in college and beyond.

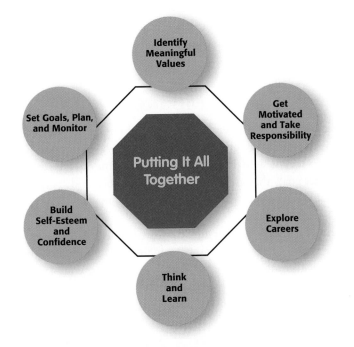

Develop Meaningful Values

Following are a list of values from Self-Assessment 2 "What Are My Values?" in Chapter 1. Now that you've almost finished your first college term or year, have your values changed? Go through this list again and check the five values that are most important to you now. Then go back to Self-Assessment 2 on page 28 and compare them with the five values you listed as most important at the beginning of the term. What have you learned?

_____ Having good friendships and getting along well with people
_____ Having a positive relationship with a spouse or a romantic partner
_____ Self-respect
_____ Being well-off financially
_____ Having a good spiritual life
_____ Being competent at my work

_____ Having the respect of others
_____ Making an important contribution to humankind
_____ Being a moral person
_____ Feeling secure
_____ Being a great athlete
_____ Being physically attractive
_____ Being creative
_____ Having freedom and independence
_____ Being well educated
_____ Contributing to the welfare of others
_____ Having peace of mind
_____ Getting recognition or becoming famous
_____ Being happy
_____ Enjoying leisure time
_____ Being a good citizen and showing loyalty to my country
_____ Living a healthy lifestyle
_____ Being intelligent
_____ Family relationships
_____ Honesty and integrity
_____ Dedication and commitment
_____ Having personal responsibility
_____ Other values

Set Goals, Plan, and Monitor

Are being well-educated and academically successful important values that have motivated you this term or are there other values that are more important? Have you linked this motivation to setting actual goals, planning, and monitoring your progress this term? Have you set goals that are challenging, reasonable, and specific? Have you set both long-term and short-term goals? Have your time management skills helped you reach your goals?

Now return to Chapter 1 and survey Self-Assessment 3 "What Are My Goals?" on page 29. Where are you now regarding your main goals in life? Are they the same as they were at the beginning of the term? In this assessment, you listed four goals you wanted to achieve this term. How have you done? If you have not reached your goals, why? What things could you have done better?

Get Motivated and Take Responsibility

How motivated have you been this term? Has your confidence been high and have you enthusiastically put your heart and mind into mastering college? Have you made a great effort and been persistent in your work? Have you been internally motivated? Do you take responsibility for your successes and your failures? How might you improve your motivation to get the most out of your next term?

Think and Learn

How have your thinking and learning gone this term? Do you understand your learning style and have you successfully mastered how to use this knowledge effectively? Have you developed effective work skills? Are you using computers to help reach your goals? Did you complete most of the Journal activities to help reinforce your learning? If so, this is a good time to look back over them and reflect on your development as a thinker and learner. How have these skills improved over the course of the term?

Build Self-Esteem and Confidence

How has your self-esteem been this term? Has it gone up and down a lot or remained relatively constant? Have you believed in yourself this term? If you have low self-esteem, do you know what the causes are? Have you linked your self-esteem with your values and the areas of your life that are important to you? Have you achieved what you wanted this term and how has this affected your self-esteem? How effectively have you coped with stress? Do you have confidence in your ability to succeed in college? Why or why not?

Explore Careers

Thinking about which career(s) you want to pursue reflects long-term goals. Have you determined one or more career areas that you want to pursue? Are your college classes and major or specialization adequately linked to your career interests? Have you improved in some of the areas many employers value in employees such as communication skills?

Revisit Your Strategies

In Chapter 1, you were asked to evaluate where you stand with regard to implementing the six strategies for success in your own life. Now revisit the statements listed below, placing a checkmark next to each one that represents you and your actions now. Leave the others blank. When you are done, go back and award yourself one point for each checkmark. Then add up the points for each of the six sections. Finally, shade the "Strategies for Success" model at the end of this section with your *total* for each of the six strategies. How does this visual model of your strengths and weaknesses compare with that on page 23?

Develop Meaningful Values

1. _____ I know what my values are.
2. _____ I feel good about my values.
3. _____ I have spent considerable time reflecting on what values I want to guide my life.
4. _____ I have discussed my values with others.
5. _____ My values are helping me succeed in college.
6. _____ My values serve as an underlying foundation for the goals I want to achieve.
7. _____ I've been in situations where my values have been tested and I stayed with them.
8. _____ I have a clear understanding of my purpose in life.
9. _____ I am flexible and realize that as I continue through college I will likely change and grow, and my values might change.
10. _____ My values are at the core of my existence.
_____ TOTAL

Set Goals, Plan, and Monitor

1. _____ I am good at setting goals.
2. _____ I have established some long-term goals.
3. _____ I have created subgoals to go along with my long-term goals.
4. _____ The goals I have set are challenging but reachable with considerable effort on my part.

5. _____ My goals are concrete and specific.
6. _____ I periodically monitor my progress toward reaching the goals I have set.
7. _____ I have set completion dates for these goals.
8. _____ I manage time effectively in the pursuit of my goals.
9. _____ I make lists of things I need to do to stay on track in reaching my goals.
10. _____ I anticipate and overcome obstacles on the way to reaching my goals.
_____ TOTAL

Get Motivated and Take Responsibility

1. _____ I am internally motivated.
2. _____ I take responsibility for my actions.
3. _____ I expect to succeed.
4. _____ I am persistent at completing important tasks.
5. _____ I am passionate about succeeding in life.
6. _____ I put a lot of energy into college.
7. _____ I have a strong work ethic.
8. _____ If I get bored, it doesn't last long.
9. _____ I have a strong desire to be a competent person.
10. _____ I am good at staying on task and not being distracted from what I need to do.
_____ TOTAL

Think and Learn

1. _____ I am self-disciplined and have good work habits.
2. _____ I have good study skills.
3. _____ I know the best ways I can learn.
4. _____ I am good at managing my time.
5. _____ I think critically.
6. _____ I think creatively.
7. _____ I have good problem-solving skills.
8. _____ I communicate effectively with good speaking and listening skills.
9. _____ I know what learning resources are available to me and how to best use them.
10. _____ I have good computer skills.
_____ TOTAL

Build Self-Esteem and Confidence

1. _____ I have a lot of confidence in myself.
2. _____ I feel good about myself.
3. _____ I have a positive self-image.
4. _____ I have a lot to be proud of.
5. _____ I am a person of worth.
6. _____ When I don't feel good about myself, I can tell why and attempt to do something about it.
7. _____ If I start to feel bad about myself, it doesn't last long.
8. _____ I have a good support system and get good feedback from others.
9. _____ My achievements help me feel good about myself.
10. _____ I have good coping skills.
_____ TOTAL

Explore Careers

1. _____ I know how much more successful I am likely to be if I complete college.
2. _____ I have several careers that I would like to pursue.
3. _____ I know what my college major will be.
4. _____ My college major matches up well with the careers I am interested in.
5. _____ I have good communication skills.
6. _____ I have good personal skills, including being able to get along with others.
7. _____ I know which college experiences will help me down the road in my pursuit of a career.
8. _____ I have talked with a career counselor about careers that might interest me.
9. _____ I have set some career goals.
10. _____ I am on the right path to reaching those career goals.
    _____ TOTAL

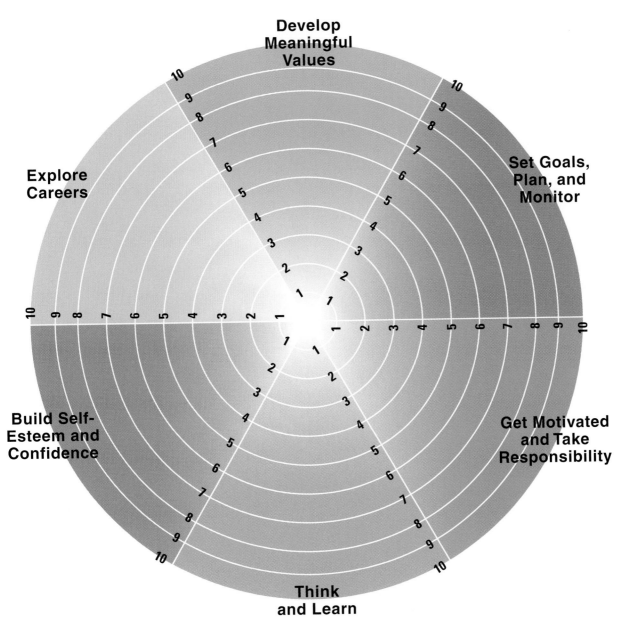

Where Are You Now?

You've just done quite a bit of reflecting about some important aspects of life. How do you feel about where you are now? Did you place a checkmark next to most of the areas listed above, or did you leave many of these blank, feeling that you need to improve? If you checked off most of the strategies above, you're likely well on your way to mastering college and developing critical skills that will help you in life after college. If you left many of the spaces blank, this is a good time to reevaluate what your values are and where you can improve.

You have a lot of change ahead of you. Developing meaningful values, setting goals, planning, monitoring, getting motivated and taking responsibility, thinking and learning, building self-esteem and confidence, and exploring careers will continue to be very important themes for you in mastering the remainder of your college years and thereafter. We wish you all the best. We have enjoyed communicating with you this term and hope that as a result of this course and book you feel well on your way to mastering college success.

References

A

Alberti, R., & Emmons, M. (1995). *Your perfect right* (7th ed.). San Luis Obispo, CA: Impact.

Alverno College. (1995). *Writing and speaking criteria.* Milwaukee, WI: Alverno Productions.

American Psychological Association (2002). *Controlling anger—before it controls you.* Retrieved from http://www.apa.org/pubinfo/anger.html

Anderson, L. W., & Krathwohl, D. R. (Eds.). (2001). *A taxonomy for learning, teaching, and assessment: A revision of Bloom's taxonomy of educational objectives.* New York: Longman.

Appleby, D. (1990). Faculty and student perceptions of irritating behaviors in the college classroom. *Journal of Staff, Program, and Organizational Development, 8,* 41–46.

Appleby, D. (1994). *Liberal arts skills at work* [Career Currents]. Hanover, IN: Hanover College.

Appleby, D. (1997, February). *The seven wonders of the advising world.* Invited address at the Southeastern Teachers of Psychology Conference, Kennesaw State University, Marietta, GA.

Armstrong, W. H., & Lampe, M. W. (1990). *Pocket guide to study tips* (3rd ed.). Hauppage, NY: Barron's Educational Series.

Astin, A. (1993). *What matters in college: Four critical years revisited.* San Francisco: Jossey-Bass.

Axelrod, R. B., & Cooper, C. R. (1996). *The concise guide to writing* (2nd ed.). Boston: Bedford/St. Martin's Press.

B

Bachar, K., & Koss, M. (2001). Rape. In J. Worell (Ed.), *Encyclopedia of women and gender.* San Diego, CA: Academic Press.

Bachman, J. G., O'Malley, P. M., Schulenberg, J. E., Johnston, L. D., Bryant, A. L., & Merline, A. C. (2002). *The decline of substance use in young adulthood.* Mahwah, NJ: Erlbaum.

Bailey, C. (1991). *The new fit or fat* (Rev. ed.). Boston: Houghton Mifflin.

Bandura, A. (2000). Self-efficacy. In A. Kazdin (Ed.), *Encyclopedia of psychology.* Washington, DC, and New York: American Psychological Association and Oxford University Press.

Bandura, A. (2001). Social cognitive theory. *Annual Review of Psychology, 53.* Palo Alto, CA: Annual Reviews.

Bashaw, R. E., & Grant, E. S. (1994). Exploring the distinctive nature of work commitments. *Journal of Personal Selling and Sales Management, 14,* 41–56.

Baumrind, D. (1991). Parenting styles and adolescent development. In J. Brooks-Gunn, R. Lerner, & A. C. Petersen (Eds.), *The encyclopedia of adolescence.* New York: Garland.

Baxter Magolda, M. B. (1992). *Knowing and reasoning in college.* San Francisco: Jossey-Bass.

Bednar, R. L., Wells, M. G., & Peterson, S. R. (1995). *Self-esteem* (2nd ed.). Washington, DC: American Psychological Association.

Beck, J. (2002). Beck therapy approach. In M. Hersen & W. H. Sledge (Eds.), *Encyclopedia of Psychotherapy.* San Diego, CA: Academic Press.

Bennett, M. E., & Miller, W. R. (1998). Alcohol problems. In H. S. Friedman (Ed.), *Encyclopedia of mental health: Vol. 1.* San Diego, CA: Academic Press.

Beyer, G. (1998). *Improving student thinking.* Boston: Allyn & Bacon.

Biasco, F., Goodwin, E. A., & Vitale, K. L. (2001). College students' attitudes toward racial discrimination. *College Student Journal, 35,* 523–529.

Blonna, R. (2005). *Coping with stress in a changing world* (3rd ed.). New York: McGraw-Hill.

Bloom, B. S., Englehart, M. D., Furst, E. J., & Krathwohl, D. R. (1956). *Taxonomy of educational objectives: Cognitive domain.* New York: David McKay.

Bly, R. (1990). *Iron John.* New York: Vintage Books.

Bolles, R. (2002). *What color is your parachute?* Berkeley, CA: Ten Speed Press.

Bolles, R. (2005). *What color is your parachute?* Berkeley: Ten Speed Press.

Bourne, E. J. (1995). *The anxiety and phobia workbook* (2nd ed.). Oakland, CA: New Harbinger Publications.

Boyer Commission. (1998). *Reinventing undergraduate education: A blueprint for America's research universities.* Retrieved June 2002, from http://naples.cc. sunysb.edu/Pres/boyer.nsf

Bransford, J. D., & Stein, B. S. (1984). *The ideal problem solver.* New York: Freeman.

Brisette, I., Scheier, M. F., & Carver, C. S. (2002). The role of optimism in social network development, coping, and psychological adjustment during a life transition. *Journal of Personality and Social Psychology, 82,* 102–111.

Brislin, R. W. (1993). *Understanding culture's influence on behavior.* Fort Worth, TX: Harcourt Brace.

Brown, F. C., & Buboltz, W. C., Jr. (2002). Applying sleep research to university students: Recommendations for developing a student sleep education program. *Journal of College Student Development, 43,* 411–416.

Brown, F. C., Buboltz, W. C., Jr., & Soper, B. (2001). Prevalence of delayed sleep phase syndrome in university students. *College Student Journal, 35,* 472–476.

Browne, M. N., & Keeley, S. M. (1990). *Asking the right questions: A guide to critical thinking* (3rd ed.).Englewood Cliffs, NJ: Prentice Hall.

Brownell, K. (2000). Dieting. In A. Kazdin (Ed.), *Encyclopedia of psychology.* Washington, DC, and New York: American Psychological Association and Oxford University Press.

C

Cacioppo, J. T. (2002). Emotion and health. In R. J. Davidson, K. R. Sherer, & H. H. Goldsmith (Eds.), *Handbook of affective sciences.* New York: Oxford University Press.

Canfield, J., & Hansen, N. V. (1995). *The Aladdin factor.* New York: Berkeley.

Carskadon, M. A. (1990). Patterns of sleep and sleepiness in adolescence. *Pediatrics, 17,* 5–12.

CNET Tech. (2002). *When games stop being fun.* Retrieved from http://news.com.com/2100-1040-881673.html

Collins, M. (1996, Winter). The job outlook for '96 grads. *Journal of Career Planning,* 51–54.

Combs, P. (2002). *Major in success* (3rd ed.). Berkeley, CA: Ten Speed Press.

Consumer Credit Counseling Service of Greater Dallas, Inc. (2000). *Credit: Information for today's consumer.* (Credit Seminar Workbook). Dallas, TX: New Vision Technologies, Inc.

Covey, S. R. (1989). *The seven habits of highly effective people.* New York: Simon & Schuster.

Covey, S. R., Merrill, A. R., & Merrill, R. R. (1994). *First things first.* New York: Simon & Schuster.

Costa, P. T., & McRae, R. R. (1995). Solid grounds in the wetlands of personality: A replay to Block. *Psychological Bulletin, 117,* 216–220.

Courtenay, W. H., McCreary, D. R., & Merighi, J. R. (2002). Gender and ethnic differences in health beliefs and behaviors. *Journal of Health Psychology, 7,* 219–231.

Crooks, R., & Bauer, K. (2002). *Our sexuality* (8th ed.). Pacific Grove, CA: Brooks/Cole.

Crooks, R., & Bauer, K. (2004), *Our sexuality* (9th ed.), Belmont, CA: Wadsworth.

Csikszentmihalyi, M. (1995). *Creativity.* New York: HarperCollins.

Csikszentmihalyi, M. (1997). *Finding flow.* New York: Basic Books.

Cutrona, C. E. (1982). Transition to college: Loneliness and the process of social adjustment. In L. A. Peplau & D. Perlman (Eds.), *Loneliness: A sourcebook of current theory, research, and therapy.* New York: Wiley.

D

Davis, M., Eshelman, E. R., & McKay, M. (2000). *The relaxation and stress reduction workbook* (5th ed.).Oakland, CA: New Harbinger Publications.

Davis, S. F., Grover, C. A., Becker, A. H., & McGregor, L. N. (1992). Academic dishonesty: Prevalence, determinants, techniques, and punishments. *Teaching of Psychology, 19,* 16–20.

DeFleur, M. L., Kearning, P., Plax, T., & DeFleur, M. H. (2005). *Fundamentals of human communication* (3rd ed.). New York: McGraw-Hill.

DeLongis, A., & Newth, S. (1998). Coping with stress. In H. S. Friedman (Ed.), *Encyclopedia of mental health: Vol. 1.* San Diego, CA: Academic Press.

Dement, W. C., & Vaughn, C. (2000). *The promise of sleep.* New York: Dell.

Diener, E., & Seligman, M. E. P. (2002). Very happy people. *Psychological Science, 13,* 81–84.

DeVito, J. (2004). *Interpersonal communication workbook* (10th ed.). Upper Saddle River, NJ: Prentice Hall.

E

Economos, C. (2001). Unpublished manuscript: *Tufts longitudinal health study.* Medford, MA: Center on Nutrition Communication.

Edelman, M. W. (1992). *The measure of our success.* Boston: Beacon Press.

Eggers, D. (2000). Commentary in Combs, P. *Major in success* (3rd ed.). Berkeley, CA: Ten Speed Press.

Eggers, D. (2000). *A heartbreaking work of staggering genius.* New York: Vintage Books.

Eggert, L. L., Thompson, F. A., Randell, B. P., & Pike, K. C. (2002). Preliminary effects of brief school-based prevention approaches of reducing youth suicide—risk behaviors, depression, and drug involvement. *Journal of Child and Adolescent Psychiatric Nursing, 15,* 48–64.

Elliott, M. (1999). *Time, work, and meaning.* Unpublished doctoral dissertation, Pacifica Graduate Institute.

Ellis, A. (1996). A rational-emotive behavior therapist's perspective on Ruth. In G. Corey (Ed.), *Case approach to counseling and psychotherapy.* Pacific Grove, CA: Brooks/Cole.

Ellis, A. (2002). Rational emotive behavior therapy. In M. Herson & W. H. Sledge (Eds.), *Encyclopedia of psychotherapy.* San Diego, CA: Academic Press.

Epstein, R. L. (2000). *The pocket guide to critical thinking.* Belmont, CA: Wadsworth.

F

Farr, J. M. (1999). *America's top jobs for college graduates.* Indianapolis, IN: JIST Works.

Frank, S. (1996). *The everything study book.* Holbrook, MA: Adams Media.

Fulghum, R. (1997). Pay attention. In R. Carlson & B. Shield (Eds.), *Handbook for the soul.* Boston: Little, Brown.

Folkman, S., & Moskowitz, J. T. (2004). Coping: Pitfalls and promises. *Annual Review of Psychology, Vol. 55.* Palo Alto, CA: Annual Reviews.

G

Garner, P. W., & Estep, K. M. (2001). Empathy and emotional expressivity. In J. Worell (Ed.), *Encyclopedia of women and gender*. San Diego, CA: Academic Press.

Gardner, H. (1989). *Frames of mind*. New York: Basic Books.

Gardner, H. (1999). *The disciplined mind*. New York: Simon & Schuster.

Gewertz, K. (2000). *Harvard University Gazette*. Retrieved from http://www.news.harvard.edu/gazette/ 2000/06.08/ ellison.html

Giles, D. E., Jr., & Eyler, J. (1998). A service learning research agenda for the next five years. *New Directions for Teaching and Learning, 73*, 65–72.

Goldberg, H. (1980). *The new male*. New York: Signet.

Goleman, D., Kaufmann, P., & Ray, M. (1992). *The creative spirit*. New York: Plume.

Gordon, T. (1970). *Parent effectiveness training*. New York: McGraw-Hill.

Gottman, J., & Silver, N. (1999). *The seven principles for making marriages work*. New York: Crown.

Grandin, T. (1995). *Thinking in pictures*. New York: Doubleday.

Griffith-Joyner, F., & Hanc, J. (1999). *Running for dummies*. Foster City, CA: IDG Books.

H

Haag, S., & Perry, J. T. (2003). *Internet Explorer 6.0*. New York: McGraw-Hill.

Haines, M. E., Norris, M. P., & Kashy, D. A. (1996). The effects of depressed mood on academic performance in college students. *Journal of College Student Development, 37*, 519–526.

Halberg, E., Halberg, K., & Sauer, L. (2000). *Success factors index*. Auburn, CA: Ombudsman Press.

Halonen, J. S., & Brown-Anderson, F. (2002). Teaching thinking. In W. J. McKeachie, *Teaching Tips* (11th ed.). Boston: Houghton Mifflin.

Halonen, J. S., & Gray, C. (2001). *The critical thinking companion for introductory psychology*. New York: Worth Publishers.

Halpern, D. F. (1997). *Critical thinking across the curriculum*. Mahwah, NJ: Erlbaum.

Hamburg, D. A. (1997). Meeting the essential requirements for healthy adolescent development in a transforming world. In R. Takanishi & D. Hamburg (Eds.), *Preparing adolescents for the twenty-first century*. New York: Cambridge University Press.

Hansen, R. S., & Hansen, K. (1997). *Write your way to a higher GPA*. Berkeley, CA: Ten Speed Press.

Harbin, C. E. (1995). *Your transfer planner*. Belmont, CA: Wadsworth.

Harris, R. A. (2001). *The plagiarism handbook: Strategies for preventing, detecting, and dealing with plagiarism*. Los Angeles: Pyrczak Publishing.

Heinrich, R., Molenda, M., Russell, J. D., & Smaldino, S. E. (2002). *Instructional media and technologies for learning* (7th ed.). Upper Saddle River, NJ: Prentice Hall.

Herson, M., & Sledge, W. H. (Eds.) (2002). *Encyclopedia of psychotherapy*. San Diego, CA: Academic Press.

Hicks, R. A., & Pellegrini, R. J. (1991). The changing sleep habits of college students. *Perceptual and Motor Skills, 72*, 1106.

Hillman, R. (1999). *Delivering dynamic presentations: Using your voice and body for impact*. Needham Heights, NJ: Allyn & Bacon.

Hofstetter, F. T. (2003). *Internet literacy*. New York: McGraw-Hill.

Holland, J. (1997). *Making vocational choices*. Lutz, FL: Psychological Assessment Resources.

Howatt, W. A. (1999). Journaling to self-evaluation: A tool for adult learners. *International Journal of Reality Therapy, 18*, 32–34.

Hurtado, S., Dey, E. L., & Trevino, J. G. (1994). *Exclusion or self-segregation? Interaction across racial/ethnic groups on college campuses*. Paper presented at the meeting of the American Educational Research Association, New York.

Hyde, J. S., & DeLamater, J. D. (2005). *Understanding human sexuality* (8th ed.). New York: McGraw-Hill.

I

Insel, P. M., & Roth, W. T. (2002). *Core concepts of health* (9th ed.). New York: McGraw-Hill.

Ishikawa, K. (1986). *What is total quality control? The Japanese way*. Englewood Cliffs, NJ: Prentice Hall.

J

Jandt, F. E. (2004). *An introduction to intercultural communication*. Thousand Oaks, CA: Sage.

Jendrick, M. P. (1992). Students' reactions to academic dishonesty. *Journal of College Student Development, 33*, 260–273.

Johnson, M. K., Beebe, T., Mortimer, J. T., & Snyder, M. (1998). Volunteerism in adolescence: A process perspective. *Journal of Research in Adolescence, 8*, 309–332.

Johnston, L. D., O'Malley, P. M. & Bachman, J. G. (1996). *National survey results on drug use from the Monitoring the Future study, 1975–1994: Vol. 2*. Rockville, MD: National Institute on Drug Abuse.

Johnston, L., O'Malley, G., & Bachman, J. (2004). *Monitoring the Future*. Ann Arbor, MI: Institute of Social Research.

Jonassen, D. H., & Grabowski, B. L. (1993). *Handbook of individual differences, learning, and instruction*. Mahwah, NJ: Erlbaum.

K

Kagan, J. (1965). Reflection-impulsivity and reading development in primary grade children. *Child Development, 36*, 609–628.

Kaplan, R. M., & Saccuzzo, D. P. (1993). *Psychological testing: Principles, applications, and issues* (3rd ed.). Pacific Grove, CA: Brooks/Cole.

Kappes, S. (2001). *The truth about Janeane Garofalo.* Retrieved from http://people.aol.com/people/ features/ celebrityspotlight/0,10950,169561,00.html

Keith-Spiegel, P. (1992, October). *Ethics in shades of pale gray.* Paper presented at the Mid-America Conference for Teachers of Psychology, Evansville, IN.

Keller, P. A., & Heyman, S. R. (1987*). Innovations in clinical practice.* Sarasota, FL: Professional Resource Exchange.

Kelly, J. (2000). Sexually transmitted diseases. In A. Kazdin (Ed.), *Encyclopedia of psychology.* Washington, DC, and New York: American Psychological Association and Oxford University Press.

Kierwa, K. A. (1987). Note-taking and review: The research and its implications. *Instructional Science, 19,* 394–397.

King, A. (2000). Exercise and physical activity. In A. Kazdin (Ed.), *Encyclopedia of psychology.* Washington, DC, and New York: American Psychological Association and Oxford University Press.

King, T., & Bannon, E. (2002, April). *At what cost? The price that working students pay for a college education.* Washington, DC: U.S. Department of Education, State Public Interest Research Groups' Higher Education Project.

Knouse, S., Tanner, J., & Harris, E. (1999). The relation of college internships, college performance, and subsequent job opportunity. *Journal of Employment Counseling, 36,* 35–43.

Kolb, D. A. (1984). *Experiential learning: Experience as the source of learning and development.* Englewood Cliffs, NJ: Prentice Hall.

Koss, M., & Boeschen, L. (1998). Rape. In H. S. Friedman (Ed.), *Encyclopedia of mental health: Vol. 3.* San Diego, CA: Academic Press.

Kurose, J. F., & Ross, K. W. (2001). *Computer networking.* Boston: Addison-Wesley.

L

Lack, L. C. (1986). Delayed sleep and sleep loss in university students. *Journal of American College Health, 35,* 105–110.

Lakein, A. (1973). *How to get control of your time and your life.* New York: Signet.

Lane, A. M., Crone-Grant, D., & Lane, H. (2002). Mood changes following exercise. *Perceptual and Motor Skills, 94,* 732–734.

Langer, E. (1997*). The power of mindful learning.* Reading, MA: Addison-Wesley.

Lazarus, R. S. (1993). Coping theory and research: Past, present, and future. *Psychosomatic Medicine, 55,* 234–247.

Lazarus, R. S. (1998). *Fifty years of the research and theory of R. S. Lazarus.* Mahwah, NJ: Erlbaum.

Lerner, H. G. (1989). *The dance of intimacy.* New York: HarperCollins.

Levinger, E. E. (1949). *Albert Einstein.* New York: Julian Messner.

Lin, J. G., & Yi, J. K. (1997). Asian international students' adjustments. *College Student Journal, 31,* 473–479.

Loftus, E. F. (1980). *Memory.* Reading, MA: Addison-Wesley.

Loftus, E. F. (1993). The reality of repressed memories. *American Psychologist, 48,* 518–537.

Lorayne, H., & Lucas, J. (1996). *The memory book.* New York: Ballantine.

M

Maas, J. (1998). *Power sleep: The program that prepares your mind for peak performance.* New York: Villard.

MacKenzie, A. (1997). *The time trap* (3rd ed.). New York: American Management Association.

Marcus, A., Mullins, L. C., Brackett, K. P., Tang, Z., Allen, A. M., & Pruett, D. W. (2003). Perceptions of racism on campus. *College Student Journal, 37,* 611–617.

Maris, R. W. (1998). Suicide. In H. S. Friedman (Ed.), *Encyclopedia of mental health: Vol. 3.* San Diego, CA: Academic Press.

Matlin, M. (1998). *Cognitive psychology* (3rd ed.). New York: Harcourt Brace.

McCabe, D. L., & Trevino, L. K. (1993). Academic dishonesty: Honor codes and other contextual influences. *Journal of Higher Education, 64,* 522–538.

McDonald, R. L. (1994). *How to pinch a penny till it screams.* Garden City, NY: Avery.

McKowen, C. (1996). *Get your A out of college: Mastering the hidden rules of the game.* Los Altos, CA: Crisp Publications.

McNally, D. (1990). *Even eagles need a push.* New York: Dell.

McNett, J., Harvey, C., Athanassiou, N., & Allard, J. (2000, July 17). *Bloom's taxonomy as a teaching tool: An experiment.* Paper presented at Improving University Teaching Conference, Frankfurt, Germany.

Mendoza, J. C. (1999). *Resiliency factors in high school students at risk for academic failure.* Unpublished doctoral dissertation, California School of Professional Psychology.

Metz, E., & McLellan, J. A. (2000, April). *Challenging community service predicts civic engagement and social concerns.* Paper presented at the meeting of the Society for Research on Adolescence, Chicago, IL.

Michael, R. T., Gagnon, J. H., Laumann, E. O., & Kolata, G. (1994). *Sex in America.* Boston: Little, Brown.

Miller, G. A. (1956). The magical number seven, plus or minus two: Some limits on our capacity for information-processing. *Psychological Review, 48,* 337–442.

Miller, J. B. (1986). *Toward a new psychology of women* (2nd ed.). Boston: Beacon Press.

Mrosko, T. (2002). *Keys to successful networking.* Retrieved from http://www.iwritesite.com/keys.html

Murphy, M. C. (1996). Stressors on the college campus: A comparison of 1985 and 1993. *Journal of College Student Development, 37,* 20–28.

Mussell, M. P., & Mitchell, J. E. (1998). Anorexia nervosa and bulimia nervosa. In H. S. Friedman (Ed.), *Encyclopedia of mental health: Vol. 1.* San Diego, CA: Academic Press.

Myers, I. E. (1962). *Manual: Myers-Briggs Type Indicator.* Princeton, NJ: Educational Testing Service.

N

Newman, E. (1976). *A civil tongue.* Indianapolis: Bobbs-Merrill.

Nichols, R. B. (1961, March). Do we know how to listen? Practical helps in a modern age. *Speech Teacher, 10,* 22.

Niven, D. (2001). *The 100 simple secrets of successful people.* San Francisco: Harper.

Nolen-Hoeksema, S. (2001). *Abnormal psychology* (2nd ed.). New York: McGraw-Hill.

Nolen-Hoeksema, S. (2004). *Abnormal psychology* (3rd ed.). New York: McGraw-Hill.

O

Occupational Outlook Handbook. (2000–2001). Washington, DC: U.S. Department of Labor.

Occupational Outlook Handbook. (2004). Washington, DC: U.S. Department of Labor.

Occupational Outlook Handbook. (2004–2005). Washington, DC: U.S. Department of Labor.

OCS Basics (2002). *Job search basics.* Cambridge, MA: Office of Career Services. Retrieved from http://www.ocs.fas.harvard.edu/basics

P

Paludi, M. A. (1998). *The psychology of women.* Upper Saddle River, NJ: Prentice Hall.

Pear, J., & Martin, G. L. (2003). *Behavior modification* (7th ed.). Upper Saddle River, NJ: Prentice Hall.

Peck, M. S. (1978). *The road less traveled.* New York: Touchstone.

Peck, M. S. (1997). *The road less traveled & beyond: Spiritual growth in an age of anxiety.* New York: Simon & Schuster.

Pennebaker, J. W. (1997). *Opening up.* (Rev. ed.). New York: Avon.

Pennebaker, J. W. (2001). Dealing with a traumatic experience immediately after it occurs. *Advances in Mind-Body Medicine, 17,* 160–162.

Pennebaker, J. W. (2002). *Writing and health: Some practical advice.* Retrieved from http://homepage.psy.utexas. edu/homepage/faculty/pennebaker/Pennebaker.html

Perkins, D. N. (1984, September). Creativity by design. *Educational Leadership,* pp. 18–25.

Perlman, D., & Peplau, L. A. (1998). Loneliness. In H. S. Friedman (Ed.), *Encyclopedia of psychology: Vol.2.* San Diego, CA: Academic Press.

Peterson, C., & Stunkard, A. J. (1986). *Personal control and health promotion.* Unpublished manuscript, Department of Psychology, University of Michigan, Ann Arbor.

Polivy, J., Herman, P., Mills, J., & Brock, H. (2003). Eating disorders in adolescence. In G. Adams & M. Berzonsky (Eds.), *Blackwell handbook of adolescence.* Malden, MA: Blackwell.

Pomerleau, O. (2000). Smoking. In A. Kazdin (Ed.), *Encyclopedia of psychology.* Washington, DC, and New York: American Psychological Association and Oxford University Press.

Poole, B. J. (1998). *Education for an information age* (2nd ed.). Burr Ridge, IL: McGraw-Hill.

Post, G. (2002). *Database management systems.* New York: McGraw-Hill.

R

Raimes, A. (2002). *A brief handbook* (3rd ed.). Boston: Houghton Mifflin.

Robeson, R. (1998). *College students on the rebound.* Unpublished doctoral dissertation. University of Indiana.

Rodin, J., & Langer, E. J. (1977). Long-term effects of a control-relevant intervention with the institutionalized aged. *Journal of Personality and Social Psychology, 35,* 397–402.

Roth, D., Eng, W., & Heimberg, R. G. (2002). Cognitive behavior therapy. In M. Herson & W. H. Sledge (Eds.), *Encyclopedia of psychotherapy.* San Diego, CA: Academic Press.

Ruggerio, V. R. (1996). *Becoming a critical thinker* (2nd ed.). Boston: Houghton Mifflin.

S

Santilli, J. S., Falbo, M. C., & Harris, J. T. (2002, April). *The role of volunteer services, self perceptions, and relationships with others on prosocial development.* Paper presented at the meeting of the Society for Research on Adolescence, New Orleans, LA.

Sax, L. J., Astin, A. W., Korn, W. S., & Mahoney, K. M. (1995). *The American college freshman: National norms for fall, 1995.* Los Angeles: Higher Education Research Institute, UCLA.

Sax, L. J., Astin, A. W., Korn, W. S., & Mahoney, K. M. (1999). *The American freshman: National norms for fall 1999.* Los Angeles: Higher Education Research Institute, UCLA.

Sax, L. J., Astin, A. W., Korn, W. S. & Mahoney, K. M. (2000). *The American freshman: National norms for fall 2000.* Los Angeles: Higher Education Research Institute, UCLA.

Sax, L. J., Lindholm, J. A., Astin, A. W., Korn, W. S. & Mahoney, K. M. (2001). *The American freshman: National norms for fall 2001.* Los Angeles: Higher Education Research Institute, UCLA.

Sax, L. J., Astin, A. W., Lindholm, J. A., Korn, W. S., Saenz, V. B., & Mahoney, K. M. (2003). *The American freshman: National norms for fall 2003.* Los Angeles: Higher Education Research Institute, UCLA.

Sax, L. J., Astin, A. W., Lindholm, J. A., Korn, W. S., Saenz, V. B., & Mahoney, K. M. (2004). *The American freshman: National norms for fall 2004.* Los Angeles: Higher Education Research Institute, UCLA.

Scott, R. L., & Cordova, J. V. (2002). The influence of adult attachment styles on the association between marital adjustment and depressive symptoms. *Journal of Family Psychology, 16,* 199–208.

Sears, D. O., Peplau, L. A., & Taylor, S. E. (2003). *Social psychology* (11th ed.). Upper Saddle River, NJ: Prentice Hall.

Sedlacek, W. (1999). Black students on White campuses. *Journal of College Student Development, 40,* 538–550.

...man, M. E. P. (1991). *Learned optimism.* New York: ...ocket Books.

...aver, P. R., Belsky, J., & Brennan, K. A. (2000). Comparing measures of adult attachment: An examination of interview and self-report methods. *Personal Relationships, 7,* 25–43.

Sher, K. J., Wood, P. K., & Gotham, H. J. (1996). The course of psychological distress in college: A prospective high-risk study. *Journal of College Student Development, 37,* 42–51.

Sherrod, L., & Brabeck, K. (2002, April). *Community service and youths' political views.* Paper presented at the meeting of the Society for Research on Adolescence, New Orleans, LA.

Skinner, K. (1997). *The MSE Oracle System.* Dallas, TX: Southern Methodist University.

Smolak, L., & Streigel-Moore, R. (2002). Body image concerns. In J. Worell (Ed.), *Encyclopedia of women and gender.* San Diego, CA: Academic Press.

Stark, R. (1994). *Sociology* (5th ed.). Belmont, CA: Wadsworth.

Stern, L., Iqbal, N., Seshadri, P., Chicano, K. L., Daily, D. A., McGrory, J., Williams, M., Gracely, E. J., & Samantha, F. F. (2004). The effects of low-carbohydrate versus conventional weight loss diets in severely obese adults: one-year follow-up of a randomized trial. *Annals of Internal Medicine, 140,* 778–785.

Sternberg, R. J. (1988). *The triangle of love.* New York: Basic Books.

Sternberg, R. J., & Lubart, T. I. (1995). *Defying the crowd: Cultivating creativity in a culture of conformity.* New York: Free Press.

Stipek, D. (2002). *Motivation to learn* (4th ed.). Boston: Allyn & Bacon.

Strong, R. W., Silver, H. F., Perini, M. J., & Tuculescu, G. M. (2002). *Reading for academic success.* Thousand Oaks, CA: Corwin Press.

Stukas, A. A., Clary, E. G., & Snyder, M. (1999). Service learning: Who benefits and why. *Social Policy Report: Vol. 13, no. 4.* Chicago: Society for Research in Child Development.

Swartz, R. (2001). Thinking about decisions. In A. L. Costa (Ed.). *Developing minds: A resource book for teaching thinking.* Alexandria, VA: Association for Supervision and Curriculum Development.

T

Tan, Amy. (1996, June 28). [Interview]. Retrieved from www.achievement.org/autodoc/page/tanoint-1

Tannen, D. (1986). *That's not what I meant!* New York: Ballantine.

Tannen, D. (1990). *You just don't understand!* New York: Ballantine.

Tavris, C. (1989). *Anger: The misunderstood emotion* (2nd ed.). New York: Touchstone.

Tavris, C. (1992). *The mismeasure of woman.* New York: Touchstone.

Taylor, S. E. (2003). *Health psychology* (5th ed.). New York: McGraw-Hill.

Tiene, D., & Ingram, A. (2001). *Exploring current issues in educational technology.* New York: McGraw-Hill.

Treagust, D. F., Duit, R., & Fraser, B. J. (1996). *Improving teaching and learning in science and mathematics.* New York: Teachers College Press.

Tyler, S. (2001). *Been there, should've done that: More tips for making the most of college* (2nd ed.). Michigan: Front Porch Press.

U

University of Illinois Counseling Center. (1984). *Overcoming procrastination.* Urbana-Champaign, IL: Department of Student Affairs.

V

van Praag, H., Kempermann, G., & Gage, F. H. (1999). Running increases cell proliferation and neurogenesis in the adult mouse dentate gyrus. *Nature Neuroscience, 3,* 266–270.

Vickery, D. M., & Fries, J. F. (2000). *Take care of yourself* (7th ed.). Reading, MA: Addison-Wesley.

Von Oech, Roger. (1990). *A whack on the side of the head: How you can be more creative.* New York: Warner.

W

Walters, A. (1994). Using visual media to reduce homophobia: A classroom demonstration. *Journal of Sex Education and Therapy, 20,* 92–100.

Wechsler, H., Davenport, A., Sowdall, G., Moetykens, B., & Castillo, S. (1994). Health and behavioral consequences of binge drinking in college. *Journal of the American Medical Association, 272,* 1672–1677.

Wechsler, H., Lee, J. E., Kuo, M., & Lee, H. (2000). College binge drinking in the 1990s—a continuing health problem: Results from the Harvard University School of Health 1999 College Alcohol Study. *Journal of American College Health, 48,* 1999–2010.

Wechsler, H., Lee, J. E., Kuo, M., Seibring, M., Nelson, T. F., & Lee, H. (2002). Trends in college binge drinking during a period of increased prevention efforts: Findings from Harvard School of Public Health College Alcohol Study surveys: 1993–2001. *Journal of American College Health, 50,* 203–217.

Weinstein, N. D. (1984). Reducing unrealistic optimism about illness susceptibility. *Health Psychology, 3,* 431–457.

Weston Exploration. (2002). *The model for exploration.* Urbana-Champaign, IL: Weston Exploration, University of Illinois. Retrieved from http://www. housing.uiuc.edu/academics/ estonex/index.htm

Whimbey, A., & Lochhead, J. (1991). *Problem solving and comprehension.* Mahwah, NJ: Erlbaum.

Whitley, B. E., Jr., & Keith-Spiegel, P. (2002). *Academic dishonesty: An educator's guide.* Mahwah, NJ: Erlbaum.

Wigfield, A., & Eccles, J. S. (Eds.) (2002). *Development of achievement motivation.* San Diego, CA: Academic Press.

Winston, S. (1995). *Stephanie Winston's best organizing tips.* New York: Simon & Schuster.

Writers Workshop (2002). *Writing resumes.* Urbana- Champaign, IL: Center for Writing Studies, University of Illinois. Retrieved from http://www.english.uiuc.edu/

Y

Yager, J. (1999). *Creative time management for the new millennium* (2nd ed.). Stamford, CT: Hannacroix Books.

Yate, M. (2002). *Knock 'em dead.* Boston: Adams Media.

Yate, M. (2005). *Knock 'Em Dead.* Boston: Adams Media.

Yates, M. (1995, March). *Community service and political-moral discussions among black urban adolescents.* Paper presented at the meeting of the Society for Research in Child Development, Indianapolis, IN.

Young, M. L. (2002). *Internet: The complete reference* (2nd ed.). New York: McGraw-Hill.

Z

Zeidner, M. (1995). Adaptive coping with test situations: A review of the literature. *Educational Psychologist, 30,* 123–133.

Zeurcher-White, E. (1997). *Treating panic disorder and agoraphobia: A step-by-step clinical guide.* Oakland, CA: New Harbinger Publications.

Credits

This page constitutes an extension of the copyright page. We have made every effort to trace the ownership of all copyrighted material and to secure permission from copyright holders. In the event of any question arising as to the use of any material, we will be pleased to make the necessary corrections in future printings. Thanks are due to the following authors, publishers, and agents for permission to use the material indicated.

Photo Credits

1: © Werner Bokelberg. **2:** © Theo Westenberger. **5:** © Bill Aron/PhotoEdit. **11:** © Bettman/Corbis. **18:** © Spencer Grant/PhotoEdit. **33:** © IT Stock Free/eStock Photo. **34:** © James Leynse/CORBIS. **39:** © Jeff Greenberg/AGE Fotostock. **48:** © Stewart Cohen/Index Stock Imagery. **63:** © Robert Cattan/Index Stock Imagery. **64:** © Duomo/CORBIS. **70:** © John Coletti Photography. **71:** (left) palmOne is a trademark of palmOne, Inc. (right) © Uripos Photography/eStock Photo. **91:** © Jose Luis Pelaez, Inc./CORBIS. **92:** © Barbra Witt. **105:** ©Spencer Grant/PhotoEdit. **107:** © Spencer Grant/PhotoEdit. **121:** © Kevin Horan/ Getty Images. **122:** © AP/Wide World. **128:** © John Coletti Photography. **133:** © Heinle Image Resource Bank/Thomson Higher Education. **139:** Courtesy of National Inventors Hall of Fame. **151:** © John Giustina/Getty Images. **152:** © Peter Kramer/Getty Images. **165:** © Francis Hogan/Electronic Publishing Services. **168:** ©Michael Newman/PhotoEdit. **187:** ©T. Kruesselmann/Zefa/Masterfile. **188:** © Stefanie Deutsch/Getty Images. **190:** © Barbara Stitzer/Photo Edit. **200:** (top left) © Daniel Acker/Bloomberg News/Landov. (top right) © Michael Germana/SSI/Landov. (bottom left) © Ethan Miller/Reuters/Landov. (bottom right) © Fred Prouser/Reuters/Landov. **217:** © Photodisc/Getty Images. **218:** © Bettman/CORBIS. **222:** © Bonnie Kamin/Photo Edit. **247:** © Pierre Tremblay/Masterfile. **248:** © Gregory Pace/CORBIS. **262:** © Paul Thomas/Getty Images. **281:** © David Young-Wolff/Getty Images. **282:** © Albert Ferreira/Reuters/Landov. **296:** © Rob Gage **297:** © Bill Losh/Getty Images. **300:** © Jonathan Nourok/PhotoEdit. **311:** © Dennis MacDonald/PhotoEdit. **312:** © C.J.Gunther. **322:** © Paula A. Scully. **323:** © Bill Bachman/PhotoEdit. **341:** © Marc Romanelli/Alamy. **342:** © AP/Wide World. **348:** © Owaki-Kulla/ CORBIS. **350:** © Photodisc/Getty Images. **353:** © Mo Wilson/ Photofusion Picture Library/Alamy. **361:** © Jay Lee Studio/Stock Connection. **373:** ©Amy Etra/PhotoEdit. **374:** Copyright © 2003, NBC Photos.

Cartoon Credits

4: © Tribune Media Services. Reprinted with permission. **6:** © The New Yorker Collection 1992, Mike Twohy, from cartoonbank.com. All Rights Reserved. **15:** © The New Yorker Collection 1990, Robert Weber, from cartoonbank.com. All Rights Reserved. **16:** DILBERT reprinted by permission of United Feature Syndicate, Inc. **17:** © The New Yorker Collection 1992, Michael Maslin, from cartoonbank.com. All Rights Reserved. **19:** © 2002. Reprinted courtesy of Bunny Hoest and Parade Magazine. **20:** © 1973 News America Syndicate. Reprinted with permission of Creators Syndicate. **35:** ZIGGY © ZIGGY AND FRIENDS, INC. Reprinted with permission of Universal Press Syndicate. All Rights Reserved. **41:** © Harald Carl Bakken. **42:** © The New Yorker Collection 1989, Robert Mankoff, from cartoonbank.com. All Rights Reserved. **49:** Reprinted by permission. www.cartoonstock.com. **52:** © Carol Cable. Used with permission of the cartoonist. **67:** © 2000 Charles Barsotti, from cartoonbank.com. All Rights Reserved. **94:** © 2003 Sidney Harris. **96:** © The New Yorker Collection 1997, Mike Twohy, from cartoonbank.com. All Rights Reserved. **107:** © The New Yorker Collection 1999, Danny Shanahan, from cartoonbank.com. All Rights Reserved. **124:** © Carol Cable. Used with permission of the cartoonist. **131:** © 2003 Sidney Harris. **136:** © The New Yorker Collection 1990, Eric Teitelbaum, from cartoonbank.com. All Rights Reserved. **157:** Reprinted by permission of Vivian Scott Hixon. **172:** © Gahan Wilson. **196:** © The New Yorker Collection 1986, J.B. Handelsman, from cartoonbank.com. All Rights Reserved. **204:** © 2003 Sidney Harris. **219:** © The New Yorker Collection 1991, Mike Twohy, from cartoonbank.com. All Rights Reserved. **225:** © Harald Bakken. **230:** PEANUTS reprinted by permission of United Feature Syndicate, Inc. **234:** © The New Yorker Collection 1990, Danny Shanahan, from cartoonbank.com. All Rights Reserved. **259:** PEANUTS reprinted by permission of United Feature Syndicate, Inc. **270:** © 2004 Leo Cullum, from cartoonbank.com. All Rights Reserved. **284:** PEANUTS reprinted by permission of United Feature Syndicate, Inc. **286:** CATHY © Cathy Guisewite. Reprinted with permission of Universal Press Syndicate. **290:** © The New Yorker Collection 1993, Frank Cotham, from cartoonbank.com. All Rights Reserved. **291:** DILBERT reprinted by permission of United Feature Syndicate, Inc. **298:** © 1994 Joel Pett. All Rights Reserved. **326:** DILBERT reprinted by permission of United Feature Syndicate, Inc. **327:** © 2000 Tom Cheney, from cartoonbank.com. All Rights Reserved. **328:** CATHY © Cathy Guisewite. Reprinted with permission of Universal Press Syndicate. **344:** © The New Yorker Collection 1999, Robert Weber, from cartoonbank.com.

Text Credits

Index

Opiates (narcotics), 321*t*
Opinion pieces, 127
Optimism, 327
Ordering, 285
Outline
    for essay questions, 230–231
    method of note-taking, 159–160,
        160*f*, 172
    for writing, 256
Overconfidence, 138*b*
Overlearning, 206

P

Paper-and-pencil planners, 70–71
Paraphrasing, 158
Parental Loans for Undergraduate Students
    (PLUS), 356
Parenting, 291
Parents, relationships with, 289–290
Pareto, Vilfredo, 67
Partial memory and recall, 206
Partner, relationships with, 290
Pass-fail systems, 234
Passivity, 286
Patterns in lectures, 156
Peace Corps, 357
Peck, M. Scott, 12
Pell grant, 355
Perkins loan, 356
Personal contact, 301
Personality
    five factor personality theory, 97–98,
        378
    career planning and, 378–379
    Holland personality types, 379, 379*f*
    Myers-Briggs Type Inventory (MBTI),
        98–99, 99*f*, 378
Personalized text method of note-taking,
    172
Peterson's National College Data Bank, 47
Phone. *See* Telephone
Physical health
    checklist, 311
    developing, 314–315
    diets and dieting, 316–318
    exercise/fitness, 315, 315*b*
    improving, 325*b*
    risks to, 314, 318–325
    sleep, 315–316, 316*b*
    summary strategies, 332
    value, 313–314
Plagiarism, 264–266, 265*f*, 266*b*, 276
Planners, 70–73
Planning. *See also* Career exploration and
        planning
    daily, 76–78

four- or five-year plan, 46–47, 59
    goals and, 8–11
    money management, 343
    reading, 167*f*
    study groups, 197–199
    study skills and strategies, 189–193
    subgoals, 69–70
    term, 71–73, 72*b*
    test-taking and, 220–223
    time management and, 69–78
    to-do lists, 76–77, 77*f*
    weekly, 73–76
    for writing, 255–256, 256*f*
PLUS loan, 356
Portfolio, 109, 263
Positive thinking, 327
PowerPoint, 51, 269*b*
Pregnancy, 324–325, 325*f*
Prejudice, 295–297
Premise, 130
Prerequisites, 40
Previewing (reading), 167–168
Primary sources, 169–170, 253–254,
        265*f*
Priorities, setting, 76–78, 76*b*
Problem solving, 133–136, 134*b*
    IDEAL method, 133–135
    maximization of, 133–135
    mindfulness, 135–136
    SCANS skills, 377
    self-assessment, 146
    summary strategies, 142
    writing, 263–266
Procedural memory, 202
Procedural tests and testing, 223
Procrastination
    checklist, 63
    described, 78–79
    excuses for, 79*b*
    overcoming, 79–80
    writing and, 264, 264*b*
Productivity, time management and, 67
Professors. *See* Instructors
Proofreading, 228, 232, 262
Props, for memorization, 206
Psychological assistance. *See* Mental
        health
Punctuation, 261
Purposeful plagiarism, 265–266, 265*f*

Q

Questions
    after speeches, 269*b*
    analytic skills, 125*b*
    answering, 101
    asking, 125, 125*b*

critical thinking, 123–127
essay tests, 230–232, 231*f*, 232*b*
journalism, 252

R

Race. *See* Culture and ethnicity
Rape, 292, 292*b*
Reading skills. *See also* Information
        processing
    active, 168–169
    analytic, 169
    comprehension, 167–169
    concentration, 165–167
    different disciplines, 170–171
    goals and, 164–165
    information processing, 153–158
    note-taking, 171–176
    planning, 167*f*
    previewing, 167–168
    primary sources, 169–170
    reviewing, 169
    SCANS skills, 376–378
    secondary source, 170
    self-assessment, 182
    for different situations, 169*b*
    skimming, 168, 183, 224
    speed, 165, 183
    strategies, 169*b*
    subvocalizing, 165*b*
    summary strategies, 208
    test-taking skills, 219
    word attack skills, 166*f*
Reading strategies. *See* Memorization;
        Reading skills
Realistic personality type, 379, 379*f*
Reasoning, 127–133
    alternatives and, 134*b*
    assumptions and, 132
    bias, personal, 133
    claims, handling, 128–131
    deductive, 132, 132*f*
    inductive, 132, 132*f*
    inferences, 127–128
    problem-solving, 133–136, 134*b*
    refining, 131–133
    summary strategies, 123
Receiver, 283
Reference materials, 255
Reflective learning, 95–96
Registration, for courses, 45, 45*b*
Relationships
    attachment, 288–289
    checklist, 281
    with children, 291
    dating, 291–292
    developing, 288–295